S0-ABE-335

THE LIFE AND LETTERS OF
SIR GEORGE GROVE

Mayall & Newman Ltd. Brighton, Photo. Swan Electric Engraving Co.

[signature]

1890.

THE LIFE & LETTERS

OF

SIR GEORGE GROVE, C.B.

HON. D.C.L. (DURHAM), HON. LL.D. (GLASGOW)
FORMERLY DIRECTOR OF THE ROYAL COLLEGE OF MUSIC

BY

CHARLES L. GRAVES

London
MACMILLAN AND CO., LIMITED
NEW YORK: THE MACMILLAN COMPANY
1903

RICHARD CLAY AND SONS, LIMITED,
BREAD STREET HILL, E.C., AND
BUNGAY, SUFFOLK.

PREFATORY NOTE

Sir George Grove, though often urged to write his Life, never did more than dictate in 1897 a number of discursive anecdotic reminiscences, filling half-a-dozen copy-books. In addition to these, he left a quantity of autobiographical material in his letters, in the diaries kept during his stay in Jamaica and his tours in the Holy Land, in his speeches and addresses, and above all in between seventy and eighty of the little pocket-books that he invariably carried about with him. In view, therefore, of his strongly expressed preference for the autobiographical method, I have endeavoured, as far as possible, to let him tell his own story in his own words.

I think it right, however, to add that this is neither a critical nor a complete memoir. The necessary detachment of view is impossible of attainment in dealing with one who died so recently : and, apart from that, I owe Sir George Grove far too much to be able to approach the task in a spirit of judicial impartiality. On the other hand, he had an immense circle of friends and acquaintances, and with the best intentions it is inevitable that I should have failed to mention many of his associates, possibly some of his intimates.

Yet, imperfect though this memoir must be, it would

have fallen still farther short of the mark had it not been for the generous assistance lent me by his relations and friends. Besides those to whom reference is made in the course of the narrative, I have to express my special indebtedness to Lady Grove, to Miss Eleanor Grove, Mr. Edmund Grove, and to the late Dean Bradley; to Mr. Walter M. Grove, Mr. Julius C. Grove, and Mr. Arthur Grove; to Mrs. Charles Bull and Mrs. Ernest von Glehn; to Miss Louie Heath, Miss Dobrée, and Mr. S. P. Waddington; to Mr. W. Barclay Squire, F.S.A.; to Mr. George Armstrong, the Secretary of the Palestine Exploration Fund; to Sir Hubert Parry, Bart., Director of the Royal College of Music, and to Sir Charles Villiers Stanford; and to Mr. and Mrs. A. Murray Smith and Mrs. Edmond Wodehouse, who greatly lightened my preliminary labours by their kind help in sorting and copying letters.

Finally, for leave to print several private letters addressed to Grove I owe my grateful acknowledgments to Lord Tennyson, Mr. R. Barrett Browning, Mrs. Sutherland Orr, Mrs. Henry Reeve, Mr. R. P. Arnold, Mr. Rudolph C. Lehmann, Mr. Otto Goldschmidt, Mr. Herbert Sullivan, and Major-General Sir J. F. Maurice, K.C.B.

C. L. G.

ATHENÆUM CLUB,
March 23, 1903.

CONTENTS

CHAPTER I

CHAPTER II

CHAPTER III

CHAPTER IV

CHAPTER V

CHAPTER VI

CHAPTER VII

CHAPTER VIII

CHAPTER IX

CHAPTER X

CHAPTER XI

CHAPTER XII

CHAPTER XIII

LIST OF ILLUSTRATIONS

LIFE OF SIR GEORGE GROVE

CHAPTER I

4

Ancestry and Parentage—"Yeoman Grove"—Thomas Grove—Thurlow Terrace—Early School Days and Schoolmates at Greaves's and Elwell's—At Stockwell and Clapham under Charles Pritchard—Early musical education—Articled to Alexander Gordon—Hobbies and recreations—Journey to Belgium in 1837—At Glasgow in 1840—Jamaica, 1841–1843—Bermuda, 1843–1846—Chester and Bangor, 1847–1849—Trip to Paris, 1848—Earliest literary effort—Reminiscences of Robert Stephenson.

THE *locus classicus* for the origin of the Grove family is to be found in Prior's *Memoirs of Edmund Burke*, vol. ii. pp. 355–6, in a passage treating of the Emigrant School at Penn, in Buckinghamshire, founded by Burke. Prior writes :—

"Penn, in Buckinghamshire, a bold promontory, to which Mr. Burke frequently resorted, at one time as the friend of General Haviland, and latterly as the patron of the emigrant school there, is situated about three miles north-west of Beaconsfield. Many of the residents are distinguished for patriarchal longevity, not a few of them attaining a century of years. The family of Grove trace an uninterrupted descent from the Conquest as proprietors of the same estate. The last possessor, Mr. Edmund Grove, died in June 1823, at the advanced age of ninety-four; and being well known in this part of the country as a fair specimen of the ancient English yeoman, may be worth noticing. When young, he had been the play-fellow of the late Viscount Curzon, and of John Baker Holroyd, who died Earl of Sheffield, and was known to most of the surrounding nobility and gentry by the name of Yeoman Grove—a name now disused for the more assuming appellation of Esquire, but formerly applied to those who farmed their own estates. Yeoman Grove was likewise known to his late Majesty, who permitted him an unusual freedom. Whenever they met in the street at Windsor, which was not unfrequent on market-day, he would grasp the royal hand with fervour, and in a way peculiarly his own, inquire—'How does your Majesty do?—How is the Queen?—How are all the children?' which commonly occasioned the Royal Personage a hearty good-humoured laugh."

The belief in the continuous residence of the Groves at Penn from the Conquest, which Prior stated on the authority of an unnamed "antiquarian correspondent," the treasurer of the Emigrant School, was by no means shared by "Yeoman Grove's" most distinguished descendant. Writing to a friend in January 1898, George Grove disposes of the legend with impatient incredulity. He alludes to the "utterly unfounded belief that the original Grove was barber to William the Conqueror and fought by his side at Hastings, for which the King gave him an estate in Bucks, and that the Groves were the oldest family in the country. Absolute fiction! Our grandfather was the 'last yeoman in Bucks': that's the nearest to the truth." As a matter of fact, the connection of the Groves with Penn can be traced by monumental inscriptions as far back as the reign of Charles II., while there is little doubt as to their being descended from the same stock as the Groves of Ferne, in Wiltshire, who migrated from Buckinghamshire in the fifteenth century, and derive their ancestry from John de Grove, of Chalfont St. Giles's, Bucks.[1] The

[1] Mr. Walter Grove, Sir George Grove's eldest son, writing on May 27, 1901, sends me the following extract from the Court Rolls of the Manor of Penn: "In the 13th year of Henry VI. [*i.e.* 1434] William at Grove is acknowledged to hold freely [*i.e.* freehold] from his father Grove's Plat [where Stonehouse, the old family house, now is] several tenements and pieces of land" at a specified quit rent. In the 1st year of Edward IV. Thomas at Grove is acknowledged to hold freely Grove's Plat and other tenements. The Penn Church registers, moreover, record the christenings of children of six Groves—William, Thomas, Henrie, Edmonde, John, and Richard—but no residences are mentioned. "We only conclude," adds Mr. Grove, "that Grove's Plat is Stonehouse, as the meadow adjoining the house is called Grove's Plat."

Penn property was never large, and seems to have shrunk somewhat in the lifetime of Edmund Grove [1729-1823]. Anyhow the resources of the family were so restricted that, as George Grove records in a note of a conversation with his brother Thomas on January 22, 1873, "our father, when he was a lad, worked as a common labourer on his father's farm on a few shillings a week. This went on until his younger brother John had gone away to London. He then told his father that he wanted to go to London too." It seems that John Grove, while still at school, conceived the notion of coming up to London to start in business. Subsequently, as we have seen, his elder brother Thomas followed his example. The story goes that he rode up to London with a guinea in his pocket, sold his horse at Hyde Park Corner, and went on to his brother's house in the City. After staying with him for a while and passing through various phases of dependence, Thomas Grove started in business on his own account at Charing Cross.

In August 1807 he married Mary Blades. For a while they lived in Charing Cross, but moved down to Clapham about the year 1819, where George Grove, the seventh of their ten children, and the sixth of those who survived their parents, was born on August 13, 1820, at Thurlow Terrace.

Thomas Grove was a man who deserves something more than a passing notice. He was good to look at: "a rather tall man," writes Miss Eleanor Grove, "and broad in proportion; very handsome, with a bright, clear complexion and brown eyes. He always wore powder, and in his blue coat with brass buttons, buff waistcoat and soft white muslin neckerchief, had a distinguished air." He was, moreover, without making any pretensions to culture or intellectuality, a man of considerable force and simplicity of character. He went blind in middle age—it is supposed from overstraining his eyes over his accounts in a strong light—but the affliction never impaired his equanimity. Never a bookish man—he read little save in his Bible—he had nevertheless a great respect for letters.

Again, though a devout Congregationalist and regular chapel-goer, his sturdy Puritanism was tempered with remarkable broadmindedness in regard to the religious education of his children. So long as they went for a serious purpose, and where Christ was preached, he made no objection to their attending other places of worship, and even subscribed, on their behalf, for sittings in the parish church, Clapham, and in another church in the neighbourhood, St. Paul's, where there was a Calvinistic clergyman. As a boy he had played the hautboy in the parish church in Buckinghamshire, and was all his life and on all occasions a great singer of hymns; for he had come under the influence of the great Evangelical revival, and by his own practice showed a wholesome regard for the view that "Those who don't sing on earth won't sing in Heaven." Mrs. Thomas Grove, *née* Mary Blades, and aunt of the author of the classical biography of Caxton, had perhaps more claim to be regarded as intellectual. Dean Bradley described her to me as "somewhat austere, but a woman of considerable brain." Amid the cares of her large household she found time—as subscriber to a Book Society—for a good deal of serious reading, and was not merely a lover of music but a proficient amateur.

Thurlow Terrace, Thomas Grove's house at Clapham, unlike most modern suburban residences justified its name, being called "Thurlow" after Lord Thurlow, who owned property in the neighbourhood, and "Terrace" from its position, for it stood on a high bank overlooking the Battersea Fields. The house itself was a large white bungalow, built by an Anglo-Indian named Corp, one-storeyed save for a portion in the middle, with a good-sized garden attached. The house itself has long disappeared, and the Wandsworth Road Station of the Chatham and Dover Railway stands on its very foundations. "The property," so Sir George told Mr. F. G. Edwards in 1897, "was about six acres; a large garden of one and a quarter acres, with big trees, thorns, curious crab-trees, &c., running down to the Wandsworth Road; a kitchen garden of half an acre behind, and beyond that a paddock running up to Larkhall Lane. . . . We could see from our upper windows the roof of the Red House[1] close to the south bank of the Thames."

All the way from Wandsworth Road to Clapham Junction the neighbourhood was a favourite residential resort for solid City people, the wealthiest living on Clapham Common. But Clapham was thoroughly rural and not even semi-suburban in the "twenties" and "thirties." Mr. Edmund Grove distinctly recollects seeing a man in the stocks at Clapham,[2] then a most picturesque village with a watch-house for the "Charlies," and old inns with timbered fronts and spacious courtyards. But the eyes of the young people were more commonly turned Londonwards. In some discursive reminiscences dictated in 1897 George Grove says:—

"In the days of our childhood Battersea Fields were almost unoccupied. There was a farmhouse about midway between our house and the Thames called Long Hedge Farm, or more commonly 'Matson's,' from the name of the farmer. Some distance to the left was a factory for chemicals which we knew as Beaufoy's, and that was a place which wakened emotions in our young minds. There was a certain secrecy about it, as nobody was allowed to get inside lest the process should be discovered, and bloodhounds were said to be kept which effectually guarded the place at night. So clear was the air across Battersea Fields that we could see the coloured sails of the barges

[1] The Red House was a place where Cockneys of the day used to shoot pigeons.

[2] In a letter printed as an appendix to *Old Clapham*, by J. W. Grover (London: A. Bachhoffner, Clapham, 1887), and dated January 17, 1887, George Grove writes:—"I was at school in a row of houses still standing near the church from 1828 to 1830. . . . The pound and stocks were, I think, near the Cock Inn, and the cage was on the same side of the Common as the spring well a little beyond. The Common was quite a wild place; one of the larger ditches had an iron girder across it, which was said to have been put there by old Brunel, the engineer of the Thames Tunnel."

going up and down the river, and could hear plainly the drums and fifes played by the Duke of York's boys in the Chelsea Hospital before they went to bed. It was an entirely open space, a good deal of it given up to corn and the rest grazing fields,[1] which were inhabited by an enormous herd of cows. We always believed that there were a thousand. The only two objects which at all looked old were the steeples of old Chelsea Church and Battersea Church, the former a tall red-brick square tower, and the latter a much more modern and pointed spire. These were always objects of immense curiosity to me on account of their presumed age."

As a child George Grove was described by his contemporaries as lively, and at times exceedingly mischievous. He was taught to read by one of his elder sisters, Bithiah —who afterwards married the Rev. Joshua Clarkson Harrison[2]—a clever, accomplished, and attractive woman. But the four youngest children, George, Edmund, Anna, and Eleanor, were specially united by their tastes and interests, as well as by their age.

"Behind our house," I quote from the anecdotic reminiscences referred to above, "there was a large paddock in which there was often a fallow deer with horns. And very often as evening was coming on, we children were allowed to go into this field and look at the deer. We often found him lying in a corner of one of the brick walls. The corner was a little lower than the rest of the field, and we could see his horns over the docks or other large-leaved plants which were in that part, and as we came near him, one felt a kind of sinking of the heart. Many years after, the paddock was bought by the London, Chatham, and Dover Railway, the house was pulled down, and the Wandsworth Road Station built upon its site. One afternoon when I was more than sixty years old, I had been in Clapham, and

[1] Dean Bradley endorses this, adding that a feature of these fields were the curious marshy ditches, in which horse-leeches were found.

[2] Joshua Clarkson Harrison [1813-1894], for forty-four years the much revered pastor of Park Chapel. Mrs. Harrison died in 1893.

had to wait at this station for a quarter of an hour for the train. I found the station-master, told him who I was, and that I had been born in the house, and asked him if I could go into the field for a few minutes to see if it was pretty much as it had been. It was about the same time of the day that I speak of above, and as I got near the corner that had remained untouched, I looked for the horns, and was amused to find exactly the same feeling reviving in my breast, which used to agitate it fifty years before."

When George Grove was about eight years old, he was sent as a weekly boarder to a school on Clapham Common kept first by a Mr. Greaves, and then by a Mr. Elwell. Greaves was a Yorkshireman, but his methods were happily different from those of the Yorkshire schoolmasters pilloried in *Nicholas Nickleby*; indeed, he was famous for feeding his boys well. A securer title to immortality was the fact that he was Macaulay's first schoolmaster.[1] At Elwell's, George Grove began a life-long friendship with George Granville Bradley, afterwards successively assistant master at Rugby, headmaster of Marlborough, Master of University College, Oxford, and Dean of Westminster. As Grove put it in an autobiographical speech in July 1880, "We met at a school on Clapham Common, kept by a man of the name of Elwell—two little mites of eight.[2] We were both in trouble. He had lost his mother, I had never been away from home before, and I recollect the first time I saw him, as well as if it was yesterday—behind a door; and I remember perfectly the feeling

[1] "Mr. Greaves, . . . a shrewd Yorkshireman, with a turn for science, who had been originally brought to the neighbourhood in order to educate a number of African youths, sent over to imbibe Western civilization at the fountain head. The poor fellows had found as much difficulty in keeping alive at Clapham as Englishmen experience at Sierra Leone: and, in the end, their tutor set up a school for boys of his own colour, and at one time had charge of almost the entire rising generation of the Common."—*Life of Macaulay*, by Trevelyan, vol. i. p. 29.

[2] As a matter of strict accuracy, the Dean was nearly a year and a half the younger. "Grove," the Dean writes, "has antedated our first meeting. I was at least ten when I went to Elwell's. The Reform Bill was then before the two Houses of Parliament and was passed while I was there."

of his hand as we walked together through the groves and wildernesses which in those early days made up Clapham Common. We took to one another at once, and I am happy to say we have never altered since. I married his sister; among his other sisters and brothers are some of my closest friends, and our own intercourse has never been interrupted for a moment."

Another schoolfellow at Elwell's was Frederick Locker, afterwards Locker-Lampson, who has left in *My Confidences*, pp. 107–9, an unflattering portrait of Elwell under the name of Wigram. Locker says that the school consisted of "some fourteen or more boys," including G. G. Bradley, George Grove, and two sons of Sir Andrew Agnew, and goes on: "We played at prisoner's base in the lean strip of a playground at the rear of the house, . . . and there was cricket once a week on the Common. It was there that I bought 'Parliament,' 'tom-trot,' and 'ginger-pop' of an old warrior with one eye and a *drôle de nez*, whose barrow of 'goodies' was our basis of such supplies." Dean Bradley tells me that George Grove, though full of life and energy, and enjoying prisoner's base and similar games, never shone at, nor cared for, organized pastimes such as cricket or football. It is worthier of note that while at Elwell's he learned the Hebrew alphabet and perhaps a little more of that tongue from a Hebrew Bible bought for him by his father.

Grove's education, however, did not begin in earnest until he went to the school at Stockwell, newly started under the Rev. Charles Pritchard [1808–1893], who from 1834 to 1862 was headmaster of Clapham Grammar School, and from 1870 to 1893 held the Savilian Professorship of Astronomy in the University of Oxford. Pritchard said of himself that, "though a divine in mind and heart," he "ultimately became, by Providence, a professional astronomer." Yet distinguished as he undoubtedly was in both capacities, his most enduring claim to grateful remembrance rests on the stimulating and enlightened conduct of his school at Clapham. After a brilliant career at Cambridge, where he graduated Fourth Wrangler in 1830, and was elected Fellow of St. John's in 1832, he was appointed headmaster of the Stockwell Grammar School, one of a number of Proprietary Grammar Schools, established in the suburbs and provinces in connection with King's College. George Grove and Granville Bradley were both pupils of Pritchard's at Stockwell, and another of their contemporaries was George Hemming, subsequently Senior Wrangler and consulting Counsel to the University of Cambridge. After a year and a half's struggle with a parsimonious committee, Pritchard threw up the headmastership. But so great was the confidence that he had inspired amongst the parents of his pupils, that the Clapham Grammar School was organised by a committee of his supporters in order to give him a free hand to carry out the plan of education which he had propounded at the opening of Stockwell School. That plan, from which George Grove derived peculiar benefits, was based on a study of the classics.[1] But it was reinforced not only by instruction in elementary mathematics, but by "a systematic scheme of instruction relating to the physical course of phenomena in the midst of which we live and move and have our being." Above all, he insisted that the main intention of early education should be the development of the habit of thinking, and he further laid great stress on the necessity of providing resources for the leisure hours of maturer life. How admirably Pritchard carried these theories into practice may be gathered from the testimony of Dean Bradley, who, in the *Nineteenth Century* of March 1884, describes the pioneer work done by this young Cambridge graduate, then "full of fire, enthusiasm, and original ability." Pritchard was one of the first to use the blackboard as an illuminating instrument of education, and to give schoolboys glimpses into the science of language. He taught

[1] The weak point in Pritchard's system was that he practically taught no modern history. Dean Bradley tells me that in consequence he was "blown up" for his ignorance when he went to Rugby.

them something of the beauty and charm of literature, old and new. Dean Bradley told me in the autumn of 1900 that he could still repeat the splendid peroration of the *Agricola*—"Si quis piorum manibus,etc."—which Pritchard made him and the other head boys learn more than sixty years before. Pritchard also set great store by intelligent reading aloud. Every Saturday the boys drew without copy, from previous study, a map of Palestine, and the Dean had no doubt that the germ of George Grove's articles on the geography and history of Palestine, as well as on general geography—perhaps the origin of the Palestine Exploration enterprise—might be traced to those Saturday maps and Saturday studies in Blunt's *Coincidences*, Laborde's *Journey in Arabia Petræa*, Keane's *Fulfilment of Prophecy*, and other works on Old Testament history, at Clapham Grammar School. Part of these studies used to consist of "imaginary travels from Clapham through Palestine, illustrated by chalk-drawn maps on the black-board." In these George Grove excelled, though his circumstantial touches were often trying to the gravity of his instructor. The weekly lessons in elementary science, writes Dean Bradley, were "eagerly looked forward to," and "there was not one among us, at all events in our teacher's class, who could not at that time draw with sufficient accuracy not merely the proverbial common pump, but a low pressure steam-engine of the day." In short, "it became impossible for any one of us to look henceforth on science as a foe." A further testimony to the excellence of Pritchard's teaching is to be found in the number of distinguished men who entrusted him with the education of their sons. The names of Airy, Darwin, Gassiot, Hamilton, Herschel, and Maurice, became familiar in the roll-call, and in 1886, the year in which Pritchard received the gold medal of the Royal Astronomical Society, and was elected to an honorary fellowship at his old College, he was entertained at a banquet by nearly 100 "Old Boys" of Clapham Grammar School, some of them grandfathers, many of them highly distinguished soldiers, lawyers, clergymen, and men of science, with the Dean of Westminster in the chair.

Under Pritchard sound and stimulating instruction was combined with rigorous discipline. While he refused—to quote his own words—to cripple boys' handwriting by "the old and barbarous practice of writing out lines," he was a firm believer in the efficacy of corporal punishment, "provided it was neither excessive, nor insufficient, nor frequent." In a little autobiographical volume, published for private circulation, he says: "An 'old boy' has recently reminded me thus—'You could hit hard!' If so, I regret it, but if *'twas sharp, 'twas short.*" Among Pritchard's many fine qualities patience was not to be numbered, but if George Grove occasionally suffered, his brother Edmund assures me that he gave great provocation. Thus one *al fresco* lecture was completely demoralized by his stealthy application of a burning-glass to the trousers of a stooping schoolmate. But along with this boyish enjoyment of mischief—Mr. Hemming tells me that he exhibited no little talent as a caricaturist—there went a genuine desire to explore and examine for himself. One day when he was about twelve years old—to quote from the reminiscences of 1897—"I got permission to take a walk and see Chelsea and Battersea Churches. I had to cross the river by the old Battersea Bridge—a curious long old timber structure. In those days in the toll-house at the entrance to the bridge I saw the words 'No tipling,' an economy of a letter on the part of the painter which made an impression on me that I have never lost. As I walked over the bridge, the planks of the floor were laid with an inch or so between each of them, and as I went along I saw the water underneath rushing down the river. I think I remember to have first felt—what is still as fresh in my mind as ever—a feeling of wonder where such a great quantity of water had come from, and a strong desire to see the bed of the stream. And I remember distinctly feeling, what Horace's rustic felt before me, that if I waited a little while, it must all run away, and then I should see without any difficulty. I did not get inside Chelsea Church, and could only have a vague sentiment of Sir Thomas More, whose place of worship it was, and of whom I already knew a few little facts. In coming back I went through Battersea, and found Battersea Church much inferior in my ideas to Chelsea."

George Grove's musical education began, so he told Mr. F. G. Edwards,[1] by hearing his mother play from the *Messiah* to her children out of an old vocal score, with "voices and figured bass only." Miss Eleanor Grove also tells me that her elder sister Eliza used to play to them a good deal. Mr. Edwards continues :—

"Then came Vincent Novello's 'Fitzwilliam Music' and Bach's 'Forty-eight.' In the latter connection we are told that the then organist of Clapham Parish Church, one John Blackbourn, always pronounced Bach's name 'Bawk.' One day Mr. Blackbourn played 'Achieved is the glorious work,' when young Grove went up to the organ-loft and asked if that was by 'Bawk.' Receiving a negative reply, he asked if a 'Bawk' fugue could be played 'next Sunday,' a request which was granted, when Blackbourn gave the Fugue in E in the second book. This so enraptured the young listener that he and his brother Edmund used to play this gem of a fugue, as a pianoforte duet, every morning after breakfast before starting for their three-mile walk to town."

There was an excellent Broadwood piano in the drawing-room at Thurlow Terrace, where the brothers and sisters sang and played to their hearts' content. Mr. Edmund Grove tells me that their musical literature consisted of choruses from the oratorios—the sheet edition of Clarke-Whitfeld ; a *Musical Library* in two volumes, edited by Dr. Ayrton ; and a *Sacred Minstrelsy*. They also subscribed to the Musical Antiquarian Society, which published Gibbons's and Weelkes's Madrigals and Morley's "Ballets," and in 1837 George Grove purchased with one of the first

[1] *Musical Times*, October 1897, "A Biographical Sketch of Sir George Grove"—an admirable monograph, most of the details in which were communicated personally to Mr. Edwards by Sir George.

guineas ever given to him a folio copy of Clarke-Whitfeld's edition of the *Messiah.* Miss Eleanor Grove vividly recalls their periodical visits to Exeter Hall to attend the oratorio concerts of the Sacred Harmonic Society. The house-key was hidden under the gate and supper left out for them on their return, which was seldom before eleven, for they footed it both ways. To secure good places in the 3*s.* unreserved seats, they had to be there long before the doors were opened, and then there was a regular hurdle-race over the benches to the front row. The interval before the performance began was spent in examining the score, or watching the players come in—Perry the leader, Lindley and old "Drag" (Dragonetti), the famous double-bass player. Throughout the oratorio "G" acted as expounder and commentator, never failing to signal attention to his favourite passages. Those were golden evenings of halcyon days; they used to sing nearly the whole way back to Clapham—a habit which led to the memorable comment of a friendly policeman near the turnpike on the Wandsworth Road. The Groves had fallen in with a noisy party from a neighbouring inn, and the policeman, who followed to keep them from being molested, and walked part of the way with them, thus delivered his soul on the subject of music: "Well, sir, some likes the pihanny, and some likes the flute, and some likes various sorts of instruments; but as for me, sir, I like the *wocal.* Indeed, sir, I may say I'm a *hog* at the *wocal.*"

These musical reminiscences have slightly anticipated the strict sequence of events. At the end of 1835, George Grove, already well grounded in the rudiments of science, natural history, and geography, with a fair knowledge of Latin and something more than a smattering of Greek, was removed from Pritchard's, and articled in January 1836 to Alexander Gordon, a civil engineer, whose place of business was at 22 Fludyer Street.

"Fludyer Street," wrote George Grove in 1897, "is now gone for ever, being covered by the India Office, but it was the next street to Downing Street, and ran parallel to it from Parliament Street to St. James's Park. An old blind woman came up the street every Tuesday afternoon. She sold what we then called matches,—thin slips of firewood about eight inches long by half an inch wide, pointed at each end, and with each end dipped in sulphur. Lights were then obtained by striking a piece of steel with a bit of flint over a round tinder-box which contained burnt rags. The sparks caught the tinder directly, and one poked the sparks with the sulphur end of the match, and by blowing, and then being nearly suffocated in the process, a light was obtained. The old woman used to say, 'Please to buy a ha'p'orth of matches from a poor stone blind.' One afternoon she had a new cry, 'Please to buy a ha'p'orth of matches, or a good Congry box from a poor stone blind.' Of course we fellows in the office wished to see what this new 'Congry box' could be. We got for twopence a small cardboard box containing, I think, fifty matches and a piece of sandpaper through which we squeezed the matches. They were friction matches, and we at once obtained a light. That was my first introduction to what is now so great a convenience. 'Congry' derived its name from Sir William Congreve, who was then, I think, Master-General of the Ordnance. . . . There was at that time no means of getting to town but by walking. There was a two-horse coach called the 'Monitor,' which ran between Wandsworth and Charing Cross, and my father always went by that in the morning, but it was too costly for us boys. It was exactly three miles from our house to Charing Cross, and I walked it in the morning and back again at night without feeling the hardship. My father would sometimes take the wherry from Vauxhall Bridge to Whitehall Stairs, and the sort of beak which was formed by the stem of the wherry is indelibly impressed on my mind. Just below Vauxhall Bridge on the London side of the river was the Penitentiary, standing almost by itself, a strange, gloomy, prison-like building. There was a little wooden building out in the river, which one understood in a vague way protected the pipes of the Waterworks. It was a dark rusty sort of colour, and covered with holes to allow the water to get in. In walking we either crossed Vauxhall Bridge and went through Millbank, or kept on the south side of the river through Lambeth, where there were several things worth noticing—gasworks, close to Vauxhall; further on, several factories, and, as we approached Lambeth Church and Palace, some very queer tumble-down streets. One or two of the names I remember: 'Digweed, Potato-merchant,' and 'Hacket, Barber.' When the Houses of Parliament were burned in the year 1834 I accompanied my elder sister and uncle Blades along that route, and we saw the earlier phases of the fire from the terrace in front of Lambeth Palace. The east end of the Houses of Parliament was formed by a large Gothic window, which at first was quite dark, and I remember the flames gradually illuminating it until the whole came into a blaze. We then went on until we came to Westminster, and before we turned up to the bridge and went over it—crowded with people—I remember the lead, or what I thought was lead, running down in a stream off Westminster Hall. . . . Quite a body of men clerks in the Treasury and in Drummond's and Coutts's Banks used to walk up every morning at the same time with ourselves. Mr. Marjoribanks, of Coutts's, drove in a gig along the road. One was less careful about one's dress in those days than one is now. Great-coats were but little worn, and one had to be satisfied with an umbrella even on very rainy days. But the boats arrived in time, and one generally took advantage of these from Vauxhall to Whitehall. The price at first was fourpence, and it was some time before they went as far as Nine Elms pier."

Alexander Gordon, to whom George Grove was articled, was, according to Mr. Edmund Grove, a "very genial man of a fine presence—almost too genial to be a typical Scot." Thus, George Grove has recorded, in illustration of his easy relations with his clerks, that he was very fond of repeating to them the nonsense rhyme, "There was a man, and his name was Dobb," &c. It was his peculiarity that while a vigorous opponent of railways—much as Lardner opposed Atlantic liners—he was a great advocate of steam traction on roads, in fact one of the pioneers of the motor-car movement. George Grove's interest in his work is sufficiently illustrated by another reminiscence dictated in 1897:—

"Battersea Fields is now crossed by three railways, the main line of the South-Western, which had a long embankment and a brick arch close to Matson's farm. I well remember the arrival of those lines. I was just articled to Alexander Gordon to be a civil engineer, and the details of the railway were naturally very attractive to me. I remember making a careful sketch of the railway, with chairs and sleepers, &c., and my disappointment when

I found that all my pains had been of no avail, as they were merely 'contractors' temporary plant.' Another thing which attracted my brother and myself was that the brick arch had different resonance at its two sides. There was a much greater echo on the side you first came to than on the other, probably because the latter had been added afterwards."

Another entry relates to two of Gordon's visitors :—

"What a quantity of snuff people used to take in the olden times! I remember when I was in Gordon's office there was an old gentleman who used to come in, known as General Birch. I think he had been in the Peninsular war. As soon as he was anchored in his chair he pulled out one of those old flat brown snuff-boxes. He would take off the lid, and fix it into one of the fingers which I believe he had lost in action, but in which the lid was perfectly secure; then he brought out from his breast-coat pocket a paper-knife, and with this paper-knife he gave himself three large helps—two up one nostril and the third up the other. I do not know that he took them very often, but it was an enormous dose each time. Another old soldier who used to come to us was Colonel Maceroni, who had been on the staff of Murat, and was in London on some mysterious errand connected with the Reform Bill riots.[1] He had, I remember, a pamphlet of instructions how to make barricades, shells, and other articles useful to rioters. He would come in about half an hour before our dinner-hour—six o'clock—and was always welcome. When he made his appearance he always seemed extraordinarily tired and excited. He would then retire into a corner of the room, and take a bottle of laudanum out of his pocket and pour out and swallow a full wine-glass. By the time dinner was ready he had entirely recovered his spirits, and used to keep us amused and transfixed during the whole meal. He lived in a cottage at or near Battersea Fields, with two very charming daughters, who afterwards became friends of my sister Ellen. They were then in the greatest poverty. What became of Maceroni afterwards I do not know, but one of his daughters married Mr., afterwards Sir Edmund, Hornby, Judge of the Supreme Court at Constantinople."

[1] Mr. Edmund Grove tells me that Colonel Maceroni was also an inventor, and had a plan for a steam carriage, which attracted Gordon. A facsimile of Maceroni's steam carriage was reproduced in the *County Gentleman* for April 19th, 1902. It is there added that Maceroni died poor in 1842.

Out of office hours music was George Grove's chief hobby. He unearthed and bought for a trifle an old spinet in a shop in Long Acre, and brought it home. He used to haunt every place where he could hear music or look at it. One of his favourite resorts was Novello's shop, then in Dean Street, Soho, where, in a back room, there was a fine large case full of scores. The choir in Westminster Abbey was not in those days what it now is, but "many an entrancing hour have I spent there in the winter months at afternoon service, with the dim candles below and the impenetrable gloom above, when I thought my heart must have come out of me with emotion and longing." It was at one of these services that he heard Richard Clark—then the chief bass of the choir, and credited with being able to take the double D—attempt but fail to descend to that depth in Purcell's "They that go down to the sea in ships." Then he used to go to the British Museum to copy music with his friend William Pickering Stevens—one of three orphan brothers, all clerks in Sir William P. Call's bank in Bond Street, and sons of an old military man—and became acquainted both with the "Museum Headache" and the "Museum Flea." Much of his spare time, again, was spent in a "mad pursuit of engravings and painters' etchings," a hobby in which he was encouraged and befriended by another friend, Mr. Holloway, the well-known printseller of Bedford Street, and owner of a fine collection. Another great friend and frequent visitor at Thurlow Terrace, who resembled George Grove in his versatility, was Robert Griffin Laing—the grandson of Mr. Griffin, a well-known Nonconformist minister of Portsea, who baptized most of the Groves—a young man of great personal charm and cultivated literary tastes, who died of consumption in early manhood.[1]

Nor was George Grove remiss in enlisting the interest of

[1] Laing, who was born August 8, 1820, kept some terms at Cambridge, and died at sea on his way home from the West Indies, where he had gone to recruit his health, on April 26, 1849.

his sisters in his favourite pursuits. As Miss Eleanor Grove says, the two boys—George and Edmund—were always "stirring up" their sisters, impressing on them the value of sincerity and thoroughness, denouncing shams in dress and elsewhere, and infecting them with their enthusiasm for books and music.

In the winter of 1837-38 George Grove got his first glimpse of the Continent. His experiences are best told in the narrative dictated nearly sixty years later :—

"While I was articled to Alexander Gordon, he was employed by the Chevalier de Brouwer, a rich manufacturer at Malines in Belgium, to survey the River Dyle with a view to see whether a better access could not be obtained from the sea to the town. The river being very sluggish and winding in its course, the Chevalier's idea was that it might be straightened and so much reduced in length. Accordingly, Gordon and his wife, with a man named Atherton as his chief assistant, and his two pupils, Pattrick and myself, migrated to Malines and took up our residence at the Hotel de Malines. It was a very respectable hotel, though probably far inferior to the best hotels there at the present time. We contracted for our living, and I remember that we paid two francs and a half a day for board and lodging, including half a bottle of *vin ordinaire* for dinner. The living was an entire revelation to us, and one or two things happened which were quite novelties. Amongst other dishes we had (and I think it was always before Pattrick) was a roasted hare. After a few days one of us noticed the head of a pin at the bottom of each of the long ears of the animal, and on investigation it turned out that the hare was nothing but a cat, which had two long hare's ears pinned on each time it was served up ! . . . When we had been a few weeks in the town the weather changed, and a very severe frost came on. The railway had only just been opened from Ghent by Brussels through Malines to Antwerp, and it was our custom to go to church at Brussels on Sunday afternoons by the train. . . . The third-class carriages were nothing but open trays with no roofs, and, if I remember aright, with no seats ; and on the first Sunday after the beginning of the frost, when we arrived at Malines it was found that three men had been frozen to death in one of these carriages. Next to the hotel was a baker's shop, and so great was the cold that the baker's apprentice was actually frozen to death in his bed ; in fact, the frost was so severe that it completely put a stop to all out-of-door work."

Grove adds that the Royal Exchange in London was burned down on the 10th of January 1838, the progress of the flames being much assisted by the extreme frost. "There was a famous chime of bells at the Royal Exchange, and the last tune played by them during the fire was said to have been 'There's no luck about the house, there's no luck at all.'" This was the great frost which made the fame of Murphy, the weather-prophet and almanac-maker, who happened to predict the day, January 20, on which the greatest cold was experienced. According to entries in a book belonging to his mother, the period of Grove's stay in Belgium extended from November 30, 1837, to January 17, 1838.

The minutes of the Institution of Civil Engineers for February 26, 1839, record that "George Grove (of Thurlow Terrace, Wandsworth Road) was admitted a Graduate"; and in February 1840 he migrated to Glasgow to gain practical experience in the factory of Robert Napier, on the Broomielaw. "I first went down to Glasgow," he wrote in 1897, "in the year 1839 [Mr. Edmund Grove says it was 1840]. In those days there was no railway further than Liverpool, and there one took a steamer—a miserable journey it was. Tom [his elder brother] took me as far as Glasgow. I remember that we had to leave the railway at Wolverton, and go for twelve or fourteen miles to Denbigh Hall on coaches or omnibuses, because there was no passage through the Kilsby tunnel. We went down first-class, and I remember that our tickets were more like cheques than tickets, and were torn out of a book, leaving a counterfoil behind. Our seat was numbered, and we had to take our numbered place."

At Glasgow, George Grove worked both in the pattern and fitting shops like a common mechanic, and, as he told Dean Bradley, had to wash his hands in oil every night before touching his books. He made friends with a Mr. Pellatt, a glassmaker, who had a good library; and an old note-book belonging to this period contains copious notes on Hallam's *History of the Middle Ages.* He also read and digested Robertson's *Charles V.*, and was so diligent a student of *The Decline and Fall* that, according to Mr. Edmund Grove, who was then at work at Greenock, his letters showed the influence of Gibbon's style. Another friend who influenced him was the Rev. Mr. Symington, who recommended him to read Coleridge's *Aids to Reflection.*

Towards the close of 1841, Alexander Gordon, having received an order to erect a cast-iron lighthouse at Morant Point, the eastern extremity of the island of Jamaica, summoned George Grove from Glasgow to superintend the construction of the plates in a yard on the Surrey side of the Thames, and appointed him as Resident Engineer during the erection of the lighthouse. In a memorandum subsequently drawn up and preserved in an old note-book, George Grove summarizes the causes which led to this decision, and the progress and completion of his task :—

"The eastern end of the island of Jamaica, as it is the most beautiful so is it to navigators the most important and dangerous part of that island—important, inasmuch as that point is the one 'made' in the inward voyage, and the one from which the homeward course is shaped ; and dangerous, from the numerous and complicated shoals and strong and uncertain currents with which it is surrounded. Not only has the want of a Lighthouse on this Point occasioned delay and inconvenience to the shipping, but many and serious losses have taken place, and have continued to take place for many years. The coast for miles round Morant Point is strewn with the wrecks of vessels of 200 to 400 tons. But, notwithstanding the obvious want of some preventive measure, the apathy which pervades the West India colonies prevented anything being done till the loss of the *New Grove*, Cousens master, a vessel of 500 tons, with a full cargo on her home voyage in 1839, between Morant Kays and the main island, from the variableness of the currents which drove her on the Kays, roused public attention, and in the early part of 1840 an Act passed the island Legislature entitled 'An Act for erecting a Lighthouse on Morant Point, and maintaining and keeping up the same.' Commissioners being appointed to carry into effect the provisions of the Act, these gentlemen, after visiting the Point and communicating with

Mr. Alexander Gordon, were by him furnished with designs for a cast-iron Lighthouse. This tower was decided on at a meeting of the Commissioners in March 1841, and having been shipped for Jamaica in November arrived there in January 1842. As there was no possibility of landing the parts of the Lighthouse at a spot nearer to the proposed site than four miles, and even this landing could not be approached by any vessel of greater tonnage than a shallop, the ship containing the Lighthouse lay at Port Morant, and much delay was incurred during the successive loadings, passages, and unloadings to and from the ship to the shallop and the wharf at Holland Bay. The first care of the resident engineer on arriving at Morant Point was to see a good or at least a serviceable line of road made between the wharf and the site. The foundation was found to be of a good solid nature: coral, a porous rock of which the whole of this end of the island would seem to be composed, covered with a superstratum of loose sand to the depth of 10 or 12 feet. The labourers procured for the erection of the Lighthouse were of a better description than the average of the negroes. They were Kroomen, and this tribe being employed much on the coast of Africa as assistants to the sailors of the timber vessels trading there, have more handy and workmanlike habits than any other tribes. The bottom of the bed of rock, having been excavated to an average depth of 18 inches and levelled, was covered with a coating of asphalte in order effectually to prevent any percolation or rise of water to the foundation. The first stone was laid on the 5th of March and the first plate on the 8th of April. After the third tier had been erected, the concrete was by sufficient tackle hoisted up and pitched into the interior, the fourth, fifth, and sixth tiers being [then] proceeded with. In fact, the filling in of the concrete was not finished till all the tiers had been put up. The derrick, crab, and tackle were the only means used in the erection of the plates of the Tower. Not a single accident of any kind occurred during the erection. On August 1 the shell of the Tower being complete and closed in, and the revolving machinery and lamp put up, a trial of the light was made, the curtains of the lantern being drawn to seaward. At a meeting of the Commissioners held in Kingston soon after this, the 1st of November was fixed on as the day for commencing the permanent lighting, and three lighthouse-keepers were appointed. Cottages have been erected at the foot of the Tower for the abode of the keepers, though the interior might have been advantageously used for this purpose."

This business-like record of the undertaking may be

supplemented by reference to the full diary which he kept during his stay in Jamaica, some details communicated to Mr. Edwards for the biographical sketch in the *Musical Times*, and several unpublished reminiscences dictated in 1897. He went out in a sailing-ship, and was met off Port Royal by the secretary to the Lighthouse Commissioners, who was astonished and somewhat dismayed to find that the engineer had as yet "no sign of whiskers." On the 13th of November 1841, he arrived at Golden Grove Estate, St. Thomas in the East, and started work on the following day. The diary—prefaced with a quotation from Bacon's *Advancement of Learning*: "It is yet a use well received in enterprises memorable, as expeditions of war, navigations and the like, to keep Diaries of that which passeth continually"—is a plain unvarnished engineer's log. The entries, with hardly an exception, relate to the business in hand, and convey no indications of the other interests of the writer. But they give a striking picture of George Grove's indefatigable energy, his close and constant supervision of his subordinates, and the obstacles thrown in his way by the climate, inadequate transport, the temperament of the coloured workmen, and "the slowness natural to the island." Grove never spared himself. He habitually rose between five and six, and there seems to have been hardly a single detail in the erection of the structure on which at one time or another he did not bestow actual manual labour. For example, the entry for February 16, 1842, runs as follows: —"Got the framework of the house up. I did it all myself, with a little help from one of the masons, and very hard work it was. I had to cut the tenons in the joists for the floor myself." Similar entries occur with regard to the making of asphalte, concrete, &c. Of the steadiness and efficiency of his skilled white labourers he speaks in high terms, but the gang of Kroomen from Kingston gave him a good deal of trouble by their fits of laziness, culminating once in a strike. In the diary itself no hint is discernible of his literary tastes, but a clue as to the way in which he spent some of his leisure moments is to be found at the other end of the same note-book, where he has copied out a number of poems by Moore, Wordsworth, Herrick, Shelley, Keats, and Coleridge. *À propos* of Coleridge, it should be mentioned that he met in Jamaica a young doctor named Porter, who had been a pupil of Mr. Gilman's at Highgate, and was full of anecdotes of the poet. Porter had also some pieces of unpublished verse by Coleridge, which Grove copied and embodied in a communication to the *Athenæum* for April 14, 1888, including therewith the story of Lamb and the pudding, also told him by Porter. It is characteristic of Grove's considerateness that he was most anxious to get his white men away from the spot on the earliest possible opportunity before the setting in of the unhealthy season, while the last entry in the diary contains a copy of a letter, urging on the Commissioners the desirability of securing another assistant to relieve the strain on the two lighthouse-keepers in attendance. Another letter of an earlier date conveys to the Commissioners his grateful sense of the manner in which they had been pleased to acknowledge his services.

In spite of the arduous and often discouraging nature of his task, Grove thoroughly enjoyed his stay in Jamaica, where he was most hospitably entertained by the planters of the old *régime*, already past the meridian of their prosperity, but still much addicted to feasting and revelry. The Creole ladies in particular he found charming. *À propos* of his stay in Jamaica I may draw upon the following reminiscence of 1897 :—

"The mango, though plentiful in Jamaica, is not an indigenous fruit there, and oddly enough the best mangoes are known as 'No. 11' and, I think, 'No. 132'; all the others had so strong a taste of turpentine that they were uneatable. But no finer fruit can be imagined than a fine 'No. 11.' I was told in Jamaica how the name originated. In one of his actions Rodney had taken a French ship, which was coming from a French settlement in India with a fine botanical collection for the public garden at Martinique or Guadeloupe. The ship was brought to Kingston, Jamaica, and no doubt the collection suffered extremely, but the two mangoes noted above were still known by their numbers in the catalogue."

Grove stated in the memorandum given above that no accident of any kind occurred during the erection of the lighthouse. But he himself had two remarkable escapes from death. He was fond in after years of telling the story, which can now be given in his own words :—

"I was very anxious to show the light on my birthday, the 13th of August 1842, and to accomplish this, which *I did*, it was necessary to hurry on the internal part of the tower, leaving it to be finished afterwards. It was in completing the floors that the first of these escapes occurred. I was on the top floor giving instructions to a carpenter, when I trod upon a short board and down I went. I struck the girder ten feet below, and bounded from that to the next one, ten feet lower still. There I hung with sixty feet clear below me, and was on the point of dropping off, when the negroes got a ladder up to me and took me off. Except for the fright and a bruise where I had fallen on the girder I was none the worse. But I remember distinctly that during the whole of the time that I was clinging to the second girder and endeavouring to twist myself up upon it, I kept repeating continually to myself the words :

"'And we seem
In running to consume the way.'

"The second escape occurred a few days afterwards. The lantern had been completed, and I, as was my duty, was in the lantern with my eyes about me. At this time, somewhere in the afternoon, a tremendous rain-storm came on, and a leak in the copper of the top covering of the lantern manifested itself. I put up a ladder and went up to discover where the leak in the copper was, when all of a sudden there came a tremendous clap of thunder and a flash of lightning at the same moment, and threw me off the ladder on to the floor of the lantern, some fifteen or eighteen feet. If the lantern roof had not been covered with water, which no doubt carried off the lightning, the flash would have certainly gone through my body."

With what pleasure Grove looked back on his sojourn in Jamaica may be gathered from a letter written to Miss

Marie Busch on August 4, 1895—more than half a century later :—

"You told me nothing more about the *Meerleuchten*. I do not know what is meant unless it is what we call phosphorescence —lovely trains and balls of light in the waves. That is familiar to me. I have seen it in the West Indies in the greatest perfection. There would be a train of twelve feet long behind the boat (a small rowing-boat in the harbour). You could see dozens of fish down in the depths, each one like a rocket, and when the water was quite smooth there would be thousands of fiery specks on the surface, like the images of stars in the heavens. How bright those West Indian days come back to me! Not only the exquisite beauty of Nature—mountains, woods, streams—but many such extra beauties as I describe above, all inspired and enshrined by the charming feelings of youth (I was only twenty-one) and novelty."

Grove seems to have remained some time in Jamaica after the lighthouse was finished, for a note in his mother's handwriting gives June 1843 as the date of his return. But his stay in England was short, for he was soon despatched on a similar job to Bermuda, where the Government decided to erect a lighthouse on Gibbs's Hill. Of his stay in Bermuda I can find but little trace amongst his papers beyond the following anecdote :—

"When I was in Bermuda the 20th Regiment was quartered there, as well as two companies of the Royal Engineers, with whom I was in closer contact, as I was under Colonel Barry, the officer in command. One day my inexperienced mind received considerable amusement. I was talking to one of the officers—of which corps I forget—and he had on some very nice white clothes, made of duck, or drill, or some such material, and I said to him, 'You don't get those clothes here, I suppose?' 'Oh yes,' he answered, 'the regimental tailor made them for me.' 'You don't mean to say that the regimental tailor can fit you like that?' was my reply. 'I should think so! He had better fit me; I would give him three days' heavy drill if he didn't!'"

A drawing of the lighthouse will be found in the *Illustrated London News* of April 20, 1844. It was first lighted on May 1, 1846; and a Parliamentary Blue-Book of the time records the fact that the Treasury paid "George Grove, engineer, £315 4*s.* 4*d.*" The delays in the erection of the lighthouse were tedious, and Grove, who had a good deal of time on his hands, struck up a close friendship with Dr. Field, the Bishop of Newfoundland, a High Churchman of very saintly character, who was much influenced by the Oxford movement. Field in turn exercised a considerable influence on Grove, who took a practical interest in the Bishop's diocesan labours, and designed him a church. Otherwise, Bermuda impressed him much less favourably than Jamaica; he seldom referred to his stay there in after years, and left without regrets in the summer of 1846, reaching home on August 6.

The influence of his association with Dr. Field showed itself at this period in a pronounced leaning towards Ritualism. He fasted regularly if not resignedly, instituted a system of doles for the benefit of the poor, and, as a not unnatural consequence, was exposed to a certain amount of not unfriendly domestic criticism. His brother Edmund was at this time occupied in putting up gas-works at Lincoln, and George Grove, whose health had suffered from his stay in the West Indies, went down by coach to pay him a visit, and in his company made a tour of exploration amongst the Lincolnshire churches. Looking back on this, the earliest of his architectural excursions, many years afterwards, he said: "Lincoln was a splendid place for churches. It contains some of the finest in the country, and there had, as yet, been no restorations!" After this Lincoln period Edmund Grove entered the office of Charles Heard Wild, in Cannon Row, near the Colonial Office, and as his brother George was out of employment, and looking for work, recommended him to his chief, with the desired result. Wild, who was one of Robert Stephenson's chief assistants, and was especially entrusted with the work of laying out stations, soon sent George Grove down to Chester to look after the erection of the "General Station" there.[1] Grove's stay in Chester left him nothing but pleasant memories. He was interested in the town, in the Cathedral and its services, and struck up a great friendship with a pupil of Gunton's, the organist, named Ffoulkes, whom he heard playing a Bach fugue in the Cathedral. As a result of their association a singing-class was started, with Ffoulkes as conductor, at which Grove had the satisfaction of introducing, amongst other works new and old, motets by Palestrina and part-songs by Mendelssohn. From Chester he was moved on to Bangor, where he served under Edwin Clark, Robert Stephenson's resident engineer at the famous Britannia Bridge over the Menai Straits, for eighteen months. His residence at Bangor, however, was not continuous, seeing that in the autumn of 1848 he made his second trip to the Continent. Wild, who, according to Mr. Edmund Grove, was a "warm-hearted man of the world," was so well pleased with George and Edmund Grove, that in September of that year he gave them each £15 to frank their expenses for a holiday trip to Paris. More than that, he furnished them with the most explicit instructions as to where they should stop, how they should live—even down to the particular dishes—and how much they should spend. Accordingly, on September 15, the brothers set off on what proved a most delightful tour, breaking their outward journey at Abbeville and Amiens to see the cathedrals and churches. On reaching Paris they found fresh traces of the Revolution in the ubiquitous trees of liberty—scraggy poplars—planted in every square and vacant space, in the remains of barricades and the unmistakable signs of street-fighting. In Paris they were joined by a London friend, Mr. J. W. Hawkins, subsequently one of the Masters of the Supreme Court, who, in January 1901,

[1] In his old age George Grove used to tell a story of an illiterate Chester tradesman, who, when asked what the letters "G. S." (General Station) stood for, replied "Julius Cæsar."

kindly sent me the following lively reminiscences of his stay:—

"In the autumn of 1848 I joined George Grove and his brother Edmund in Paris. Lamartine was then President of the Republic, and considerable excitement prevailed in the city. Sir George, who was perhaps the most versatile man whom in a long life I have ever known, was full of eagerness to see and hear everything, and one of the first things we did was to go to the Embassy and endeavour to get admission to the Assembly to hear Lamartine speak. The *Attaché* we saw gave us no hope: we were 'nobodies in particular,' as Theodore Hook said. He suggested the President's secretary as the most likely person. To him we went. He shrugged his shoulders—it was impossible; but George assured him that we should be desolated if we were not permitted to hear the eloquent and poetic statesman-President, and the secretary relented and said that if we came to the Assembly half an hour before they sat he would ask the President to allow one at least of the enthusiastic young Englishmen to have admission. We went, and got the permit: George, of course, was voted to be the one, and at night he gave us a wonderful account of what he saw and heard.

"Another day we went to Notre Dame, and ascended the tower into the belfry, where there is a bell with, so George told us, a good deal of silver in it. He accordingly proposed that we should try how our voices would sound in the bell, so we three crept underneath—it hung very low—and when inside sang 'God save the Queen.' It was the dinner-hour of the workmen who were repairing the tower, and while we were in the bell they returned to their work. On our emerging we found a number of them standing round who had heard us singing, and one of their number asked what we had sung. George replied, 'Our National Anthem,' and asked some of them to get under the bell and sing the 'Marseillaise,' which they did, and then asked us to repeat our anthem. We did so, though I can speak for one of the singers that we did not sing the second as cheerfully as the first time. I feared that their Republican susceptibilities might be offended by our singing a monarchical song, but no, they assured us of their love and affection for the free British nation, and begged us to give them the notes of our anthem. George took out his notebook, wrote down the notes, and with many bows and good wishes we parted from them, accompanied, however, by a foreman who volunteered to take us over any part of the Cathedral which was actually closed to the public. George's love of fun and keen sense of humour were shown one afternoon at the Palais Royal. Some boys were playing and skylarking, and a *sergent de ville* drove them off. George, hat in hand, approached the magnificent official, and begged him to say why the young *gamins* were not allowed Liberté, Egalité, and Fraternité. 'Oh,' he replied, 'the *gamins* disturb the citizens.' 'But they are brethren,' said George, 'they are equal, they have liberty. Now we English have great liberty. Look here what we do in England,' and turning to me he said, 'Give me a back, Hawkins.' I gave him one, and over he went. The policeman looked at us with some amazement, and simply said, 'Ah, Messieurs les Anglais sont toujours drôles.' I cannot adequately convey George's manner and humour in these reminiscences. He was an admirable *cicerone*. We took the *diable boiteux* up the tower of Notre Dame, and made out every spot mentioned, and then went up the Arc de Triomphe to see that side of Paris from a height. Indeed, in the course of our short stay in Paris—I think only ten days—we must have seen every old and many new churches, every public building worth seeing, all the galleries of course, and got home each evening dog-tired, but inspired by George with enthusiasm for everything we saw, and amused by his rollicking fun. I remember one recital, chiefly by him, of the Falstaff scenes in Henry IV. after we had gone up to our bedrooms."

Music was not forgotten in this Paris visit. Mr. Edmund Grove remembers in particular a visit to St. Roque, where they were much struck by the singing of Gregorian hymns, the accompanying of the organist, and the procession with men playing the "tone" on serpents of the old pattern. And I find in the 1897 reminiscences the following allusion to Parisian street nomenclature :—

"The names of the streets of Paris are peculiarly interesting. I was very much struck by some of them during my early visits there. Full as my mind was of the Bible at that date, it was curious to find the Clos Saint Lazare, where there was so much fighting in 1848 lying between the Rue Paradis and the Rue d'Enfer. I also remember, though they are not so obvious in their origin, the 'street of the dry tree,' the 'street of the naughty boy,' the 'passage des deux sœurs,' and the 'street of the washerwomen of St. Opportune.' The 'new street of the little fields,' immortalized by Thackeray, has, I think, been done away with."

Bangor remained his headquarters till the summer of 1849, and when the first floating of the tubes of the bridge was successfully accomplished, George Grove wrote a popular account of the work, which, according to Mr. James Forrest, formerly Acting Secretary of the Institution of Civil Engineers, was sold on the spot. He also sent the following account of the operation to the *Spectator*, then edited by Mr. Rintoul, which appeared in the issue of that journal for June 23, 1849:—

"The operation of floating the first tube of the Britannia Bridge [over the Menai Straits], from the place in which it was constructed to the foot of the towers by which it is at last to be supported, came off on the evening of Wednesday [*i.e.*, June 20, 1849]. The preceding evening was the one originally fixed on; but, a capstan breaking after hauling out a few feet, it was necessary to put off doing more till the following day. The tube was built at a distance from the bridge of about 2,000 feet, and in a position along the shore, at right angles to the line of railway. It had, therefore, after being borne down by the tide to very near the towers, to be slewed round across the stream, and finally adjusted into its place on the projecting shelf of stone at the foot of the piers. These evolutions were accomplished by ropes from capstans and crabs on the two shores and on the Britannia Rock; the men in charge of which were signalled to from the top of the tube. The final adjustment was a very delicate piece of work, as the width of the recess into which the end of the huge mass had to be inserted is only an inch greater than that of the tube itself: however, it was managed with complete success.

"The whole operation occupied exactly one hour and three-quarters, the order to haul out being given at 7.36 and the Anglesey end entering its recess at 9.22.

"On the tube with Mr. Stephenson were his two assistants, and Messrs. Brunel and Locke, who acted as his honorary assistants, Captain Claxton, and Sir Francis Head. There was a general gathering of engineers, and a vast concourse of spectators, who lined the shores and platform on both sides of the Straits.

"The raising of the tube through the 100 feet between its present and its ultimate position will probably take place in the course of a few days. Its length is 472 feet, height at the centre tower 30, and its weight between 1,700 and 1,800 tons."

This was George Grove's first appearance in print. Curiously enough, it was reserved for him some twenty-seven years later, as editor of *Macmillan's Magazine*, to accept the first contribution of Mr. St. Loe Strachey, the present editor of the *Spectator*.

At Bangor, George Grove, as we have seen, came chiefly in contact with his immediate superior, Edwin Clark. But he also saw a good deal of the great "Chief" himself, Robert Stephenson, and in this context the following reminiscence of 1897 is worth recording :—

"Mr. Robert Stephenson once told me a very interesting story about a dream of his. A workman was killed at the Britannia Bridge by the bursting of the hydraulic press for lifting the tubes, and Clark sent me up to tell the Chief what had happened. He was very kind, kept me to dinner, and told me the following story. Some time in the 'twenties,' his father and he came up to town to watch the Liverpool and Manchester Railway Bill through the House. Robert was then three-and-twenty, and of a cautious frame of mind. His father had never been in London before for any length of time, and was resolved to see everything. Amongst other things which he was anxious about was a menagerie in the Strand called Exeter Change, which stood where Exeter Hall stands now. It did not open till twelve in the day, and he was told that this was because the keeper gave the lion a walk every morning inside the enclosure of the cages, and nothing would satisfy George but he must go and tip the keeper and see the lion at large. The proposal only put Robert into a great state of agitation. 'My father is sure to stroke the lion, or do something rash of that kind. He will be killed, and then what will become of our Bill?' For everybody knows that George Stephenson's wit and confidence were the main things which got the Bill through the Committee. . . . While the Bill was in deliberation, Robert had to go down to the North—of course by coach. He left early in the morning, and the night before he left he had an extraordinary dream. He dreamed that he and his father went to Exeter Change by appointment with the keeper. When they got there, the keeper said to them, 'Now, gentlemen, I am going to let the animals out.' 'But,' said Robert in a great fright, 'what are we to do?' 'Oh, all right, sir, no danger, just you stand in that corner, and if any animal happens to molest you, say 263 to him, and you will see he will turn round and go off.' He stood there in a great fright, and presently a hyæna came up to him making demonstrations. In a broken voice he said '263,' as he had been told, and immediately the hyæna turned on its heels and made off. Robert went down to the North, and in about a week he came up again, and on going to his lodgings, where he had slept the night before leaving, he found a book turned down on the table beside the bed, which he had been reading before he went to sleep. It was *Hood's Comic Annual*, and was open at a picture of a man in the corner of a farmyard, with all the oxen pointing their horns at him, and the page was 263."

CHAPTER II

Appointed Secretary to the Society of Arts in 1850—The Great Exhibition of 1851—Marriage—Life in the Adelphi—The Christian Socialist Movement—Appointed Secretary to the Crystal Palace, 1852—Translates Guizot's *Études sur les Beaux Arts*—Move to Sydenham—Reminiscences of Paxton—The von Glehns and Scott Russells—Friendship with Tennyson and Stanley—Introduced by Stanley to Dr. William Smith—Work on the Bible Dictionary—Music at the Crystal Palace—Origin of the Analytical Programmes—Reminiscences of Cotton and Spurgeon.

With the close of his engagement at Bangor, George Grove was once more on the look-out for a job. These were the lean years that succeeded the great railway panic of 1846; there was not enough work to go round, and though Grove had proved his capacity as an efficient, conscientious, and hard-working subordinate, it is by no means so certain that he possessed the qualities required to achieve distinction in the higher walks of his profession.

"Looking back over the scattered course of my life," so he said in a speech delivered in July 1880, "it is curious to see how many of the points in it have been determined by my friends. My whole London life, and all that came out of it, is due to three of them, now gone—Mr. Robert Stephenson, Mr. Brunel, and Sir Charles Barry. I was then, in 1848, in a subordinate engineering post, in Mr. Edwin Clark's staff, on the Britannia Bridge, with no confidence in myself, and little chance of getting on. They used now and then to come down to watch the operations at the bridge, and these distinguished men used to notice me, and were as good as gold to me. They counselled me to go to London, and (there is no treason in saying so now) they forced me into the secretaryship of the Society of Arts, just then vacated by Mr. Scott Russell."

This was early in the year 1850, the Council Minutes of the Society of Arts showing that George Grove was in the first instance appointed joint secretary with Mr. Scott Russell on February 6, 1850. On the 6th of March of the same year the Minutes state that Mr. Scott Russell "was to accommodate Mr. Grove in his house," and on the 18th of March the following resolution was passed: "That the Council being fully satisfied with the competency of Mr. Grove fully to discharge the duties of Secretary, the resignation of Mr. Russell be accepted, and that Mr. Grove be nominated as Secretary for the ensuing year." The salary of the post being small, it was agreed that Grove should be at liberty to continue in practice as an engineer, and during the next few years he frequently acted as inspector of permanent way materials of various railway companies, while his engagement with Edwin Clark did not terminate until February 1852. For these two years Grove lived in the house attached to the Society of Arts in the Adelphi, and, after his wont, made troops of friends. The Great Exhibition of 1851, which was really originated by the Society of Arts, was then in active preparation, tickets were sold at the Society's office, and this brought him into contact with numbers of influential people, who naturally enough were attracted by the vivacious and enthusiastic Secretary. Amongst these were Mr. Francis Fuller, a land agent, one of the chief promoters of the Exhibition, Mr. Scott Russell, Grove's colleague and predecessor, and Joseph Paxton. One of the relics of this period is an autograph application from the Duke of Wellington ordering two season tickets, beginning with "London, March 1, 1851, at night," and containing a glaring fault in grammar.

One of the Council of the Society of Arts, and a good friend to George Grove, was Henry Weigall, the sculptor, whose relations with the Duke were more like those of Goya than of Count d'Orsay:—

"Henry Weigall," wrote Grove in 1897, "who then lived in Somerset Street, Portman Square, was one of the few people who could boast of having had an apology made to them by the Duke of Wellington. He was a good-looking man, with a very shiny bald head, who prided himself much on his manners, was an extremely sensitive, particular person, and it must have wounded him dreadfully to be always addressed and spoken of in public by the assistant-secretary, Davenport, as Mr. Wiggle. He had a friend, named Mrs. Jones, of Pantglâs, a rich Welsh lady who was a good deal in London, and drove a very stylish curricle or phaeton. Mrs. Jones was also a friend of the Duke of Wellington's, and nothing would satisfy her but that his Grace should have his bust executed by Weigall. The Duke had a very low opinion of sculptors, and is said to have spoken of them as 'damned busters'; however, Mrs. Jones's influence was sufficient to prevail on the Duke to visit Weigall's house with her one day. They were shown into the studio, and the Duke seems to have had some difficulty in taking off a *paletot* which he wore. Weigall, who was the very pink of politeness, stepped up to him, and placing his hands on the Duke's shoulder said, 'Allow me to assist your Grace,' upon which the Duke was very wroth, and turning sharply round he said, 'G–d d—n you, sir! take your hands off me!' which Weigall immediately did, and went out of the room, nor could he be brought back unless the Duke would consent to make him an apology for such an improper mode of address. As the Duke could not be prevailed upon to do this, Mrs. Jones and he left the house with their purpose unfulfilled. However, a few days later they reappeared, and then the Duke did grumble out something like an apology, with which Weigall was fortunately satisfied, and the bust was made, and very successful it was. It is the only bust that I remember to have seen which shows the extraordinarily deep furrows in which the Duke's eyes were set. At a visit paid by Her Majesty to the Guildhall in 1851, at which I was present, there was a jam in the crowd, and I was wedged in immediately opposite and close to the Duke, and I remember this particular feature in his face struck me very much."

After the close of the Exhibition, George Grove was married, on December 23, 1851, to Harriet Bradley, fifth daughter by his first marriage of the Rev. Charles Bradley, of Glasbury and of St. James's Chapel, Clapham, and sister of his schoolmate and life-long friend, George Granville Bradley, subsequently Dean of Westminster.

After spending a short honeymoon at Clevedon in Somersetshire, George Grove brought his wife back to the house in the Adelphi. Though anything like formal entertainment was impossible on their slender income, the house was the hospitable centre of much interesting society, including Septimus Hansard, the well-known rector of Bethnal Green, F. J. Furnivall, J. M. Ludlow, and Tom Hughes. Two of this group are happily still left, and I am indebted to them for the following notes on his connection with the Christian Socialist movement. Mr. Ludlow writes, January 11, 1901 :—

"I became acquainted with George Grove in, I think, 1849. He was brought to dinner in my then house in Cadogan Place by the Rev. Septimus Hansard, then a curate under Mr. Hampden Gurney in Marylebone, who died rector of Bethnal Green, Grove being a member of the congregation. It appeared that a little publication, entitled *Politics for the People*, which represented the initiation of the Christian Socialist movement, had been sent out by some friend to him in Jamaica, where he was superintending the building of a lighthouse, and had aroused his sympathies (which in later years died out altogether). I found him very pleasant and intelligent, and saw him pretty frequently for some years. I do not think he ever joined the 'Council of Promoters of Working Men's Associations,' for prudential reasons connected with his profession, but he delivered in the Hall of Association, Castle Street East, Oxford Street, on April 18, 1853, a lecture on 'Mathematical Principles exemplified in Common Things,' which I thought the best of the year's series. This included as lecturers Charles Kingsley, Mountstuart Grant-Duff, Charles Pearson, and Tom Taylor."

Dr. Furnivall writes that he only recollects Grove as

"a latish comer into our set [Maurice, Tom Hughes, Ludlow]—a cheery, bright, dear little fellow, with a merry twinkle in his eye, who said a good thing whenever it was possible. . . . I remember him only at our meetings; and I was, alas! too busy with other things to see anything of him, a busier man than myself, in after life. But I always read and heard news of him with great pleasure, and now and then wrote to and heard from him. During my seventy-five years of life I've never come across a happier-natured, cheerier-souled fellow than George Grove. Blessings on his memory!"

An interesting evidence of Grove's practical share in

this movement is furnished by the following letter from Carlyle, dated Chelsea, May 7, 1852 :—

"SIR,—I beg a thousand pardons! I perceive your former letter, not judged to be very pressing, had fallen aside, and has never been answered at all. You may believe me it was not indifference to the honour done me, nor want of good-will to the object you have in view. But this perverse east wind has quite lamed me, of late; and I have been too willing to shirk any writing, or other duty, that was not quite peremptory.

"How the *wind* may blow eleven days hence, we cannot say; but I have too clearly no prospect of being at once well enough and disengaged enough to do myself such a pleasure as you propose for the 18th; and must therefore, with much regret, and with many cordial thanks, beg to be excused on that occasion.

"Surely if you can achieve anything to resuscitate the decayed vigour of *Mechanics' Institutes* it will be well done.

"With many thanks and regards, and regrets for my own inability, I have the honour to be,

"Your most obedient,
"(Signed) T. CARLYLE."

From an old letter-book containing transfers in copying-ink of Grove's correspondence between 1852 and 1864, it appears that the negotiations which led to his appointment as Secretary to the Crystal Palace were opened in May 1852, a few weeks after the death of his father, who passed away on April 2. A company had been formed to re-erect the Hyde Park Exhibition building at Sydenham, and Mr. Francis Fuller, one of its chief promoters, made an informal offer of the secretaryship to Grove. On May 13, Grove wrote to Fuller referring to their conversation, and stating his inability, on the basis of the inadequate information vouchsafed him, to return a definite answer. Satisfactory assurances were evidently at once given by Fuller, for we find Grove writing on the following day, May 14, to accept the offer of the post, on the terms that a salary of not less than £600 per annum should be guaranteed him for ten years. He asks for a reasonable time to wind up his affairs at the Society of Arts, and stipulates that he shall be allowed full liberty to accept any private practice that he may be able to conduct without prejudice to the interests of the company. These demands were evidently conceded, since the same letter-book shows that for some time after taking up his work at the Crystal Palace he continued to inspect permanent way materials for the Great Northern and East Indian Railway Companies, besides acting as auditor to an Insurance Company. Grove did not take up his residence at Sydenham until the autumn, and we find him apologizing in August for not having cleared out of the Adelphi, the reason assigned being the dilatoriness of builders in executing the necessary repairs in his new house. The entries in his letter-book furnish sufficient evidence of his multifarious occupations. Besides winding up at the Society of Arts, hurrying on the procrastinating British workman at Sydenham, making journeys to Peterborough and Manchester to inspect railway materials, he was simultaneously engaged in negotiations with Bosworth, the publisher, and the late Mr. G. Scharf, the illustrator, of his first publication—a translation of Guizot's *Études sur les Beaux Arts*. The terms were arranged to Grove's satisfaction early in October, and the book saw the light early in 1853. That M. Guizot had no reason to complain of translator or publisher may be gathered from the letter which he addressed to Grove a few months later :—

"PARIS, 24 *Avril*, 1853.

"J'ai été si occupé, Monsieur, depuis quelque tems que je n'ai pu encore répondre à votre lettre du 3 Février dernier. J'ai relu votre traduction de mes *Etudes sur les Beaux Arts*, et je l'ai trouvée très satisfaisante ; elle est exacte en même tems qu'élégante. Et Mr. Bosworth de son côté a mis, à l'exécution matérielle du livre, un soin qui en fait un fort joli volume. Je serois charmé de vous confier la traduction de mes autres travaux ; mais j'ai, depuis longtems, contracté à cet égard des engagemens avec Mr. Bentley, et il m'a donné pour traducteur Mr. A. Scoble, qui est venu me voir ici, qui a déjà traduit deux ou trois volumes de moi, et de qui je n'ai qu'à me louer.

"Recevez, je vous prie, Monsieur, avec l'expression de mon regret, celle de ma considération très distinguée."

By October 1852, Grove and his wife were installed in their new house, Church Meadow,[1] Sydenham, for it was not until 1860 that they moved into the picturesque old wooden house where he spent the last forty years of his life. Paxton's name has already been mentioned as one of those with whom Grove was brought into contact, and at this point of our narrative it may be convenient to insert Grove's reminiscences, never before published, of that remarkable man, for whom he cherished a deep respect :—

"Very few people know the origin of the Crystal Palace building. Sir Robert Schomburgk, when travelling in South America, discovered the *Victoria Regia*, and sent a plant of it to his friend, the Duke of Devonshire, at Chatsworth. The Duke was extremely gratified, and ordered Paxton to build a house for it. The house was a square of 24 feet, divided into nine squares of 8 feet each, and secured by cross-ties from the top to the foot of the pillars, so that it was extremely substantial. Each of these squares can be treated as a cell or unit, and added to on each side, and that is practically the Crystal Palace, neither more nor less.

"Paxton's introduction to the Duke of Devonshire has never, perhaps, been properly told. The Royal Horticultural Society used then to occupy a large part of the Duke's gardens at Chiswick. The Duke went to Russia to represent our Sovereign at a marriage, or some other function, as Ambassador. While he was there, he sent over to the Royal Horticultural Society on several occasions some Russian plants or other botanical specimens, and when he returned was anxious to know how they had progressed. Nothing seemed to be known about them, until at last some one recollected that they had been given into the charge of 'young Paxton,' who was then in the Society's employment as an ordinary gardener. Paxton was found, had an interview with the Duke, and pleased him very much by his intelligence, his general good manners, and his clear voice, which just suited the Duke's slight deafness. The Duke, having thus got to know him, used to see him now and then, and occasionally spoke to him at his work. One morning the Duke went down after breakfast, and, finding Paxton bedding out plants, or engaged in some such job, said to him, 'Mr. Paxton, I want to speak to you. I have had a letter from Chatsworth, saying that my head gardener is dead. Will you undertake

[1] The house, now called 1, Church Meadow, was then the first house past the Church, St. Bartholomew's, close to Sydenham Station.

to succeed him?' 'I shall be very glad and proud,' said Paxton. 'When can you go down?' said the Duke. 'By the night mail,' was the answer. This pleased the Duke, who naturally expected some delay for preparation. Paxton accordingly went down, and arrived early in the morning at Bakewell, from whence he walked over to Chatsworth. Nobody was up. He waited some time, walked over the gardens, and at length got in through an open window; and when the housekeeper came down to breakfast, she found her room in possession of a stranger—of course, armed with his credentials. This was, I believe, his first introduction to the house that he served so well. The Duke's property at that time was in considerable disorder, overburdened by mortgages, &c. Paxton, however, began to put things in order, and before the Duke died his property was in the most flourishing condition, and he himself a very rich man. When the Emperor Nicholas I. of Russia came to England in the year 1844, he went down to Chatsworth to see the Duke of Devonshire, and there was a large party to meet him. Paxton arranged a great display of fireworks, and illumination of the tall fountain which played against a background of cliff covered with foliage. Paxton had collected a large party of gardeners, who were concealed behind the palm-house and other greenhouses; and, as soon as the fireworks were finished, and the guests had withdrawn to the house after midnight, these men issued forth, and removed all the rocket-sticks and other traces of the fireworks, Paxton superintending them until after daybreak, when everything was in perfect order. He was just going away to get some sleep and a bath, when he saw a door on the terrace open, and the Duke of Wellington come out and look cautiously about him as he went out into the grounds. Paxton at length thought it would be well to show himself, and did so, wishing his Grace good morning. Upon which the Duke said, 'Well, Mr. Paxton, I am trying to find the dead men, but I can't see any of them.'

"Paxton's oddities came out strongly in his language. One afternoon, during a great crisis in the City, he had been up to town to see somebody at Overend Gurney's, and had been very much disturbed by some stories he had heard of the misery into which country clergymen and others were thrown by the bankruptcy. 'When I hear these things,' said Paxton, 'it makes my blood broil'! On another occasion he spoke about a great 'plothora' of money which there was in the City at that time. I was breakfasting with him one morning when Milner made his appearance. He was superintending some alterations at the Rothschilds' house in the east of France, and came over to consult Sir Joseph on the arrangement of the fountains on the terrace.

'Well, Milner, what did you propose?' 'Why, Sir Joseph, I thought something like the top terrace at the Crystal Palace.' 'Palace! Milner, what do you mean? Liliprussians to giants!'—which was quite a gardener's mistake. Another day I remember his saying, after a long explanation, 'Now you understand my plan in all its ramnifications.'

"The attachment between the Duke of Devonshire and Paxton was very great. On one occasion, about the time of the opening of the Crystal Palace, the Duke came on a visit to Rockhills, and there was no mistaking the feelings which animated him towards Sir Joseph. But the most remarkable instance happened at the time of one of his illnesses, and was told me on the very best authority. The Duke was lying ill at Brighton, and two eminent London physicians came down to hold a consultation. After they had made up their minds, they returned to the bedroom and told the Duke the result. He heard them out and then said, 'Would you oblige me, gentlemen, by ringing the bell? *I should like to hear what Paxton thinks of it.*'"

To this period also must be referred the beginning of Grove's long and intimate friendship with the two families who formed the inner circle of the Sydenham society of which Grove was the intellectual centre—the von Glehns, of Peak Hill Lodge,[1] and the Scott Russells, of Westgate. Robert William von Glehn [1800–1885], a native of Revel, the capital of Esthonia, one of the Baltic provinces of Russia, established himself in London as a Russia merchant in 1835, became naturalized as a British subject, married a Scotch lady named Duncan, and was deeply attached to the land of his adoption. As a young man, being tall and distinguished-looking, very musical, a great linguist and a beautiful dancer, he was naturally very much sought after in London society. Later on in life he repaid his welcome by the generous and graceful hospitality which he dispensed to a large circle of friends and acquaintances. Herein he was admirably assisted by his wife, who was not only clever and well read, but shared her husband's devotion to music, and shone as a conversation-

[1] It was on Peak Hill that Campbell, the poet, lived; and there he was visited by both Byron and Scott.

alist. About the year 1844, the von Glehns took Peak Hill Lodge as a summer residence, and some ten years later made it their home for good. Of their twelve children, ten are still living, including Mrs. Creighton, widow of the late Bishop of London ; Ernest von Glehn, who married Miss Marian Bradley, a half-sister of Grove's wife ; Oswald, the artist ; William, who married the well-known singer Sophie Löwe ; and Miss Olga von Glehn, to whom the writer of this memoir is indebted for much valuable information in regard to the Sydenham phase of Grove's life. By general consent of those best fitted to judge, none of this gifted family was more attractive or accomplished than Mary Emilie (Mimi) von Glehn, the goddaughter of the famous Mrs. Somerville, the mathematician. So remarkable was her musical talent that Hans von Bülow declared her to be the best amateur player of Beethoven and Chopin he had ever met with. And so keen was the interest that he took in her musical development that for two winters running she went for six weeks to Hanover, where von Bülow gave her three or four lessons a week for nothing.

The third household in this triple alliance was that of the Scott Russells. John Scott Russell—who had preceded Grove as Secretary to the Society of Arts, and who was now brought into closer connection with him as one of the first Board of Directors of the Crystal Palace Company, and as his near neighbour at Sydenham—was the well-known engineer and builder of the ill-starred *Great Eastern*—a very handsome, brilliant, and unsuccessful man. Married to a beautiful and clever Irish lady, he had five children, two of whom—Madame Rausch and Mr. Norman Scott Russell—still survive. The three daughters all inherited the talent and good looks of their parents ; and compelled admiration by the irresistible union of beauty and intellect. It is sad to relate that Louise, the eldest, and the special friend of Miss Mimi von Glehn, died, like her, of lingering consumption.

Other near neighbours and close allies were Mr. Henry

Phillips, a portrait painter of great merit, and his wife, who were deeply attached to the Groves; Mr. Mayow Adams (son of a private secretary of William Pitt), his wife, an unmarried sister, and a widowed sister-in-law (Mrs. Herbert Adams); and two clever and charming unmarried cousins, the Misses Wynell Mayow. Mr. Mayow Adams's aunt, Miss Adams, had been lady-in-waiting to the Duchess of Gloucester, and his wife (*née* Hodge), was the daughter of an officer who fell at Waterloo. With her brother, who fought in the Crimea, and is mentioned in Kinglake's *History*, Grove delighted to discuss the battles and incidents of that campaign.

The foregoing paragraphs are to a great extent anticipatory, since, at the period which we have reached, many of the most brilliant members of the Sydenham set were still in their teens—some not yet out of the nursery. The brightest days of Grove's long connection with Sydenham did not dawn till the "sixties," when the younger generation were beginning to grow up and to respond more readily to the stimulus of his enthusiastic and vivid personality. But even in these earlier days the influence was at work, and Grove had begun to infect all around him, young and old, with that cult of hero-worship —in religion, art, and letters—to which he dedicated the best energies of his life.

The preparations for the opening of the Crystal Palace naturally occupied a great deal of Grove's time. But now, as always, he contrived to keep a great many irons in the fire. Thus we find him making extensive purchases of the works of Bach, which led to another letter from Carlyle, dated Chelsea, January 28, 1853:—

"DEAR SIR,—Your excerpt about Sebastian Bach is worth something; and the kindness with which you communicate it is worth a great deal. I am very much obliged to you.

"According to 'Rodenbeck's' book the visit in question occurred on the '7th April' (1747), and the concert, that evening, was at the *old* Schloss in Potsdam, Sansouci being just in the birth-throes, and not yet born, for such objects. 7th

April, 1747, that was the evening on which Sebastian tried the pianos.

"If you fall in with any other such notions in your reading, of course it can do me no harm to receive them, whether I ever write on Frederick or not, and it may do me good in either contingency.

"Believe me, dear Sir,
"Yours with thanks,
"(Signed) T. CARLYLE."

Later on, over the signature of "Constant Reader," he is found inditing a long letter to the *Spectator* of June 11, 1853, *apropos* of the performance by Vieuxtemps of "Old Sebastian's" Chaconne at a recent concert of the Musical Union. In it Grove energetically protests against the notion then current, that Bach "was a man who *wrote fugues*; that he was prodigiously learned, and equally crabbed and difficult to comprehend; and that, in consequence, to all but professionals and the most initiated of amateurs, his pieces are utterly uninteresting." Grove, on the other hand, stoutly maintains that Bach's learning was a very subordinate thing, and that "not *it*, but feeling, tender passionate sentiment, a burning genius, and a prodigious flow and march of ideas, are his characteristics."

The two years that followed were notable landmarks in Grove's life. On April 25, 1853, was born his eldest child, Lucy Penrose, a singularly attractive and lovable girl, whose premature death in 1863 caused her parents deep and abiding grief; while in 1854 he made the acquaintance of Tennyson and Stanley, the introduction in both cases being effected by his brother-in-law, Granville Bradley. As regards Tennyson, it appears that the Directors of the Crystal Palace—no doubt at Grove's suggestion—were anxious to secure an inaugural Ode[1] from the new Laureate's pen. Grove accordingly was

[1] It is an interesting evidence of Grove's catholic tastes that the champion of "Old Sebastian" should have favoured the choice of Hector Berlioz—then bracketed with Wagner as a veritable musical Anarchist—as the composer to whom Tennyson's Ode should be entrusted.

despatched to the Isle of Wight, and what followed may be told in his own words :—

"Tennyson was very kind and good to me," so Grove told Mr. Edwards in 1897. "He received me with the greatest cordiality, but he could not see his way to writing the poem ; and the net result of my visit was the beginning of a truly delightful and valuable friendship, and his explanation of the difference between a 'cowslip' and an 'oxlip,' which I asked him *apropos* of his line—

> "'As cowslip unto oxlip is,
> So seems she to the boy.'[1]

This he answered by picking one of each in the copse behind the house, and showing me how the one stood erect and the other drooped its head."

Grove's admiration for Tennyson's poetry was both deep and lasting. Later on, as we shall see, he published some admirable studies of Tennyson's lyrics in the *Shilling Magazine* and *Macmillan's Magazine*—where under his editorship "Lucretius" first saw the light ; he knew "In Memoriam" practically by heart ; he took the deepest interest in the preparation of Professor Andrew Bradley's monograph on that poem ; and in choosing Christmas presents for his particular friends Tennyson's latest volume of poems was easily first favourite. Tennyson, as we have seen, could not see his way to write the proposed inaugural Ode, but the formal opening of the Crystal Palace by the Queen took place with great *éclat* on Saturday, June 10, 1854. Costa had charge of the musical programme, which included the "Hallelujah" Chorus given by 1500 singers, the band being "monstrously strengthened," as Chorley put it, by upwards of 200 brass instruments ; and Madame Clara Novello electrified the audience, in "God save the Queen," by a high B flat which was heard right at the other end of the building. The *Times* of the following Monday (June 12) devoted a long descriptive article to the ceremony, from which it may be not amiss to transcribe the following passages :—

"Even the huge semicircular orchestra prepared for Mr. Costa's

[1] "The Talking Oak," line 107.

band of 1,600 performers was a work of no small difficulty to finish in a week. . . . .

"Soon after one o'clock the majority of the visitors had assembled, and the vast interior of the building presented a sublime spectacle. The area of the centre transept, filled with a grand representation of English Society, and having the throne in the midst, was in itself a remarkable sight. On the north side the semicircular orchestra swarmed with the celebrities of our musical world—the instrumental performers below, the vocalists, with old Lablache in front, on the upper benches, a military band on the crest of this harmonious 'mountain,' and below, Costa, with Miss Clara Novello by his side. . . . .

"Scarcely had the illustrious party taken their places, and the cheers with which their arrival was welcomed subsided, when the music of the National Anthem was rolling in rich volumes of sound over the length and breadth of the Palace. The solo parts were sung by Clara Novello with most thrilling effect, while the reverberation of a Royal salute fired from the park served to mark with additional grandeur the powers of the great orchestra and chorus. Never, perhaps, was this noble anthem heard with more overpowering effect. Many shed tears, many more found it difficult to restrain them, but one result was even more remarkable. There is a rule that under no circumstances shall a policeman uncover while on duty. The strains of the National Anthem, however, were too much for them on Saturday. One communicated the contagious influence to another, until a large proportion owned the power of present Royalty by taking off their hats. While in this state an awful glance from Captain La Balmondiere reminded them of their breach of discipline, and the headpieces were at once resumed; but it shows the effect of the music, and was nearly as great a compliment to Mr. Costa and Miss Novello as the condescending recognition which the former subsequently received from the Queen."

Addresses were subsequently read by Mr. Laing and several heads of departments, and a procession was formed of the officials, heads of departments, and Directors,[1] headed by the chief superintendent of the works, Mr. Belshaw, and brought up by the Royalties, Cabinet

[1] The Directors present were Sir Joseph Paxton, and Messrs. Laing, Calvert, Lushington, Geach, Anderson, Scott Russell, and Farquhar. The list of heads of departments includes the names of Fergusson, Layard, Scharf, Penrose, and George Grove.

Ministers, and Foreign Ambassadors. After a formal progress round the building, the Queen returned to the main transept, the Hundredth Psalm was sung, the Archbishop of Canterbury offered a prayer, followed by the "Hallelujah" Chorus, and the Queen declared the Crystal Palace open.

But the introduction to Stanley was far more momentous in its consequences. It not only brought Grove into contact with the man whom of all he ever knew he reverenced most highly, but it practically determined the main course of his life for the next dozen years. The story of their meeting is best told in the interesting autobiographical speech delivered by Grove in July 1880. After giving various instances of the manner in which the turning points in his career had been determined by his friends he continues :—

"To take another instance. What was it that started me with the study of the Bible? I had been brought up to know the Bible well, and a great deal of it I knew by heart, but the study of it was quite distasteful to me. What was it that altered my feeling? Why, the bitter complaint of my dear old friend James Fergusson[1] (then a new friend) that there was no index of the proper names of the Bible. He was engaged then, as he has been ever since, in an internecine warfare with everybody who doubted his splendid theory that the round church in Jerusalem—the Mosque of Omar—was the church which Constantine built over the tomb of our Lord, or rather, what Constantine believed to be the tomb of our Lord. Fergusson and I used to meet at the Assyrian Court of the Crystal Palace and talk about many things, and this among them; and it was in one of these talks that he lamented that he could find no such list to support his argument. Well, we set to work at once, my wife and I, and we made a complete index of every occurrence of every proper name in the Old Testament, New Testament, and Apocrypha, with their equivalents in Hebrew, Septuagint Greek, and Latin. There it was; what was to be the next step? Soon after this came a

[1] James Fergusson [1808–1886], the distinguished antiquarian and historian of architecture, adviser of the Crystal Palace Company in regard to the erection of the Assyrian Court, and from 1856 to 1858 general manager of the Company. He was succeeded in this post by Robert Bowley, another intimate associate of Grove's.

great event in my life. I saw the Dean of Westminster (Dean Stanley) for the first time. He was then Canon of Canterbury, and it was there I saw him in 1853 or 1854. I had heard of him often from Bradley and other men, but had never met him. It was in his house at Canterbury, and he was finishing *Sinai and Palestine*, and I recollect as well as yesterday the way he came forward to me, with his hands out, as if he were welcoming an old friend, and how he showed me what he was engaged on [the Appendix to *Sinai and Palestine*]. He showed me that in Hebrew there were distinct words for all the different kinds of natural objects; for mountains and hills, and rocks and plains, and rivers and torrents, and that while in Hebrew these terms were never interchanged, in the English Bible they were used indiscriminately, and that a great deal of light might be thrown on the narratives if these were set right in our Bibles, and other things of the same sort rectified. He set me alight in a moment, and I fairly blazed up. I rubbed up my Hebrew, of which I had learnt the alphabet at Elwell's school, I got up German enough to plough through Ewald and Ritter, and plunged with delight into a sea of Biblical research. Now the Dean would have you believe that it was I who invented the appendix to his book, in which the Hebrew topographical terms are described and catalogued. But that is only his way of putting it. It was *he* who invented it, and I just carried out what he devised, and did the mechanical part of the work for him."

The value that Stanley set upon Grove's assistance is sufficiently indicated in a letter to Dr. Jowett in 1856, in which he says: "I ought never to write a book without a Grove or Albert Way to correct references and proofs." At first Grove offered his services as a volunteer and gratuitously; it was only when the labours of revision assumed much larger dimensions than were originally contemplated, that, at Stanley's insistence, he accepted remuneration for the services so frankly acknowledged in the prefaces to *Sinai and Palestine* (1856 and 1864).

It was to Stanley also that Grove owed his connection with the *Dictionary of the Bible.* Dr. William Smith, the lexicographer, had already conceived the scheme of his greatest work, and was organizing a staff of contributors. To quote Grove's own words in 1880:—"Dr.

Smith had proposed the Dictionary, and was looking about for help, and Stanley told him of me [1] and of my list of proper names, and there we were. That introduced me to my excellent friend Mr. John Murray, to the Archbishop of York, to Mr. Lightfoot, now Bishop of Durham, Mr. Thorold, now Bishop of Rochester, to Aldis Wright, and to half a hundred good men and true. It was hard work, no doubt, but it was lovely work, and it was a double pleasure to be one of such a team, and to be driven by such a first-rate coachman as our Editor."

The zeal with which Grove threw himself into the work may be judged from a letter to Smith dated Crystal Palace, January 16, 1857, in which he submitted a list of upwards of two hundred names and words in A and B alone. He twice visited Palestine—in 1858 and 1861—so that his topographical and geographical articles might rest on the solid basis of close personal survey, and according to his own account wrote no fewer than 1,100 pages of the 3,154 contained in the Dictionary.[2] It should be explained, however, that Grove's services in connection with the Dictionary were very far from being confined to the articles which appear over his initials. Not only was he entrusted by Dr. Smith with the task of revising such articles as his expert knowledge fitted him to test and check, but he actually re-wrote a good many contributions without formally claiming their authorship. Thus we find him in one letter to Smith offering to let an article which he had written go in over the initials of another writer whose article had been withdrawn, on the understanding that the other man should have the pay for it. It is pleasant to be able to add that the relations which prevailed between Grove and Smith throughout their

[1] According to Dean Bradley, Stanley said that Grove was the best Old Testament theologian he knew.

[2] Mr. John Murray, to whose courtesy I am indebted for valuable information on the subject of Grove's connection with the Dictionary, has, by reference to the books of the firm, made it clear that this estimate evidently covered articles revised for other writers, as well as those written by himself. The latter may be roughly set down at from 800 to 850 pages.

long and intimate association were of the utmost cordiality. There was an occasional difference of opinion, once or twice a slight breeze, but never anything approaching to serious friction. Dr. Smith early recognized the value of Grove's assistance by conferring on him privileges not accorded to any other contributor: to him, and to him alone, were the finished sheets entrusted. He also constantly consulted him with regard to the choice of contributors, as their correspondence abundantly proves, and treated his suggestions with the utmost attention and consideration. Special recognition of Grove's work is made in the preface to the completed work. But while Grove was the most voluminous and industrious contributor to the Dictionary, he, as we have seen, fully acknowledged the claim of Dr. Smith to be regarded as the directing and supervising intelligence of the whole undertaking. Partly owing to his Nonconformist antecedents, partly to the alleged rationalistic tendencies of some of his contributors, Dr. Smith's *Dictionary of the Bible* was subjected to severe animadversion in certain quarters. The *Record*, January 18, 1864, roundly declared that "the ostensible Editor seems to have done no editing at all." Whereupon Dr. Smith replied to the effect that the whole undertaking entirely originated with him; that he selected the contributors, apportioned the work, suggested, where necessary, the mode of treatment; omitted some articles, altered others, and revised the whole; and in conclusion appealed to his contributors to verify his statements. No attempt was made to impugn the accuracy of this crushing rejoinder, for the sufficing reason that it was strictly and entirely in accordance with the facts of the case.

Grove's work on the *Dictionary of the Bible* occupied the bulk of his leisure, from first to last, for nearly seven years. But during this period, which covered the years 1857–1863 inclusive, he contrived not only to prosecute his musical studies with great zeal, but to play a part in the organization of the musical performances at the

Crystal Palace far larger and more important than was demanded of him by the ordinary discharge of his duties as Secretary. For several years, absence from England or London and the pressure of professional work had curtailed his opportunities for hearing music. In this way he missed the chance of seeing or making the acquaintance of Mendelssohn in the "forties." But, once settled in London, Grove began to add to his musical library—in particular purchasing the works of Bach and Palestrina—and to frequent the concert halls. When Berlioz conducted the first series of the "New Philharmonic Concerts" at Exeter Hall in 1852, Grove attended the performance of Beethoven's Ninth Symphony, though he candidly confessed that he "could make very little of it." From the letter to the *Spectator* already quoted, we have seen that he frequented the concerts of Ella's Musical Union. The Crystal Palace was opened in June 1854, and Mr. August Manns, who had originally occupied the post of sub-conductor to the Crystal Palace band—then a wind band only—till October 1854, was reappointed full conductor in the autumn of 1855.

"The music at the Crystal Palace"—we quote from Grove's own account in the *Dictionary of Music*, vol. ii., p. 207,

> "was at that time in a very inchoate condition; the band was still a wind band, and the open Centre Transept was the only place for its performances. Under the efforts of the new conductor things soon began to mend. He conducted a 'Saturday Concert' in the 'Bohemian Glass Court' the week after his arrival; through the enlightened liberality of the Directors, the band was changed to a full orchestra, a better spot was found for the music, adjoining the Queen's rooms (since burnt) at the north-east end; and at length, through the exertions of the late Mr. Robert Bowley, then General Manager, the Concert Room was enclosed and roofed in, and the famous Saturday Concerts began."

The origin of the analytical programmes which made Grove's name a household word amongst all friends of music, and endeared the familiar abbreviation of "G." to two generations of concert-goers, is happily described in the autobiographical speech of July 1880:—

"Well, at the Crystal Palace, as I need hardly tell you, over and above my special duties as Secretary, there was the music, to which I soon began to attach myself particularly. And here, again, the analytical programmes, of which Mr. Sullivan has spoken so much too kindly, originated entirely from the suggestion of a friend. We were going to celebrate the birthday of Mozart in 1856, when the Crystal Palace music was just beginning to struggle into existence, and Mr. Manns said to me how much he wished that I would write a few words about Mozart himself, and about the works to be performed. I tried it, and that gave me the initiation; and after that, as the Saturday Concerts progressed, I went on week by week. I wrote about the symphonies and concertos because I wished to try to make them clear to myself, and to discover the secret of the things that charmed me so; and then from that sprang a wish to make other amateurs see it in the same way. My friend Sullivan, in his affection for me, has, I think, overrated the value of these analyses, and has also given me more credit in respect to the Crystal Palace music than I deserve. No doubt I have devoted myself very much to it, and perhaps I was the means of obtaining Mendelssohn's Reformation Symphony, and some works of Schubert's, which, otherwise, we might not have been the first to play. But what is the use of possessing music, or of analysing it, unless it is played to perfection? No, ladies and gentlemen, the great glory of the Crystal Palace music is the perfection in which it is played. There is no doubt that we play many of the greater works better than they do anywhere else in England. I say this notwithstanding some recent events. And to what is this due? To the devotion and enthusiasm, the steady, indefatigable labour of my friend, Mr. Manns. Probably no one but myself is in the position to know really how very hard he has worked, and how much he has done behind the scenes to ensure the success of the performances that do him such infinite credit. And here I may say that one of the special advantages that music has been to me is the number of young friends that I have made through it. I welcome every one of them as they arrive. I hope I may always keep abreast of them and never sink into an old fogey."

The concert in question took place "in the music-room of the Queen's apartments, North Wing," on Saturday, January 26, 1856, and from Grove's annotations—which, as he told Mr. Edwards in 1897, "I remember writing in my dressing-room in our first house in Sydenham, near the church,"—we may quote a characteristic passage from the notice of Mozart's Symphony in E flat, which concluded this Commemoration Concert. After referring to Mozart's extraordinary productivity in the year 1788, he continues :—

> "The circumstances which necessitated such fearful exertion on this and many other occasions in Mozart's life we have no means of ascertaining. [This was before the days of Jahn's 'Mozart.'] Whatever they were, they were in accordance with a common custom of Nature. She seems to delight in condemning her most gifted sons to an ordeal the very reverse of that which we should anticipate. It seems equally true in Art and in Morals, that it is not by indulgence and favour, but by difficulty and trouble, that the spirit is formed; and in all ages of the world our Davids, Shakespeares, Dantes, Mozarts, and Beethovens must submit to processes which none but their great spirits could survive—to a fiery trial of poverty, ill-health, neglect, and misunderstanding—and be 'tried as silver is tried,' that they may become the teachers of their fellow-men to all time, and shine, like stars in the firmament, for ever and ever."

For upwards of forty seasons Grove contributed the lion's share of the analyses to these programmes, those of the works of Beethoven, Mendelssohn, Schubert, Schumann, and Brahms being with hardly an exception from his pen. The analyses of the nine Symphonies of Beethoven were eventually expanded into the important volume published in 1896, but he rarely allowed any of these commentaries —which can be reckoned by the hundred—to appear twice in the same form. His researches at home or abroad, his conversations with musicians, his general reading, were constantly drawn upon to supply fresh and illuminative matter, whether in regard to musical or literary parallels, details of construction or anecdotic reminiscences. That he was not the inventor of the analytical programme Grove has himself frankly admitted. He had forerunners in Thomson, the Professor of Music at Edinburgh, *circ.*

ann. 1840, in John Ella, who started the *Musical Union* in 1845, in John Hullah, when he prefixed biographical notices to the book of words of his historical concerts at Exeter Hall in 1847, and in Dr. Wilde, who compiled the programme books of the New Philharmonic Society, started in 1852—to which, it may be added, Grove himself contributed in subsequent seasons. But "G" combined all that was good in his predecessors with a freshness, an enthusiasm, a charm of exposition, and a wealth of illustrative detail that were all his own. There have been better analysts, anatomists and dissectors of the organism and structure of the classical masterpieces; there has never been so suggestive and stimulating a commentator upon their beauties. "G's" purple patches were always ingenious and often delightful. Ella's "synoptical analyses" abounded in egotistic irrelevances—*e.g.*, "As I was sitting one day sipping my cup of incomparable Viennese coffee in such and such a restaurant, Liszt suddenly tapped me on the shoulder"—stilted rhapsodies, arid technicalities, and a constant abuse of conventional epithets. It is no part of our present purpose to belittle the admirable work which Ella achieved, but as an annotator he certainly failed where Grove succeeded in enlisting the sympathy of the amateur.

The record of these early years at the Crystal Palace, clouded in March 1856 by the death of his mother, may be rounded off by two extracts from Grove's unpublished reminiscences of 1897. The first relates to a "very interesting person named Cotton," who had been Bishop Selwyn's chaplain in New Zealand, and who appeared in Sydenham towards the end of the Crimean War.

"Cotton," writes Grove, "was an enthusiast about bees, and had not only written a very interesting volume 'My Bee Book,' but while at Oxford had kept two hives of bees in his rooms, allowing them to go out by a hole in the top of the window. He made his appearance in Sydenham quite casually, coming straight from the Crimea with a very large bag and a large knapsack or bundle across his shoulders containing a photographic apparatus and various other impedimenta. He introduced himself at the parsonage, where the Rev. Charles English was always hospitable. Besides, his father, Mr. William Cotton, was Governor of the Bank of England, a very good Churchman, and renowned for his charities to the Church, so that his name was an 'open sesame' to any parson. Cotton's request was a very modest one (if he had kept to it)—that he might be allowed to take a photograph of the chancel of English's church from the lawn of the parsonage. 'I shall only be a few minutes over it, and I can assure you I shall make a beautiful picture or it.' 'By all manner of means,' said English. However, it ended in Cotton's residing there for, I think, the next fortnight . . . . His story of some circumstances attending his voyage to New Zealand was very interesting. He went out, I think, in a sailing ship with the bishop. Cotton's intention was to take a hive or two of bees with him to introduce them to New Zealand, but as he and the bishop were to go by railway to Falmouth and meet the ship there, he contented himself with depositing the hives on deck, and giving the sailors strict directions not to knock them about, assuring them that if left alone they would molest nobody. When they got on board the ship at Falmouth, they found that the hives had been jostled, and the bees had got out and stung some of the sailors, upon which they were promptly thrown overboard. 'Never mind,' said Cotton, 'there will be no difficulty, we will get some more bees at Falmouth, and we will take them out *in ice*,' which was very creditable to his ingenuity, and completely answered the purpose. The result of the experiment, however, was very curious. The native bees of New Zealand were stingless, and were soon exterminated by the English intruders; and not only the bees, for there was a bird called the 'bee-eater' which subsisted on these stingless bees, and attempting to make a prey of the English variety, was also exterminated. This, at any rate, was Mr. Cotton's version."

The second reminiscence relates to Mr. Spurgeon, who came down to see the directors of the Crystal Palace with reference to his preaching a sermon on the General Fast, October 1857.

"After his interview with the Board was over, I took him to my room in the passage close to the board room to get his hat and coat. As soon as we had got inside my room he said: 'You haven't a place here where I can have a smoke?' 'Oh yes, I have,' said I, opening the door of the little room behind my office. He then lit up, and I was emboldened to say, 'Then you do not mind an occasional cigar, Mr. Spurgeon?' 'Oh, yes I do, young man,' he replied. 'It is the regular cigar that I like.' I do not remember that I ever heard more than one sermon from him. That was at Exeter Hall when he was preaching there, I think, when the Tabernacle was building. It was interesting, but not very flattering to his scholarship. The text was: 'They shall never perish, neither shall any pluck them out of my hand.' He said: 'You will observe here how definite the promise is. It does not say they *will* never perish, but it is the definite form of the future—they *shall* never perish.' It gave me rather a shock because I was well aware that there is no definite future in Greek, and whether the English is 'shall' or 'will,' it is the plain future in the Greek. But one thing struck me very much—the singing of the hymns. He gave them out two lines at a time, and often accompanied his reading with an observation such as '*Now* with all the devotion you are capable of.' Then the congregation sang very low and solemnly. '*Now* with all the vigour of your lungs.' And then they made as much noise as possible. It gave great vitality to the hymns."

Of Maurice mention has already been made in connection with the Christian Socialist Movement, but it may be added that Grove's eldest son, Walter Maurice, born on January 27, 1857, derived his second name from the great preacher, who had written to his father the following interesting letter on October 29 of the previous year, in connection with the Sunday Question at the Working Men's College:—

"I have been thinking very earnestly of this Sabbath question ever since our conversation on Sunday, and I have fully convinced myself that I ought to do something; for this clamour, I foresee, will lead to more practical unbelief than almost any which the devil could have stirred up, and if we, the clergy, should really contribute to keep the people of London in the gin-shops, God, I am sure, will visit us for this sin. I think that in such a case sermons, which are in general the most helpless kind of literature, may be the most helpful, because the weapon which is used in attack should be used in defence, and because any person tolerably impressed with his responsibilities as a preacher will feel that he is not to plead a cause, but to set forth as well as he can the whole principle involved in the dispute. Above all, I still feel that I was obliged to rest the whole argument on Scripture to vindicate the Jewish as well as the Christian Sabbath from the abuse that is put upon it, and to oppose the course the clergy are taking as contrary to the principle which is contained in both, and that is interpreted to us by the highest authority. I had made up my mind to begin the subject next Sunday, and to preach three sermons on it before I went to Eversley on Wednesday. I talked over the whole matter with Kingsley, and found him very earnest about it . . . . but we agreed that as a country clergyman he was less called on to work than I was . . . . There is no sort of moral courage required to bring the subject before a Lincoln's Inn congregation. I shall have an audience favourably inclined to your cause, and the thing I shall be anxious for in their position is that they shall not think they are acting as worldly-wise men in following their instinct, and that Christianity is opposed to it, a most dangerous sentiment I am sure. At the same time it is an audience before which one can go with many points that would be out of place or unusual in an ordinary parish, and if you should think I have said anything which can do any good I will print it afterwards. Kingsley begged me to write this to you that you might not think he was inattentive to your wishes.[1]

"Affectionately yours,

"F. D. M."

[1] General Sir Frederick Maurice calls my attention to the first allusion to the Sabbath Question in his father's correspondence in a letter to Daniel Macmillan, dated October 25th, 1852. (*Life*, Vol. II. p. 144). Maurice writes: "My dear and excellent friend Grove is the secretary of the New Crystal Palace and is greatly agitated by the violent denunciations of the Evangelical clergy against him and it. They are trimming the pulpits for a regular assault. They command us all to preach against the Palace on peril of our souls." Maurice adds that while his reverence for the Sabbath was extreme he saw infinite danger in the acceptance of Pharisaic views on the subject. "The modern fanaticism will drive hundreds of literary men far from ill-affected to Christianity (such as Thackeray) into positive hatred of Christianity."

CHAPTER III

First visit to the Holy Land in 1858—Jaffa, Jerusalem, the Dead Sea, Bethhoron, &c.—Impressions of Egypt—Work on the Bible Dictionary—The Wooden House at Sydenham—Sydenham acquaintances—Visit to Oberammergau—Edward Lear and the Toadstools—Mr. Gladstone at the Crystal Palace—Second visit to the Holy Land in 1861—Nâblus, Carmel, Damascus, &c.—Grove's Note-books and their contents—Arthur Sullivan and Franklin Taylor—Death of Grove's elder daughter.

GROVE's letter-book for 1857—1858 contains little correspondence beyond that in connection with his work for the *Dictionary of the Bible*, at which he laboured with unremitting diligence during his hours of leisure. Indeed during one summer Lady Grove assures me that he hardly ever went to bed before daylight. It is difficult to fix the precise date at which his long-cherished desire to visit Palestine took practical shape. It was doubtless stimulated by his association with Stanley and Fergusson, and soon became a positive necessity in view of his topographical and geographical contributions to the Dictionary. In May 1858 he let his house at Sydenham and came up to live in town for five weeks. The early part of August was devoted to preparation for his start, and in the last week of that month he set off on what Dean Bradley calls his "first dash to the East."

From an entry in his note-book, dated Friday, August 27, it appears that on board the steamer that conveyed him from Marseilles to Alexandria no fewer than eleven nationalities were represented, including Arabs, Armenians, Corsicans, Maltese, and the King of Oude and his suite. Grove had a good deal of coversation with a number of French priests on board and observes, "these good fathers seem to have no conception of any other motive for going to the Holy Land but *un pèlerinage*, *une pieuse intention.* 'Ah!' said one of them to me last night, 'vous avez laissé votre femme et votre famille! C'est une pieuse intention.' I have tried hard to explain to the most sensible of them that my object is not one of devotion or sentiment, but without success. 'Ah, les voyages scientifiques ne sont pas mon métier.'" He adds, "Few things divide foreigners from English more than their habits at table. I believe that the first trace of orientalism one meets with out of England is the custom of 'dipping their fingers in the dish' that even Frenchmen are given to."

Grove was on deck at 5.30 A.M. on the morning of Sunday, August 29, when land was sighted, and has recorded with minute precision his first impressions of the coast, the Pharos, Pompey's Pillar, the windmills "standing up like great plants of prickly pears," adding, "and this is the East, yet not the veritable East, till we reach Jaffa. How I strain to the left to catch a glimpse of the mountains of the South of Palestine. . . Here's the pilot boat, the boat a plain English one, the pilot in turban and jacket and his two men, very dark-complexioned, in fez. The one in the stern squatting crosslegged on the thwart. A real turban, not of Paris make, with rolls of linen all sham, like that of the Spahi in the train to Marseilles."

The next entry is dated "Wednesday, September 1, 4.30 A.M., one mile off Jaffa," and is remarkable alike for the enthusiasm and exactitude with which he records his first view of "the real East." After noting the appearance of the coast line and the town, he continues, "A hoopoe (bird beloved of Solomon) has just lighted on a rope close to my hand and flown away to land towards the sun, which has this instant made his appearance."

In Jaffa he visited the bazaar, but pushed on almost immediately to Jerusalem, the rough jottings pencilled in his note-book describing what he saw at the moment that he saw it. Nothing escaped his omnivorous interest in these scenes at once so fresh and so familiar,—the creaking of the shadoofs, the chirping of crickets, the changing colour of the sand, the configuration of the distant hills. A short pause at Ramleh enabled him to note the architecture of the Christian Church turned into a Mosque. Arrived at Jerusalem—where he records that the first name he had heard called, that of the waiter of the hotel, was *Isa* (Jesus)—he devoted himself with characteristic energy to a careful and minute study of the topography and architecture of the city. On September 2 he visited and made a careful sketch of the pool of Bethesda, with notes on the masonry, hydraulic work, &c., examined the wall of the Haram enclosure—eight pages of notes and several diagrams drawn on the spot attest his minute observation—rode out before dinner to the consul's house with "Rogers of Haifa and Sandretzky," and on his return examined the aqueduct or canal between the Birket Mamilla and the Pool of Hezekiah. On Friday, the 3rd, he rode before breakfast with Mr. Rogers to the Mount of Olives, and Bethany, visiting the Seraskier's house after breakfast. Next day he began his excursions in the neighbourhood; and the spirit in which he set to work may be gathered from the following entry:—

> "Standing on this rugged hill, east of Bethel, we had to the east, and nearer than B., a hill of about equal height crowned by a remarkable mass of grey ruin—a positive 'heap' of building stones, called by the peasants of the neighbourhood Tell er Rijmeh = 'the mound of the heap.' The top has several olive trees on it; but its aspect is most desolate. This must be Ai. The name is exact, and the situation with regard to Bethel and the hill ot Abraham's view perfectly suitable."

On the morning of Monday, September 6, he started in company with Mr. Rogers on a trip to the Dead Sea—which he saw in something like a storm. "The sea was running high, there were white waves all over the surface and breakers on the shore," the Jordan Valley, and Jericho. Leaving Jericho, he notes that "on the road leading to the ascent to Jerusalem there is a clump of a dozen large fig-trees which may be the legitimate successors of that in which Zacchaeus stood."

On the return journey, on Wednesday, the 8th, Grove describes an incident which may be given in his own words :—

"After leaving the well behind Mukhmâs we were very much refreshed and rode more briskly on towards the village. We crossed two ridges and then up a long broad shallow Wady of tilled ground planted with old olives in full bearing. This Wady sloped gradually upwards (say S.W.) and at the head of it we came to the back of the village. We were immediately led to the house of what seemed to be the head man of the place and were glad to dismount. The house formed two sides of a sort of court, the other two being completed by a stone wall; between the wall and one of the sides a light roof was thrown, and under this were three or four men sitting. They did not get up very quickly when we came in, for which they were well scolded by the woman of the house, who made them rise and put pillows and carpets on a piece of matting which occupied one side of the shed, and on this we sat down, Rogers taking off his boots and squatting. I (thinking it best not to try to do the oriental) keeping mine on and lying down. Rogers then gave the woman four paras to buy eggs and figs. She was a very tall, bony, hard-featured woman in blue calico, but with a pleasant look, and evidently well to do, as the coins all round her forehead were dollars. Her husband was an old man with a white beard and moustaches and a thin, querulous look. Yussuf now came in with the saddle-bags and cloaks, and we unpacked the precious remains of our bread, also our tea, sugar, salt and the big bag of tobacco. The wretch had managed to break one of the bottles of Jordan water.[1] While we waited for the eggs people began to drop in, all fellahin in abbas, some with very good countenances, tall (as usual) fine clean-limbed, strong fellows. Two of them were spinning with the curious teetotum-looking spindle which I have seen two or three times. These fellows all squatted on their heels along the wall opposite to us—except one old man, a pushing person, who came and sat down by me on the divan. I dozed, being very tired. Soon a man brought in coffee without sugar—

[1] Before starting for Palestine Grove made a memorandum to fetch bottles of water from the Fountain of the Virgin, near Siloam, and other sources.

very good, though—and served it round to all, after we had first taken what we wanted. We had waited so long for the eggs that I got Rogers to go out and look after them, and it was just as well, for, not being given to boil eggs, they had been in the water half an hour and were like stones. They came in on a flat basket or lid, and then came a similar one having a quantity of small green figs. They were all capital, and we did them justice. Our bread excited great astonishment, and various pieces were pinched off for the children and for some of the elders. Our Bedawy (an old acquaintance) was made very welcome and an Arab fiddle fetched for him to play on. After we had eaten our fill we prepared our tea and made an excellent brew. . . . All the world now began to smoke, and Suleiman, after much pressing, began to play and sing ; the fiddle had only one string of horsehair, the belly was of leather. His first tune was in the minor key and the second was like the mueddin's call, the voice being in unison with the instrument. The words were very antique, and from that and the accent often placed on the wrong syllables for the sake of the metre, Rogers said neither he nor any one else could understand it. The subject was a man asking a girl in marriage from the father. Then he sang some of Antar the Bedouin poet's recitations, interspersed with a bit of tune very like the first. It was now time to repack and be off. I strolled out and in a shed found a woman grinding. . . . In another shed was a woman who had just taken a batch of loaves from the oven, and was covering the lid up with ashes. I had my glass and was looking about at the hills and ground round about, which caused great curiosity. Our hostess looked through, but did not at all like the sight. 'God preserve us !' said she, 'give the people back their things and let them be off,' so we went, sending Yussuf and the Bedawy over to Jeba, while we took two men to the Wady Suweinît, the wildest ravine I have seen."

On his return to Jerusalem on the 9th he resumed his topographical and archæological investigations, and his note-book is full of details and diagrams relating to various places of interest. On Friday, the 10th, he visited the "Wailing place" in the morning. There were eight persons present, four men and four women, "some sitting on the ground, some standing and leaning against the wall ; murmuring a sort of chant and knocking their heads against the wall. The mueddin's call was over all, and the whole effect was very striking."

On Saturday he visited Bethlehem and Hebron, and at the latter place went into the synagogue in the evening, in the crypt of an old Gothic Church. Though it was "disorderly and offensive in the highest degree," the scene was striking. "The wine and snuff for the coming year were blessed amid the tumultuous Amens of the congregation." He adds, there is "one uncommon and very good feature at Hebron—nothing less than an English common of short turf, which lies on the west of the town, and reaches from the houses for some distance up the hill." On Monday he returned to Jerusalem from Hebron by Bethlehem at 3 P.M., and records in his note-book how much he was struck by the "leaden ashy hue of the whole city" as it came into sight at the well by the Greek Convent of Mount Elias.

The remainder of his stay was spent in surveying, and sketching. He notes in particular a fine view of the Mountains of Moab from Dr. Sandretzky's house at sunset on Tuesday afternoon, and on Thursday, the 16th, he left Jerusalem for Jaffa, returning by Beit 'Ur [Beth-horon]—the ascent to which is most minutely described in his note-book—Jimzu, Lydda,—where he was specially struck by the number of blind and one-eyed people—and Ramleh. Jaffa was reached on the 17th at 9.30 P.M., after a slow and fatiguing day's ride from Ramleh; and on the following day—the heat of which was excessive—he started for Alexandria at 5 P.M. Only those who have seen and studied his note-books can realise the amount of sight-seeing, minute observation and actual physical exertion crowded into the space of seventeen days, and that during a month usually avoided by travellers owing to its excessive heat.

"With Jaffa itself," he notes in his last impressions, "I was as much struck as before, bating the novelty of the scene. It seems to me on the whole the best specimen of an oriental town of the three I have seen—less altered by European influence than Jerusalem, brighter and gayer and busier than Hebron, while it surpasses both in its entourage and its proximity to the sea. . . .

As the sun went down I had my last view of Palestine, a long line of low sand cliffs—Jaffa the only eminence—relieved against a dim background of grey mountains from behind Jaffa downwards *as straight as the wall of Moab itself*. Such was my last impression."

From Alexandria, which he reached on the following Sunday, Grove went on immediately to Cairo. With the city itself he was rather disappointed. "It has not," he notes, "the same burnt look as Jerusalem, but it is almost as ruined looking, and everything has the air of being unfinished . . . half the mosques are in ruins, and that not ruins like deserted churches in Europe, but, owing I suppose, to the soft nature of the material, in absolute decay. The new mosque of Mehemet Ali is splendid enough, but its *entourage* detestable." But he thought the country wonderful :—"My eyes never rested on such green as that of the doura fields between the Nile and the Pyramids. Miles and miles of nothing but gardens. It must have been a bondage indeed that drove out the Israelites from such plenty to the waste broiling desert of Sinai." On his homeward voyage he saw, on Friday, October 1, the Comet set off the coast of Spain. "Nothing can exceed the effect of the rush of its huge tail—curved to the orbit of the Comet, and as long as the tail of the Great Bear—down to the sea. This evening we are passing Malaga. The Sierra Nevada in the background, with one of the most jagged outlines possible. How different from the level and monotonous outlines of Palestine are these varied hills!"

Grove reached England on October 7, and shortly afterwards resumed his impressions of Palestine and Holy Land in a letter addressed to his brother-in-law, G. G. Bradley :—

"CRYSTAL PALACE,
October 26, 1858.

"I have left you too long without telling you of my return. It took place on the 7th, exactly seven weeks after my departure, and I believe that never were seven weeks better employed. From beginning to end my journey was one bright success. I started from Marseilles on Sunday, 22nd August, and reached Jaffa on September 1st, passing, but not landing at, Malta and Alexandria. On the 1st, then, I set foot in the Holy Land. On the 2nd at day-break I was under the walls of Jerusalem, and there I stayed as a centre of operations till the 14th, when I left it, to return as I came by Jaffa. In those fourteen days I managed, besides exploring the town itself—not, of course, thoroughly, but to a great degree —to go to the Dead Sea, Jordan, Jericho, and back by Gibeah, Michmash, Anathoth, &c. (three days) to Bethlehem, Hebron, Solomon's Pools, and the Mountains of Judah (three days)—Nebi Samuel, Bîreh, Bethel, and Ai (one day), besides rides to Bethany and the Mount of Olives; and in returning to Jaffa I went by the Bethhoron road, past Gibeon, Bethhoron, Lydda and Ramleh, and saw a country not often visited by English people. I was very fortunate in finding a man in Jerusalem to whom A. P. S. had given me a letter, but who generally resides so far off that I had despaired of finding him. His name is Rogers, Consul at Haifa, and if I had searched the whole country through I could not have had a more thoroughly efficient man in every respect, nor one more delightful and fitted for my purpose. I had him and his horses to myself for eight days till some business obliged him to leave me, so I was thus far in excellent hands. For the remainder of the time I did not fare so well, but still not amiss. It has all made an immense impression on me—not one which I can tell out at once, but which I am sure will have great influence on me and on everything I write on the subject for the future. Knowing the country before by books so well it was not so great a surprise to me as Egypt (of which I will tell you presently), but still there was all the difference between knowing it at a distance and coming face to face with it, and at every turn something or other came out which I had not looked for.

"The country was, at the end of the summer, very much burnt up and parched, and I don't wonder at any one who sees it in autumn giving a report of its barrenness and monotony, but I am still glad to have seen it at that time, because if I ever go again (as please God I will), it will no doubt be in spring, when the whole look of the place must be very different. Stanley's statements about that as about everything else were corroborated by every one, and here I may say that much as I thought of him and his book before, my admiration for them both has been immensely increased by my visit. It is impossible for anything to be better or truer than the book, or to have caught more exactly the very air and atmosphere, as it were, of everything. It is as true as it is delightful, and I don't think one can say more. I had a long walk with him on Friday, and am going to Oxford for a Sunday very soon. But to go back. After leaving Jaffa I went to Alexandria to take the English boat, and then, owing to the Indian mail being late, I had six whole days in Egypt entirely beyond what I had ever expected or thought possible. Indeed it never entered into my head. Of course I never could go away for more than three or four hours lest the mail should come in, but still, by a judicious use of horseflesh I managed to see the Pyramids, and, using Cairo as a centre, to make acquaintance with the Nile and the land of Egypt itself. After all, I believe the land and the river are more wonderful than anything which is contained *in* the country. It was high Nile during my stay, and fortunately I found an old chum resident engineer to the big bridge over the River, and from his house got it well into my memory, and to see that great strong even flood—flowing as still and calm as a meadow stream in England and like them full up to the lips—and meandering about in 'links' as they do—with the white-sailed, winged boats always going up and down—is a thing I shall never forget. And then the fields through which it flows: no green *here* seems to me comparable to it—all laid out in squares like a garden—'a garden of the Lord, like the land of Egypt'—flat from end to end with all the forms so familiar to me in the hieroglyphics, men, women, children, camels, buffaloes, birds in flocks—altogether I believe that Egypt has struck me more than even Palestine. But here's Post, and I must stop. . ."

One of his earliest letters after his return relates to his purchase of a number of duplicate scores of Palestrina at a sale of Lord Shrewsbury's effects. But he was chiefly absorbed by his work on the Dictionary, into which he plunged with renewed vigour, as his correspondence with Dr. Smith and Stanley abundantly testifies. Additional evidence on this point is furnished by his friend Mr. W. Aldis Wright.

"So far as I can recollect," he writes, under date November 12, 1900, "I first met the late Sir George Grove in the year 1858. We were both engaged upon the *Dictionary of the Bible*, and soon found that we had much in common. He had just returned from a visit to the Holy Land, and was full of enthusiasm at all he had seen. His interest in the topography of Palestine marked him out as the contributor to the Dictionary to whom articles bearing on this subject could be most fitly entrusted. Indeed they were for the most part written by him. But his contributions were by no means confined to topographical or geographical subjects. The articles on Elijah and Elisha were written by him, as well as the history of Jerusalem down to the taking of the city by Titus. In addition to these, he wrote the majority of the articles on the more obscure names in the first volume; and, though perhaps not formally, was really sub-editor of the whole work. He had a fair knowledge of Hebrew, without being in the technical sense of the word a Hebrew scholar. But his native intelligence and acumen enabled him to turn his knowledge to better account than many who were better equipped. I am sure I do not exaggerate when I say that he was the life and soul of the whole book. All that he wrote was full of the same enthusiasm which characterised himself."

The solidarity of the undertaking was agreeably strengthened by the institution of Bible Dictionary dinners, at which all contributors had the right to attend on the payment of a small fee, the difference being made good by Mr. Murray, to whose generosity and enterprise Grove often alludes. These dinners, which were continued for several years, were mostly held at the United Hotel in Charles Street, at the back of Her Majesty's Theatre in the Haymarket, but others were given at the Crystal Palace, at Windsor, and elsewhere, entirely at Mr. Murray's own expense. Grove's share in all that concerned the Dictionary gave him the liveliest satisfaction, but the strain on his energies proved almost more than he could stand. His days being "consumed with deliberations, Boards, &c.," he was driven to devote a great part of his nights to his work on the Dictionary. In November 1858, and again in April 1859, we find him writing to Dr. Smith to relinquish certain articles that he had undertaken to contribute, and adding, on the latter occasion, "I cannot go on any longer being torn to pieces as I am now, even for the Bible Dictionary." But his wonderful elasticity, which never failed him until his final breakdown, soon enabled him to shake off these momentary fits of depression. On June 1, he went to the

Derby with his friend and fellow contributor, F. Ffoulkes, and the next day, writing to Smith, records the fact, and adds, "we talked Dictionary whenever the race would allow." And he would always find time to do a kind service to a friend or subordinate. In November 1859, he writes at length to Mr. John Bergheim, the son of one of his Jerusalem friends, then working as a civil engineer in England. Grove had consulted Nasmyth (of steam-hammer fame) and Scott Russell in his young friend's behalf, and his letter is full of good advice about the best modes of preparation for that career. He lays great stress on the advantages of a practical training in the fitting and pattern "shops" over that to be obtained in a civil engineer's office, and continues: "in the meantime read as hard as you can at your mathematics, and pick up all the knowledge you can—chemistry, geology, photography, *anything practical*—it will all help." So, too, earlier in the same year, he had written to a number of influential friends to enlist their interest on behalf of his chief messenger at the Crystal Palace, George Armer, who was about to emigrate to New Zealand. The trouble he took, and the length at which he wrote are truly characteristic. All his life long Grove was ready to speak up for his *protégés*, his subordinates, his pupils and his friends, so long as they were in earnest.

In the course of the next few years Grove was repeatedly sounded with a view to his accepting other appointments. One of the first of these suggested candidatures was that for the post of Director of the Patent Museum, with regard to which we find him in correspondence with Mr., afterwards, Sir Henry, Cole, in January 1860. It is evident that Grove thought seriously of the change, but it would have involved serious loss of income, and there were also other drawbacks. Besides he was by no means dissatisfied with his position at Sydenham. As he put it in a letter to Mr. Cole, on January 14, 1860:—

"Here I am independent of every one but the Directors; and, moreover, from circumstances which have lately happened, I feel myself stronger in my seat than I have done for some time past. I don't say that this would tempt me to stay—but it certainly is a reason why I should try for a *good* post."

What he really wanted was a post which, while securing him a fair income, would leave him more leisure to devote to literary work. In March 1860, by which time the first volume of the Bible Dictionary was ready for the printer, and Dr. Smith had submitted to him the proof of the Preface, Grove was suffering severely from overwork. He complains to Smith of exhaustion, want of sleep and rest, and showed an irritability over an editorial emendation in his article on Jerusalem—Dr. Smith had altered the word "shell" as applied to the assault of the legions to "batter"—which was hardly warranted by the facts of the case. Happily the friction was speedily removed, for on March 26th, 1860, he writes to Dr. Smith in the most cordial strain. After expressing himself as extremely gratified by Mr. Murray's liberality he continues :—

"But gratifying as that part of the business has been, your note was far more so : and the money really seems to me *as nothing* compared with the sincere and heartfelt expression of praise and satisfaction which accompanied it. It is a pleasure to work with all one's heart and might for an object : it is a pleasure to be well paid : but the appretiation [Grove always spelt the word thus] and satisfaction of one able to appretiate—so kindly and honestly expressed as you have done it—are far beyond either."

Further on he admits that his temper has been tried by the strain : "I find that now the excitement is all over, I am very shaky, so nervous and irritable that I am a torture to myself and to every one round me. However this will soon go off, no doubt."

On the 27th a dinner was held to celebrate the completion of the first volume, and on the following day Grove wrote to Dr. Smith as follows :—

"My dear friend—How can I thank you enough for all that you have said of me and for the extremely pleasant and delicate manner in which you said it ? If anything could have added to the value of your praise it was the fact of your mentioning me in connexion with Stanley, and then evoking further laudations from him. I think I have a right to be proud of such testimony as was given in my favour last night, and I confess to being so—and more—if you will allow me to say so—I am proud of having you for my friend, and trust that the relation thus happily begun may long be continued. I made a poor return last night in the few words I spluttered forth. Directly after I sat down, everything I ought to have said came fast enough into my mind. Gratitude to you for all your kindness and forbearance; pride—as a layman and a most secular one too—at my connexion with so many scholars and divines: renunciation of all claim to praise, since if it had not been for Stanley, I never should have had my attention turned to this particular line at all, &c. &c. But I shall never be a speaker and I fear it is of little use to attempt it. I wish my wife could have been there, for she has suffered so much from my absence from her on dictionary matters, that it would have been fair for her to enjoy the trifling recompense of hearing her husband's praises."

Grove's temporary fatigue, however, implied no slackening of interest in his Biblical studies, or any other field of mental activity. Only a week later we find him writing to Stanley about the next volume of the Dictionary, and the possibility of securing Jowett's co-operation; about a scheme for abridging *Sinai and Palestine*, and various other cognate topics. Another scheme, unfolded in a letter to Mr. John Murray, bearing date May 2, 1860, was that of a "Dictionary of Persons (embracing contemporaries), giving in a condensed form the most prominent dates and facts of the lives of all persons at all known to the world." Grove was ready to undertake the compilation of the Dictionary, and suggested a single volume of the size of the *Dictionary of the Bible*, but as the scheme is never mentioned again, it may be assumed that Mr. Murray was able to offer irrefutable objections to its realisation.

The question of a new post was twice mooted this summer. On May 31st, he announced his intention of standing for the secretaryship of the Eastern Bengal Railway Company, just then resigned by Fergusson, but only if Leith, the chairman, gave his friend Farquhar to understand that Grove was certain to be appointed. "The reason why I should prefer that post to this," he writes to Mr. A. P. Fletcher, "is that I can't stand the constant worry and high pressure here as I used to do, and that as *that* would give me more time to myself, it is practically a more lucrative berth." The assurance was presumably not forthcoming, for nothing came of the candidature, though he was still prosecuting it in December 1860. The nature of the other appointment is not declared, but, in a letter addressed to Mr. Fuller on June 19, 1860, he declines the proposal that he should undertake, at an increased salary, the secretaryship of what was evidently some projected enterprise of a kind which involved rivalry with the Crystal Palace. To do so would be, he argues, a breach of good faith and good feeling towards his board, "who, however I may dislike some of the individuals, have always as a body, behaved thoroughly well towards me." Another characteristic letter is that addressed a month later to the Rev. George Williams, the eminent authority on the topography of Jerusalem, with regard to the publication in a folio facsimile *édition de luxe* of the Codex Sinaiticus recently discovered by Tischendorf. It was proposed only to publish the New Testament in a cheap form, and against this exclusive dealing Grove vigorously protested, offering to start a memorial, either to the French Emperor or to Tischendorf.

It was in the summer of 1860 that Grove and his family —his second son Julius Charles had been born on April 8th, 1859—moved into the quaint wooden house that was to be his home for the remaining forty years of his life.

"I have always understood," he wrote in his unpublished reminiscences of 1897, "though I cannot remember who told it me, that this house in which we live was at one time inhabited by Charles James Fox, who invited some one to come down and see him, and, on his friend inquiring its whereabouts, said: 'Drive to Dulwich'—evidently the extreme of civilisation in this direction—

'and ask for the prettiest cottage in Kent.' I asked Sir George Trevelyan if he could give me any support for this story. He said that he had never heard it before, but it was exactly the kind of thing Fox would have said. . . . This house and the next below it belonged at a later date to old Mr. Cowburn, who was remarkable for the affectionate way in which he used to end his notes on any subject; but he was at the same time very punctilious in matters of business. Miss White, a cousin of Mayow Adams's, was one of his tenants, and Cowburn on one occasion was

GROVE'S HOUSE AT SYDENHAM.

extremely annoyed to find that her rent had not arrived on the day on which it was due. The same evening he wrote to her as follows: 'Dear Miss White,—Your rent was due this morning. Yours most affectionately, George Cowburn.' Miss White was naturally much annoyed at this reminder, and the next quarter she resolved to be in time, and sent the money a day too soon. She then got the following note: 'Dear Miss White,—Your rent was this time as inconveniently early as it was last time disgracefully late. Yours most affectionately, George Cowburn.'"

To this period or a little earlier belongs a reminiscence of another neighbour, Captain Ford, who lived at 62

West Hill, and like another old sailor friend of Grove's, Captain Richardson, was one of the officers who looked after salvage for Lloyd's :—

"Early in the history of the Crystal Palace, in fact not very long after the opening, we came in one Sunday after afternoon church to our house in Church Meadow and found somebody there anxious to get some ice for Captain Ford. It appeared that Ford had been suffering from an abscess on his knee, and a young homœopath doctor in lancing it had cut too deep, and the old gentleman would bleed to death unless some ice could be got to stop the hæmorrhage—would it be possible to get some at the refreshment department of the Crystal Palace? I promptly gave him a note and a small handbag, and started him off up the hill. The ice proved effectual, and a few days afterwards I called to see the old Captain and say how glad I was to have been of service. 'Yes, sir,' he said, 'I have had very little the matter with me: this is the first time anything has gone wrong with me since I died of the plague at Alexandria.' 'You died of the plague, did you?' said I. 'Yes, I was in the navy in those days, and we were lying off Alexandria, and the plague came on board, and I died—or they thought I did; and they took me on shore and threw me into the dead pit. The night was cool, and some time before daybreak I came to myself. It was so dark that I could not see anything, but I felt round me, a knee here and a nose there, and soon realised where I was. I was young'—only about sixteen, I think he said—'and I soon scrambled out, and when the ship's boat came on shore for water after daybreak, they found me sitting on the wharf.'"

Another of his early Sydenham acquaintances was Mr. James Braidwood, who started the first fire brigade at the Crystal Palace, and used to come down occasionally to inspect it.

"Braidwood lost his life at the great fire in Tooley Street, close to London Bridge, in June 1861, by a wall falling upon him and several of his men. That fire took place on a Saturday night, and I went up after dinner by train at about eight o'clock. It was an extraordinary sight. I forced my way over the bridge and went down Thames Street, where the heat was intense. At length we got to Tower Hill, which was crowded with people, though it was between twelve and one o'clock—not only people looking at the fire, but the ordinary entertainments of a holiday. I remember a man with an electrical machine, 'three shocks a penny,' doing a very brisk trade. The trains were running all night, and we got back to Sydenham at about four in the morning."

In the early autumn of 1860 Grove set off for the Continent with his wife, reaching Brussels on August 16. His note-book shows how carefully he studied the pictures in the Musée at Brussels, the inscriptions and relics at Cologne and the monuments at Coblentz. Fresh from his tour in the East, he was always on the look out for traces of Oriental influence in architecture. At Cologne he made a drawing of the jar brought by S. Helena from Palestine to Rome, and thence to Cologne by Otto I; at Würzburg and elsewhere he notes and sketches the oriental dome-shaped spires. Passing through Frankfurt, Aschaffenburg, and Würzburg to Nuremberg he there describes the stations of the Cross between the cemetery and the Pilatus House, and comments on the Syrian look of the citadel hill. His next pause was at Munich; thence he travelled by steamer from Starnberg to Seeshaupt, giving a full account of the picturesque national dress of the peasants from Dachau, and reached Oberammergau at midday on Saturday, August 28th. The experiences and impressions of his visit were embodied in a long letter which appeared in the *Times* of September 5th, 1860, the first detailed description of the Passion Play addressed to the English public in an English newspaper. A "meagre sketch" he modestly calls it, but in reality it is a most vivid *résumé* of the impressions of a sympathetic yet keen-sighted observer, full of valuable and practical hints as to route, accommodation, etc., for intending visitors. Two points in this letter are worth notice. One is Grove's account of the "last dreadful scene—the uprearing of the three crosses with their living burdens and all the cruel incidents of that most cruel and living death." Of this he says:—

"I know not how to speak. I only know that irreverence or incongruity was a feeling which never once entered my mind. It certainly was not perceptible on any of the faces within my reach, and the long-drawn sob or sigh which escaped from the whole mass of spectators as from one man, when the sacred corpse was at last carried out of view, was one of the most genuine and remarkable tributes to the reality of the whole representation that can be imagined. The fierce blaze of the afternoon sun, in the full heat of which the two last scenes took place, gave additional vividness to the representation of sufferings which derived half their torture from the fever and thirst by which they were accompanied."

Grove also speaks of the unconventional conception of Judas developed at Oberammergau. He was represented,

"not as a hardened villain, but rather as a narrow-minded, impulsive, vindictive man, really puzzled and annoyed at what he conceived to be the 'waste' of the 300 pence on the precious ointment, and stung to the quick by the reproof so publicly administered to him by Christ. Under the influence of these feelings he at last consents to the suggestions and entreaties of the priests and money changers. But he never really believes that what does happen will really come to pass, and his violent self-murder is the sudden result of his discovery of the certainty of the dreadful catastrophe in which he has been a chief actor."

Grove goes on to say that this view of the character of Judas has, if he remembers aright, the support of the Archbishop of Dublin and of Horne, the author of *Orion*, who adopted it some years previously in a dramatic poem on the subject. He sums up by describing his experience as one of the most interesting of his life :—

"I could not have believed, and I am quite sure that no one who has not seen it can conceive, how thoroughly real and impressive it all was—how unconscious one became of its being acting at all. It is the nature of things that, with advancing civilisation and additional publicity, this simplicity and reality will wear off; it can hardly fail to do so, to a certain extent, before the next representation arrives. I therefore strongly advise all those who can do so to be present at one of the two remaining performances, which are fixed for the 9th and 16th of September."

A more intimate account of his impressions is given in a letter written to Stanley on August 30th :—

"We arrived at the village (Oberammergau) in a heat which

no tongue can describe; Syria, Jamaica, nothing that I have ever felt came near it, and for some time I thought that I should have fainted under it. The two Zwinks and Thaddeus, Petrus, Judas Iskariotes, all the Apostles, had their homes full, and though they behaved like angels themselves, could not afford any substantial consolations. However, at last we were received by an old woman, of neither whose cleanness nor hospitality can I speak as you did. However, all that has been long ago effaced. Who do you think should come tearing through the village in a chaise and pair just as night fell? Who but the very next person to yourself I should have wished for? Madame Mohl! You can imagine how she added to the enjoyment of the next day.

"Of the play I hardly know what to say. It far surpassed in interest and in merit (though of the *merit* I never thought till afterwards) anything I had ever conceived. I would not have missed it on any consideration, and it has left an impression and given me a vivid idea of the scenes which I shall never lose. I think the things which struck me most, though it is hard to particularise when all was so excellent, were (1) the long procession carrying the crosses, with the farewells to Mary, S. Veronica, etc. (to this and the next scene the tremendous heat gave a reality which perhaps you missed); (2) the debates in the Sanhedrim; I could not make out what was said, but how true and natural the action throughout was! how perfectly free from all cant or consciousness! (3) the Ecce Homo (Pilate I thought admirable, so also Herodes, though in a different way); the scenes after the crucifixion I thought not so good. They were more artificial, and *anything* after that crisis must be an anticlimax. The tableaux were most interesting, and *how instructive!* but I think they would be better with motion. As to chorus and music, I found them perfection. Two or three things were omitted which might be added with advantage; (1) there ought to be some plan of darkening the stage, and then the dramatic incident of Peter being discovered by his coming too near the fire would find its place. Naboth, too, was stoned at night. The *two witnesses* in Naboth's case would make the parallel more exact. (2) The *race* of Peter and John, and the 'stooping down and looking in'—these ought not to have been forgotten. (3) 'When they had sung an hymn.' This should have been done. (4) I think that Ithai's profession of adherence to David would make a good tableau.

"I have written a longish letter to the *Times* recording (very imperfectly) my impressions, but the whole thing has so religious a cast that Delane will hardly, especially in Dasent's absence, put it in. Look out for it, however; I posted it yesterday. I could not help writing, for I am sure there are hundreds who would be thankful to be told of it. . . . We go to Innsbruck this afternoon. I hope to join Papillon. Madame Mohl is at Vienna, *longing* to see you. I have made a discovery here that they sell and *am billigste* the duplicate books in the Royal Library. Halm, the director, is charming. I have bought several books for which I remember hunting in London for years. Good-bye. How I long to see you and talk about Ammergau.

"Yours ever,

"GEORGE GROVE."

From Oberammergau he returned to Munich by Murnau and a village where he saw a skittle ground with the skittles set up in the wall of the churchyard close to the west-door, and spent some interesting hours in the company of Halm, the director of the Munich Bibliothek. Halm had been at Oberammergau in 1850, and told Grove that the Christus of that year was "so perfect a figure that you could hardly resist adoring him." Thence by Kufstein, Volders and Hall, always noting the churches and spires as he went, he passed on to Innsbruck, which "constantly reminded me of Jerusalem," and so by Landeck, Mals and Trafoi to Bormio, and thence over the Stelvio to Chiavenna, reaching Zürich Saturday, September 8th. After a field day in the public library, he went on to Lucerne, and Basle, returning to Paris on September 12th. In Paris he spent most of his time in the Louvre, copying inscriptions, and examining Vandyck's etchings, and crossed from Boulogne. His experiences on the continent are graphically summarised in the following letter to his brother-in-law, G. G. Bradley :—

"CRYSTAL PALACE,

"*September* 19, 1860.

"MY DEAREST G.—We arrived in England on Friday night, finding our children perfectly well and happy. We have had a most delightful journey of exactly four weeks. . . . The one drawback has been the necessity of travelling so fast, but even that has brought its compensation, as without it we should infallibly have missed a midnight and moonlight scramble through the Splügen, which has been one of the most remarkable things of the whole journey. Remember that it was the first time I had ever seen Rhine, Germany, or Alp. Every day brought its novelties and surprises; but the points of the journey by which it was most admirably accentuated were three: (1) The Ammergau Play; (2) the Stelvio, with an unrivalled view of the Ortlerspitz; and (3) the adventure in the Splügen.

"(1) Of the play I need not say anything, because no doubt you saw my letter in the *Times*, and also because the next *Macmillan* will contain an account by A. P. S. He was there the Sunday before us. . . .

"(2) The Ortler was *wonderful*. We left Mals in a one-horse trap in pouring rain, but our faith was amply rewarded, for before we had gone an hour the rain stopped, and after passing Trafoi (where, by-the-bye, we met with a man named J. F. Baird, who was at Rugby with you, and one of the VIth when Arnold died) the clouds completely cleared away, and the mountain stood bare for the remaining four hours of our ascent of the Pass. In form I should think it differed from any other mountain in Switzerland. It stood out as a huge square fort, cut off on each side from all neighbouring heights by an enormous glacier descending into the valley in front, and crowned by two or three horizontal layers serving as a base to a small but perfectly formed pyramid—like a tent. It was covered with the fresh snow of the night before, and as the clouds suddenly gave way and left the whole standing up before a very pale blue sky—the square mass and the horizontal layers in gray shadow, and the pyramidal peak shining in the sun like a diamond, it was one of the most beautiful and awful things I ever saw. It was exactly like the sacred tent which the Deity Himself might inhabit. This was the first time it had been seen for more than three weeks, and we had it in view, opposite, on our left during the whole ascent.

"(3) The Splügen was entirely different. This was a *nocturnal* adventure. There had just been a furious storm of rain in the mountains which had carried away five or six miles of the road in the lower end of the Pass, and made it quite impossible for any vehicles to proceed. We were therefore turned out of the diligence at 1.30 A.M. at the lower end of the river, and left to scramble and climb our way to the other end where a fresh carriage was waiting. The whole of this part of the Pass is bordered with thick woods of large chestnut trees, and into these, wherever the path was entirely swept away—and that was of constant occurrence—we had to penetrate. It was bright moonlight; and the gloom of the woods—the illusions of moonlight—the curious scene on our left, where the bed of the torrent was filled with great blocks of stone as large as the chancel of a church and heaps of débris in the wildest and most fantastic ruin, glittering like snow in the moonlight—the strange hour and the flavour of risk, not to say danger—altogether formed one of the most extraordinary adventures I shall probably ever go through. The water had of course long since subsided, and the scene of the desolation without a trace of any agent, was not an unimportant element in our feelings. Harriet stood it—as she did all our other hardships—most bravely. We had been virtually travelling the greater part of the time in a blazing sun—since five on the previous morning—and, after the excitement of this scramble was over, I fear we were not quite in cue for the Via Mala. However *that* may be seen at any time; *this* probably not for another half century. . . .

"I am told that my letter is attributed to *Grote*, whose initials are G. G. Milman rushed off at once after reading it, and I hope got in time for last Sunday. . . I did it in monstrous hurry and could very much improve it, but Stanley's article will of course supersede every other. . . ."

On his return to Sydenham, Grove was at once engaged in the preparations for the Flower Show, held at the Crystal Palace on September 20th, when he was specially attracted by the Gladiolus exhibit. Next day he remarks in his note-book that "the round hills about Caterham struck me as not unlike *Benjamin*. For the smooth rock-like flagstones see the East Hill at Hastings half way up," and the possibility of his paying a second visit to Jerusalem is mentioned in a letter written a month later to his friend, Mr. Bergheim. Entries in his note-books prove him to have already begun to take an interest in the music of Schubert—who afterwards became "his existence"—while a further proof of his Solomon-like versatility is shown by a sudden desire to collect toadstools, evidence of which is forthcoming in the following highly characteristic illustrated letter from Edward Lear, the artist and humorist, to whom he had been attracted by their common interest in the East:

"OATLANDS PARK HOTEL,
"WALTON ON TEMMS, SURREY,
"15 *Novr*. 1860.

"DEAR GROVE

"I HASTEN to inform you that in a wood very near here, there are Toadstools of the loveliest and most surprising colour and form:—orbicular, cubicular and squambingular, and I even thought I perceived the very rare Pongchámbinnibóphilos Kakokreasópheros among others a few days back. You have therefore nothing better to do than to come with Penrose and hunt up and down St. George's Hill for the better carrying out of the useful and beastly branch of science you have felt it your duty to follow. Provided also that you bring your own cooking utensils you may dine off your gatherings though I won't partake of the feast, my stomach being delicate.

"Seriously, however, I should indeed like to see both F. Penrose and yourself here:—couldn't you send a line first, and come over to luncheon? though it would be far better if you came and dined and slept and then toadstooled all the next day—back to Sydenham or as you pleased. Saturdays and Sundays are my only insecure days, but those are the days also you would be least likely to think of coming. Daddy [*i.e.* Holman] Hunt writes to me that he is coming soon:—it would be very nice if we could all combine.

"Besides the seedars —you would see 11 other unfinished vorx of art—not to speak of a good many sketches. My life passes daily in a different place, Lebanon, Masada, the Tiber,—the Cervara Quarries,—Philates, Zagori,—Philae,—S. Sabbas,—Damascus, Bethlehem, Beirût, and Interlaken. But I confess that a little more society would sometimes be pleasant—for painting, Greek, music, reading and penning drawings are all used up by the end of the day. Various friends, however, write and come—so I don't complain.

"If you let me know—shall I send out and gather toadstools in hampers for you? You can sit and pick them in the large hall.

"O! that I could get back to Jerusalem this spring!

"Goodbye.
"Yours,
"EDWARD LEAR."

Meantime Grove had resumed his work on the Dictionary with unabated vigour, and early in 1861 we find him expressing his regret to Dr. Smith, that he had ever let any of the geographical articles on Palestine proper out of his hands: "I have," he goes on, "a perfect enthusiasm for exploring the subject and attach an importance to these minor places and names which no —— or —— can feel." The letter concludes with an interesting tribute to the scholarship and literary power of Dr. Westcott. By July he had definitely resolved on making a second trip to the Holy Land in the early autumn. There were difficulties in the way, as appears from a further correspondence with

"Remarkable Fungus discovered in the woods near the Oatlands Hotel. Supposed to be the Pongchámbinnibóphilos Kakokreasópheros of Naturalists."

Dr. Smith, but Grove writes on July 24th that he had gone so far with regard to his journey that he could not retreat. He could not get away in 1862, and besides "I feel such great reluctance at writing about parts of the country which I have not seen, that I should be very loth to give up going before the close of the Dictionary would prevent my journey being of any use." The postscript to this letter refers to Blondin's first appearance at the Crystal Palace, when he walked from end to end of the building on the tight rope, and goes on: "Gladstone has been here looking at Blondin. He congratulated me on my share of the Bible Dictionary, and said he thought *that* a no less unique performance than *this!!* Robert Cooke[1] should print that panegyric." In after years Grove used to relate how on the same occasion Mr. Gladstone said that Blondin's feat gave a Chancellor of the Exchequer a very good lesson in *balancing*—one of the very few puns that Mr. Gladstone ever perpetrated. Blondin's visit, it may be added, had a further humorous outcome in the shape of a paragraph in one of the papers alluding to Grove as a very remarkable man, "the author of *Have you seen Blondin?* and of that truly interesting article on 'Elijah' in the *Dictionary of the Bible.*"

Grove left Marseilles on September 29, 1861, in the steamer *Hydaspe.* His diary opens with a note characteristic of the ex-engineer :—

"Engines by Fawcett and Preston (No. 1754), vibrating cylinders . . . . My berth is the top on the left side below was an *inconnu* for Alexandria. Opposite is his holiness, Gregorio 'Ata, the Archbishop of Hamath, in N. Syria, of the Catholic Greek Church, with his secretary. 'Monseigneur' can speak only Arabic, but the secretary also some French. The Archbishop is not sick but *enrhumé*, and he lies in his berth all day in his purple, like Jesse, the father of David, at the root of the Jesse trees . . . . a fine, tall old man with a benevolent good face and a large grey beard. He escaped with his life in the massacres of Damascus only by the assistance of Aga Salîm, who had an ancient friendship for him. Their breviary is in Arabic, printed in the Lebanon at one of the convents."

Amongst other fellow passengers was Sir Victor Houlton, the Colonial Secretary of Malta, from whom Grove heard some strange anecdotes of Pelissier on the occasion of his visit to Malta in the governorship of Sir W. Reid, and from the Archbishop's Secretary he obtained full details on the relation of his Church to the Orthodox Greek Church. At Malta he crammed a great deal of

[1] Mr. Robert Cooke was at that time a partner in Murray's, with special charge of the advertisement department.

sight-seeing into a few hours, and at Alexandria, which was reached on Sunday, October 6, made a special study of the architecture and decoration of the Coptic Church. Jaffa was reached on the 9th and he seems to have set out almost immediately for Nâblus in order to be there for the Day of Atonement. The notes of his journey thither are unusually full, though often illegible, being written in pencil at the moment that any interesting object met his view. The lie of the land, the structure of the houses, the crops, the birds—all appealed to his devouring gaze, and the pages of his note-book are crowded with outline sketches of the hills, drawings of water-jars, and records in musical notation of the songs sung by the guides. Under date October 11th we find a full account, with really excellent sketches, of his investigation of the Holy Place of the Samaritans on Mount Gerizim, of the method of killing the lambs, given him by the Samaritan, Yakub Esh-Shelaby, at whose house he stayed during his sojourn in Nâblus, and of the curious physiographical parallelism between the two summits of Ebal and Gerizim.

Grove arrived in Nâblus on October 11th and put up at the house of Yakub Esh-Shelaby,[1] to whom he was indebted for all that he saw and heard on the following two days. One object of his visit was to witness the rites of the *Yôm Kippoor*, or Samaritan Day of Atonement, and a most vivid account of his experiences is given in a letter written at the time, and subsequently expanded into an article in Francis Galton's *Vacation Tourists and Notes of Travel in* 1861 (Macmillan, 1862). From the sunset of Thursday the 11th to that of Friday the 12th was the Sabbath of the Samaritans, and from sunset of the 12th to that of the 13th, the *Yôm Kippoor*. On the evening of the Sabbath he entered the Synagogue at 5 o'clock to watch

[1] The personal history of the family of Yakub Esh-Shelaby, as dictated by himself to Mr. Rogers, formerly Consul at Damascus, may be found in a small book, entitled *Notices of the Modern Samaritans* (Sampson Low and Co., 1855).

the conclusion of the ordinary service and the commencement of the Fast. Grove's narrative is an admirable pen-picture. He describes the structure of the venerable building ; the numbers, dress and posture of the congregation, all squatted on the ground, all gazing towards the recess of the Torah, or Book of the Law, which points in the direction of the Kibleh on Mount Gerizim, the one holy place of the Community ; and the priest reading the service "in a loud, harsh, monotonous chant or plain-song, varied by occasional jerks or *barks*, and by strange gestures, as if he were trying to bite violently something immediately in front of him." Equally impressive is his account of the recital of the whole Pentateuch by priests and people, interspersed with common prayers and creeds or professions of faith, which constitute the service of the Fast :—

"All stood up, and the storm of harsh voices raged round. They seemed to repeat very fast, and with a metrical, jumping sort of measure which converted it almost into a gallop. Now and then—at what particular passages I could not discover—they roared or barked still more loudly ; now and then they prostrated themselves at certain portions of the law, such as the Ten Commandments . . . . Though the attitude of the people was in the main devout and absorbed, there was a good deal of talking amongst the general body in my neighbourhood. It was not, however, the talking or minor interruptions that struck me, so much as the hard, undevotional, violent character of the proceedings. Not a soul seemed to be touched or interested. It was not disorderly, nor undignified, but seemed a service without worship."

During the Fast neither meat, drink, smoke nor even medicine is tasted (however grave the case) by man, woman, child, infant or suckling, and "the wails and screams of the unfortunate infants in the neighbouring houses during the whole of the evening and night" afforded painful evidence of the rigour with which the ordinance was carried out.

Next morning Grove paid a visit to the village of 'Awertah, a few miles off, which contains the traditional sepulchres of Eleazar and Phinehas, the son and grandson of Aaron; and a cave, the reputed residence of Elijah. In the afternoon he returned to the synagogue to witness the close of the Fast:—

"The *sound* of the service was much the same as it had been last night, only, if possible, more discordant; but the *aspect* of the scene was most pleasing, and struck me even more than at first. Many of the men were models of manly beauty, tall and dignified in form, and with lofty, open and most engaging countenances. There is no posture in the world more noble and graceful than that in which orientals sit on the ground. But all these were not sitting. A few were standing, if possible, in a still more striking posture, propped up against the wall, like Belisarius in the well-known picture, on long staves, and holding out both hands in an attitude of deprecation, or adoration. Then the pure white dresses, just relieved by the little dash of colour in the red caps emerging from the turbans, or of a red or yellow scarf escaping here and there; the quaint charm and glitter of the antique chandeliers, the venerable vaults above, and the rich solid hue of the carpets underfoot, all tempered by the sweet, soft light of the Eastern afternoon as it flowed in at the door or wavered down from the apertures overhead: these things combined to form a picture which, to a *deaf* man, would have been without alloy, and which was so beautiful as to make even me (who am not deaf) forget the discordant voices for a few moments as I contemplated it."

Lastly, after the recitation had increased to a "perfect race," and the two great songs with which Deuteronomy concludes had been reached, the priests came forth from behind the red veil in dresses of pale green satin with the two great rolls, "the desire and despair of European scholars since Scaliger's time," and exposed their cases for the congregation "to kiss and stroke" and the twenty-four hours of almost incessant vociferation ended with a tumultuous succession of prayers and catechisms between priest and congregation. Grove's very interesting comments on the Fast may be found in the volume of *Vacation Tourists* already mentioned, pp. 337–356, but one may be given here:—

"I could not help recollecting the great Christian spectacle at which my wife and I had been present last autumn at Ammergau, and wondering at the force of the principle which had been sufficient to raise that miracle of ordered beauty, fitness, reverence and intelligence, out of such chaotic beginnings as those before me."

Later on in the evening, in consideration of a liberal backsheesh to the priest, Grove was allowed to examine and make some rubbings of the case of the Great Roll, which was subsequently pronounced by experts at South Kensington to be Venetian work of the 14th or 15th century. He also obtained from Yakub Esh-Shelaby a copy of the Roll which he brought back for the Comte de Paris.

On October 14th Grove left Nâblus for Carmel and Damascus. Here again his sketches of Tabor, of the hills beyond Jordan and of Bedouin tents, though only executed in outline, are uncommonly well done. On October 16th he reached the headquarters of the Sheikh Abreik, and after encamping on the village threshing floor went up on the hills to the west to look at Carmel:—

"We crossed one valley and climbed the next hill commanding a splendid view of the plain of 'Akka, Carmel on the left with the palm grove of Haifa just visible at the further end, the Kishon winding below with shining water in its pools. In front were the regular rounded hills gradually breaking down into a perfect English park, with a smooth turf-like surface, dotted with clumps and single trees; beyond them two *tells* in the peaceful beauty of the evening sun; beyond these the noble plain seven or eight miles wide, broken only by the faint trace of a stream crossing it to the Kishon; in the distance the bounding main with the reefs of foam distinctly marked. On the right, the hills of Galilee thickly wooded, sloping down to the plains, and the towers of 'Akka just appearing above them. The park-like character (it is the exact word) extends up the slopes of Carmel, and the whole formed as lovely a picture as I wish ever to see."

The interest that Grove felt in Carmel and its surroundings may be readily imagined by those who are

George Grove in 1861.

From a portrait by Henry Phillips.

familiar with his vivid and enthusiastic articles on Elijah and Elisha in Smith's *Dictionary of the Bible*. On ascending the mountain he satisfied himself, with a view to verifying the Bible narrative, that the guide could run down to the well by a straight path and back in a short time, and that he could ride to Sôlam in four hours without difficulty—"this," he adds, "with a view to Elisha the Shunamite." He took away with him, as mementoes, acorns, wild figs, hawthorn and myrtle-berries. At the convent he was received with the utmost courtesy and kindness by the Prior and Friar Bruno, who expressed their surprise at his courage in coming alone to Palestine, and having ventured to visit the place of sacrifice, and he sympathised deeply with their complaints against the strangers who disfigured the visitors' book by tearing out its pages. Grove was at pains to transcribe some of the amazing entries, which are perhaps unequalled in this branch of literature for their bigotry, vulgarity and ineptitude.

On October 19th he left Haifa for Damascus, spending the night at Nazareth, where he made several supplementary notes to Stanley's description, and mentions the cell at the Franciscan convent with the inscription "cellule honorée de la demeure du Général Napoléon Bonaparte en 1799." On his journey northward we find him, as on so many other occasions, correcting inaccuracies in Porter. He was struck by the quantities of fish, diving birds, and kingfishers in the lake of Tiberias, and made careful notes and sketches of the architecture of the Temple at Tell Hûm. The night of the 21st—the hottest day of his ride—he spent at Safed, "the most isolated place I ever saw," with the ruins of the earthquake of 1837 still unrepaired. Next day he came in view of the Hermon, and on the 23rd rode from El Mellâlah to Banias, noting *inter alia* the abundance of blackberries. At Banias he made, as usual, careful notes of the masonry and structure of the castle, and gives a striking account of the Cave of Panium—"the first natural source of a river I have ever seen." On

October 24th he pushed on from Banias to Damascus; thunderstorms earlier in the week had affected the temperature, and the mornings were very cold, and he noticed that the crocuses were coming out thickly. On the morning of Friday, October 25th, he had his first sight of Damascus, and arrived at the British Consulate at 6.40 P.M. The entries in his note-book during his stay are characteristic of the wide scope of his interest. He records at length the quaint legend of the grapes of Daraiyah; various local traditions of Elijah and Elisha; notes the peculiarities of the new Moslem sect founded by Sheikh Ali, a Moghrebbi; describes with full detail the architecture of "Naaman's House," the Bâb Esh-Sherki, and the Synagogue and Cave of Jôbar, where, according to tradition, Elijah was often wont to live. Lastly, we may transcribe a characteristic passage on the olive:—

"The olive tree is a great instance of the power of nature and of the impossibility of judging from first appearances. As you ride through them in the scorching mid-day sun, they look so profoundly torpid—so pleasantly, smilingly imbecile, and to have outlived so completely all their productive force, that it is not till you get up to them and find their branches almost breaking beneath the weight of the fruit—literally as many olives as leaves—that you discover how mistaken you were, and in what vigorous health the old gentleman is who seemed to you so senile and so good-naturedly fatuous. These trees have a most human look. Their regular rounded form is like the head of an old *fogey*, and the dust upon them, with their own natural grey, gives them a *powdered* look which helps the illusion."

On October 31st, Grove witnessed the performance of the whirling Dervishes, which has been too often described to justify quotations from his account of the ceremony, animated and detailed though it is. It gave him the impression, he observes, of "a solemn kind of amusement more than of a religious worship, and the absence of excitement or fanaticism was very striking." On Sunday, November 3rd, Grove turned his face homeward, leaving Damascus at 8.15 in the morning, and reaching Baalbek at 4.35 P.M. on Monday afternoon. He took the Zebedâni route, and while finding Porter's rhapsodies ludicrously exaggerated, was greatly impressed by the "magnificent wall of Lebanon—the white mountains rising out of the wooded slopes of the lower spurs, below which spread out the curiously tossed and furrowed forms of the lowest outliers—and below all the rich and many-tinted plain." From Baalbek he made his way to Beirût, duly recording his admiration for the splendidly engineered French road from Damascus, and the beauty of the gardens and groves. Grove left Beirût on Thursday, November 7th, with a strangely mixed assortment of fellow-passengers, including the Patriarch of Jerusalem, returning from his summer visitation in the North, and a quantity of pilgrims—some of them old Russian women—for Jerusalem, as well as Turks and Greeks bound for Alexandria. There were also on board a number of greyhounds—"dogs from Tarsîs," Grove adds in brackets—destined for Said Pasha, dogs with hairy ears and tails, and, like the pilgrims, in a very miserable and squalid condition. Travelling by Alexandria and Malta, Grove reached Marseilles some ten days later, and after a pleasant journey, during which he notes that he never saw the line, "autumn laying here and there a fiery finger on the leaves," more gorgeously exemplified before, reached home on November 20th.

For the best part of two more years—1862 and 1863—the Bible Dictionary was destined to occupy Grove's best energies. His correspondence deals with little else, and his note-books are full of memoranda, extracts, and references connected with this absorbing subject. Thus the first letter in his letter-book after his return is addressed to Captain Washington, the Hydrographer, asking for the latitude and longitude of a number of places in Syria, and various meteorological details. That he was not easily pleased with his own work is sufficiently shown by a letter—undated, but probably written in February, 1862—in reply to one from Dr.

Smith begging him to lose no time with his article on Palestine :—

"Last night," he writes, "I did down to the fall of Jerusalem (Nebuchadnezzar), but it did not come out right, and it has vexed me so, that while lying awake this morning I resolved to relinquish it, of course provided I have your sanction for so doing. This—considering that the article will be signed by me, and that the public (if they ever care sufficiently about the subject to think at all about it) will hold me responsible for its incompleteness —you will, I trust, not refuse : especially as the effect of so doing will be to release the vast machine from that inaction which has so annoyed you and Murray (and myself). I have come to this resolution only after great hesitation, and with very sincere regret. But I see clearly that the alternative lay between a mere skeleton cribbed from Milman and a serious delay, provided I made the article really an original one, as I did in the case of the *Annals of Jerusalem.* I could not now blink the difficult questions of chronology, or of the discrepancies between Rawlinson's discoveries and the Bible—and in the late periods of the Roman occupation, the Moslem conquest and the Crusades, etc., I must investigate the subject entirely afresh. It was easy when doing Jerusalem to evade some of these difficulties, but in connection with the history of the entire country they would have to be fairly looked into : all which would take a very long time to do as I should like to do it. I feel that I owe you this explanation, not merely because I am very deeply sensible of the kind way in which you have acted towards me during the last three months, always treating me like a *friend*, and never like a *contributor*."

In February, Stanley started for Palestine with the Prince of Wales, and the entry, "Books wanted for Stanley," which preceded his departure, in Grove's pocket-book gives place to "Questions for Stanley" on his return in June. From this point onward Grove began the habit, continued for many years, of making out lists of books in his pocket-books, and crossing through those which he read. The list for 1862, which is characteristic of his catholic taste, is too long to be given in full, but contains the following : *Wheat and Tares ; The Four Georges ; The Dutch at Home ; Stanhope's Pitt ; Mendelssohn's Letters ; Hurd's Works ;* G. C. Lewis's *Astronomy of the*

Ancients; Muir's *Mahomet*; *Aids to Faith*; *East Lynne*; Rossetti's *Translations from old Italian Poets*; Carlyle's *Frederick the Great*; *The Danes in England*; books on Hungary, Hawaii, North America and Egypt, and Spedding's *Bacon's Life and Letters*. Another book which he read and delighted in early in 1862 was the *Amours de Voyage* of Clough, who died at the close of the preceding year. The same pocket-book also contains the rough draft of one of his early analyses of Beethoven's Eroica Symphony, and a number of the good sayings and anecdotes in which Grove delighted. The quality of these stories and jokes varied, but certainly most of them deserved recording. From the 1862 pocket-book comes the story of the then Master of Trinity's comment on a sermon in which Canon Wordsworth had attempted to prove at great length that the measuring rod (Κάνων) in the Revelation was the Canon of Scripture: 'He need not have said so much to prove that a Canon may be a stick.' Another entry relates to the importance of the letter *r* in French eloquence: "When Guizot was accused in the chamber of communicating with Louis XVIII., he replied, "Oui, j'étais à Gand (great uproar). Oui, j'étais à Gand (renewed uproar). Accumulez injures sur injures, outrages sur outrages, ils ne s'éleveront jamais au hauteur de mon dédain."

A third relates to an old lady and her maid who, terrified by a thunderstorm, had betaken themselves to prayer and were overheard at the words, "especially for the Houses of Parliament." Other entries deal with philological curiosities, links with the past, stories of Sydney Smith, Lords Melbourne and Lyndhurst, printer's errors, and every conceivable kind of topic, frivolous and weighty. Of domestic events, the most interesting in 1862 was the birth of his younger daughter Millicent Stanley Grove on January 28th, while of his new friendships not the least pleasant and fruitful was that struck up with Arthur Sullivan, just returned from Leipzig, where he had been studying in company with

Walter Bache, Carl Rosa, John F. Barnett and Franklin Taylor. The beginning of his friendship with Sullivan, with whom he remained on the most intimate terms for the rest of his life, as related by Mr. F. G. Edwards on Grove's own authority, is worth recording :—

"Sitting one day in the gallery at a concert in St. James's Hall, Sir George espied some one peering through the glass panel of the gallery door. 'Who is that engaging looking young man ?' he enquired. 'Oh, that's Sullivan,' was the reply, 'he's just come back from Leipzig.' A friendship between the two men was quickly formed and soon became very steadfast. It was at the Crystal Palace that Sir Arthur was really first brought before the English public as a composer, where his charming *Tempest* music was performed, April 5, 1862, and repeated on the following Saturday.[1] While Sullivan was writing his *Sapphire Necklace* he took rooms over a shop in Sydenham Road, to be near his kind friend Grove, at whose house he almost lived. At a later period another of Sir George's 'young men' stayed, with Sullivan, under his roof. He was a fellow student of Sullivan's at Leipzig, and the two young musicians made much music together, always sure of a deeply sympathetic listener."

The name of the other young musician was Franklin Taylor, the distinguished pianist and professor, another lifelong ally of Grove's, and in later years, like Mr. J. F. Barnett, one of the staff of the Royal College of Music. Grove did not leave England in 1862, owing to the stress of his work on the Dictionary, but in September he and his wife spent a most interesting ten days at Oxford with Stanley, then Canon in residence at Christ Church, and met Ewald, who afterwards dined with the Groves at Sydenham. It is worthy of note that in July, 1862, he was asked by Mr. Beresford Hope to join the staff of the *Saturday Review*, but declined owing to the pressure of his other engagements. His note-books show that he was in constant communication with Stanley, and his

[1] Sullivan wrote on the 25th, "I will not bore you with a long epistle, but *I must* tell you how grateful I am for all your kindness during the C. P. affair, and I know how much I am indebted to you with regard to the success of the *Tempest*."

correspondence relates almost exclusively to the Dictionary, now approaching completion. That Grove's relations with his editor and publisher continued to be of the most satisfactory character may be inferred from a note to Dr. Smith dated "Crystal Palace, November 25, 1862":—

"The cheques have arrived and I confess to being very much gratified by Murray's liberality. Of course I have worked hard and believe that I have fairly earned my quota—but that is no law for Mr. Murray; especially is it no reason for the increase which he has given me over the sum which he understood I was to have. I shall write a little note of acknowledgment to him for this: meantime I am not unmindful of the share which you have had in this matter and for this and so many other kindnesses am truly grateful."

At the same time the hold that Beethoven had already taken on him is conclusively shown in a letter to his sister-in-law Miss Emma Bradley, undated but belonging to this year, *à propos* of the sonata Op. 106:—

"Why, my dear child, it's the most *awfully difficult* thing! You perhaps don't know what an event it is, having heard it at all. I recollect when Miss Goddard played it (for the first time it was ever heard in London[1]) in 1853 and the extraordinary sensation it made. There is no doubt whatever, it is she we have to thank for Beethoven's latest and most difficult sonatas having become so popular as they now are. But the gem of them all (and playable too) is the arietta which is the subject of the last movement of Op. 111. You will find no difficulty in playing the arietta itself and the first or two first variations, and if they don't make you cry, I shall be astonished. Taking into account that it was B's last P.F. composition and that he was then stone deaf, and alienated from every one though as full of love for every one as any man that ever lived, the tenderness of this little air is most overcoming."

The early months of 1863 found Grove busily engaged on his article on the Salt Sea, on which, to judge from his note-books, he lavished more care and research than on

[1] As a matter of strict accuracy, it was played for the first time in London by M. Alexander Billet, on May 24, 1850, at St. Martin's Hall.

any of his contributions to the Dictionary, supporting the candidature of his friend John Hullah for the post of Gresham Professor of Music, and taking up the cudgels for Stanley (*Morning Post*, January 17th, 1863) when a Professor Simjanki had attacked his Hebrew scholarship. There is also good reason to believe that he sided with Stanley over the Colenso controversy in the same spring as he undoubtedly did in the case of Dr. Jowett. But his life, so fully occupied with congenial interests, was suddenly clouded with a great sorrow. On April the 18th his daughter Lucy, then just ten years old, began to take pianoforte lessons from Mr. Franklin Taylor. On May the 15th she received a charming note from Arthur Sullivan thanking her for a gift of a walking stick. The weekly lessons, duly entered in Grove's diary, continue till May 30th, when they closed for ever, an attack of scarlet fever proving fatal on the 15th of June. She was buried on the 18th, and these two sad anniversaries, noted with melancholy precision for many years in his diaries, never failed to remind him of a bereavement to which he was never entirely resigned.

Grove did not often speak of this loss, but letters written to intimate friends twenty years later prove how indelible was its trace, and even in his gayer moments he was fond of using a Malapropism—"I cannot exclaim to you" for "I cannot explain to you"—borrowed from the childish talk of his daughter Lucy. In one of his note-books he gives the context: "One Sunday I was taking L. out for a walk and she said in a tone of deep emotion, 'Oh, papa, I cannot *exclaim* to you how much I like walking with you on Sunday afternoons.'"

CHAPTER IV

Arthur Sullivan, Madame Schumann and Stephen Heller—Dickens at the Frederick Lehmanns'—Visit to Stanley at Oxford—F. D. Maurice on Renan—Reception of the *Dictionary of the Bible*—Stanley's marriage and appointment to Westminster—The Pierotti Controversy—Holiday trip to Switzerland—Anecdotes of Lord Houghton—Grove and the house-breaker—Origin of the Palestine Exploration Fund—Grove's energy as founder and advocate of the scheme—Reminiscence of Costa—Visit to Paris—Anecdotes of Wilberforce and Helps—Grove's championship of Schumann—Proiected Life of Shelley—Papers on Tennyson's Lyrics.

TURNING to the musical side of Grove's life we find, first, that his acquaintance with Arthur Sullivan had already ripened into a cordial friendship. On May 13th, 1863, Sullivan celebrated his twenty-first birthday, which is all that is needed by way of introduction to the letter written to Grove on that day :—

"47, CLAVERTON TERRACE, ST. GEORGE'S ROAD, S.W.
"*May* 13, 1863.

"MANY many thanks, my dear good friend, for your affectionate letter and for the substantial proofs of your regard—you are right when you speak of the happy year we have had since we knew each other, but I go still further and acknowledge with gratitude the immense advantage which your friendship has been to me—I have learnt more from being with and talking to you, than you can ever well know, for you have taken good care not to let my Art alone absorb me, but have interested me in other equally, if not more instructive matters. I should not have said this, but you impute so much to me that it is but right to tell you what I owe to *you*—Long may our friendship last!

"The arrival of the Family parcel caused an immense sensation here to-day. Everything was eagerly examined and admired, and the clear and explicit key drawn out by you, studied with immense interest. The umbrella has been the theme of universal admiration in town, and the trade has profited accordingly. I have not yet received the deputations from the various Public Offices, Colleges &c., but shall doubtless have a hard day's work tomorrow. One of my presents has been a locket with Beethoven's hair in it. What do you think of that, you old ravenous Beethovenite?

"Tell dear Mrs. Grove I will write to her tomorrow, and also to the children, whose presents pleased me beyond measure. Goodbye, dear old fellow,

"Ever yours affectionately,
"Arthur S. Sullivan."

His long friendship with Madame Schumann also dates from this year, in which she appeared with great success at the Crystal Palace. In a quaintly worded note dated June 4th, 1863, in which she apologises for her "bad English," Madame Schumann writes to express the great pleasure she experienced in playing her husband's concerto "with your distinguished orchestra. Pray say to Mr. Manns that the delight by the fine accompaniment let me forget quite at all the trouble and noise of the visitors walking outside the room. I shall be very glad to play again in one of your concerts next year."

Stephen Heller he had got to know the year previously, when Heller and Hallé played Mozart's double concerto at the Crystal Palace, and Grove was very fond of telling the story of the young lady at Manchester—where Heller had visited Hallé—who, when informed that M. Heller could improvise on any subject that was given to him, ingenuously asked, "Do you mean to say that if he was given a *sponge*, he could improvise upon that?" In 1863 also he began to be a visitor at the house of Mr. Macmillan, with whose firm in after years he was so long, intimately, and honourably associated ; and he was already a *persona gratissima* at the pleasant gatherings organised by Frederick Lehmann and his wife, whose house in Westbourne Terrace was a focus of artistic, literary, and musical activity. It was here on May 31st in this year that Felix Moscheles gave him the details of Mendelssohn's visit to Buckingham Palace, and the following letter, addressed to Miss Olga von Glehn a few weeks later, gives a fair notion of the quality of the company gathered under the Lehmanns' hospitable roof :—

"C. P. *Saturday morning.*
[No date.]

". . . . The next day (Sunday) we went to London at 10, first to the church near Victoria where Taylor played—a very Pusey place indeed—nice music and plenty of it—and heard a very dull sermon. Thence we walked across the Park to Westbourne Terrace. Here we found Dannreuther and two other fellows, and after lunch started with the L's and their boys, some in a carriage and some on horses, for their country house at Muswell Hill. A very pretty neighbourhood and a very pretty new house —everything regardless of expense, but in very good taste. Back again to Westbourne Terrace. At dinner were Robert Browning, F. Moscheles, Mr. and Mrs. Benson, and Miss Enequist—a débutante singer—besides the former party. On Thursday we went to a great dinner-party there, followed by a musical 'at home.' At dinner were Dickens and his sister-in-law, R. Browning, R. Chambers, Miss Gabriel and ourselves. It was very pleasant. Dickens was very amusing, but not the least forced, and Browning was also interesting. Dickens was full of a ship of Mormon emigrants which he had been seeing ; 1200 of the cleanest, best-conducted, most excellent looking people he ever saw. No doubt there will be an account of it in *All the Year Round*. After dinner came a host. Sullivan with Dannreuther and Taylor and Lotto, a new violinist. Ward R. A. and his wife, Holman Hunt, Deichmann, Miss Enequist—besides others whom I did not know. Chorley, Rathbone, Deutsch, &c. &c."

Grove's expectations as to the account in *All the Year Round* were duly fulfilled. In the number for July 4th, 1863, "The Uncommercial Traveller" describes his visit to a Mormon Emigrant Ship "on a hot morning early in

June," thus approximately fixing the date of the foregoing letter.

The winding up of the Dictionary prevented Grove from taking an extended holiday in 1863, and writing to Dr. Smith in the autumn he complains of low spirits: "whether it is want of holiday or some deeper reason I don't know, but I can't get over my loss. It pursues me everywhere, and the sad memories of my dear child take possession of me directly I cease from active occupations." He did, however, occasionally get away to the country, and there is a characteristic entry, showing his intense interest in local tradition, relating to a visit to Bulverhythe on July 6th:—

"'The landlord of the inn' he writes 'cannot recollect any sign or picture with a bull's hide on it. It has always been a *Bull*, formerly red, now black. . . . The old story is, that William the Conqueror landed down below, and bought or obtained as much land as a bull's hide would cover. He then cut it into thongs and it reached to Battle. (The cabman said it reached round Bulverhythe, and that the old sign at the inn was a bull's skin hanging in strips.) The whole place is full of stories of W. the Conqueror. An old stone used to be shown where he dined. 'Bo Peep' was so called because they spied there at him as he landed. *Silver hill* because there his horse was shod with silver. *Turnbridge*: there the women met him armed with boughs of trees, and he said he must *turn* as the women had come against him."

Stanley, with whom Grove had been in close correspondence in connection with his article on the Dead Sea, paid a visit to Italy this autumn in company with his sister Mary Stanley and Hugh Pearson. On his return at the end of October, Grove was one of his earliest guests at Oxford, where Stanley was at this time Professor of Ecclesiastical History and Canon of Christ Church, and has left in one of his note-books full notes of their conversations.[1]

[1] It was probably to this visit that Grove referred in a reminiscence dictated in 1897: "I stopped once with Arthur Stanley at his house in Christ Church, at the same time with Lord Monteagle. Their method of farewell was very good. 'Well, good bye,' said Stanley, 'you've been a charming guest.' 'And you,' rejoined Lord Monteagle, 'have been a host in yourself.'"

Stanley's reasons for rejecting the offer of the Archbishopric of Dublin, as reported by Grove, correspond closely with those given in his letter to Tait (Stanley's *Life*, vol. ii. pp. 131–132), but the account of the interview with the Pope adds a good deal of amusing detail to the more decorous narrative given in the *Life*, vol. ii. p. 358. This is how it runs in Grove's report :—

"Our interview with the Pope was very pleasant. I knew his Chamberlain, an English convert, and he managed it all for us. The aspect of the rooms leading to the Pope's room was splendid —state on state—such servants I never saw for splendour, number, and variety; some in red velvet, others in black and so on. Nothing at all poverty-stricken, but quite the reverse. He was standing reading papers and so immersed in them that he did not turn round when the official announced us. At last he was made aware of our presence and then turned round. We kissed his hand. Catholics kiss his foot in acknowledgment of his spiritual sovereignty, but we kissed his hand as any other sovereign—we treated him like any other king. He then began to say that he must talk in French. He had not had the opportunity of learning English when he was young. To this I assented. He then began to speak of the P. of W.: he had heard that I had been with him, and then ensued the curious blunders I told you of in my letter. 'You know Weelberforce; he is a professor of Oxford?' (I burn to tell the Bishop that, he will be so dreadfully mortified.) 'I know two of his brothers, one of whom died at Frascati.' Pearson mentioned Faber and he said F. was a great loss, so much given to works of charity. 'I have to thank the University of Oxford, for it has given us *le célèbre Newman.* Manning, was he of Oxford?' He then asked, as I thought, if our professors were married (*épousés*) to which I replied that some were and some were not. 'Yes,' he said, 'but I speak of Pousi [Pusey] *très âgé*. . . .' When we went he said, 'I pray God bless you in all your relations and I pray for you now and always as I do for all Christians.' We backed to the door which seemed to please him. We kissed his hand also at parting. H. P. [Pearson] took great pains to kiss the fisherman's ring. He was much more impressive than any of his portraits—more broad and massive in face, with a very large nose."

Stanley also gave Grove the following account of a

chance meeting with Lord Shaftesbury in France on his return from Italy :—

"He had been in North Italy, and told me apparently, quite to his satisfaction, that the religious sentiment was quite extinguished there—probably he meant the Romanist sentiment, but he seemed not to look for anything to take its place. . . . He told me too that Lord Palmerston's idea was to have two Italian kingdoms—North and South—but that it was frustrated by Garibaldi."

In this context it may be noted that a sermon preached by Stanley towards the close of the year led to the following striking letter from Frederick Denison Maurice :—

"2, BRUNSWICK PLACE, YORK TERRACE,
"*December 7th.*

". . . I partly thought he might mean Renan in that passage. Now that I know he does, I don't agree with it. I have read Renan[1] with care, I wished to find the bridge. I have utterly failed to find it. I cannot read his book as I can the letters of the Savoyard or a number of books by professed infidels clutching at the truth of our Lord's character, though unable to describe it as divine. Renan seems to me to consider Him essentially untruthful and to like Him the better for being so. It is the Jesus of a Jesuit. I do not say that he may not have realised by his visit to Palestine the actual existence of a Person who had been to him the mere dream of a shadow before—and the disagreeable dream of a dark shadow. I do not say that the graceful Galilean impostor who died 1800 years ago may not be on the whole a better and healthier object of contemplation to him than the mere picture or image of a sufferer. Let that be so. I rejoice if it is. But the only good I can get out of the book for us is this. It tells English Churchmen how much they have become believers in a dead and not a living Christ, how much they have polluted Him with their trickeries and falsehoods. As the result of that habit of mind, it may serve as a warning; but oh, surely a man, who lives and is ready to die for the truth like Stanley, who wants all young men to live and die for it, must not circulate the opinion that a man is a bridge for us who believes that a teller of lies is the highest model of human excellence, the author of the most blessed worship in the world. Such a doctrine is to me accursed, the parent of all curses. I

[1] Renan's *Vie de Jésus* was published in 1863.

have written this in an article for *Macmillan*.[1] I do not know whether it will be inserted this month, but it was a necessary outcome of my own soul. I shall be bitterly grieved if on the whole it does not carry your sympathy with it.

"Ever yours affectionately,

"F. D. M."

The references to music which occur in his diary for 1863 show that he was steadily enlarging his acquaintance with the compositions of Schumann, with those for orchestra at the Crystal Palace, while for the pianoforte pieces—for Grove was no executant—he found an admirable interpreter in his friend Franklin Taylor. His work on the Bible Dictionary was now finished, but how unabated was his interest in the subject may be seen from the elaborate list of questions, dated October 2nd, prepared for the Rev. H. B. Tristram, who started for Palestine towards the end of the year at the head of a small scientific expedition to explore the geological, zoological and botanical aspects of the Holy Land. Even before the publication of the Dictionary in its complete form, Grove's reputation as an authority in the department of Biblical research was so far established that he was approached by more than one publisher to undertake work of a similar nature. Thus we find him on November 28th, 1863, declining to edit a Bible for Messrs. Dalziel Bros., as the scheme suggested did not commend itself to his judgment, while the negotiations opened by Mr. John Rivington about the same time, in connection with another projected Dictionary, were discontinued as soon as Grove ascertained that Mr. Murray was resolved to proceed with his scheme for a Dictionary of Christian Antiquities. With regard to the former scheme Grove wrote, "As I am not likely to be able to edit more than one Bible in my life-time, I see no alternative but to reserve myself for a more favourable opportunity." The notion of a Bible Commentary is

[1] Maurice's article, "Christmas Thoughts on Renan's *Vie de Jésus* will be found in *Macmillan's Magazine* for January 1864.

more than once mooted in Grove's correspondence on Dictionary matters with Dr. William Smith, before the announcement, in the *Times* on November 13th, 1863, of the scheme of the Speaker's Commentary. I find some notes of a conversation at Dr. Smith's on November 17th in which the following passage occurs, "The time will come when we will do a commentary on a very liberal and satisfactory basis—not anything of Colenso, but really liberal and first-rate. You and I and Stanley—and you and I will have our names on the title-page as joint-editors." Writing to Mr. John Murray a month later, on December 15th, he incidentally mentions that the Commentary—presumably the Smith-Grove Commentary—had been dropped.

Meantime the second and third volumes of the *Dictionary of the Bible* had appeared, and a survey of the notices which appeared in the leading papers make it agreeably clear that Grove's services met with adequate recognition. The *Times* (Dec. 26, 1863) notes that "the greater part of the minor biographies are furnished by Mr. Grove, who on many grounds occupies a very high position amongst his fellow labourers." The *Saturday Review* (Dec. 12, 1863) praises the treatment of the purely geographical, physical and historical subjects, and adds, "Mr. Grove's co-operation and superintendence in all that relates to the knowledge of the Holy Land of itself adds great value to the book." Special and honorific mention of Grove's work was also made by the *Reader*, the *Daily News*, the *Nonconformist* and the *Record*, the last-named remarking that "Mr. Grove and Mr. Wright have been the Nethinim of this vast undertaking, discharging those minute laborious offices absolutely essential to any work of the dictionary species. The ability of these modest labours is truly honourable to them." As for the abiding value of Grove's work in this branch of inquiry I am glad to avail myself of the expert testimony of the Rev. William Addis, who, in the later years of Grove's life, discussed Biblical and theological problems more frequently with him than any other of his friends. Mr. Addis writes :—

"If I try to estimate the permanent value of his Biblical work, the result is apt to seem disappointing. For what work is of permanent value in this field? In a sense none, for Biblical work, if scientific, is like all scientific work, and of course scientific work is perpetually superseded by the advance of research. Sir George Grove was certainly a chief authority on the geography of Palestine, but enormous pains have been spent in the exploration since his time, and these have added greatly to our knowledge. Again, Sir George was, like all the scholars of his time, a disciple of Ewald. Now it would be difficult to mention a greater name than Ewald's in the annals of Hebrew learning; but a new school, led by men like Wellhausen and Kuenen, has arisen since Ewald's day, and nobody stands nowadays where he stood. There is, however, a truer and deeper sense in which scientific work has an abiding worth: it prepares the way for fuller truth: it is the condition of all subsequent advance. Judged by this equitable standard, Sir George Grove's work will always deserve grateful recognition. He rendered valuable service well nigh half a century ago to Dean Stanley's *Sinai and Palestine*, not only by verifying the references, but still more by arranging the appendix on Hebrew geographical terms. Far more signal was the service done for Biblical scholarship by the part he took in Smith's *Biblical Dictionary*, a really epoch-making work, for it is not too much to say that it inaugurated a new era in Biblical study, that it was in fact almost the beginning in England of such Biblical study as deserves to be called scientific. Of this work Sir George Grove was the very soul. He began it by compiling a concordance of proper names in Bible and Apocrypha, he wrote most of the articles on obscure names in the first volume, and corrected the proofs, and revised the whole book. This would have been labour enough for most men. But besides all this, he wrote many articles of first-rate importance. Among these I may mention a long and learned article on the geography of Palestine, till lately the best account which we had, and still worth careful study, with two brilliant biographies of Elijah and Elisha. Canon Driver, the present celebrated professor of Hebrew in the University of Oxford, has called attention to the felicitous sagacity with which, in his article on Moab, Sir George Grove divined the stage of civilization which the Moabites had reached. At that time the data for an opinion were scanty enough, but the discovery of the Moabite stone with its famous inscription, turned Sir George Grove's conjecture into ascertained fact."

What Grove felt himself about his share in the Dictionary is very well summed up in a few rough memoranda—probably notes for a speech at the Bible Dictionary Dinner, held after the completion of the work. He says that, though his work throughout had been of a humble and mechanical kind, it had been to him both a pride and a pleasure. Dr. Smith had treated him with entire confidence, and the other contributors had generously helped him when his scholarship was exhausted.[1] Finally anything of any real value in his articles had been due to the inspiring influence of Stanley.

In Stanley's appointment to Westminster he naturally took the deepest interest, and writing to his brother-in-law, Granville Bradley, describes his first meeting with Lady Augusta:—

"CRYSTAL PALACE, *Dec.* 7, 1863.

"I was very fortunate yesterday. I rushed up to town in the afternoon hoping to catch sight of him at Grove End Crescent. Finding him not there, I thought I would try Vere Street, and there he was with Lady Augusta, so that I saw him and her and heard Maurice all at once. She is charming to look at—a thoroughbred lady, without a particle of affectation and a most loveable countenance . . . . He, archangel that he is, looked more like an old clothes-man than I ever saw him before, and yet, looking at him and Maurice standing before that little Bethel of M's, the thought crossed me that the dingy street ought to have blazed with eternal splendour, for these were certainly the two greatest men in the Church of England in it then! The marriage is to be on the 16th at the Abbey; no one invited, but he will be very glad to see any of his friends."

Notes of the first sermon preached by Stanley as Dean of Westminster in the Abbey on January 10, 1864, appear on an adjoining page of the same note-book, and further on occurs the draft of a letter evidently intended for the press, in which Grove asks whether "something could not be done to make the Dean of Westminster audible to a larger part of the great and important congregation whom he has now to address." The defect, according to Grove,

[1] Here he had, no doubt, Mr. Aldis Wright specially in his mind.

was not in the Dean's voice, but in the position of the pulpit, and he suggests that it should be moved from the East to the West corner of the Transept.

On February 8th, 1864, the judgment of the Privy Council in two of the prosecutions occasioned by *Essays and Reviews* was delivered, and led to the following comments from Grove in a letter to Miss M. E. von Glehn :—

"Crystal Palace, S.E.,
"*February* 10, 1864.

"... The great news of the week to me, is the judgment of the Privy Council, on the trial of two of the *Essays and Reviews* men, which is in fact to settle *for ever* (for members of our Church) that speculation and free inquiry into the nature, inspiration and authority of the Bible is allowable, and may be pursued without fear of penalty. Coupled with it is the appointment of a Royal Commission to inquire into the present regulation of subscription to the Articles, the Act of Uniformity, &c. This is the question raised by Stanley in his letter to the Bishop last year. The Commission is not all that one could wish, but nothing but good can come from it. Stanley has preached twice since you went, (1) on the mission of the Church of England, (2) on the Prayer Book as the expression of that mission."

In the same month Grove was approached by Tom Hughes on behalf of Hutton and Townsend of the *Spectator*, with a view to his undertaking the review of Signor Ermete Pierotti's *Jerusalem Explored*, but wrote to Hughes on February 22nd explaining the obstacles in his way, the chief being that his review could not fail to be in great part an exposition of Fergusson's theory about the Mosque of Omar. Grove did not review Pierotti's work in the *Spectator*, but he started a very lively controversy by a letter to the *Times* of March 7th, charging Pierotti with a number of plagiarisms from the illustrations of Fergusson's *Essay on the Ancient Topography of Jerusalem*, from Mr. Tipping's plates in Traill's *Josephus*, and from other authorities. Pierotti, who had made his *début* at the British Association in October

1862—when the Rev. George Williams read a paper of his on "Recent Notices of the Rechabites"—retorted with a general and emphatic denial of these charges, and the controversy raged for a month or more, Grove being backed by Tipping and Fergusson, who challenged Pierotti to submit the whole question to the Council of British Architects, or any other competent tribunal. On the other side the Rev. George Williams, already alluded to above, wrote a pamphlet in Pierotti's defence, but his private letters to Grove, written after a visit to the Crystal Palace, where Grove had laid out all the documents and books involved in the controversy on his table, for the inspection of all concerned in it, show that his confidence in his *protégé* was a good deal shaken. A large number of antiquaries and architects availed themselves of Grove's invitation, with the result that the balance of expert opinion unquestionably declared itself against Pierotti.

Another and more notable controversy—the long-standing dispute over the endowment of the Greek Professorship at Oxford—had come to a crisis in the same month. On March 8th Convocation had rejected the grant to Dr. Jowett, though recommended by Dr. Pusey and Keble, on the score of Jowett's heterodox religious views. Grove's attitude is well expressed in the letter which he wrote on the following day to Miss von Glehn, a letter which deserves to be reproduced if only for the striking tribute to Stanley at the close :—

"CRYSTAL PALACE, *March* 9.

"... The question of Jowett's salary was brought on at Oxford again yesterday, and (I am ashamed to tell you) lost by a large majority. The late judgment of the Privy Council, acquitting the *Essays and Reviews*, and promising *finally* (so that it can never be gainsaid, but is a step gained *for ever* in the history of England) that the Church of England does not require its members to hold every word and letter of the Scriptures as absolutely and infallibly dictated by God, and that there may be differences of opinion as to the everlasting duration of future punishment—this judgment had caused such a panic amongst the ignorant country clergy, and the opportunity had been so skilfully made use of by the leaders of both High and Low Church, that they moved up to Oxford, and in spite of the fact that Pusey and Keble both recommended the measure for raising Jowett's salary, and that all the intelligence of the University was for it, they negatived it by a majority of 72 in about 700 votes. On me and on many others it has come quite unexpectedly, for we were in hopes that at last justice was going to be done and the very angry feeling of many laymen throughout the country, and especially of the students at Oxford, appeased. It will only hasten the day for Parliament to interfere, but meantime it is a monstrous thing that such a dreadful piece of dishonesty should be continued, or that the most eminent Greek scholar in Oxford should be allowed to hold the office of Regius Professor at £40 a year, while all the others are raised to £500 and some even to £1200. I have not heard from Stanley since it happened, but I can well understand how grieved and enraged his righteous soul must be at such a flagrant thing, and one against which he has striven so steadily for seven or eight years. Stanley's sermons since he was made Dean have been most admirable. The first was on sacrifice, the real meaning of a 'reasonable, holy and living sacrifice.' Then followed one on the Church of England, its comprehensiveness and moderation and practical character; then one on the Liturgy, its uniting old and new, its breadth and depth; and then there was one out of the course on Abraham sacrificing Isaac (which I did not hear) and then two Sundays ago he resumed the former set with one on Hymns—their various origins, their virtues and usefulness. You would have been amused at the characteristic way in which the Dean of Westminster preaching in the great Abbey of Westminster showed and exulted in the fact, that the best known and most valued hymns had been written by *heretics*—non-jurors, dissenters, Calvinists, Wesleyans, or if by members of our Church, yet by men who at one time were disliked and shunned (as Keble's *Christian Year*) though now their hymns are household words; and he quoted in the course of his sermon a passage on the use of hymns to repeat in quiet odd moments, from a man who to many persons is the typical heretic of the day—Francis Newman. There never was such a good Samaritan, such a praiser of other good Samaritans, such a pourer of oil and balm into the wounds and rents of his brethren, as this dear Dean of mine."

Though Grove had begun to take things a little easier now that he was released from the pressure of the

Dictionary work, he was never allowed to be idle even if he had wished to be so. On March 25th Dr. Smith wrote asking him to undertake the editing of a Biblical Atlas for Murray, and a week later Mr. Murray followed this up by a letter in which he expressed the hope that he would consent, adding: "You are the proper person to preside over such a work. No one else can do equal justice to it from your reading and practical experience." Eventually Grove undertook to act as sub-editor or coadjutor with Dr. William Smith on the Classical Atlas, giving his special attention to the Biblical maps.

From a letter addressed to Mr. (afterwards Sir Henry) Cole, C.B., dated February 23rd, 1864, it appears that Grove had decided not to apply for the vacant Keepership at South Kensington, as Mr. Cole had suggested he should, and several years elapsed before he seriously contemplated a move. In the interval between the conclusion of the Dictionary and the initiation of his Palestine Exploration Fund Campaign, Grove began to make more of his social opportunities, and his diary for 1864 shows that he dined out a good deal, went frequently to the Opera—where he saw *Fidelio*, *William Tell*, *Faust* (twice) and *Mireille*—visited Ascot on the Cup Day and was a frequent guest at the entertainments, musical and otherwise, organised by his friends the von Glehns and Scott Russells. Now that Stanley was installed at Westminster, Grove was a constant visitor at the Deanery, and amongst the new names that appear in his correspondence are those of Dean Milman; the Lushingtons; M. Lartet, the distinguished palæontologist and geologist, his "dear Jesuit," as he called him, the author of works on the Hauran and the Tribe of Judah; Joachim, who stayed at his house in July; Dannreuther and Ernst Pauer. Besides the other Sydenham friends already noticed mention may be made of the Charles Davidsons and the David Rowlands. Of the Directors of the Crystal Palace at this period the three whom he saw and liked most were Mr. James Low, a Deacon of Spurgeon's, Mr. Ionides, the Greek Consul, and

Mr. Bicknell. Of the last-named he wrote as follows in the reminiscences of 1897 :—

"The Directors had very often something to say about the programmes of the Saturday concerts. On one occasion I remember Mr. Bicknell expressed his extreme dislike of Wagner's overture to *Tannhäuser* which in those days was almost the only orchestral piece of Wagner's that was heard at the Crystal Palace. Indeed Bicknell went so far as to say that if we continued to give that 'vile overture' he would bring the matter before the Board, and have it stopped. I was not very much better than he was in regard to *Tannhäuser*, but I reasoned with him for Manns's sake, and said that I thought when he had heard it once or twice more, he would alter his opinion. What I prophesied actually came to pass, for—I think it was about a year later—he made a confession to me that by that time his feelings had altered so much that he would as soon hear it as anything else."

On March 18th, Grove wrote to the Secretary of the P. & O. Company asking whether they would grant free passages to and from Alexandria to the four Sappers[1] who were going out to survey Jerusalem and the environs—the cost of the survey was defrayed by the Baroness Burdett-Coutts—a request which was met by a liberal reduction of the fares. Room may here be found for an interesting letter dated March 31st, from his friend Mr. Procter Wright[2] of Leipzig about his pet scheme of a new music school at Sydenham :—

"If the objections to making Sydenham the site of the new music school are insuperable, could it not, to some extent, be supplementary—the pupils, for example, be admitted to the

[1] Headed by Mr. (now Sir Charles) Wilson.

[2] "Procter Wright," writes Mr. Dannreuther, "was a friend of Moscheles and H. F. Chorley. The son of a 'land agent to the University of Cambridge,' he came to Leipzig to study medicine and music—for which latter he had much love and no aptitude. He lived with his mother and sister, and their rooms were the meeting-place of the English-speaking colony generally, and particularly of young musical people—such as Sullivan, Walter Bache, Franklin Taylor, and myself. Wright was about fifteen years our senior—a warm-hearted man, always ready to lend a hand and give friendly advice, so we all liked and respected him. He was known as 'the man who couldn't raise his fourth finger over an

orchestral performances, and those who are forward enough, taking part in them? Such regular and persistent immersion in a musical atmosphere (which is not allowed to stagnate) seems to me absolutely essential to a thorough musical education. And where is such an atmosphere at present to be found in England except at the Crystal Palace? . . . . It makes me very happy to hear of the progress and success of 'my children.' It is curious how important a month April is to them: Sullivan—Dannreuther—Taylor, all April children, so far as their Crystal Palace *débuts* are concerned."

On July 22nd Grove's youngest son Arthur was born—the godparents being Arthur Stanley, Arthur Sullivan and Miss Olga von Glehn; and early in August Grove set out for a holiday trip to Switzerland in company with Mr. and Mrs. von Glehn and their daughter Ida, taking with him by way of holiday reading *Esmond*, Clough's *Poems*, Tennyson's *Princess*, Schumann's songs and two sonatas of Beethoven. Basle, Lucerne, Andermatt, Brieg, Chamonix, Geneva, Lausanne, Berne, Interlaken, Basle, Strasbourg and Paris were the successive stages of a trip which lasted a little over three weeks, and gave him almost unmitigated pleasure. At Lucerne he fell in with his brother-in-law Granville Bradley and his wife, and his sister-in-law Miss Emma Bradley (now Mrs. Charles Bull). The last named contributes the following reminiscences of their meeting:—

"'G,' who came to dine with us at the Schweitzerhof, was just like a boy let out of school, bubbling over with enjoyment and rollicking fun, and our little dinner was quite uproarious. Then we took a boat and went out in the moonlight on the lake, and 'talked of many things.' 'G' had just 'discovered' Mrs. Browning's Sonnets from the Portuguese and was delighted to

F sharp,' and his knowledge of music, like Sam Weller's 'vision,' was limited. When I knew him he had given up the pianoforte, and was devoting his time to the translation of such works as Plaidy's *Technical Studies*, Gunther's *Anatomy and Pathology*, and Hauptmann's difficult *Harmonik und Metrik*—the last-named proved too much for him. The reports on musical events at Leipzig, which appeared in the *Athenæum circa* 1860–1865, were extracts from the letters he wrote to Chorley. He died a few years ago."

find I knew them well. I can hear the tones of his voice now as he repeated, with all the passion it expresses, the noble lines 'Go from me, yet I feel that I shall stand, &c.,' almost choking over the last two lines. It was such an evening as one never forgets. Next day we just met for a few minutes, and went our several ways."

From the rough journal of impressions—generally scrawled down at the moment in his pocket-book—we may transcribe the following extracts :—

[Arrival at Andermatt] "We came through a dark tunnel, and on emerging therefrom at 5 p.m., a sight burst on us, which, like the view of Damascus from the Kubhet en Nasr, was quite peculiar and worth coming any distance to see. We had before us a perfectly level and perfectly green meadow of apparently about a mile square, surrounded on every side by high mountains, snow-capped and sloping steeply down with peaceful green slopes and sparse pine copses to the still greener meadow. In the very centre was a largish church with a tall campanile and a few other buildings all perfectly white. The sun, fast sinking, was streaming with mellow afternoon radiance over the western side of the basin, and threw a deep shadow over the side of the meadow nearest us, but the whole of the rest of the meadow, the church and the buildings, were in the brightest and most cheerful light. The yellow green of the floor so brightly illuminated, so well accentuated by the pleasing forms and the sparkling white of the church and the other buildings, and contrasted with the shadow on the foreground and the darkness from which we had emerged, and the peaceful background of the enclosing mountains, all combined to form a picture of strange charm which filled me with rapture. This was Andermatt—the village 'on the meadow.'"

The look of the waterfall opposite Faido inspired him with this fantastic parallel :—

"The water enters sideways behind a great screen of rock, so that nothing is seen but a mass of white foam, innocent and joyous, tumbling in like a *baby*. This at once opens out into a wide clear basin without a ripple on the surface, and with the clear candid transparent look of *youth*. To this succeeds a rough hurrying portion over stones between rocks—full of noise and clamour, like the turmoil and strife and business of *mature manhooa*, and from this it lastly sweeps down into its grave below the bridge like the exit of *age*."

Grove speaks of the *Mer de Glace* as "coming down like an army on that peaceful valley of cornfields," but the impression was impaired by the spectacle of a "middle-aged tourist in knickerbockers with a Tyrolese hat and feather, red striped stockings and a bright mauve flannel shirt." But he did not spare himself either :—

"No spectacle is more pitiably ridiculous than a man without either whip or spur . . . with an umbrella in one hand and an opera glass in the other, doing his best by clicks, hisses, motions of his body, and kicks, to make a mule go on. At last I discovered that by opening my umbrella quickly, or fluttering it close to his ear, I could rouse my mule to madness, but then he went off so furiously that his driver set up an unearthly yell, and his rider was seriously inconvenienced by the jolting."

On August 23rd he notes a curious colour effect on Mont Blanc :—

"That wonderful effect which clouds seem to have, towards evening, of shedding over a spot of snow a light far superior to that on any other spot not so covered, of a specially bright, white ethereal kind—such a light I saw on the glacier on Saturday night and on the spot above the Grands Mulets to-night. The darkish glacier and the darkish clouds above, added to the effect, which is something more bright, heavenly and ethereal than anything I ever saw or could have conceived. It has the effect of increasing the extent of the spot to an indefinite degree and making it appear to stretch away into infinity. It makes it faint and therefore distant."

At Berne he fell in with Vernon Lushington, from whom he heard the following anecdotes :—

"A millionaire bought a place in the country. His first appearance in church was anxiously looked for. The clergyman waited a decent time, and then began the service. During the Litany the rustling of a silk gown was heard in the aisle, on which the parson faltered. But the clerk speedily undeceived him 'Only the upper house-maid, Sir. *Good Lord deliver us.*'"

"Tennyson speaking to Lushington of Tintern, mentioned that he had not seen it since he wrote there 'Tears, Idle Tears.' Then some one repeated it. 'Ah,' said Tennyson, 'it seems to me as fresh and as beautiful as it did the day I wrote it'; thus confirming my view as to the power possessed by artists of contemplating their own work apart from themselves."

Grove reached home on September 1st, and one of the letters awaiting him on his return was from Madame Schumann, dated Rigi-Kaltbad, August 26, 1864, thanking him for his championship of her husband's compositions, which had encouraged her to pay another visit to England in the ensuing season, and asking for his advice in the matter. In this context mention may be made of the first performance at the Crystal Palace, of Arthur Sullivan's *Kenilworth* music on November 12th. But the most interesting entries in his pocket-book at the end of the year all relate to Stanley. One is an amusing list of *errata* in the first proof of Stanley's lectures, vol. ii:

MS.	Proof
Practical sermons	Penitent sinners
Each to each	Crest to tail

Another relates to the reception of the Dean in the Senate House at Cambridge; while a third, dated December 30th, 1864, records "Dr. William Smith's story of A. P. S. and Lord Houghton," the authority being Mrs. Grote, who told it to Smith:—

"Lord Houghton met A. P. S. sometime after he had become Dean, and said, 'Arthur, you'll excuse me telling you that you preach too much; you don't do it well, and it's a great pity you should do what all your friends think a mistake.' Stanley thanked him. In the afternoon he called on Lord Stanley of Alderley in Dover Street and told him, on which Lord Stanley was very much astonished. In the evening Lord Stanley met Milnes in the House of Lords, and asked him, 'Did you really say so-and-so to A. P. S.?' 'Yes, I did' replied Milnes. 'I thought it a kindness to tell him what I really thought.' 'Well,' rejoined Lord Stanley, 'I'm astonished to hear it; but it emboldens me to tell you something which has long been on my mind, only I have not ventured to say it, which is, that you speak a great deal too much in this House. You don't do it well, and it bores us all immensely.'"

With this may be bracketed another story of Lord Houghton and Sydney Smith, which Grove noted down a few days later :—

"Monckton Milnes, when a very young man, was dining in company with Sydney Smith. He was going to dine next day with Archbishop Howley, and took care to proclaim the fact. A little later he leant across the table and in a loud voice said to Smith, 'Smith, a glass of wine with you.' Smith much amazed said nothing and took his wine. Soon after there came a pause and then Smith said—the whole table listening—'I think, Mr. Milnes, you said you were going to dine with the Archbishop of Canterbury to-morrow.' 'I am.' 'Then if you want to take wine with the Archbishop, I advise you not to say across the table, "Howley, a glass of wine," because he's much older than you are, and having a particular dislike to being so addressed, would be sure not to take it.'"

Against the date November 17th, 1864, in Grove's diary occurs the entry, "Our house robbed." The story of what actually happened—a story curiously characteristic of the narrator, is worth telling, and can happily be told in Grove's own words from the unpublished reminiscences dictated in 1897 :—

"The story of 'our thief' was not at all a bad one, and was for some time one of the Sydenham legends. One night I was reading in the drawing-room by the light of a 'moderator' lamp, when it suddenly occurred to me that it was rather late. My wife had already gone to bed, so I took the lamp in my hand, opened the drawing-room door and went out into the hall, when I put the lamp on the slab. As I did so, I heard the door leading into the pantry and the kitchen bang. Why, I thought to myself, the maids have not gone to bed, though it is a quarter past twelve. I called out: 'Haven't you gone to bed yet?' but there was no answer. I accordingly went to the door leading down into the store pantry, and to my surprise the back-door, which opened on the shubbery, was wide open, and I saw the moon shining distinctly among the trees. Hallo, I thought, those girls must have left the back door open. I then fetched the lamp from the hall, and found that the cupboards in the pantry had been broken open. There was a thick pair of boots on the floor, and a small carpet bag, which contained some very small silver articles. I shut and locked the back-door, and went upstairs to inquire if the maids had locked the door or not. Yes, they certainly had. I then went into my wife's room and told her what had happened, thinking that the thief had no doubt escaped while I was fetching the lamp. I came down stairs still carrying the lamp in my hand and Punch, a little yellow terrier we had, following me closely. When I came into the hall I went into the dining-room, and there to my surprise, behind the door was a man without either hat or shoes. 'Hallo' said I, 'what are you doing here?' 'Well,' said he, 'that is more than I can tell you.' 'Well, show me where you got in,' I said. 'Just let me get my hat,' said the man, and went over to the other side of the room, and crept under the sofa, and pulled out his hat. We then went into the kitchen, and he showed me that he had got in by the window of the larder, that he had discovered a cold shoulder of mutton and the remainder of a large rice pudding and had kindly left us an old umbrella in the corner of the larder. I brought him back to the store pantry and he immediately said, 'You will give me my boots, won't you, sir?' which I had put on a shelf. Here was a difficulty: what was I to do? The locks in the house were very old, and if I locked him up in one of the rooms he would very easily get out again, and I did not feel either able or willing to knock him down and stun him, which was the only other course that suggested itself to me. So I gave him his boots, and took him out to the front gate of the garden. 'Now you had better be quick,' I said, 'or you will have the bobbies after you.' He then made the following singular request: 'You haven't got a shilling about you, that you could give a poor fellow?' 'No,' said I, 'I have not,' but I believe that if I had I should certainly have given it him. I saw him vanish up the road, shut the gate, went back into the house, told my wife what had happpened, and set the maids to look out of their window at the top, and call a policeman if they saw one pass. The moon was bright as day. In about three-quarters of an hour two policemen came strolling up the road, and I went out and told them what had happened during the last hour and a half or so. 'Well, sir, it is no use talking about that, but show us where he got in.' We went back into the house through the front hall door, and I noticed immediately a strong smell of tobacco which I thought had been left by the thief before I turned him out. 'What very strong tobacco that man must have had,' I said. 'Never mind, sir, show us where he got in?' We went through to the larder, and as I was showing them I heard a faint noise in the kitchen. We went into the kitchen and sure enough there was the man back again squeezing the front part of his body into a cupboard and doing all he could to light a pipe. The policeman of course took him off to the station in Upper Sydenham, I with them, and the next day we went to Greenwich police court where he got a year's imprisonment. I must say I was afraid, for a long time, lest some night he should come back again. I have said that this was one of the legends of Sydenham, for it also had its mythical side. I happened at the same time to have bad rheumatism in my left arm, and had to carry it in a sling for some time, and one of the stories circulated (I believe by Paxton) was, that while I was talking to the thief and he was asking me for the shilling at the gate, my wife had looked out of the bedroom window and had fired a pistol, which unfortunately hit me in the left arm."

To the close of this year may also be ascribed an interesting review[1] of a book by the Rev. John Mills, "Three months' Residence at Nâblus," which reveals with great frankness Grove's whole attitude in regard to Biblical criticism:—

"People are at last beginning to see that the Bible is not only the 'handbook of salvation' but that it is the most interesting document in the world. Its narratives have more liveliness than those of Herodotus, more detail than those of Homer. But, unfortunately, the manners were so utterly different from those of the West—especially the West of the nineteenth century—that it is quite impossible for the unassisted reader to realise them. Every one can feel the force and beauty of the broad traits of humanity set forth in the stories of Joseph and David, but the details which give the pictures their special and peculiar interest are lost or misconceived. Who does not feel what a point is added to the tenderness and faith of David's Psalms, when we remember that they were the genuine expression of the man who was barbarous enough to count the people he had killed in the strange fashion related in 1 Sam. xviii. 27; who sent one of his

[1] The cutting containing the review gives neither the date nor the name of the newspaper. But Mills's book was reviewed in the *Athenæum* on December 3, 1864.

faithful servants to death while he himself was seducing his wife; and who drove the luckless Moabites by hundreds into blazing brick-kilns? Who can understand the actions of the prophets—their walking barefoot and naked, their cries of woe, their restless, incessant interferences, without having seen their descendants the dervishes? Here, if anywhere, is that saying of Goethe true:—

> 'Wer die Dichtung will verstehen
> Muss in 's Land der Dichter gehen.'

But it is impossible for us all to visit the Poet's Land, and therefore any descriptions which set the modes of thought, life, and feeling of its inhabitants before us as they are (and therefore as they were in the unchangeable East) are cordially welcome."

À propos of the project of the Greek Church to adorn Jacob's well and build a splendid church over it, Grove reveals his attitude with no less precision:—

"Better a thousand times that the well should remain choked and neglected as at present, but in all other main respects the same as it was when our Lord sat on its edge, and talked to the woman of Samaria—than that it should be surrounded by the glitter and sham that have oppressed and destroyed the house of Nazareth and the manger of Bethlehem, and in the last case have actually rendered the birthplace of Christ inferior in interest to the contiguous cavern of St. Jerome."

The record of the year may be closed by a brief reference to Grove's book list. It is far too voluminous to be quoted in full, but in proof of his wide range of interest, it may suffice to mention Matthew Arnold's Poems, Landor's *Imaginary Conversations*, *Eothen*, Austen's *Faust*, Lewes's *Goethe*, Engel's *Music of the Ancients*, Lecky's *History of Rationalism*, Herder's *Spirit of Hebrew Poetry*, the *Chronicles of Carlingford*, and *Our Mutual Friend*. From a memorandum relating to the Christmas presents given by Grove to his friends this year, it appears that he mostly gave books, and that his favourite choice was the Poems of Tennyson.

If Grove devoted more time than usual to recreation in 1864, he certainly made up for it in 1865, by the energy with which he threw himself into the Palestine Exploration Fund movement. The origin of the scheme cannot be better described than in the words of Major-General Sir Charles Wilson, R.E. In the course of the brief memoir which is printed in the Quarterly Statement of the Palestine Exploration Fund for July 1900, Sir Charles writes :—

"Sir G. Grove, during his tour in Palestine, was much impressed by the close agreement between the natural features of some of the localities he visited, and the allusions to them in the Bible; and he greatly felt the want of accurate maps of the districts which we was unable to examine. At one period he had as his assistant, at the Crystal Palace, the late Mr. James Fergusson, who was deeply interested in the topography of Jerusalem, and the possibility of carrying out surveys and scientific researches in Palestine and Jerusalem was frequently discussed. The first opening came when Miss (now Lady) Burdett-Coutts wished to supply Jerusalem with water, and it was decided, as a preliminary measure, to make an accurate survey of the city. Contrary to general expectation, the survey was successfully completed without the slightest interference by the Turkish officials, or the Moslem population. The success of the survey, some discoveries made during its progress, and an acrimonious controversy respecting the sites of the Holy places, aroused general interest and gave an opportunity which Sir G. Grove was quick to seize. He determined to raise funds for the scientific exploration of Palestine, and to enlist the sympathies of his many friends in the enterprise. No one could resist his enthusiasm."

Mr. Walter Morrison, who became acquainted with Grove in 1864 in connection with the exposure of Pierotti, tells me that he remembers paying a visit to Sydenham to examine Grove's Pierotti *dossier*, as it might be called, and meeting James Fergusson and Mr. David Roberts in Grove's office :—

"This led to a discussion as to the extent of our knowledge of the Holy Land. Mr. Grove was one of the highest living authorities on this subject, as he had written most of the topographical articles in Smith's *Dictionary of the Bible*. Suddenly with alert gesture and look he said, 'Why should we not found a Society for the systematic exploration of Palestine?' Thus the Palestine Exploration Fund was begun."

Grove set the ball rolling in a letter to the *Times* on January 3rd, 1865, based on a letter from Sir Henry James, which had appeared a few days previously, describing the good work being done by Captain Wilson in his Survey of Jerusalem. Grove pointed out that there were several vexed questions which it was most desirable should be settled by Captain Wilson and his party before they left, and continues:—

"There are doubtless many persons who would contribute towards the accomplishment of such objects as these by an efficient and responsible party, like that of Captain Wilson, if some proper channel were found for their liberality. The Assyrian Excavation Fund, formed in 1853 by Mr. Layard, M.P., and the late Mr. S. Phillips, is still in existence, and I believe I am correct in saying that an unexpended balance is in the hands of the treasurer, Mr. John Murray. The original occupation of this fund is gone, but why should it not revive to the kindred work of Palestine Exploration?"

The question was answered rapidly, and in a very satisfactory way, for writing on January 12th to a friend Grove says, "Already, before making an announcement, I have had £300 given me. Fancy that! Of course I am to do all the work, but that I don't mind if any good to that dear little country is to come out of it." On Friday May 12th, a preliminary meeting was held in the Jerusalem Chamber, Westminster, with the Archbishop of York in the Chair, and attended by Stanley, Dr. Pusey, Sir Roderick Murchison, Professor R. Owen, James Fergusson, Henry Reeve (editor of the *Edinburgh Review*), John Murray, W. Tipping, Walter Morrison, the Rev. A. W. Thorold, Dr. J. W. Hooker, and others, at which a strong Committee was formed, with Grove as Honorary Secretary, while the Archbishop of York, the Dean of Westminster, and Professor Owen were appointed as a sub-committee to draw up a statement of the general objects of the Association. The public meeting at which the Palestine Exploration Fund was formally embodied, was held at Willis's Rooms on June 22nd. The Archbishop of York again presided, and the principal speakers were the Bishop of London, Lord Strangford, Sir Roderick Murchison, W. Gifford Palgrave, the Dean of Westminster, Mr. (afterwards Sir Henry) Layard and the Count de Vogüé. The resolutions submitted to the meeting were as follows :—

"That a Fund be formed for the purpose of promoting the Exploration of the Holy Land."

"That the exploration of Jerusalem and many other places in the Holy Land will probably throw much light on the archæology of the Jewish people."

"That, in addition to the praiseworthy researches which have recently been made by Frenchmen, Englishmen, and others, in the Holy Land, it is highly desirable to carry out such a systematic survey as will completely establish the true geological and geographical characters of that remarkable region."

"That it is desirable that the animals, plants, and minerals of the Holy Land be collected ; and that facts requisite for their systematic history be noted by competent observers on the spot."

"That Biblical Scholars may yet receive assistance in illustrating the sacred Text from careful observers of the manners and habits of the people of the Holy Land."

The last resolution, it may be noted, was proposed by Dean Stanley. In his opening address the Archbishop of York laid great stress on the fact that the P.E.F. was not going to be a religious society, or launch into any controversy. "We are about to apply the rules of science, which are so well understood by us in other branches, to an investigation into the facts concerning the Holy Land." He was also able to announce that the Queen had consented to become the Patron of the association, and that the Honorary Secretary had already received—almost without solicitation—the sum of £1,500, amongst the first names on the list of subscribers being those of William Tipping, Walter Morrison, Dr. William Smith, James Fergusson, the Archbishop of York, and Dean Stanley. Grove's name hardly appears in the report of this meeting, but fortunately there is no lack of first-rate testimony as to his share in the movement. At a meeting of the P.E.F. held at Cambridge on May 8, 1867, Dean Stanley said :—

"Mr. Grove described the persons who originated this society as the Archbishop of York, the Dean of Westminster and other eminent persons. He (the Dean) assured them that these gentlemen did nothing of the kind, and that the person who started the fund and caused its progress was Mr. Grove himself. Indefatigability was Mr. Grove's characteristic, and he it was who had enabled other people to take the question up and form a society; Mr. Grove was the head and front of the whole proceeding, and without him it never would have been undertaken."

Stanley's tribute is fully borne out by the Rev. George Williams, who at the same meeting said :—

"There could be no doubt that to Mr. Grove belonged the credit of originating the scheme; though with characteristic modesty, he had put forward the names of the Archbishop of York, the Dean of Westminster and others, who would probably have never thought of organising such a society unless it had been suggested by Mr. Grove."

Sir Charles Wilson is no less explicit. "To Grove," he wrote, in the memorial notice already alluded to, "the foundation of the Palestine Exploration Fund is due."

The public meeting, in June 1865, bore immediate fruit, and though public interest was somewhat distracted by the General Election, by August arrangements were completed for sending out a small party in charge of Captain Wilson, as he then was, to explore and excavate in Palestine. The function that Grove fulfilled in the early years of the Fund has been very happily described by the late Sir Walter Besant. "In George Grove," he wrote in 1892, "the Society had an advocate eloquent, of burning enthusiasm, and full of his subject." He was indefatigable in his appeals, public and private, witness his letter to the *Bible Dictionary* contributors, asking for assistance in a work which is "so directly a result of the great work on which we have been engaged together"; his frequent letters to the *Times*; and his paper read before the Geographical Section of the British Association on September 8th, 1865. After the close of 1866, Grove shared the secretarial duties with the late Rev. F. W. Holland, and the absorbing nature of his other duties compelled him to resign in 1868. But he never lost his interest in the active work of the Fund, and to the end remained a member of the general committee.[1]

His work from first to last was literally a labour of love, but he was amply repaid by the many friendships which it brought him. As Sir Walter Besant has said, "the list of the whole General Committee from the beginning is almost a list of English worthies between the years 1865 and 1892 [the year in which he wrote]." By November 1867, Grove, in one of his periodical appeals to the *Times*, was able to report that the Society had made an Ordnance Survey of 2,300 square miles, to say nothing of many important discoveries and excavations, at the modest outlay of £3,242. By 1892 Sir Walter Besant was able to say that the Palestine Exploration Fund had by its researches restored the splendours of the Holy City, and restored the country for the world for ever by its map and by identifying the places and names of the Bible. Of the many distinguished officers and civilians engaged in the work of Exploration and Survey, it may suffice to mention the names of Wilson, Anderson, Warren, Conder and Kitchener; of Palmer, Clermont-Ganneau, Hull, and

[1] Mr. Walter Morrison, who speaks of him at this period as "a delightful man to work with—so quick, so intelligent, so amiable and tolerant, without being in the least weak," says, "I think the Palestine Exploration Fund continued to hold the second place in his thoughts after the work of the Royal College of Music."

Flinders Petrie. The last name in our list reminds us that the indirect results of the formation of the Palestine Exploration Fund were not less remarkable than its direct achievements. Such was the impetus that it gave to exploration, that it may fairly claim to be the parent and progenitor of the later movements—which have met with such splendid success in Egypt, Asia Minor, Greece, and Crete. To the present generation, Grove is best known as a musical educator, but when one surveys this great work of the scientific reconstruction of the past to which he gave a fresh and electrifying impetus in 1865, one cannot help feeling that he has established a more enduring title to immortality by launching the Palestine Exploration Fund.

In one of Grove's pocket-books for 1865—internal evidence proves the entry to have been made in January or February—there occurs a list of bulls, including one of Costa's "He will walk on crotchets." The context is furnished in Grove's 1897 reminiscences. "Costa's friend, Captain Lyon—an old Queen's messenger who lived with him—had broken his leg, and on one occasion I asked him if he was getting better. 'Oh, yes,' said Costa: 'he will walk on crotchets.'" Grove's acquaintance with Costa dated from the year 1856 when, after the burning down of Covent Garden Theatre in March of that year, Costa conducted a number of Opera Concerts in the Nave of the Crystal Palace, and their association was periodically renewed for upwards of twenty years at the triennial Handel Festivals, which Costa conducted from 1857 until his retirement in 1880. Of their early acquaintance Grove wrote thus in 1897:—

"I was a good deal astonished by him at first. I was just coming to some knowledge of Beethoven, and remembering the lovely melodies in the E♭ Concerto I was astonished to hear him say, as he walked up and down the Nave of the Palace, 'Beethoven has no melody,' by which I suppose he meant melody in the sense of the Italian school. Neither had he much opinion of Mendelssohn; he looked upon the Chorales in *St. Paul* as mere pieces of plagiarism. 'I had to introduce a piece of that sort in *Eli*,' he said, 'but it is entirely my own. I should never have thought of borrowing it from any existing psalm tune.' Once he told me an anecdote which was probably questionable so far as Mendelssohn was concerned. He went into a room in the old Queen's Theatre and found Mendelssohn, Moscheles and Meyerbeer together. 'What are these old Jews about?' was his manner of addressing them, which I do not think would have pleased Mendelssohn particularly. One day he said to me, 'Is there any overture or other piece which you would like to hear at the opera concerts? because if so, I should have great pleasure in putting it into the programme.' Now I had heard a few months before Beethoven's *Coriolan* overture and was thirsting to hear it again, and accordingly suggested it. 'Oh, I do not know it,' said Costa, 'but I will put it in for you,' and he inquired the name a second time. In those days Costa did not *rehearse* the opera concerts himself—that was done by Sainton, his leader. *Coriolan* closed the concert and I went into Costa's room with a bursting heart to thank him for it. 'I will never play that piece again,' he said in his harshest voice. 'It ends *pianissimo*, and it is impossible to make any effect with it.' Costa was a most strict disciplinarian. He had ordered his librarian at Covent Garden never to lend any parts or pieces from the Library. On one occasion, however, Manns had borrowed from the librarian in question the parts of *Fidelio*, but to his surprise he found the *obbligato* horn parts pasted over. Of course he tore them off. Costa required them within a day, and his wrath may be imagined when he found that the cancels had been destroyed. He discharged the librarian on the spot and never employed him again."

These reminiscences of Costa may be supplemented by the interesting paper which Grove contributed to the *Pall Mall Gazette* in May 1884, entitled "The Secret of Sir Michael Costa's Success." Grove maintains that Costa's great plan was "'make yourself safe.' Surround yourself with the best possible agents, the best assistants that you can obtain, quite regardless of expense, and success is certain. In the zenith of his career Sir Michael never moved without such men as Bowley, to prepare the whole scheme of the transaction for him, Sainton, Blagrove, Hill, Lucas, Howell, Pratten, Lazarus, the Harpers,

Chipp, and others of equal eminence at the principal desks, Peck and Henry Wright to distribute the parts. With the perfect organisation and efficient execution of such lieutenants, failure was impossible,"—though, as Grove adds, the method was horribly expensive and crippled the Sacred Harmonic. But Costa was quite unable to train and develop second-rate materials—to educate an orchestra like Richter, Manns or Rosa. His interpolations were "shameful": his additions vulgar, unnecessary and brutal, and his ignorance astounding. Grove very justly adds that in spite of all drawbacks we owe Costa a debt. "He was a splendid drill sergeant; he brought the London orchestras into an order unknown before. He acted up to his lights, was thoroughly efficient as far as he went, and was eminently safe."

At Easter Grove paid a flying visit to Paris in the company of his friend Emanuel Deutsch, the distinguished Orientalist, one of the many friends he owed to his work on the *Dictionary of the Bible.* In a letter to Miss Olga von Glehn on his return, dated April 18th, he writes:—

"I saw all the savants in Paris—Renan, de Vogüé, De Saulcy, Mohl and Madame Mohl (*savante* and *spirituelle* enough for a whole Academy), Lartet, my dear Jesuit, Gifford Palgrave, and heaps besides. . . . Renan alone disappointed me—a short, mean, unpleasant-looking person with whom I tried in vain to talk. Of course his books show what he is, and his appearance is only curious as showing how little one can judge from looks. . . . Garibaldi is here to-day. He is *splendid*—the most noble, *happy*, ingenuous countenance you can conceive. I saw and spoke to George Eliot too (Adam Bede), a *divine person*, with large features, but wonderful eyes and the sweetest smile."

That he was greatly impressed by De Saulcy—the French explorer in Palestine—is sufficiently shown by some rough notes in his pocket-book, in which he pays a generous tribute to De Saulcy's inexhaustible devotion to his subject, his enterprise, and the splendour of his achievements, and continues :—

"In that fierce hand to hand fight which is raging around the ruins of Jerusalem and in which, like the fight of the Horatii and Curiatii, the three are arrayed against our own doughty champion, De Saulcy is the leader, and a noble chivalrous leader he is."

A further reference to the Paris visit is to be found in a letter to Mr. (afterwards Sir Herbert) Oakeley, dated Crystal Palace May 11th :—

"CRYSTAL PALACE,
"*May* 11, 1865.

". . . . I did go to Paris after all, though in the end at five minutes' notice. A man came to dine with me on the Saturday night, and in the middle of dinner, at half past seven, one of us said, 'What a pity we could not hear the Concerto on Sunday,' on which we both started off at once just catching the train, enjoying ourselves *ad infinitum* under Joachim's hospitality and returning on Monday. The Band is wonderful, especially the wind—the delicacy and certainty of which is absolute perfection. The fiddles not so good, wanting in the fire and sentiment of ours. The Concerto did not go quite so well as on the famous night at the Philharmonic last year, but still was wonderful and impressed me more than ever. I should perhaps say it was 'the finest thing in the world,' if I had not just now been *entranced* by the scherzo to the 9th Symphony which certainly is so. I wish you could have heard the performance of it here. . . . The second performance was honoured by the presence of Madame Schumann. . . . Try to meet her in private if possible, and get her to play her husband's smaller compositions—Noveletten, Nachstücke, Humoreske, &c.—and you will be delighted beyond measure. On Monday morning she played to me Bach's Prelude in B minor, (Organ Pedal Fugue),[1] the Chromatic Fantasia, and a heap of things by R. Schumann. I can't conceive anything finer. . . . I envy you your return at this season. If it were but warmer, England would at this moment be a heaven on earth. Spring strikes me every year with more force and more moral significance. So may it be always! I long to keep my freshness and my youth: to enjoy the beauties of Nature and Art more and more

[1] Of which the autograph is in possession of Sir Herbert Oakeley.

every year, never to get stiffened against novelty or *blasé* with antiquity, but to keep a boy's heart to the end of life. And what I wish for myself I wish for you and for all my friends.

"Yours ever sincerely,
"G. GROVE."

Of the musical events of the year in which Grove was specially interested, two call for special note. On February 18th Mr. Franklin Taylor made a successful *début* at the Crystal Palace in Hiller's F sharp minor pianoforte concerto, and on June 1st an extra concert was held in which Madame Schumann played her husband's pianoforte concerto, the vocalist of the occasion being Madame Joachim. From Grove's miscellaneous private correspondence for 1865, three characteristic letters may be here inserted—one on the need of the Higher Criticism, one on Victor Hugo and Swinburne's *Chastelard*, and a third on Mendelssohn's relations with Schumann :—

[*To* MISS M. E. VON GLEHN.]

"CRYSTAL PALACE, *Monday Morn.*
"[No month, 1865.]

". . . I was furious with E— for having interpreted in the most literal way one of the most poetical texts in the Revelation, and in the course of talking about it, said that one harm which such slavish exclusive devotion to the Bible had done was, that probably it had prevented us from having by this time a modern Bible of our own, which should contain the experiences and aspirations of our modern Christian Saints and prophets and in which the conceptions of God, and of the next world, formed in a dark ignorant age, by *Eastern* people, would be superseded by others more in accordance with the progress of the world and the continual revelation which God is making to us through nature and life and events. . . . Everything in the world seems to advance—science, philosophy, metaphysics—all are miles ahead of where they were 1000 years ago—and yet not one of them may be applied to religion because the Bible is set up as an idol, or as a final gauge and measure for all times to come. It's only because we are so accustomed to it, that we don't see it,—but think of the crude, horrid ideas of God that many of the books contain :—anger, revenge, hatred, and all other bad passions are attributed to Him. I think of such passages as the worm that dies not and the fire that is not quenched—of poor Dives longing for a drop of water—*and being refused*, and it's impossible not to see that these are merely expressions such as people in that ignorant, sensuous age could comprehend."

[*To the same.*]

"CRYSTAL PALACE, S.E.,
"*November* 29, 1865.

"... I have begun to read French poetry—begun with Victor Hugo's *Chansons des Rues et des Bois*. There is a vast deal that shocks and frightens an Engländer and that no Engländerin could by any possibility read, but there is a vast deal that is very calm and pure and beautiful, and it is such a new world to poor ignorant me. It is all so bold and broad, and such a sweep and an aplomb! I remember being struck in the same way with the French pictures in 1862 in walking out of our gallery into theirs. They were full of faults of taste, but the subjects were all so much *bigger* and more broadly and confidently treated than our domestic paintings which looked quite feeble by their side. I get the same impression always at the Luxembourg. To return to Victor Hugo. I have also read some *Chants du Crépuscule* which charmed me very much. There is some new English poetry too for you to see when you come back, by a certain Swinburne—*Atalanta in Calydon* (a Greek story) and *Chastelard, a Play*—a young man but a very promising poet.

"Chastelard was one of Mary Queen of Scots' lovers, who, in despair and madness when she married Darnley, hid himself in her room with the object of being killed for it—which he was, *in her sight*. It is very sensuous—like Keats, but most wonderfully beautiful and affecting. It carries you away like a flood—perhaps afterwards one may reflect and see its faults, but at first it's too enchanting. . . .

"I hope soon to go and visit Tennyson and talk to him. A man who can write such a gospel as there is in *In Memoriam*—you know how I value that book—must know all about it, but where, I ask, did he get the art to build so vast and bright an edifice out of such slender materials and so gloomy a foundation?"

[*To* MR. E. M. OAKELEY.]

"CRYSTAL PALACE,
"*December* 30, 1865.

"The charge against the editors of Mendelssohn's Letters is wider than you seem aware of. They have suppressed *all mention* of many of the most prominent of his contemporaries and the dearest of his friends. It is hardly credible that the names of Jenny Lind, Joachim, Sterndale Bennett, J. W. Davison, Robert Schumann, and Clara Wieck, with whom he was in the closest intimacy and constant correspondence, should either not be found at all in either of the volumes or else only be mentioned in some such terms as 'the Schumanns are here' 'Bennett has just arrived,' and so on. What the motive for this exclusion is, I do not know. I can only observe one fact :—that Mendelssohn had a very high opinion of all these persons, and that therefore if he had mentioned them, it would always be in terms of praise. Now very few of the letters printed contain praise of his contemporaries; blame of Meyerbeer and Auber and others is occasionally to be found, but praise of anybody rarely if ever. This seems to have been one guiding principle in selecting the letters, and it is a very reprehensible one, because it not only suppresses Mendelssohn's good opinion of the various persons, but also leads one to believe that he was jealous of his rivals—which is the reverse of the truth. Quantities of letters exist *full of praise* of Jenny Lind, Joachim, Schumann, &c.

"An instance of the bad use that may be made of the omissions is found in a criticism on Schumann in the *Saturday Review* of June 3rd, in which the writer says, 'Mendelssohn and Schumann have been compared. If the public wishes to know what Mendelssohn's opinion of Schumann was, let them remark the significant fact that the published volumes of his letters do not contain a single reference to Schumann or his music.' The idea of suppression of appreciative or laudatory letters about Schumann out of regard to Madame Schumann is, as you say, 'too absurd.' I don't believe any good will be done by any criticisms or representations *here*. The family is quite impervious to such remarks. But it may evoke letters from the possessors of these in England. . .

"Yours ever, G. Grove."

The year 1865, as we have already seen, brought a great accession to the numbers of Grove's already extended circle of acquaintance. As Secretary to the Palestine Exploration Fund he was brought into contact, besides those already mentioned, with Murchison, Sir Gilbert Scott, Milman, Pusey, and Wilberforce. Of the last he tells an amusing story in the reminiscences of 1897 :—

"Bishop Wilberforce of Oxford was always very good to me.

He took a great interest in the Palestine Exploration Fund and made one or two speeches at the meetings. He wrote me several letters on the subject, generally from a railway carriage, and when he had an opportunity, never omitted to come into my room at the Crystal Palace. One day he had been doing some business at Penge, and came up to my room with his chaplain, and after a little while he said: 'I have got to buy some toys for one of my grandchildren, so you must take me out and show me where the toy-stall is.' We went together and I showed him the stall not far from the private door near Wood's ticket office in the centre transept. There was the usual difficulty in choosing; so I took up a little black doll, which squeaked when it was pinched, and said: 'There, my Lord, that ought to be interesting to a Wilberforce.' 'Oh, no,' he answered, 'take it away. I have heard about nothing else all my life.'"

In January 1866 Grove paid a short visit to Tennyson at Freshwater, but no record of the visit remains beyond a few fragmentary notes in his diary of the pieces which Tennyson read aloud in the evening, and a reference to a discussion of Goethe's sonnets. But he left long notes of stories chiefly told him by Arthur Helps at the house of their common friend Hullah on February 12th. "On the evening of Westbury's appointment as Chancellor, Helps had to see him, and said, 'Lord Chancellor, you've a troublesome task before you, for to-morrow morning at nine you've to charge the Jury of the Pyx, and give the history of the coinage.' This he did, and at nine next day made them a lucid, accurate, and admirable speech on the coinage of all countries, debasements, &c. Another time while arguing before the Privy Council, Bethell asked Helps to get him a Pindar, and looking up an appropriate passage quoted it with great effect. Helps also told me that Lord John Russell was the best company in England whether on a journey or elsewhere." To this may be added another story of Lord John, which Grove had in 1865 from Dr. Williams, Helps's secretary:—

"Mr. Helps, being with the Queen and Earl Russell, heard the Queen say how tiresome it was sometimes in writing, when one got into the middle of a long sentence from which one could not extricate oneself, adding 'I often do so,' on which Russell replied, 'Yes, Ma'am, so I perceive.'"

The friendly relations that existed between Grove and Helps were pleasantly described in the fragmentary reminiscences of 1897 :—

"Arthur Helps and I were very sincere friends, and saw as much of one another as two such busy men could. He was a great friend of my wife's as well, and used to come down occasionally on Sunday afternoons, and he was also a great friend of Hullah's with whom I was then very intimate.

"I wish I could recollect more of his conversation. But one story I shall never forget. It was of a good weak-minded clergyman who overworked himself unnecessarily in his parish and was accustomed to take counsel with an old lady somewhat below his station but with much more common-sense than he possessed. One day he went into her house in the afternoon to get some tea. 'Well, Mr. ——, and how are you?' 'Not at all well,' said the clergyman, 'I'm afraid I shall not be with you much longer.' 'Oh, nonsense,' said she, 'You work very much too hard, and do a number of things that are not necessary.' 'Well,' said he, 'It was what my Master did, and I cannot do better than try to imitate Him.' 'Oh, yes,' said she, 'no doubt, but then you see it was His 'obby.'"

Grove's interest in the theological controversies of the day is shown in the following letter to Mr. E. M. Oakeley :—

"CRYSTAL PALACE,
"*February* 12 [1866].

"I am ashamed to say I do not know what your No. 1 is from. I fancy from R. S., but I was too lazy all day yesterday to look. ἀνήριθμον γέλασμα is a very happy rendering of his 'tausend verschiedenen Weisen.'"

"I have got 'Ecce Homo,' and I need not tell you that it interests me extremely. But I should have said its *style* is its weakest part. It is rambling and feeble, and really makes the book difficult to read. But there is no doubt of its ability and goodness. It is most instructive to observe on what a truly English tentative method he has gone, as compared with French or Germans—Strauss or Renan! The 'Law of Mercy' chapter strikes me as the best.

"J. H. Newman's letter to Pusey[1] I read yesterday, and was fairly enraptured. What a style—what a tone—what a loving affectionate heart! Add to all these the magic of that great name. It is a most charming work.

"Perhaps you are not old enough to care for that wonderful time 1840–45. *I* lived through it all—not at Oxford, alas, but with the keenest interest in as much of the struggle as an outsider could know about. . . .

"Yours ever, G. GROVE."

In 1866 Liddon was Bampton Lecturer and in May Grove wrote to his young friend Ernest von Glehn, then an undergraduate at Christ Church, who had asked him to spend a Sunday at Oxford and hear Liddon preach :—

"C. P., *Wednesday*, *May* 9, 1866.

"Thanks for your note. I'll come down if I can, but it is very doubtful. Oxford has lost its main charm to me since A. P. S. went away—not that that would keep me from coming, but something invariably intervenes when I want to get off on a Saturday, and there is no Sunday morning train. I did not mean to imply that you had depreciated Stanley. He is to me one of the greatest preachers I ever heard : but then I am peculiar in two things. (1) Manner goes for nothing with me, and matter, style, and certain little traits are everything :—you'll appreciate this when I tell you I would walk any distance to hear (and see) Jowett. (2) The fact of a man being my friend, or of my having learnt something from him biasses me tremendously. Then again I should *go* with Stanley far more than with L[iddon], because although once a great ritualist and High Churchman I was more so in taste than doctrine, and *now* have left the doctrine altogether. But why compare the two men at all? Each is great in his own way and Liddon probably one of the greatest preachers that ever lived in our church. It's like Mendelssohn and Schumann—enjoy both without what Mrs. Malaprop called 'odorous comparisons.'

Yes it *is* a dear place and at this time how lovely! Do you know Hinksey ferry? I wonder if you care for it as I do, and if you would be touched by *Thyrsis*, a poem of Matt Arnold's in *Macmillan* for April as I am. I fear not, but still read it. Shall I send you Clough's Letters? They are full of charm and

[1] In response to Pusey's *Eirenicon*. This reply was reviewed along with Newman's "Dream of Gerontius," in the *Spectator* of March 3, 1866.

interest. I am so glad you liked my Elijah [in the *Dictionary of the Bible*]. It was good when I wrote it, for no one had ever tried it before, but now A. P. S. has swept me clean away in his second volume of the Jewish Church. . . . Your mother and father, and Olga went to the opera last night—a revival of Gluck's *Iphigénie en Tauride*—very fine indeed."

The musical significance of 1866 to Grove was largely centred in the progress of his young friend Arthur Sullivan, who during this period was a constant visitor at his house and at those of the von Glehns and Scott Russells. On March 10th Sullivan's Symphony was produced at the Crystal Palace, on which occasion Grove described the pleasure he felt in the production of "an important work by my friend Mr. Arthur Sullivan," which thus added "another link to that chain which already connects him with the Crystal Palace, a chain which began when his *Tempest* music was first performed there." On May 13th he notes going to "Cox and Box," on July 11th to "Arthur's Concert," and on October 17th we find him again at Freshwater in the company of Sullivan. The motive and events of the visit are thus described in a letter to Miss Olga von Glehn dated October 28th, 1866 :—

". . . I have had no holiday and do not think I shall get one beyond perhaps a week in Paris before Christmas. But my life is not without its alleviations. Last week I went down to Freshwater and had a charming afternoon and evening with Tennyson. He was at his very best, and made a much deeper and more favourable impression on me than ever before. I had proposed to him to write a *Liederkreis* for Sullivan to set and Millais to illustrate, and he had caught the idea at once and had done three songs out of seven—very charming songs and very good for music. Sullivan went down with me, and pleased both Mr. and Mrs. Tennyson extremely. In the evening we had as much music as we could on a *very tinkling* piano, very much out of tune, and then retired to his room at the top of the house where he read us the three songs, a long ballad, and several other things, and talked till two o'clock in a very fine way about the things which I always get round to sooner or later—death and the next world, and God and man, etc. I must tell you about it all, for it is too long to write. I am going to write to him to-morrow to ask his pardon for having done another paper on his song in the 'Princess'—'Tears idle Tears' which is to be in *Macmillan* for November. It is longer than the other. I want also to tell him to write a second poem to Maurice, as a companion to the one at the end of 'Maud.' *That* was written when Maurice was turned out of King's College, for venturing to hope that God was good enough not to let men burn for ever and ever. And now he has actually been made Professor of Moral Philosophy and Theology at Cambridge! Isn't it a triumph, not only for him, but for the cause of goodness and justice and the progress of all that's right? I can't tell you how delighted I have been. It is an occasion worthy of a poem from Alfred Tennyson."

The mention of Maurice may justify the insertion of the following fragment of a letter dated October 31st, 1866:—

[*From* F. D. MAURICE.]

"The thoughts which you express about the past and the hopes you encourage me to entertain as to the future console me much. Although I am delighted at what you say of Tennyson, I am convinced that the shocks you allude to, however terrible to him or to you, are meant to make you feel the eternal standing ground more firmly; that which lies beneath all opinions and criticisms, and anything else which is of the earth earthy, or of the water watery. If I can but lead any of my pupils to believe that Truth is and must remain, whatever clouds may come over the practice of it, I think I shall not care how much darkness we had to traverse together. Your brother-in-law's death[1] was very sad, but I am sure there is light—" [The conclusion of the letter is missing.]

For the rest Grove heard a great deal of music this year, not merely at the Crystal Palace, but at the Popular Concerts, the Musical Union, and at the Philharmonic. Always catholic in his tastes, he went twice to the Pantomime, where he was always fond of taking his young friends, and several times to the Opera, where he heard the *Reine de Saba*, *Faust*, and in company with Henry Chorley Gluck's *Iphigénie en Aulide*. There was a good deal of

[1] Mr. John Bradley was drowned on October, 24, 1866.

informal but excellent chamber music at his house, in which Franklin Taylor, Daubert, and others took part, and amongst other works of note he heard the *Paradise and the Peri* by Schumann, a composer in whose music he took a great and ever-growing delight. Writing to Miss Paget—(now Mrs. Henry Thompson)—the elder daughter of Sir James Paget, on August 8th, 1866, he says:—

"Your note has pleased me wonderfully. I knew you would like the Schumanns, and it is so true what you say about liking them better and better the more you try them. No music in the world improves more on acquaintance and discloses *more to the worshipper*. In this (as in many other things) it is like Beethoven's. *Allnächtlich im Traum* is a lovely song (not so fine as Mendelssohn's, though). But look at the *Frauenliebe und Leben* set—the last in the book—*Er der herrlichste: Der Ring: Hilf mir, Schwester*. Also make instant acquaintance with the *Nussbaum*. The accompaniment may bother you, but get your mother to play it, and you'll go nearly out of your wits. Now I'll tell you what you must do. You are sure to come across pianos on your journey: wherefore, send to Ewer's for the Schumann album (3/-) and take it with you and learn 'May-song;' 'Recollection' (with a date); 'Sylvester-lied' (the last of all) and all those with *** to them. It is a little thin work, no trouble to carry. I wish you *bon voyage* with all my heart, and only regret I can't go somewhere myself, but I am poor, and also overwhelmed with arrears of work. Kindest regards to your father and mother. P.S. Your choice is excellent. The *Hidalgo* is quite a fine *piece*, isn't it? with that dashing accompaniment, while *Mondnacht* is quite the opposite side of Schumann. What rubbish to call him obscure and unmelodious!"

These criticisms may sound very obvious now, but at the time when they were written, the two leading musical critics—J. W. Davison of the *Times*, and H. F. Chorley of the *Athenæum*—were decidedly hostile to Schumann, and it took all the missionary enthusiasm of Manns Grove, and a few others to make headway against the coalition of Philistines and prejudiced experts. As Grove's musical heroes for 1866 were Sullivan and Schumann, his literary idols were Tennyson and Shelley. Indications of his admiration for the latter up to this point are not numerous, but it suddenly became acute and inspired him with the desire to write Shelley's life. His notebooks abound with memoranda on sources of information, lists of "people who may have known Shelley," &c., but the scheme evidently received a sudden *coup de grâce* from Dean Milman, who, writing to Grove "in the strictest confidence, and entirely from the most friendly feelings," effectually dissuaded him from undertaking a task which, in the opinion of Milman—who had known Shelley both at Eton and Oxford—ought never to be carried out. The letter, for obvious reasons, cannot be reproduced, but it is worthy of note that in it Milman peremptorily disclaims the authorship of "the celebrated and orthodox, and of course very hostile, article in the *Quarterly*" on Shelley.

Grove's personal friendship for Tennyson is shown by the two visits already mentioned. His admiration for his genius is attested by two papers, one "On a Song in 'The Princess,'" which appeared in the *Shilling Magazine* for February 1866 and the other on "Tears, idle Tears," which appeared in *Macmillan's Magazine* for November in the same year. The former is interesting as being practically Grove's first venture into the domain of literary criticism. He begins by calling the song—"Ask me no more"—a Drama in three Acts, which he names Indifference, Hesitation, and Submission; and follows up his exposition of the meaning of the poem with some remarks on its form—the peculiar stanza, with its slight variation on the *In Memoriam* quatrain—the artistic significance of the burthen, "Ask me no more," the music of the lines, the notable fact that the poem is almost entirely composed of monosyllables—in the whole fifteen lines there are only six words of two syllables—and the sparing but most effective use of alliteration. He concludes characteristically:

"In this Mr. Tennyson may be compared to the great musicians, who delighted to produce some of their finest effects with the scanty materials of quartet or trio, and to show that they could move their hearers as greatly with those imperfect means as with all the resources of the full orchestra ; or to others—Mozart for example—who in the full orchestra itself persistently rejected certain instruments, with the help even of which other musicians in vain strive to reach his pinnacle of greatness.

"In considering, to conclude, the first impression which this masterly composition leaves on one's whole being—ear, heart, intellect, imagination, memory—I find myself continually tempted to compare it with some of the masterpieces of the musical art, some of the slow movements of Beethoven's symphonies for example, which present the same astonishing combination of beauty of subject and beauty of general form with perfect delicacy of detail, the same consummate art with the same exquisite concealment of it—and which, like it, form a whole that satisfies both the intellect and the imagination, and, once known, haunts the memory for ever."

Over the paper on "Tears, idle Tears," Grove expended a great deal of thought and trouble, as may be gathered from a letter written by him during the autumn to his sister-in-law, Mrs. Bull :—

". . . . Your notes do me good—because, if you will allow me to say so, they are so much above the general run of such productions. Women are much pleasanter critics than men because they are more sympathetic, but then they are often too docile and too much biassed by their fondness for their friend to form a fair judgment. You—my dear—while you possess the sympathy to the fullest, possess also that clearness of head which so many of your lovely sisters want.

"I have now done my paper, and there it must stand. I know that it contains too much of myself and too little of Tennyson, but I can't reconstruct it, and it must stand or fall. You will find something put in about 'Break, break.' It is a rare favourite of mine. I regard it as the first poem of *In Memoriam*, as 'All along the valley' is the last, and it expresses as nothing ever did before the listlessness which is the first result of such a stunning blow—what are hills, or stately ships, or fisherman's boys, or sailors to one touch of the vanished hand, one word from the still voice? I don't think it would be impossible to analyse it, and your doubt almost inclines me to try.

"You are right as to T.'s power of *touching* inexpressible things.

Did you ever notice the wonderfully subtle way in which he manages by words which are anomalous or contradictory, or almost unintelligible, to raise a feeling in you which no clear words would raise?

> "'The milk that bubbled in the pail,
> And buzzings of the honied hours.'

"'Buzzings of the honied hours' means really nothing definite, but it conveys, as hardly anything else could convey, the sounds of insect life—bees and the kindred of bees, and the warm evening and the hives somewhere near, and the sweet hour of the day—and everything else you like. Connected with this is his way of describing a thing by incongruous words, as

> "'And strangely on *the silence smote*
> The *silent-speaking words*; and strange
> Was love's *dumb cry* defying change
> To test his worth.'

"No words are *uttered* the whole time, but by the expression 'silent-speaking' and 'dumb cry' you have an impression made on your mind which conveys everything you want, and which no more laboured or more *regular* language could convey of the agitation the letters caused in him. Allied to this again is his habit of joining words belonging to two different senses and getting at one blow the impression of both, as

> "'And bats went round in *fragrant skies*.'

"Of course it ought correctly to be fragrant *air*, but by the use of the word skies, which addresses itself to the eye (inward and outward) you have a whole world of new significance imported, and relations of all kinds brought into play."

The paper, as we have seen, appeared in the November number of *Macmillan*, and will repay careful perusal. One may specially note the musical analogies which Grove discovers for the desolateness of the images in the third stanza:—

"Wallis's picture of Chatterton is full of desolation; but it is far below this poem, because *there* the struggle is over—*here* it is still going on. Schumann's overture to *Manfred* is equally gloomy, and equally touching. It is, however, a more extended work in every way. The nearest parallel in music must, perhaps, be looked for in Schubert's works—at the base of which, almost without exception, there lies a profound melancholy. The songs of 'Das Wirthshaus,' or the 'Todesmusik' (Op. 108), are those which occur to me as the most suitable. But, indeed, such parallels are never quite satisfactory, if only from the fact that owing to the necessary form, there are fewer ideas in music than in poetry, though perhaps as many emotions."

"Tears, idle Tears," as Grove points out, dwells exclusively on the melancholy aspect of memory. For the contrary view he happily quotes Jean Paul's dictum, "Memory is the only Paradise out of which nothing can ever drive us," and Dryden's famous lines :—

> "Come foul, or fair, or rain or shine,
> The joys I have possessed in spite of fate are mine ;
> Not Heaven itself upon the past has power,
> But what has been has been, and I have lived my hour."

Tennyson himself, as he adds, "has elsewhere enforced this view in the noblest, most complete manner . . . *In Memoriam* and the few scattered pieces connected with it contain the most complete answer to the sweet seductions of 'Tears, idle Tears.'"

But perhaps the most striking thing in the paper is the vehemence with which he combats the view expressed in the phrase "deep as first love," asserting that,

> "brilliant and fresh as it may be, it cannot be so 'deep' as the love of a man of ripe age and maturer powers, who has kept his 'boy's heart' so long as still to love ardently, but joins to his ardour the knowledge, the firmness, the persistence, the power, with which years have endowed him. These—and they are not of infrequent occurrence—these are the grand 'deep' passions of life, so powerful as to modify, and sometimes completely to change, even a character long fixed and settled."

Grove adds some excellent remarks on the peculiarity of the stanza, the use of the refrain, and very truly and happily says that in this poem,

> "owing to some hidden secret of workmanship, which I am unable to discover, save by its effects, some subtle fragrance

breathed over the song, so perfect is the cadence of the lines, and so sweet the music of the syllables, as to give all the effect of the rhymes which the stanza-form naturally suggests, and which the ear, in this case, fails to miss."

Grove's published appreciations of Tennyson ended with this paper, but from various entries in his pocket-books it is evident that he not only contemplated a complete commentary on "The Princess," but had gone some little way in the execution of his scheme. Other entries prove him to have been reading Heine and Mrs. Browning, and his own thoughts, as the following extract may show, were often poetical in spirit if not in form :—

"I sometimes have a glimpse of religion and such things in this way—as if we were in darkness and cold and misery under a veil on the other side of which was a bright light and great warmth and comfort and happiness and everything good. Then now and then there comes a chink in the veil, and sometimes it comes so that the ray comes right in on one, sometimes only a faint light; sometimes a puff of warm air or sweet smell—sometimes a burst of music. Well, the Bible and all the poetry of the world and all the good thoughts and all the sweet lovely ideas that one gets from the women one knows, and that make one cry for nothing, press one's tears all for nothing out of one's eyes—these are the chinks in the veil."

CHAPTER V

Voyage of Discovery to Vienna with Sullivan in 1867—The generosity of Herr Spina—Visits to Döllinger and Brahms—Prague, Dresden, Leipzig and Berlin—The Life of David—An adventure in the train—Editor of *Macmillan's Magazine*—Relations with contributors—Testimony of Sir Wemyss Reid—Tour in Italy in 1868—Ascents of Vesuvius—With Liszt in Rome—Miss Mayow's and Sir Frederick Gore-Ouseley's stories—Reminiscences furnished by Mr. Ernest von Glehn, the Bishop of Lichfield and Rev. A. T. Davidson—An invitation from Tennyson.

IF in 1866 Grove fell largely under the spell of poetry, music reasserted her sway in 1867, the year of his memorable visit to Vienna. Joachim and Madame Schumann both played at the Crystal Palace in March, and in July Grove met and heard Rubinstein. At the end of July he went over to Paris for the opening of the Exhibition, and spent a few days to his entire satisfaction in the company of Arthur Sullivan, who has left a pleasant picture of his travelling companion :—

"What shall I say of Grove? It would be painting the lily to try to describe his goodness and charm, so I refrain. We take great care of each other, are very economical, haggle over centimes and get on famously." [*Sir Arthur Sullivan.* By Arthur Lawrence. London: James Bowden, 1899. Letter quoted on p. 68.]

But the great event of the year was the visit to Vienna. Grove's devotion to Schubert was of long standing. The famous C major Symphony, the subject of one of the most charming of his analyses, and the most ingenious of his theories, had been given at the Crystal Palace for the first time on April 5th, 1856, and with every year Grove's affection for "der einzige Schubert," as Schumann called him, grew and strengthened. The publication in 1865 of the *Life of Schubert*, by Dr. Kreissle von Hellborn, with its incomplete Catalogue, inspired Grove with the desire to gain every possible information about the unpublished and unknown works of Schubert. To this end he entered into a correspondence with Herr Spina, the well-known music publisher in Vienna, with the result that the *Rosamunde* music and the "Unfinished" symphony were given for the first time in England at the Crystal Palace. The *Rosamunde* music, however, was incomplete, and the thought that Vienna must be full of such hidden treasures decided Grove to make a voyage of discovery in the hope of unearthing some of them. He accordingly started on September 24th, was joined by Sullivan on the 27th, and travelling viâ Baden, Munich, and Salzburg, reached Vienna on October 5th. The results of the visit, which more than fulfilled Grove's most ardent expectations, are recorded in the appendix to Mr. Arthur Coleridge's translation of Kreissle von Hellborn's *Life of Schubert*, but may be supplemented by the following letters to Miss Olga von Glehn :—

"VIENNA, *October* 9, 1867.

". . . My last letter was from Baden. I must skip the intervening distance between there and here and tell you of our extraordinary good fortune since we came to Vienna. It has been quite wonderful : everything has happened to our wish and advantage. Spina the magnificent has behaved like a prince, really like the most thoroughbred gentleman. We have got from him three more pieces of *Rosamunde* music, an overture, a Stabat Mater, a Trio for Violin &c., all most interesting and some of them first rate (all by Franz Schubert), and he has given me many pieces of printed music, a bust of Schubert, an original letter of Beethoven's and has behaved in the most charming and kind way. Another man who has the reputation (like Nabal) of being a cross-grained curmudgeon, has been all kindness and we have now from him, here on the table, two grand symphonies and a lovely overture. Also I have got every information about all the other symphonies and made myself thoroughly happy. This is a wonderful place, far finer and more interesting and beautiful than Paris. I like it much better. The old town lies in the middle of all, and round it are the new suburbs and the interest of it comes from the great people still continuing to live in the old town, which is full of wonderful palaces and houses. The churches except S. Stephen's are not so much, but there is a quantity of fine sculpture and monuments about. Every square or street almost has a statue or group of statues in it, and not mere dummies, but beautiful interesting works, really lovely to look upon. The shops are gorgeous and the people charming. I am quite in love with South Germany and hope the Prussians will come up to them.

"We leave on Friday for Prague and Dresden and Leipzig, where we hope to be on Monday or Tuesday. The dreadful scramble of this note is occasioned by my having utterly mistaken the hour and thought it was 4 instead of 5, and thus leaving myself no time, but I will continue after the post has gone."

"VIENNA, *Wednesday Night*,
"Hotel der Kaiserin Elisabeth.

"I now go on with my letter, interrupted by the Post. I don't think you have any idea how hard we work. To-day for example we went to Spina's house 1½ miles away—half an hour is spent in mutual compliments, hand-shaking, lighting cigars, &c. then Spina produces a pile of MS. music about as big as a portmanteau and says, 'Here is all I have that you wish to see. You shall go into my room with it and do what you like.' More compliments, more handshaking; then we go out of the office into the house, into a drawing-room, opening into a *Nebenzimmer* and that into another drawing-room with a Clavier, and then he leaves us with the books. First we spend an hour in incoherent raptures, then we get more reasonable and part it all into lots and begin to go through it thoroughly. Then we take the things we like into the other room, and Arthur plays, and we decide to have or not to have. After settling about the instrumental things we open a bundle of about 60 songs, 40 of which at least have never been printed. Some of them turn out *charming*, equal to anything of Schubert's or any one else's, so they have to be played over and over again. Meantime I have got awfully cold and the stove not being alight, our noses get positively blue and our hands have to be kept constantly in our pockets, and it is some exertion to put off this frigid aspect and be cheerful when Spina pops in, as he does three or four times in the course of the entertainment, to talk and purr and press on us endless cigars as big as sausages! At last all is examined and related and written down in note books, and sorted, and then Spina comes for a final talk and we play him about 10 of the best of the things, and he has his raptures and pats Arthur on the shoulder, and says how much gratified he would be to hear something of *his*, on which Arthur plays some 'Day Dreams' and Spina embraces him and says 'ganz ausgezeichnet,' 'reizend, ganz reizend,' 'charmant' 'sehr nett,' and brings out several pieces by protégés of his which have to be played and praised and talked over. By this time it is 4 o'clock and Spina says, 'I am now going to show you something of *real* interest, come down with me.' And he produces about 12 letters from Beethoven to his firm (Diabelli)—never printed or seen before by profane eyes—and reads them all to us, which, as they are worse than Hebrew to make out, is a work of time and a cause of more raptures (for they really are very curious and interesting and show him to be, what I have always believed, but never could get Arthur to acknowledge before, so like Tennyson in everything—his fondness for friends and dislike of strangers and his constant mention of the 'honorar' for his pieces). At last Spina selected one with a clearer signature than the rest and begged me to keep it as a souvenir; more raptures, more bad German from the happy recipient, more handshaking. Then this prince of music-sellers gave Arthur a quantity of things and then on our happening to ask if Schubert's bust on his tomb had ever been copied, produces one immediately and insists on my having it, then hurries me into another room to see a portrait of Liszt and then into another to see 'a Mr. Jungmann of Leipzig.' We got away at last at 4.30, as cold, spent and hungry as ever in our lives. . . . In the evening we went on to Spina's shop (not his house this time) to look over two or three book-cases of pamphlets and music and to ask a few questions. Amongst other things we talk to an old lame man on the other side of the counter who is always called Herr von Doppler by the other shopman—an old German creature, so old and so cheerful and *gemüthlich* with the oddest cap on! and suddenly we find out that he *knew*, *knew intimately* and *for years* Haydn, Beethoven, Seyfried, Stadler and all the rest. He shows us the best portrait of Beethoven, and describes his 'queer Polish coat with tassels and his tolerably (ziemlich) bad hat' and his short answers and all the rest. 'And Mozart, Herr Doppler, did you know him?' 'No, he died in '91 and I was not born till '92.' 'And Schubert, how about him? you must often have seen him?' 'Seen him! I should think so! why I was at his christening. I am five years older than he was and was his father's *schüler* and knew the whole family well.' Of course this sets all our fireworks off: we go up into the air at once and burst and explode with enormous reports. Then we make a plan of operations for to-morrow, which being probably our last day is important. How we are to get possession of this dreadful opera book of *Rosamunde*, without which all the pieces are unintelligible, and now I remember that I have a letter to the Emperor's secretary, who can compel the opera people to disclose all their secrets, and how we will go from there to-morrow morning. Of course it is all very jolly, though I make it out to be hard work: it is really the pleasantest thing: the place is interesting and new, and Arthur is pleasant and the seeking and finding the Schubert things so exciting that it will be very charming to look back on. . . . Our day in Baden was very pleasant, it was very fine and there was everything to see. We walked to the Schumanns' and were very well received and saw the album which R. S. and she kept full of the most interesting letters and portraits and locks of hair of every composer and poet and painter from Jubal and David downwards. We had a lovely walk and sauntered and finished up the day at Madame Viardot's—so clever and so unaffected and pleasant. The next day was quite delightful. We took the train not at Baden, but at a country station eight miles off, to which we drove across in an open trap starting at half past seven with the same lovely straight road; the air was delicious as an English October morning. It soon got hot though, and kept so all the way from Baden to Munich. For about twenty miles after Essling it was about the loveliest thing I have seen—such a country! a splendid valley, up the side of which the train kept climbing, and winding in and out through the wooded slopes, but always up higher and higher. Underneath was the lovely valley with the mountains embracing it all in the bright sun and, as the afternoon got on, the shadows grew longer and longer and smoother and smoother and we felt more and more *sentimentalisch* and enjoyed all the pleasures great and small of that lovely frame of mind. At last we came to the top of the mountains and there lo! and behold was the Danube, nothing less, flowing along, a great broad stream right up aloft on the 'roof of the world.' You can't think how strange and unexpected it was to come upon a great river in such an improper place! . . . At Munich were all the picture galleries to see next day, and the sculpture gallery and the churches; and I had several people to call on: the distances are tremendous and the people were out, and my visit had to be made twice and it came on to rain and we were very cold and unhappy. One of the visits turned out well, as we found Döllinger the great professor and champion of liberty and toleration, like Arthur Stanley is in England, though he is a Roman Catholic and a priest, a most interesting old fellow—I had two hours' talk with him and we never flagged a moment. Fortunately he talks English perfectly. Next morning we left Munich in a fearful snow-storm and got to Salzburg at twelve. It was such a sell, for we could not see a hundred yards each side of the train, and the view is splendid in fine weather. At Salzburg it didn't snow, it was kind enough not to do that, but it rained hard and was wretched, and tho' we behaved like men and went to the Castle and the Mozarteum and everywhere we ought to have gone to, it was very miserable and we nearly quarrelled. Somehow everything was gloomy. The great sight in the Castle is the view, but when you can't see that, they take you by way of a pleasant thing to the torture chamber and there you realise, at least I did for the first time, what dreadful things men have done to one another in cold blood—a battle or a murder is bad enough, but to see the actual winches and wheels and pulleys by which men were pulled to pieces and killed by hideous slow agonies because they could not help thinking differently from their torturers is too dreadful and made a tremendous impression on me. Thank God, it is all over now ; over never to return. We can torture badly enough even now, Heaven knows, but it is in quite a different way, and Colenso and Jowett, after all that even they have gone through, are very different objects and much less to be pitied than the poor creatures who were turned out of the chamber at Salzburg, with their flesh in ribbons and not a whole joint in their bodies. . . . . There being nothing to see at Salzburg, we gave up our plan of going to Linz and sailing down the Danube and travelled all that night instead. And for once my charming state of mind fled, but only for a bit. Vienna soon revived it, and on Sunday I was the gayest of the gay again, and laughing at all my troubles. We conducted ourselves in an appropriate manner that day, and went to hear a fine Mass at the Dominican Church in the morning, and in the afternoon rode to the Belvedere Gardens and then to the Währinger Friedhof to see the tombs of Beethoven and Schubert and it was very sweet and cheerful in the setting sun and we felt very nice and *ruhig*, and brought home our grass and ivy from the said graves, and thought of our friends at home and were quite happy."

The above was written on Wednesday night, and it was

Grove's intention to leave in a couple of days for Prague. The sequel is told in the narrative given in the Appendix to the English translation of Kreissle von Hellborn's Life alluded to above :—

"So far, success—brilliant success. But I had failed in one chief object of my journey. The *Rosamunde* music was almost dearer to me than the symphonies. Besides the *entr'actes* in B minor and B flat, the 'Ballo, No. 2,' and the 'Ballet Air, No. 9,' which we had already acquired in 1866, we had found at Mr. Spina's an *entr'acte* after the second act, and a 'Hirten-Melodie' for clarinets, bassoons, and horns ; but we still required the accompaniments to the Romance and the two choruses, as well as the total number of pieces and their sequence in the drama. To quit Vienna without these would have been too cruel, and yet neither from Dr. Schneider, nor Mr. Spina, nor in the library of the Musik-Verein—where the admirable librarian, Mr. C. F. Pohl, was entirely at our service—had we succeeded in finding a trace of them.

It was Thursday afternoon, and we proposed to leave on Saturday for Prague. We made a final call on Dr. Schneider, to take leave and repeat our thanks, and also, as I now firmly believe, guided by a special instinct. The doctor was civility itself ; he again had recourse to the cupboard, and showed us some treasures which had escaped us before. I again turned the conversation to the *Rosamunde* music ; he believed that he had at one time possessed a copy or sketch of it all. Might I go into the cupboard and look for myself? Certainly, if I had no objection to being smothered with dust. In I went ; and after some search, during which my companion kept the doctor engaged in conversation, I found, at the bottom of the cupboard, and in its farthest corner, a bundle of music-books two feet high, carefully tied round, and black with the undisturbed dust of nearly half-a-century. It was like the famous scene at the monastery of Souriani on the Natron lakes, so well described by Mr. Curzon : 'Here is a box !' exclaimed the two monks, who were nearly choked with the dust ; 'we have found a box, and a heavy one too.' 'A box !' shouted the blind abbot, who was standing in the outer darkness of the oil-cellar—'a box ! where is it ?' 'Bring it out ! bring out the box ! Heaven be praised ! We have found a treasure ! Lift up the box ! Pull out the box !' shouted the monks in various tones of voice. We were hardly less vociferous than the monks, when we had dragged out the bundle into the light, and found that it was actually neither more nor less than what we were in search of. Not Dr. Cureton, when he made his truly romantic discovery of the missing leaves of the Syriac Eusebius, could have been more glad or more grateful than I was at this moment. For these were the part-books of the whole of the music in *Rosamunde*, tied up after the second performance in December 1823, and probably never disturbed since. Dr. Schneider must have been amused at our excitement; but let us hope that he recollected his own days of rapture; at any rate, he kindly overlooked it, and gave us permission to take away with us and copy what we wanted, and I now felt that my mission to Vienna had not been fruitless."

No time was to be lost, so Grove summoned Herr Pohl to his assistance, and with his aid and that of Sullivan, the missing accompaniments were copied out then and there. The task was not finished until nearly two in the morning, but Grove and Sullivan were fresh enough at the end to indulge in a game of leap-frog. The acquaintance with Herr Pohl—the biographer of Haydn, author of *Haydn and Mozart in London*, and in after years one of the most valued and informing contributors to Grove's *Dictionary of Music and Musicians*—ripened into the closest intimacy; indeed it may be said that of all Grove's numerous German friends, none corresponded with him so freely, affectionately, and regularly as C. F. Pohl.

On Saturday, October 12th, Grove heard Gluck's *Iphigénie* at the Opera, and on the following day Schumann's Mass, "heavenly sweet and touching," at the Hofkapelle. On the same day he went to the picture gallery in the Lichtenstein Palace, and paid another visit to the tombs of Beethoven and Schubert in the Währinger Friedhof. Finally, on the last morning of his stay in Vienna, he called for the first time on Brahms, whom he found unlike his portraits: "hair short, face more practical and less sentimental. He showed me wonderful MSS." of Schubert, Beethoven, Mozart, and Schumann. At 1.30 he left Vienna, the faithful Pohl "in a tall shiny hat," coming to the station to see him off. Tuesday was spent at Prague chiefly in the library, Wednesday at Dresden among the pictures, and on Thursday he rejoined Sullivan at Leipzig, in time for the Gewandhaus concert. On the 20th, Sunday, he went over to Dresden and heard *Rienzi* at the Opera, went to Rubinstein's concert on the following day, dined with Baron Tauchnitz on Tuesday, and travelled to Berlin that night, summarizing his experiences for the previous ten days in a letter addressed to Miss M. E. and Miss Ida von Glehn, dated Hotel du Nord, Wednesday night, October 23rd :—

"... I can't at all tell if you have heard anything of me since my last letter, and I have not time to go on with a chronicle of events, only to tell you, that I stayed in Vienna two days after Arthur. Thence on Tuesday to Prague, then to Dresden—picture gallery, Raffaelle's Madonna, &c., and then to Leipzig, where I rejoined Arthur. They played his overture on the Thursday night—a fine performance but a horrid audience. They clap no one hardly and are quite unmoved by orchestral performances—however they made a little exception in his favour and recalled him at the end. The Symphony they rehearsed on Sunday morning, but I don't think they cared very much for it. I begin to understand the difference between the Germans and us in the matter of music, and to see the reason why they don't like Mendelssohn. To please them, everything must be dreadfully grim and earnest, and as soon as a bit of tune comes, they think it all '*ganz trivial*'—a state of mind which I hope we shan't get into...."

On the following day (the 24th), Grove visited the grave of Mendelssohn in the Alte Dreifaltigkeits Kirchhof, outside the Hallethor, sketching the tomb in his pocket-book and adding the comment, "It was a fine bright afternoon, sunny and cheerful, and yet everything told of decay—just what it should be for a visit to the tomb of that bright sweet nature . . . I picked three twigs and then came away." He attended Joachim's concert on the 25th, and started for home the next morning viâ Cologne and Paris, reaching Sydenham on the night of the 27th.

The year 1867 was marked by the making of a number

of new friendships at home and abroad, and the loss of one of his best Sydenham friends, the Rev. Charles English, who died in May. Throughout its course Grove was unremitting in his duties as Secretary to the Palestine Exploration Fund, and in his public advocacy of its claims, the *Times* of August 5th containing a long statement of the operations of the Society from his pen, concluding with a fresh appeal for funds for "the first organised effort to do what four-fifths of the educated Englishmen of the last 50 years have longed, have tried to do for themselves." In the spring, as appears from a letter from Tennyson dated April 21, 1867, and another to Henry Cole on the following day, he contemplated standing for the post of librarian to the House of Commons, but nothing came of his candidature, in spite of the influence and support of Stanley.[1] Two literary projects took shape in his mind in the course of the summer, and for some time to come occupied his thoughts and pen. One was an introduction to the study of the Bible, which never got beyond the stage of a general sketch, and the other a popular Life of David, the first germ of which appears in his pocket-book—some time between the end of May and the beginning of July—in the following words: "I am going to tell you the story of a boy who began his life very poor in a small country village, and yet when he grew up became a great king, and one of the best and most famous men the world has ever seen." His pocket-books for some time to come are filled with passages from the projected life, but perhaps the best notion of Grove's unconventional treatment of

[1] Matthew Arnold had also stood for the post, as appears from a letter dated May 7, 1867, beginning, "Neither did I know *you* were standing when I first came forward. I was put out of my pain sometime ago by hearing, on Sir T. Erskine May's authority, that an arrangement was in progress by which the Assistant-Librarian would have the place, and Erskine May the *house*. This is the arrangement which has been finally come to, and as without the house the librarian's place would not have suited me, I feel easy in my mind at seeing another man get the place. . . . I hope before long you will succeed in getting some employment which leaves you a little more leisure than you can get at the Crystal Palace."

his subject may be gained from two letters to his sister-in-law, Mrs. Bull :—

"CRYSTAL PALACE,
"*August* 10, 1867.

"Many thanks. David was a mixed character, I suppose—very interesting, because so human and natural, but surely with a good deal of the hero about him. His sparing Saul over and over again in the teeth of the ferocity with which S. pursued him is surely very fine. I think you will like my treatment. *All the women* do—bless them, and all the men too for the matter of that, but the difficulties are all to come—the rebellion and the great love passages and *those* are the difficult parts. I take him to be the great instance of a man who waits till mature life before he has his 'grand passion.' Abigail and Ahinoam and Eglah, etc. were only women he picked up in the villages 'to make his establishment.' Michal was his first love, but when she came back to him they were both so altered and all the circumstances so cruelly against Michal, that it was impossible for it to end except as it did—and then came the grand event of his life, and poor fellow, it wrecked him. Ah! how many a man has been wrecked on the same reef. . . ."

[*To the same.*]

[*Same year. No date.*]

"Your note has quite touched me and tho' dreadfully busy, I can't help saying a few words. I confess I was puzzled by your judgment about David—because it was quite unlike that of anybody else. I have read it to about thirty people of intelligence, and taste, and knowledge, and no one before found it 'comic' and if I had left out some colloquialisms in the first part I don't think that you would have used that adjective either. Comic I certainly never meant it to be, though about much of the history of Samson and the Philistines I am sure there's a great deal that's grotesque. The fact is, we invest everybody in the Bible—even the bad men—with such a sanctity, that to tear that off and show them in their real colours gives a shock. The colloquialisms are the consequence of my original plan being to write for children. I have altered that and must alter the style *tant soit peu* but only *peu*. I have also got to bring in the Psalms—the poetry of David, which will cast a new light over all. But still, if Samson and the Philistines were grotesque—nay even if they were *comic*—I don't see why we should shrink from realizing the fact. My dear child, do you suppose that a man like David went through his life without a joke? I don't believe that our Lord himself did. I feel quite sure that when the Pharisees asked Him a sign from '*heaven*' and he put them off the scent by pointing to the *clouds* and their indications of the weather—it must have been with a *very keen* sense of humour, heightened of course by the fact that they did not 'see' the point. But as for the rough people of David's days—for rough and fierce they were beyond anything we can realize in their words and ways—I adhere to my view. *In their hearts* some of them were tender enough—David was when he came to write his poetry, but then he was a different man from what he was in action—though indeed I don't think that I have shewn him hard and coarse at all. I have not felt him as that, but have conceived (and *seen; for I have often seen him*) him as a very refined person (for his times). What I have not done, is, I have not made him so full of religion as we always think he was—and this for two reasons. (1) Because I believe our impression is derived in great measure from the form of words he used. 'God bless you,' 'good-bye,' 'good evening,' though all invocations of the name of God, don't really convey that to us: an Arab says Wallah, Bismillah, etc., constantly—every third word, but he don't mean it. It is their form of language—and so were the constant references to Jehovah in David's language. Men are men, and are very much like one another, all the world and all history over. You to your descendants will be what St. Peter's ancestors were to him—one of the 'holy women of old.' (2) You get that view in the Bible and from your cradles. I want to present a view which is over-looked in that blaze of sanctity but which is as real—I believe more so. I am not hurt about the failure of D., for 'failure' it was, but *instructed* and strengthened. I am sure (cheeky though it may sound) that even now there's no book like it in the world. I mean it's nearer the true figures of the men and women, and I'll go on and do it thoroughly well at last. . . ."

Some of the entries in his pocket-books on this subject are curiously illustrative of Grove's fondness for parallels. Thus we find

> Saul was like Mr. Tennyson
> Absalom . . . Mario
> Benjamin and Judah . . . Saxons and Normans

But in spite of his resolve the Life was never completed,

partly no doubt as a result of the criticism of his friends. After his death, however, it was printed for private circulation, with a brief Preface by his friend the Rev. William Addis, under the title "The Story of David's Early Life." We may close the record of Grove's literary activities in the year 1867, by extracting from one of his pocket-books the following suggestive little essay entitled "A Plea for the Vague:"—

"I suppose it is a mere commonplace to say that what is vague has much more power on the mind than what is precise, but as I have lately come to realize it, it is a very fresh and new truth to me. The first time I remember noting it, was at the Britannia Bridge, where I was for some time employed during its construction, when the disadvantageous contrast between the effect of one of the great towers after the scaffolding was removed and its truly grand appearance while the scaffolding was standing, struck me extremely. Of course the tower was a bigger object with the scaffolding than it was after it was down, but it was not the size alone that made the difference. It was the vague hazy texture of the timber framing surrounding the solid case within, and making a gradual transition from the hard lines of the stone-work to the soft clouds or sky. And also there was the fact—and I am sure there is a great deal in this—that the imagination was excited by the dim vision of the tower standing there in the midst of all that shadowy encasement. It was something difficult and half forbidden to approach, which therefore brought one's sense of mystery into play. When I returned after an absence of a few weeks and found the scaffolding gone, and the tower standing alone in all the clearness of its outline and precise form, I shall never forget how disgusted I was, and also how interested. It was a new discovery. The same thing attends the learning of a new language and makes it so interesting and attractive to a beginner. I am but a poor scholar, but I like to try to find out the meaning of Goethe and Heine, and I would not exchange the power which their poems have over me from their vagueness, from the scaffolding which my mind casts round them, for the more accurate appreciation which greater knowledge would give me, because at last I do get to find out the full meaning, and then I enjoy both—all. I have my mysterious wonder: I have the poet's exact meaning, and I have had the delight of gradually extracting it—of pulling down the scaffold bit by bit, and so becoming thoroughly aware of every minute beauty of the image within. It is the same with objects seen through a mist. But what is vagueness in all these departments to what it is in the two highest regions of human [intelligence], Poetry and Music?"

Grove was always anxious that others should share his pleasures and enthusiasms, and many people met him half way. As an instance of the more cautious temper, one may quote the characteristic letter he received at the end of this year from Samuel Sebastian Wesley, the gifted but eccentric organist of Gloucester Cathedral, to whom he had sent an arrangement for 4 hands of Schubert's Symphony in C major. Wesley wrote on December 11th, 1867:—

"My Dear Sir,—As soon as your kind present of the Symphony reached me, I put it in the hands of a pupil that he might be able to play it with me, so that I might learn its quality. He has never yet come to me to play it (I have been much from home), and I waited to write to you until I had tried through the Symphony, as the duet form is not quite convenient for affording, by reading, a knowledge of a new work, as you will, I think, allow. I will make an effort to get up to town on Saturday. I suppose I can get where the Symphony is to be heard. I am not much acquainted (strange to say) with the building. I beg your acceptance of my best thanks, and am, Yours very truly,

"S. S. Wesley."

Of eccentric correspondents Grove had no lack, and he left behind him a curious collection of strange applications and begging letters received for the most part when he was Secretary to the Crystal Palace. The following undated letter was probably received in this or the preceding year:—

"Seeing from the newspapers that you are in want of a Secretary for the Palestine Exploration Fund, I hasten to offer my services. I must begin by informing you that I am of the female persuasion, and a member of the Society for the Employment of Women. Excellent references to be had of John Stuart Mill. My appearance is agreeable and manners retiring. I unite a sufficient amount of intelligence with the handwriting you perceive. Any but a merely nominal salary would be acceptable. Any amount of sympathy in private affairs given without extra charge. Being one of a large family of paupers a small payment in advance would be acceptable. Hoping one day to go myself to the New Jerusalem, I enclose six stamps for the Exploration Fund. Wishing to remain incognito I do not feel myself bound to sign this."

In this context we may record in Grove's own words the romantic incident which occurred before he gave up the Secretaryship to the Crystal Palace. It forms part of the discursive reminiscences dictated in 1897 :—

"When I was at the Crystal Palace, I had a very curious adventure one afternoon in the train. There was then a quick train which left the Palace every afternoon at about half past three, and did not stop until it reached London Bridge. I often went up by this train. One afternoon I caught it just as it was starting, and got into a compartment which contained a young lady. She at once began to complain loudly against my intrusion, as she wanted to be in the compartment by herself. The train, however, was moving and there was no alternative. She proceeded to tell me that she was not happy at home, that she was going to run away and she wished to change her dress in the carriage. I said 'Well, there can be no difficulty about that. I will look out of the window until you tell me you have finished.' When she did so, I turned round, and to my astonishment she had turned herself into a very good imitation of a sailor. I had a long talk with her and did everything in my power to induce her to give up the idea of running away, but without success. She assured me that there was no young man in the case. She had put her own clothes into a bundle, and when the train drew up at London Bridge station, she went off unaccompanied by any one. I never found out who she was."

About the New Year Grove paid Tennyson a short visit at Farringford and recorded his impressions in a letter to Dr. Bradley on his return :—

"CRYSTAL PALACE, S.E.,
"*January* 8, 1868.

"I only got your note on Monday morning, too late to fly to your arms. I was very bad on Wednesday, as crooked as <, but on Thursday I made a shift to go to Farringford, where I passed Friday in great contentment, coming back on Saturday. A. T.

was very charming. He did not say a word I wished unsaid: and he said a great many I would fain remember. He is working hard at Hebrew, and thinks the Psalms and Isaiah the finest poetry there is. Moreover, he was very religious and *Christian* in all his talk about life and politics, &c. He has been pleased to promise me *Lucretius* for *Macmillan*. The subject is not pleasant, but it is a grand poem: *one of the grandest of all his works*. (Tell M. I have just dipt my pen into the tea instead of the ink which is a bore.) Also I hope that you will see in our February number a poem by him called *Wages*, more characteristic and more lofty (though shorter) than either of those in *Good Words* or *Once a Week*.

"They are expecting you there in ten days or so. The boys please me much. Hallam is growing very manly: and with plenty of humour. . . Harriet has gone to Hastings to-day with two children: one other is in the North, and Baby with me. I am seizing the opportunity of her absence to work like fifty steam engines. . ."

In the following May, after having acted as assistant editor to Professor David Masson for several months, Grove undertook the sole editorship of *Macmillan's Magazine*, to which he had already been a contributor, and retained the post for fifteen years. With his wide range of interests, and his extensive acquaintance among the leading men of letters, science and art, he was admirably fitted for the post, and, while securing the co-operation of many writers of established repute, he was no fetish-worshipper of names, but always on the alert to recognise and encourage young and unknown writers.

The list of contributors prefixed to the half-yearly volumes afford a good notion of the quality of *Macmillan's Magazine* under Grove's *régime*. Thus for 1868 he had Henry Fawcett, Arthur Helps, Thomas Huxley, Norman Lockyer, F. D. Maurice, Christina Rossetti, Aubrey de Vere, and Tennyson. In 1874 the list contains the names (amongst others) of Samuel Baker, Mandell Creighton, Bret Harte, Professor Freeman, W. H. Lecky, Goldwin Smith, A. P. Stanley, and R. L. Stevenson—who here made one of his earliest appearances. In 1878—a very brilliant year—Grove's contributors included George Eliot, George Meredith, Matthew Arnold, Walter Pater, Stanley, and Freeman; and in 1882–3 the list contains the names of Tennyson, J. A. Symonds, Mrs. Oliphant, J. H. Shorthouse, Stanley, Matthew Arnold, William Morris, John Morley, Dean Church, W. Gifford Palgrave, Mrs. Woods, and Mrs. Humphry Ward, who had made what was pratically her *début* in *Macmillan* in 1871 in a paper on the Poem of the Cid. The most constant contributors during Grove's editorship were Tom Hughes, Stanley, Matthew Arnold, Kingsley, Freeman, and Goldwin Smith. Music was represented by Ferdinand Hiller, Dannreuther, and Hubert Parry, a contribution from the last named (in 1875) taking the form of a group of poems: while of the other writers not previously mentioned it may suffice to give the names of R. H. Hutton, J. R. Green, W. K. Clifford, Andrew Lang, C. G. Leland, F. W. H. Myers, Stopford Brooke, M. Guizot, and Mr. Gladstone. Grove's labours as editor brought him into contact with, or correspondence with, a number of interesting people, and while it is permitted to no editor altogether to avoid giving offence, Grove's geniality and freedom from partisan acrimony reduced the friction to a minimum. Thus though Freeman was a frequent and valued contributor to the Magazine, Grove not only invited Froude to contribute, but made it clear that he in no way associated himself with Freeman's methods of controversy.

From the correspondence that grew out of the Magazine work, we may select the following characteristic letter from Matthew Arnold:—

"London,
"*May* 29, 1878.

"My Dear Grove,—I read Mrs. Masson's delightful papers. I daresay poor Mrs. Thrale has had hard measure, but Macaulay's biography of Johnson remains a capital piece of work notwithstanding.

Voltaire has several times passed through my mind, but I cannot undertake him. *Il faut savoir se borner*, as the great

Napoleon said. I wish you would say to Craik on Monday that the printing of the title-page seems to me to be ugly and straggling, and I wish it could be made to look more slender, *élancé*, and pleasing, but the thing is not worth bothering about.

"Look out the Beethoven passage for me, when you have time. All that sort of thing interests me much. I see he died at fifty-six; I shall be fifty-six next Christmas, and am not loath to depart, but I hope I shall not have dropsy first, and be punctured, and the punctures turn to sores. But 'an enduring heart have the Destinies given to the sons of men,' as Homer says.

"Ever sincerely yours,

"MATTHEW ARNOLD."

Grove's enterprise as an editor may be illustrated by his attempt early in 1868 to secure a contribution from Tourguénieff. Madame Viardot-Garcia, whose acquaintance he had made in the previous year, had written to him in February, on behalf of a German baritone singer in whom she took a great interest, and in his reply Grove had entrusted her with a message to Tourguénieff, suggesting that an authorised translation of one of his stories should appear in the Magazine. Tourguénieff wrote from Baden on March 13th, sending a copy of a French translation of one of his books, revised by himself, offering to send the Russian original to the English translator if he knew Russian, and expressing his appreciation of Grove's flattering offer. He continues :—

"Ce qui me touche surtout—c'est l'idée de contribuer à repandre dans le public anglais des notions plus exactes sur la société et la littérature russes. Je serai très heureux de voir que la tendance prononcée de la meilleure partie de notre public vers l'Angleterre rencontrât quelque chose d'analogue chez vous. Vous pouvez m'écrire en anglais, Monsieur. Je connais très bien cette langue ; j'éprouve seulement quelque difficulté à l'écrire.

"Recevez, Monsieur, l'expression de mes sentiments distingués."

"J. TOURGUÉNIEFF."

Grove was not merely enterprising : he had the editorial virtue of importunity. People expostulated like Mark

Pattison, when he wrote "Why do you try to bring water out of a dry and barren old rock, when all this young talent is flushing up on all sides of us?"—but generally succumbed to his powers of persuasion, or declined with reluctance, like Robert Browning, when he wrote (Nov. 24, 1869), "I feel very unwilling to deny you anything, but I have no other method of defence from the importunities of people of quite another sort." Finally in this context it may be permitted to anticipate the strict chronological course of the narrative by the insertion of the following interesting estimate of Grove as editor, kindly furnished me by Sir Wemyss Reid:—

"My friendship with Sir George Grove began in 1876, when I was introduced to him by William Black. The purpose of the introduction was that I might propose a series of articles on Charlotte Brontë for *Macmillan's Magazine.* I had no sooner met the distinguished editor than I felt drawn to him irresistibly by the delightful cordiality and grace of his manner, the brightness of his intelligence, and the goodness of his heart. He duly printed my articles in *Macmillan's*, and they were subsequently expanded into a monograph on Charlotte Brontë. This was the beginning of my business connection with Grove, and although I was not a very frequent contributor to his magazine, I had sufficient experience in that capacity to be able to judge of his qualifications as an editor. He struck me at the time—and I have not modified my opinion since—as being on the whole the most delightful editor I had ever known. He was certainly sympathetic and appreciative to no ordinary degree. He was the first editor of any position from whom I ever heard words of generous commendation, and manifestly it delighted him as much to utter such words as it delighted his contributor to listen to them. When a man did well in any work he had undertaken for him, Grove's first purpose was to tell him so, and he always told him in the most generous terms. If an article did not suit him he would convey his decision regarding it in language which only served to raise him in the esteem of his contributor. Then he showed such a genuine interest in everything that affected the welfare of a contributor that it was quite impossible to remain on merely formal terms with him. You felt that he was your friend, and by an inevitable and natural process you became his. Thus he set up the pleasantest relations, both personal and professional, with the men who worked under him during his editorship. Like many another contributor to *Macmillan's*, I have delighful memories of evenings at Sydenham, when the host, crouching before the fire in his favourite position, made the whole company gay with story and reminiscence, and quaint, but never ill-natured, jest, and when he never failed to gladden the heart of any contributor who was present by some outspoken word of praise of his work, evidently meant to commend him to the general company. If the chief end of an editor is to secure the affection, as well as the respect and loyalty, of his contributors—and I see no reason why it should not be—then indeed was Grove successful beyond most editors whom I have known.

"He could not understand the jealousy and bitterness which are not always conspicuous by their absence in our critical reviews. 'I am very sorry for the article in the ——,' he wrote to me once, 'or rather for the temper of mind which prompted the attack. Something like a man not liking the outside of my house, and therefore accusing my wife of infidelity! Thank God, I can hardly understand that kind of disposition: the illogicalness would be so glaring to me, though I am no logician.'"

Returning to the course of events in 1868, I find under the date of February 2, some rough notes of "Mr. Tennyson's Stories" the best of which Grove afterwards dictated in 1897:—

"There was a certain Mr. Phillips, a rich attorney and member of the corporation of Shaftesbury. Every year the corporation had a haunch of venison given them by the Duke of Westminster or some large landowner in the neighbourhood, and it was their rule to devour it at an inn at a village some three or four miles distant from the town. Phillips was a great gourmand and very full of fun, and these occasions were thought a great deal of. At one of these dinners, just as the venison was brought in, Phillips got up and said, 'I must go.' There was a universal protest at this, but he was firm and said something was drawing him home, he could not tell what. The horse was accordingly put into the trap, and off he went. When he got to his house in Shaftesbury, he found his wife sitting in the parlour with her jaw dislocated, in floods of tears, and with the bell-rope in her hand. She had gaped and put out her jaw. She then pulled the bell, but the bell-rope had come down in her hand, and she had no alternative but to fling herself into a chair and think of her husband, which brought him home! Lord Tennyson told me that he heard this story from the man himself and had every reason to believe it."

On the 23rd of March Grove left England for a six weeks' holiday tour in Italy, crossing Mont Cenis on the night of the 25th, and reaching Florence on the following evening. Leaving Florence on the night of the 27th, he caught his first sight of Vesuvius "with the left hand side of the top broken away like a broken tooth." The mountain was in eruption, and as the train drew nearer to Naples great jets of dark red flame shot up out of the smoke and glowing patches of lava were distinctly visible. He stayed at Naples just ten days, and made no fewer than three ascents of Vesuvius—on March 30th, April 1, and April 3—embodying his experiences in a letter to the *Pall Mall Gazette*. At the first and second attempt he got to the rim of the great crater, but it was too full of smoke to admit of anything being seen below his own level. On the third ascent he was again disappointed, but saw "enough to be thankful for." His pocket-book contains pages and pages of notes on the three ascents, the most striking passage being that in which he describes the last part of his climb on March 30th :—

"We then continued the ascent coming to a small funnel-shaped hole not more than forty feet [across] and some twenty-five feet deep. It was full of vapours of sulphur, so strong, that it was all we could do by stuffing pocket-handkerchiefs into nose and mouth, and holding breath, to stand it. It was only now and then, when the wind blew stronger than usual, that we could manage it. It was a horrible little pit—brown and dry and sandy—it looked merciless and hellish—dead. The guide rolled down some stones to the bottom, and in a few moments eight or ten bubbles appeared and blew up (like a crater) a horrid sulphurous vapour."

From this they advanced to the edge of the real crater, but it was full of thick vapour, and only very rarely could they see down into it.

From Naples, where he met and dined with Mrs.

Somerville (the famous mathematician), Grove made excursions to Salerno, Amalfi, Posilippo and Pozzuoli, moving on, on April 8th, to Rome, where, with characteristic loyalty, he put up at Mendelssohn's lodgings, and nearly poisoned himself in consequence of his allegiance. It goes without saying that he saw all the sights, and has left many of his impressions on record. Some are amusing, as when he discovered likenesses to his friends amongst the busts at the Capitol—notably those of Aristotle and Cleopatra—and there is a good note on the dresses and physiognomy of the Papal Court, as observed when he was received in audience on the 11th :—

"Here you see the same figures that you [used] to admire in the pictures of the Italian painters. All those wonderful velvet and brocade mantles and ruffs and doublets, and not only the dresses, but the very men themselves are there, exactly the heads to suit the court—keen-eyed and cool-faced, with long oval faces and short black hair."

Grove not only saw the Pope, but made friends with another great potentate—Liszt, of his first visit to whom he gives a lively account in a letter to Miss Olga von Glehn :—

"ROME, *Monday Night*,
"*April* 20, 1868.

"... Fancy my being still in Rome! When I first came, I meant to leave on Easter Tuesday or Wednesday, but my going was dependent on the fêtes at Turin and Florence, and as they do not begin till Sunday and Wednesday, there is no reason why I should run away from this most delightful of places. I feel inclined to stay in this royal place and see all I can and complete my conversion and get my Cardinal's hat at once, instead of coming back, as the Pope presses me to do, next year. . . .

"I forgot all about Liszt's being here till Saturday, when the thought suddenly flashed into my head. So I discovered his address and wrote a note, humble, but fragrant with incense asking him to deign to receive his slave. Then I went to the convent at which he lives, yesterday morning, and got an answer,[1]

[1] Liszt's answer, which Grove kept, began, "Il me sera très agréable de faire votre connaissance, et de recevoir aussi des nouvelles de Mr Walter Bache, qui j'estime et affectionne sincèrement."

saying he should be glad to see me to-day between three and four. Guess if I were punctual! I had just before called on Father Mulhooly at the Convent of San Clementi, whom I found in a wretched little room, without carpet or fire or any furniture but a table and a spittoon, and a deadly fear possessed me that Liszt might be in an equally forlorn case, but no, he was capitally lodged[1]—a jolly drawing-room with a grand piano—a library beyond, and a bedroom beyond that. He was awfully kind and nice. I stopped with him for nearly two hours and never enjoyed myself more. We talked of all kinds of things, music, religion, Germany, England, the people we mutually knew, etc., and it pleased me, as you will understand, to find him quite simple and good-hearted, a thorough accomplished man of the world, without spite or conceit, no forcing forward of his own music, or abuse of other musicians, etc. At last I looked at the name on the front of the piano 'Chickering, Boston'; and then he told me that Mr. S. had come from America, bringing the piano with him, that all his establishment, books, pianos, music, etc., were at Weimar, and only a few things here. I asked if I might be allowed to hear him, and after a little resistance—'Croyez-moi, monsieur, je ne prétend pas à jouir beaucoup le piano'—he began and played for about five minutes. Can you understand how I felt when I heard the first notes? It *was* so sweet to hear the dear piano once more, for I am so tired of strong men's voices and screaming organs dreadfully played! Then we talked again, and then he took me into the library to give me a note of introduction to a lady in Florence. Then some people were announced—a blind man with his daughter whom Liszt had kindly asked to come and let him hear her play. (Blind man rather interesting by-the-bye, an amanuensis of Bunsen's, speaking English and knowing a friend of mine, Jacobson, Bishop of Chester.) The girl played her two feeble little pieces, and you can't think how kind he was—without a morsel of humbug. And then he said he would play to her and she would sit by "pour me corriger, vous savez," so down we all sat, he in the middle and she and I on the two sides and he played away most charmingly for a quarter of an hour. Of course it was modern style, but not the least extravagant, and lovely to hear: loud, then soft, and then loud again, and so easy and graceful, no *tours de force*. Then he said in German that we should have something 'lustiges,' and, turning to me, as I had been asking about his transcriptions of Schubert's songs, said he would play the Soirées de Vienne—Schubert's Waltzes, and he played two, most lovely. I never was

[1] At Santa Francesca Romana.

so delighted and he saw I was pleased and liked it. I had a capital opportunity of looking at his face, for he kept turning round to me, as he played, to see how I liked it. Three things occurred to me—which I will tell you as I thought them at the time. 1. A great general likeness to Napoleon when young. The instant I shook hands with him, the words came to the tip of my tongue, 'the young lieutenant of Engineers' (Carlyle, somewhere about Napoleon). 2. The mouth just like Kingsley's. 3. He was not tall, but in that limited space was concentrated the pluck of thirty battalions. He was in an Abbé's dress, long black coat and knee breeches, with buckles in his shoes; which became him well. His hair is grey, his face very refined and *luminous*, and his hands the perfection of delicacy. It was quite different from Rubinstein or any of the great players, and I could have listened for ever. We parted with great effusion and he entreated me to come again ('wet or dry, come early') which is evidently a favour, as he told his servant that I was to be let in."

The acquaintance, so pleasantly begun, led to further meetings on the following Thursday, and on Sunday the 26th, when Liszt invited Grove to a "petite réunion musicale," at which he played compositions by Bach, Raff, and von Bülow. For his sight-seeing Grove had the best of cicerones in Lanciani and Parker, while amongst other Roman friends mention may be made of the Storeys, W. B. Richmond, and the Conte di Bentivoglio. Altogether the visit to Rome was a great success. As he says: "I could not have come at a better time. The weather during the last week was everything that it could be, and the spring advanced, and the trees burst and blossomed in the most charming manner." On the 28th of April he left for Florence, where he came in for a round of festivities which began on the 30th with the entry of Prince Humbert—processions, horse-races, a regatta, and fireworks on which Grove, long familiar with such displays at the Crystal Palace, descanted with the enthusiasm of an appreciative expert. He spent a good deal of his time in the picture galleries, left for Turin on the 5th of May, and started for home the next night, reaching home on the 9th. In his absence he had applied by telegram for the post of Secretary to Lloyd's, and that he prosecuted his candidature seriously is shown by the draft of a letter copied into his pocket-book, signed "Thos. Hughes, Chairman of the Board of Directors of the Crystal Palace Company," and addressed to the Chairman of Lloyd's, setting forth Grove's qualifications in eulogistic terms. The application however proved unsuccessful, and Grove remained for nearly five years longer at the Crystal Palace. The entries in his diary during the summer relate chiefly to meetings with Stanley, social engagements, the Handel Festival and the excessive heat, for July and the early part of August were in Horace Walpole's phrase veritable "mastiff days." On July 30th his eldest son Walter went to school for the first time, and on August 2nd we find a record of two stories told him by his friend Miss Ursula Mayow which seem worthy of preservation :—

"Colonel Jacob of the Indian army was in India during the Mutiny. He had a brother in Worcestershire and two sisters living about twenty miles off. One of the sisters was a widow with several daughters, and the other was unmarried. The two sisters slept together one night, the widow woke and said, 'Heigho ! what an unpleasant dream I have had. I dreamt that I looked at my watch and it had stopped, on which a voice said to me, "Your watch has stopped but that's not all, your brother's life has stopped too."' She then looked at her watch and found that it *had* stopped. The other sister who had been listening all the time, said, 'Well, I have not been asleep, and I have been distinctly conscious of the presence of something in the room, and just before you woke I felt it pass over me and quite lightly kiss my lips, and it was *his* kiss.' In the morning they made a note of what had happened and so anxious were they, that they sent one of their old servants over to the brother who lived twenty miles off to ask how he was. The answer was 'quite well : it's a pity you have nothing better to do than to send your people on such useless errands.' They then knew that if the occurrence referred to any one, it must be to the brother in India. Not long after came the telegram announcing Jacob's death. The date, however, was different. The dream had been on the 16th, the telegram gave the 12th as the date of his death. The sisters like sensible women accepted the discrepancy as a proof that the dream was merely a dream. 'They had been thinking a great deal of their brother and it was natural that they should have dreamed about him, but the difference in date showed that it could be nothing more.' In a few days, however, came the full dispatch, and letters from friends, and then it turned out that the dream was right after all, and that Colonel Jacob had died on the same day on which his sisters had received warning of it."

Miss Mayow's second story was apropos of Lord Cardigan's stupidity and ran as follows:—

"My brother Colonel Mayow was in the Crimea under Lord Cardigan's command, and like a good Churchman he used to read prayers on Sunday to his regiment. Of course he never read the Absolution. Lord Cardigan always came, and he never failed to say after prayers were over, 'There was no hurry, Mayow, you need not have left out the Absolution,' though my brother as regularly explained why he had left it out."

On August the 12th Grove dined with Sullivan in the company of Mr. Manns and Herr Ferdinand David, the distinguished violinist, who illustrated the advance in technical accomplishment by the following remark: "When I began to play there were some pieces such as Lipinski's military concerto and Ernst's Hungarian Fantasia which only two or three men in Europe could play. Now all my pupils play them."

Grove attended the meeting of the British Association at Norwich on August 19th and 20th and at the end of September paid a visit to Sir Frederick Gore-Ouseley at Tenbury, recording while they were still fresh in his memory on September 30th the following stories told him by his host:—

"Before I came here I lived in a house at Langley in Bucks, with Fyffe and several boys. A friend of mine heard groans and strange noises and was changed by them from profligate bad ways to a better mind. I had never heard the noises myself, but one night—the 21st September—I had stopped [up] late to read till two o'clock, and before going to bed, while walking down a long passage to my room, I was—in the dark—all of a sudden startled by the whole place becoming illuminated quite brightly, and I saw at the end of the passage an old man in a dressing-gown with a very forbidding countenance. He was quite plain to be seen. I was very much startled, but I had the presence of mind to rebuke him in the name of the Holy Trinity, on which he vanished at once, and he never reappeared since. I made search in old parish registers, and I found that an old man had strangled his wife and killed himself in that part of the house on September 21st. No one else saw the apparition, though they heard noises and saw doors open and shut apparently without any visible agency. The date was the same on which my friend heard the groans. The house now lets for £300, three times as much as when I had it."

"When I was an undergraduate my father was taken ill, and I went to see him. In the train all along, I had constantly before me on the opposite seat the image of my aunt, his sister, weeping. I did not know her well and had not thought about her till I saw her there. Did I try to touch her or sit on the same place? No, I hadn't the courage."

"My father had been dead some years and my mother was on her death-bed with an incurable complaint. It was quite hopeless, and the doctor had given her an opiate to make her sleep during the last [night]. I went away to my own room to bed. There I saw in the room sitting on a chair as plain as I see you, my father, and while I looked my mother came in and took his hand, and they went away together. She had just then died."

"My father and mother were in India and my father was taken ill and it was thought so serious that his sister was sent for —the aunt I mentioned just now. There were no overland routes then, and she had to come by the Cape. While she was coming my mother one night sleeping by the side of my father saw my aunt appear with wet clothes and all her hair cut off. She had died during the voyage of a fever and her hair had been cut off before her death as a remedy. There was a discrepancy, however, in the time of her death, but on calculating the longitude it agreed to a minute. My mother said nothing about it to my father but resolved secretly to intercept the letter that he might not be frightened, but he knew it beforehand, and mentioned it to her."

By way of contrast to these ghostly narratives almost the next entry in his pocket book relates to some grotesque but *bonâ fide* mistranslations given him by his brother-in-law Dr. Bradley, then headmaster of Marlborough College. —*impedimenta vomuit* for "he brought up the baggage" and *transenna homo medicina non video* for "A blind man does [dose] not see."

The intense interest that Grove felt in his heroes and his friends, in art and letters and life, has been already illustrated in these pages. The stimulating influence that he exerted on others, and especially his juniors, may be gathered from the following graphic sketch from the pen of Mr. Ernest von Glehn, who in 1868-9 was in residence at Christ Church, Oxford. After dwelling on his wonderful sympathy for the young, Mr. von Glehn continues :—

"To me, to know him as I did was indeed a liberal education. There was no one to whom I could so freely pour out all my youthful thoughts and feelings, however crude, or with greater certainty of a sympathetic hearing, and nearly always of real help and guidance. Many and many a time did I walk and talk with him far into the night between my father's house and his. I would start to see him home after an evening spent at Peak Hill; then on reaching his house, about a mile and a half off, he would turn and walk back with me, and so on and so on. He never seemed to weary and it was generally I who said 'Now G. we really must go to our homes and beds.' Truly he *was* a riend for a young man: there was no room for anything mean and squalid in his mind: it was too full of keen interests, enthusiasms, and delights in everything good and beautiful. And then those delightful Saturday evenings at his house after the Crystal Palace Concerts, when he gathered round his table eight or ten intimates, and generally one or two artists from the concert —that was the time of his prime, his gaiety, his fun; and his stories—how they flowed! And then when music followed—a trio or a quartet—what a listener he was! I am sure the artists always went 'one better' than their best in that low old-fashioned drawing-room. Most people seem to me to listen to music without showing anything of their enjoyment in their faces, but how wonderful it was to watch his dear old face as he sat and listened."

The "intimates" referred to by Mr. von Glehn were practically common to Grove's house and Peak Hill and at this period included J. R. Green, Canon Ainger, Emanuel Deutsch the orientalist, Arthur Sullivan, Franklin Taylor, and Lionel Lewin, a young man with great social gifts and a happy knack of improvising verse that was always amusing and often witty, who died in early life. Later on were added Jules Stockhausen the famous singer, Hans von Bülow, Robert Hausmann—the admirable 'cellist of the Joachim quartet—Anna Mehlig, Scharwenka, Otto Goldschmidt, Hubert Parry, and many other musicians painters and literary men. The present Bishop of Lichfield, then Vicar of St. Bartholomew's, Sydenham, whose long and unbroken friendship for Grove dates from this period, gives a charming picture of these gatherings :—

"No one who has enjoyed the hospitality of Sir George and Lady Grove in their picturesque old wooden house in Lower Sydenham can forget the delightful Saturday evenings when friends, and men of letters, and musicians would meet at the table of the Editor of *Macmillan's Magazine* and Secretary to the Crystal Palace. But however interesting and eminent the guests might be, it was the host who was the soul of the company. He literally bubbled over with anecdote, enjoying his stories as much as any member of the party. He was always ready at repartee. His humour was abundant, his versatility remarkable. There were few subjects on which he could not discourse; and he was able to produce his knowledge, not only without effort, but with a certain enthusiasm which enlisted the keen interest of all who heard him in the particular matter in hand. There were quiet Sunday evenings as well, when he welcomed his more intimate friends, and held sweet converse with them on the highest and deepest subjects."

A brief note addressed to Mr. E. M. Oakeley, then a master at Clifton College, at the close of the year is worth reproducing not only as illustrating Grove's divided allegiance to music and letters, but on account of Mr. Oakeley's interesting account of the article that prompted Grove to write :—

"CRYSTAL PALACE, *Dec.* 3, 1868.

"How fares it with you? Did you see the *Pall Mall* of Monday, November 30th? If not, get it and read an article in it on Schumann[1] which marks an era in English musical criticism.

"Have you seen Browning's new poem?[2] And can you tell me any man to ask to review it? I want to find a new, but also thoroughly competent hand, and I look wildly in every direction. Tell me if any one occurs to you. My kind regards to T. E. Brown.[3] Yours ever truly,

G. GROVE."

The entries in the early months of 1869 show that Grove was assiduous in his attendance at the Palestine Exploration Fund meetings, and that besides the concerts at the Crystal Palace he attended musical functions so widely differing in character as Miss Arabella Goddard's recital, Walter Bache's concert and a performance of Offenbach's *Grande Duchesse*. In June the Sydenham coterie was reinforced by the advent of a welcome newcomer in the person of the Rev. A. T. Davidson, who has kindly furnished the following interesting paper of reminiscences :—

"My acquaintance with Sir George Grove dates from June 1869, when I became curate to the present Bishop of Lichfield, then Vicar of St. Bartholomew's, Sydenham. On letting one's

[1] This article (writes Mr. Oakeley) was an amusing piece of "hedging," by someone (probably, from internal evidence, Mr. J. W. Davison, the *Times* critic) on whom, after a Crystal Palace performance of the E flat symphony, it had begun to dawn that the attitude of British criticism towards Schumann was indefensible. A previous article by him in the same paper, one of the four he employed to disseminate his views on Music, shows him beginning to harbour doubts whether Schumann was, after all, only "a sincere but most dreary and unmelodious mystic," as he had recently been described in the *Athenæum*. The *Athenæum* knew no "hedging"; its critic, Mr. Chorley, died impenitent, and made it a point to the end of his life to walk out of the concert-room at the beginning of the second movement of Schumann's Quintet, to mark, it is said, his high disapproval of a certain chord in the eighth bar! The *Pall Mall's* "hedging," however, does not go very far, Schumann, we read, "mistook music for a branch of metaphysics." But "the domain of music is a wide one, and affords ample room for him"; and Mr. Davison "does not charge anyone with unfairness or prejudice in this matter: the fault lies with Schumann himself" (of course; not with the Chorleys and Davisons!) "who chose to write caring less for the beauty of his work than for its faithfully reflecting certain trains of thought." And so on!

[2] *The Ring and the Book*. It was reviewed by J. R. Mozley in *Macmillan* for April, 1869.

[3] Author of *Fo'c'sle Yarns*, &c

memory go back to that time, it is not difficult to recall the strangeness I felt in the midst of such a society as I found gathered together in the quaint old house in Lower Sydenham the first time I visited it, being then altogether unaccustomed to anything of the kind. There was Sir George, or Mr. Grove as he was then, bustling about with a cheery word for everyone, leaving nobody out, talking to me, who had only that very moment been introduced to him, as though my arrival in the parish and my work therein were matters of the keenest interest to him:—there was his wife setting us all at our ease, bright, sparkling, amusing, giving one the impression 'nothing you do will make any difference; we are accustomed to all sorts and conditions of men here; there is a great noise; everyone is talking at once; but you will get accustomed to it presently:'—there were distinguished people of all kinds, travellers connected with Palestine Exploration, a musician or two, and friends who had come to dine after the afternoon's concert at the Crystal Palace. Everybody seemed to be cheerful and happy. There was no pretence about anything: no starch or stiffness, no dulness. After dinner we all went out into the garden. We talked, and smoked, and had tea. There were endless stories, and endless jokes, Sir George taking the lead, but just as good a listener as he was a talker, till at length came eleven o'clock—what might be described as 'closing time' on Saturday evenings at Lower Sydenham—when the Londoners had to leave in order to catch the 11.22 train to Victoria. Each party, nay each individual if he went alone, was accompanied to the gate by our host—a parting word on his lips for everybody. I can see him now:—to those he was fondest of, his usual valediction, seizing one's hand in both of his, was—'good-bye, good-bye, God bless you!'

What I have just said may be taken as the picture of the man as I knew him, and as I venture to think most others knew him, in his lighter moments. I had a standing invitation to dinner for Saturday evenings—on which nights he might specially be considered to be at home to his friends—and as I certainly went there, when I was not bound to go elsewhere, on most of the Saturdays I was at Sydenham, I may, without unduly magnifying myself, claim to speak with some authority. Many were the distinguished people I met—Arthur Sullivan, John Hullah, Henry Leslie, Joachim, L. Straus, Stockhausen, Gounod, Ferdinand Hiller, W. H. Lecky, F. W. Myers, Holman Hunt, to speak of no others prominent in art, science, and literature. But to all 'G,' as he was styled by his intimates, was the same. For everyone there was the welcoming smile, and cheery word. I suppose there must have been those who bored him, for such are nowhere absent. But I am bound to say, I don't think anyone was allowed to be conscious of his powers of boring on those Saturday evenings. There was an infection in the atmosphere. Everyone seemed to be at his ease, and to find something to say and something to interest him. It was impossible for it to be otherwise with a man and his wife who seemed, at such times, to hold the world as a place to kick up one's heels in, and to be gay to one's heart's content.

"Not that Sir George could not be serious enough. Sometimes, though to be sure not often, there might be no one but oneself at dinner on Saturday evening; then the talk would be ot graver matters. He was quite willing, nay indeed eager to discuss my work with me, to talk on theological points, to suggest books I should read, to illustrate what he said by references to favourite authors of his, Wesley, Newman, Arnold, Stanley. Also we clergy of St. Bartholomew's got into the habit of going down to Lower Sydenham after church on Sunday evenings. We had tea, and much talk with our host on many kinds of subjects but—as perhaps fitted the day—mostly of the weightier sorts. If the time was summer, we would wander about in his delightful old garden, with pipes and cigars, while he tackled us, perhaps, about our sermons preached that day—approving here and disagreeing there—doing it in that genial, affectionate tone, which made us all so pleased he had spoken, and in my case at any rate, only adding to the love I soon got to feel for him.

"And then there was another point about him. There never was such a man as 'G,' for not letting you feel unwelcome. You might go to him at any time, or any day, and he was always glad to see you. If he could not attend to you, he would say so, but with such pleasantness, that you never felt you had had a walk for nothing. If on the other hand he had a minute or two to spare, he would throw himself into your news or your difficulty, whichever it might be, sympathize with you, cheer you up, promise to write to this person or that person for you (promises which he always amply redeemed)—in fact he always illustrated practically the direction to consider not merely one's own things, but those of others as well. And it was not only to personal friends that he was willing to devote himself. Although one of the busiest men I have ever known, he was quite ready, nay eager, when it was possible to spare an evening to enliven a parochial entertainment with a reading from Dickens, or by taking a share in any music that was made. I should say, as far as Sydenham was concerned when I knew it, that no man was more in request, just as I am sure there was no one among the residents who was more ready to help in anything that was going on, or to think it the most natural thing in the world to do what he could.

Enthusiasm, geniality, affection which never wavered for an instant when once he had bestowed it—these seemed to me, when I was working in Sydenham, as the prominent features of his character. I am bound to say I found him the same whenever I went back to see him. '*Davidson*,' he would say, with a sort of emphatic surprise, each syllable of my name well drawn out, '*how* glad I am to see you! When will you come and dine? Is your wife with you? Bring her too of course.' There were the jokes and the stories all ready when I went: there was the keen interest in my Lancashire parish: there were questions as to whether I heard much music, as to what I was reading, and so forth:—all his sayings and mannerisms, if I may venture to call them so, making you think, which in truth was the case, that while you were with him no one could be more interesting to him than you, and nothing better worth talking about than your life and its concerns.

Of course I have only set down what numbers of others could have written as well as, or better than I. But I am sure the conclusion we should all come to is—that he was a unique personality, and for warm-heartedness, loyalty, and zeal, we shall not easily look upon his like again."

The Bible Dictionary Dinners were still kept up and on July 8th there was a special dinner at Windsor, while on July 14th occurs the first mention of his attending the meetings of the Metaphysical Society[1] of which he was an original member. Early in July Tennyson wrote to Grove asking him to make a fourth in a three weeks' trip to Mürren, the others being the Rev. S. Eardley and

[1] The Metaphysical Society was founded in 1869 by Tennyson, Mr. Pritchard, and Mr. James Knowles (who first mooted the idea) for the free discussion of Christian evidences by those ranged both on the side of faith and unfaith. The earliest members were Dean Stanley, Seeley, Roden Noel, James Martineau, W. B. Carpenter, Hinton, Huxley, Pritchard, R. H. Hutton, W. G. Ward, Bagehot, Froude, Tennyson, Tyndall, Alfred Barry, Lord Arthur Russell, Gladstone, Manning, James Knowles, John Lubbock, Dean Alford, Alexander Grant, the Bishop of St. David's (Thirlwall), Frederic Harrison, Father Dalgairns, George Grove, Shadworth Hodgson, Henry Sidgwick, Edmund Lushington, the Bishop of Gloucester, Mark Pattison. See the *Memoir o Lord Tennvson*, by his son, chap. xxx.

Frederick Locker-Lampson.[1] Grove was unable to go but his cordial feelings towards Tennyson found vent a few weeks later in a letter which elicited the following characteristic answer :—

BLACK HORSE COPSE, BLACKDOWN,
August 12th.

"MY DEAR GROVE.—I am in a house 800 feet above the sea —no roads and no post—or I would have thanked you earlier for your proposed glass of Locker and Co. to be drunk in my honour on the 8th [Tennyson's birthday]—day which I always feel inclined to pass like a Trappist without speaking—or to keep it sitting in sackcloth and ashes. . . .

"Ever yours,
"A. TENNYSON."

[1] An account of this trip is given by Mr. Frederick Locker-Lampson in chapter xxvi. of the *Memoir of Lord Tennyson* by his son.

CHAPTER VI

Visit to Italy in 1869—The miracle of S. Januarius and the Santa Casa at Loreto—Grove's accounts in the *Times* and *Spectator*—His merits as a travelling companion—Anecdotes of Mr. Denison—The story of Purley—Visits to Paris and to Penn—Grove and his contributors—Election to the Athenæum Club—With Sullivan in Paris, June, 1871—Visit to Switzerland in the autumn—Correspondence with Tennyson—Death of Deutsch in 1873: Grove's tribute—At Rippoldsau with Thompson of Trinity—Study of Chinese Porcelain—Grove resigns the Secretaryship of the Crystal Palace to edit the *Dictionary of Music.*

In the first week of September 1869 Grove went to Worcester for the Festival of the Three Choirs, at which Sullivan's cantata *The Prodigal Son* was produced with great success, Titiens, Trebelli, Sims Reeves, and Santley taking the solo parts. Immediately afterwards he started for Italy on the 11th, travelling viâ Mont Cenis, Turin, Bologna, and Ancona to Loreto, where he spent the 14th examining the Santa Casa, proceeding to Naples on the following day. The object of his visit was to witness the miracle of the liquefaction of the blood of S. Januarius, and his experiences were embodied in a long letter "from an occasional correspondent" which appeared in the *Times* of September 28th, 1869. Beginning with a description of the state of Naples on the eve of the *Festa*, which opened on Sunday, September 19th, and lasted seven days, he continues :—

"The cause of it all [viz., the excitement, crowds, fireworks] is that the 19th September is the Feast of St. Januarius, and that on that day and the seven days following, his blood, which is reputed to be preserved in the Cathedral of Naples, in a solid form, resumes its original condition on being exposed to the sight of the faithful."

Grove goes on to say that he has seen the "miracle," and with every disposition to do it justice and be impressed by the dignity, pathos or virtue of the ceremony, he is profoundly disappointed. He describes most elaborately the two bottles in which the blood is preserved in the *Capella del Tesoro* or *Capella San Gennaro* in the Cathedral of Naples—the dark opaque appearance of the contents, the reliquary in which they are enclosed, the monstrance in which it is conveyed in the procession, "the whole looking not unlike a small circular carriage lamp"—the place where the reliquary is kept, the process of exhibition, and the alleged liquefaction with all the accompanying demonstrations of delight—scattering of roses, letting loose of sparrows, pealing of the organ, and the kissing of the reliquary. After commenting on the time taken by the process of liquefaction—which varied on three days mentioned from six to thirteen minutes—Grove proceeds to give the results of his minute observations on each of the three days. He notes that it is not possible to have the reliquary in one's hands, and that it is difficult to see clearly, but is satisfied on several points, e.g., that there is no motion in the smaller bottle, that in the larger the fluid in its motion left no trace of its presence on the glass : that there was no colour of blood on the glass or in the fluid ; no frothing or agitation in the liquid.

He acquits the participants of any juggling, and dismisses various explanations of the alleged liquefaction—by the heat of the candle or the priest's hand—but notes the unconcerned unmoved attitude of the chief actors concerned. "It was a 'transaction' which had to be got through in regular course."

He further tested the alleged miracle of the stone with red marks at the Church of the Capuchins at Pozzuoli, on which St. Januarius was said to have been beheaded, the marks on which are alleged to sweat blood at the same time as the liquefaction at Naples, but nothing was seen. The whole account is a remarkable illustration of Grove's powers as an observer, his indefatigable interest, his endurance, and his gifts of minute and circumstantial description. What the resultant sum of his impressions was may best be gathered from a passage in his pocket-book not incorporated in his letter to the *Times* :—

"I will not deny that on the last day I was more touched than before, but it was by the eagerness of the people whom I saw crowding round the rails of the choir in the afternoon. The 'miracle' remained to the last as mechanical and unspiritual as before. How long is it to be so? How long are a great people so full of fine qualities as these Neapolitans to be condemned to such senseless rites, to have such stones given them for bread? Doubtless it is all part of a scheme too wide for us to embrace even if we could."

Grove's companions at Naples during the Festival were the Rev. Augustus Legge [the present Bishop of Lichfield] and his wife, and Mr. F. A. Eaton, Secretary of the Royal Academy, with whom he made a trip to Ischia, commemorated in a set of verses in the visitors' book on the summit of Monte Epomeo, from which we may quote the two last stanzas :—

"'Now who were these writers
These doggerel inditers?'—
Will scornfully ask the next comer.
Would you know it, my friend,
Just read to the end,
You'll never see anything rummer.

The party consisted of four,
And we certainly wanted no more:
Two *Legges* never beaten,
A luncheon well *Eaton*,
And a *Grove* ever green to the core."

At Naples Grove put up at the Hotel "Belle Vue," then kept by an old man named Zavota, of whom he left an interesting account in his reminiscences of 1897 :—

"In the early part of the great war Zavota had enlisted in the Marines, in the English Navy. From the Marines he was transferred to the regular army, was present at the battle or Corunna, and was one of the men who took Sir John Moore to his grave. After this he was established at Naples chiefly through the kindness of the Duke of Devonshire, victualled the yachts of the duke and his friends, and in time made a considerable sum of money. With this he bought the land on which he had been born, built an hotel, and subsisted by keeping the hotel and making wine. Before this, however, and after leaving the army he had been private servant to Sir Hudson Lowe, then resident in the south of France, and told me some curious stories illustrating Lowe's secretiveness of character. On one occasion his master told him to come with a carriage at eleven o'clock at night, as he wished to take a drive. Zavota, from previous experience, provided himself with a bag of clothes, but Sir Hudson had no luggage. They got into the carriage, and he was told to drive to a town about ten miles distant to the north. When they arrived there they got other horses, and went on until they finally reached Paris, where his first occupation was to buy clothes for his master. They then continued their journey until they reached London, and as they drove into London Sir Hudson said : 'Do you know what I have come here for?' 'Not at all,' said Zavota. 'I am going to be married.' Accordingly they drove to a small hotel at the bottom of Albemarle Street, Piccadilly, where the marriage took place in due course."

On October 3rd Grove breakfasted with Costa at Casamicciola on the island of Ischia, where he was much impressed by the spectacle of the conductor and his brother eating mountains of macaroni out of an enormous basin, and on the 6th returned to Loreto to continue his investigations into the Santa Casa. Of these he has left long and interesting notes in his pocket-books, from which I borrow the following passages :—

"It is barely three weeks since I saw the miracle of the liquefaction of the blood of St. Januarius at Naples, and I am now in contact with a miracle still more strange, still more opposed to all our ordinary beliefs—I mean the Santa Casa or Holy House at Loreto. This is, I suppose, the most frequented place of pilgrimage in Christendom, and surely not without reason if its pretensions are sound, for it purports to be the actual house at Nazareth in which the annunciation of the birth of Our Lord was made to the Virgin, and in which Jesus Christ lived with his family till He left them for his own independent life. I say the actual, very, house itself—carried across the sea by angels' hands and set down, after some hesitation, on the spot it now occupies."

After describing the basis of documentary evidence—Papal Bulls and ordinances, &c.—on which the story rests, Grove gives an account of the splendid Church in which the house stands, and of the house itself—an oblong room entered by three doors—its method of illumination, the gorgeous altar, and the walls of ordinary rubble stonework, with some brickwork in the N. wall, he continues :—

"Everything has been done to dwarf the house and make it look more insignificant than it originally was : the great cumbrous lamps, the tawdry altar, the ugly cross, all have this effect, and a very bad effect."

He then gives full details of the history of the house, the alterations effected by Leo X., the ornaments, functions of the Capuchins, the rites observed at the Feast of the Translation of the House, the ornaments, bells, &c., and the various movements of the Santa Casa.

On October 8th, Grove was in the Church at 6.30 a.m. :—

"The scene was a busy one. Early as it was the Holy House was crammed, and the chapels surrounding were also crowded with groups of *contadine* in their clean gay (elsewhere they would be gaudy but here everything harmonizes) red and yellow headgear, crimped white jackets and brown high-waisted skirts—kneeling or sitting on the steps round the confessional boxes waiting for the confessor, or watching with more or less care the course of the magical process which is being transacted at the altar. Some Zingari from the encampment on the common with long wild hair innocent of the comb, high boots and most forbidding looks, did not make the scene any less strange. The tinkling of the bells of the altar attendants was incessant."

Grove was reminded of the Vatican and St. Peter's by the way the Church dominated the whole town :—

"It is like the Vatican in another thing—the wealth and completeness of its establishment. There is an establishment of singers as at the Vatican and there only, besides St. Peter's, are there confessionals for all nations. . . Two only are wanting to make the number equal to those of the Vatican—the Hungarian and the Portuguese."

After noting the cosmopolitan character of the congregation, and its constant influx during the twelve hours—from 4 a.m. to 4 p.m.—the Church is open, Grove summarizes his impressions in the subjoined passage :—

"There is something appalling in the completenes and perfection of the whole, in the efficient smooth way in which the whole immense machine works—no failure or weakness or hesitation in any part, however small, remote, or insignificant. I remember being struck with that at Rome in the Easter ceremonies when it seemed as if every one from the lowest friar to the Pope himself was ready at once to take any part in any ceremony however complicated. And it has been confirmed at Loreto. The quantity of things to be done, the number of motions and minute acts to be kept in one's head is so great, and yet every one seems to perform them without faltering or forgetting. And then the whole appears so perfectly suited to the wants of a peasantry like the Italian or the Indian.

"No one who has been in the Holy House and is open to impressions of the kind is likely to forget what he saw. I have been at the Holy Sepulchre, at the Grotto of the Nativity of Bethlehem and Nazareth, but none of them at all equalled this. . . . But then the effect is materially lessened on reflection by two very important considerations. First it is not religious but theatrical. Everything has been done to rob the place of its real interest. . . It has been grossly altered. How far better if it had been left to the simplicity in which, wherever it really came from, it originally stood.

"But secondly and lastly there is the terrible consideration that it cannot be what it pretends to be. It is impossible . . . the four flittings. In such a case the *onus probandi* rests with those who assert so violent a contravention of the laws of nature, and the proof has never been given."

On the moral of these miracles Grove writes as follows:—

"The problem of the nature of such miracles sinks into nothing compared with the problem of the temper of mind which can accept them and find food from them. Few things seem more puzzling to one's notions of right and wrong, than to find large countries or even individuals subsisting and deriving all their spiritual sustenance from that which we know to be not only erroneous but absolutely false. Interpret the sacrifice of the Mass in either sense—in that of the ignorant Catholic who believes that the wafer and wine are converted into the actual veritable tangible flesh and blood of Christ, or in the strict theological sense that their substance is changed into the substance of flesh, while their accidents remain those of bread or wine—both are wrong. The first there is no need to refute. The second is refuted by the fact that the old metaphysic of substance and accident is as dead as the Ptolemaic system of astronomy. And yet there are millions of men and women who derive all their religious life, from day to day and week to week, from believing this change to take place. The learned and pious Hindoo who prays before a rude and obscene symbol with as much agony and emotion as ever a Christian did to the image of Christ in his mind and gains as real and lasting peace from the answer which he then believes himself to have received, is but another instance of the same thing, and what is the explanation—that so long as the religious emotions are excited, the means by which they are excited are immaterial. One means is as good as another. Or is it that these are all means by which God connects himself with the soul and spirit of man? In either case what becomes of objective truth? And one rises from the consideration of the question with an uneasy feeling that the symbols and documents of Christianity may be as baseless as those of the Hindoo."

On the 8th of October Grove started homewards *viâ* Bologna and Turin, spending a day in Paris at the Louvre and the Exposition Industrielle, and reaching home on the 11th. The *Spectator* of October 2nd having commented on his narrative of the miracle of St. Januarius in the *Times*, Grove contributed a long supplementary letter to the *Spectator* of October 23rd, reciting his experiences on the later days of the Festival. He describes the ceremony on the Monday when the party divided—Mr. and Mrs. Legge and Mr. Eaton going to Pozzuoli to test the miracle of the Stone, while Grove went again to the Cathedral. He notes the progress of the "miracle" with the same minute attention to detail—the time occupied in the liquefaction being longer, 13 minutes—describing the closet where the reliquary is kept, and giving a fuller description of the reliquary itself. He went into the sacristy to see the jewels—St. Januarius is extraordinarily rich in busts, collars, crosses, chalices, &c., and ornaments set with magnificent stones. After this follows a picturesque account of the Capuchin Church at Pozzuoli, the bust of the Saint with its resemblance to Pio Nono, its miraculously restored nose, and the Stone which his friends had watched on the Monday from 9 till 9.45 without observing any of the alleged changes. Grove also describes his visit to Fiorelli, the Director of the Museum, who could give him no information. On the Tuesday the indefatigable Grove was again in the Cathedral—the Legges had gone on to Sicily, and Eaton to Ischia—occupying himself more this time with the people and the general scene. Most of the people had a "strongly professional air," and gave one "much the impression of *claqueurs*," but some of those present—women—showed genuine and even touching emotion. He also describes the bearing of the old Cavaliere Tesoriere—the Archbishop's representative—a dignified old man, a thorough gentleman with a decided look of Newman. In the afternoon Grove went again to the Cathedral and was much struck by the ceremony of the kissing of the reliquary by the general crowd:—

"By the way," he adds, "what a splendid decoration lighted candles make to a church! I mean the long thin ones that one sees abroad. I saw it first at Vienna, in the church of the Franciscans; then at Rome in the convent chapel of the French nuns; again at Loreto last week; and now at Naples. There may be from 80 to 150 lights—all the back of the altar is formed of them; and the long thin, soft-white vertical lines of the candles, and their golden flames, have a grace and splendour about them unspeakably beautiful in themselves, and suggestive of all that one connects with light and glory. And, like gold, they harmonize with everything, and are effective in sunlight no less than in twilight or darkness."

On Sunday, the 26th, Grove was once more in Naples, and could not resist going to San Gennaro again, to take his farewell. This was his fourth visit, but he found no reason to modify his observations or impressions. He sums up by saying that, if he has been minute in his account, it is because he desires to record every trait of so curious a spectacle :—

"It is a scene which the march of events and opinions will inevitably extinguish before many years are over, as it has recently extinguished the Doseh at Cairo, and the dancing before the high altar at Seville, and which will yet always be interesting and characteristic. And if I have given no summing-up—passed no judgment on the 'miracle of St. Januarius'—it is because I prefer rather to state my impressions as they came to me, and leave my readers to draw their own conclusions."

No better summary of this most successful holiday trip can be given than that kindly contributed by the Bishop of Lichfield :—

"If George Grove was a most entertaining host, he was also a delightful travelling companion. In the autumn of 1869 I had the good fortune to visit Loreto, Ischia and Naples with him. He threw himself with all the joyousness of a boy into the little incidents of travel. Out early in the morning at Loreto he came back laden with figs to tell us with glee that they were to be had for a penny the dozen. Afterwards at Ischia he was wild with delight at accomplishing the ascent of Monte Epomeo with the help of a patient moke, and recorded his feelings in doggerel in the visitors' book on the summit. His spirits never flagged. His only regret was that his wife could not be with him to share his pleasure. With all this he was always observing, always enquiring, always giving life and interest to everything we saw. He noted with much satisfaction that Balaam was amongst the prophets sculptured on the marble casing of the 'Santa Casa' at Loreto. He extracted every detail of the legend of the 'Santa Casa' from a young English priest attached to the Cathedral establishment. The stream of pilgrims delighted him. His sympathetic nature made him feel what a very real thing this expression of their devotion was to the simple peasants.

"At Ischia the wonderful beauty of the scenery, the glow of the sunset, the stillness only broken by the singing of the gatherers of the vintage on the plain below, completely fascinated him.

"Every odd moment was occupied with reading or writing, and he would come in to breakfast in the morning full of some story or novel that he had read since the evening before. His power of reading rapidly and his memory of what he had read were both surprising.

"But these are a few dry facts which present most inadequately his living personality. A genial and sympathetic companion, a firm and most affectionate friend, George Grove was a man of loving and reverent spirit, who would spare no pains to be thorough, whether in finishing off any work that he had in hand, or in helping any one whom he felt he could help out of a difficulty, or to make a good start in life, or to improve his position. His memory is cherished by all who knew him and felt his influence for good, and appreciated the simple guileless character which lay behind so much enthusiasm and so much experience of men and things."

On his return to England Grove went down to Newark on November 8th to attend a meeting on behalf of the Palestine Exploration Fund, and put up for the night with Mr. Denison, then Speaker of the House of Commons. Of their conversation he has left the following notes:—

"Amongst other things, we talked of the changes in manners which had taken place of late years and in particular how much less swearing there was, and he told me a story of Lord Melbourne which illustrated how common oaths were even among the most highly educated people. During a debate in the House of Commons on, I think, the Poor Law Bill, which Denison had charge of, some fact or date was wanted which nobody knew exactly, and Denison left the House and ran up to the Home Office to ascertain it. As he got there he found Lord Melbourne just getting on to his horse on the edge of the pavement, and at once told him what was wanted. 'Oh, you must ask my brother George,'[1] he said. 'Well, I have asked

[1] George Lamb, Melbourne's youngest brother, Member successively for Westminster and Dungarvan, and in 1830 Under-Secretary to his brother in the Home Department.

him,' said Denison. 'And what did he say?' was the reply. 'Well,' said Denison, 'he damned me, and he damned the Bill, and he damned the paupers.' 'Well,' said Lord Melbourne G–d d—n it, what more could he do?'"

Grove's work on the *Magazine* and the Palestine Exploration Fund, to say nothing of his multifarious duties at the Crystal Palace, kept him busy for the rest of the year. He also undertook for Mr. Murray to direct and superintend the preparation of the *Biblical Atlas*, which formed part of Dr. Smith's *Atlas of Ancient Geography*. He dined out, however, pretty frequently, and added to his store of strange stories one which he never wearied of telling. He recorded it in one of his pocket-books at the end of 1869 and afterwards dictated it in 1897. The present version is collated from the two MSS. :—

"The following story was told me by Mrs. Mayow Adams and was confirmed by Miss Ursula Mayow. A labouring man who belonged to the parish of Purley near Croydon, was coming home one evening, and as he passed a pond on the boundary between Purley and Addington, he saw some boys fishing something out of the water. 'Hallo! boys,' he cried, 'what have you got there—a cat?' 'No, it ain't a cat, it's a baby and a dead 'un.' 'Let me see it,' said the man, and he at once buttoned it inside his coat and set off running home. His wife brought the little creature to, and the first thing next morning he took it to Dr. C— who was then the vicar of the parish, to know what to do. 'Take it to Purley Parish' said the vicar, but Purley Parish said it was found on the Addington side of the pond, and the Addington people found some similar excuse, and neither would have the child. So in the end Dr. C— said he would take it and promptly baptized it Purley C— giving it his own name. In a year or two the child, which turned out very well and became a great favourite, began to appear in the dining-room, and then it became necessary to decide what was to be done with it. Mrs. C— said to her husband, 'We must make up our minds whether the boy is to be brought up for the kitchen or the parlour.' 'Well, my dear,' said C—, 'God has been very good to us, and we have plenty of money but no children. Suppose we adopt it?' She readily consented, and C— made out his will leaving the whole of his property to Purley. But seven or eight years after Purley was first found, Mrs. C— herself had a baby—a girl, and the will was accordingly altered, the property being divided between the boy and girl. In due course of time Purley was sent to a public school and to Oxford, took orders, and became his reputed father's curate. Miss C— became engaged to be married and the wedding took place in the church which was only divided from the parsonage by the garden. Purley was the officiating clergyman and after the service they all went back to the parsonage for the wedding breakfast. As they were about to sit down, 'Stop,' said the bride, 'we can't begin till Purley is here to say grace. Where is Mr. Purley?' 'I saw him go across the lawn only a few minutes ago,' said one of the servants. From that moment Purley was never seen or heard of again. It is supposed that he had fallen in love with Miss C—, knowing that he was not really her brother, but that he had never mentioned the fact. Poetic justice would demand that he should have been found in the pond where he first made his appearance, but that was not so. No trace of him was ever discovered afterwards."

To judge from his note-books and scrap-books, no subject interested Grove more deeply in 1870 than that of Revision, in regard to which he seems to have entirely sympathized with Stanley, to whom he pays the following memorable tribute in a letter to a friend written early in 1870:—

"All that you said this morning fell with double force on me. You must have noticed how silent and ignorant I was with ——. In this (as in all else) I learn from A. P. S. His eagerness to ask questions of any one he meets is a continual lesson to me. He never minds confessing that he is ignorant.

Grove was also much impressed by Stanley's speech at the public welcome to Baboo Keshub Chunder Sen, when he endorsed Gladstone's view that "it is our duty above all things to avoid the error of seeking to cherish the Christianity of isolation," and his collection of newspaper cuttings shows how carefully he followed and preserved Stanley's contributions—over the signature of "Anglicanus"—to the *Times* and other journals. Grove's own contributions to the Press in 1870 were mainly concerned with the "Moabite Stone." In a letter to the *Times* of February 8, he had spoken of Captain Warren as "the discoverer," but in reply to M. Clermont-Ganneau, he wrote in the issue of March 24th to explain that the real discoverer was "Mr. Klein, of the Prussian community in Jerusalem, who first saw it many months ago." But he goes on to say that as Captain Warren was the first to obtain good working impressions of the stone, he was not so far out in his use of the word "discoverer." This was followed by a letter to the *Pall Mall Gazette*, dated April 18th, and enclosing a letter from Klein giving a narrative of the discovery of the "Moabite Stone" in August 1868, and testifying to the energy and zeal subsequently shown by Captain Warren and M. Clermont-Ganneau. Besides the ordinary meetings of the Palestine Exploration Fund, Grove attended special public gatherings at Windsor and Oxford, and took an active part in promoting the appeal for fresh funds to aid the new operations of the Society.

On its musical side 1870 was chiefly noticeable for the steady accumulation of material relating to the symphonies of Beethoven and Mendelssohn. Grove was a regular attendant at the Philharmonic Concerts, and specially notes the impression made on him by the performance of the E♭ pianoforte Concerto of Beethoven on April 25th; Joachim was his guest in February after playing at the Crystal Palace; and there was no lack of music at the Hullahs', the Frederick Lehmanns' and his own house. Grove took no regular holiday in 1870, but a few weeks after the declaration of war between France and Germany took a run over to Paris, where he spent his birthday, August 13th. Of this visit, however, I can discover no record beyond the clear and unmistakable entry in his almanac of the date of his departure and return to England. It was probably paid in the company of his friend Mr. C. A. Fyffe, who subsequently acted as the Paris correspondent of the *Daily News* and narrowly escaped execution as a spy under the Commune. Mr.

J. C. Grove well remembers how in the course of the war his father used to run out in the morning to buy the *Daily News* and read Fyffe's letters.

Grove sustained a severe loss on August 20th in the sudden death of his old friend Bowley, the general manager of the Crystal Palace, with whom he had worked on terms of great cordiality from the outset, and of whom he never spoke afterwards save in terms of the heartiest goodwill. Bowley appealed to Grove in a variety of ways; as one interested in music; as a genial colleague; and lastly as the unconscious perpetrator of sundry Malapropisms and "bulls" which Grove never tired of relating—a special favourite being the translation of *secundum artem* as "second rate."

In October he spent a couple of days at Margate, a place associated with an anecdote which he was very fond of telling, and recorded in 1897:—

"Dr. Price, an old Margate man, used to say that he had heard the old incumbent of Margate Church preaching on the future delights of the blessed in heaven, and on the certainty that every one would have what he could best appreciate, winding up with the words: 'And for those who prefer light refreshment, there will be light refreshment.'"

Another short visit paid towards the close of the year was to his brother Thomas at Penn, and here again we may draw on the 1897 reminiscences:—

"One Sunday at Penn Church the sexton was ill, and the vicar, Mr. Grainger, brought in his stableman to take the communion alms. My brother sat in a large square pew and the groom not being experienced missed him out and then went back for his alms. But he could not make Grainger understand whom the 5*s*. came from, and therefore, pointing back over his shoulder said, 'From the gentleman in the loose box, sir'! On another Sunday I first saw the yew tree *smoking* in Grainger's garden. When the tree is shaken by the wind at that particular time of the year, the pollen ascends really like the smoke of an altar. Tennyson evidently did not know so much about the yew tree in the early part of his life as he did later. I hink he notices the 'smoking' first of all in one of the *Idylls of he King*, 'I have seen this yew tree smoke for many a year.' But e also mentions it in the second interpolated poem in *In Memoriam*, where he also notices the fact that the yew tree does ;et a little green in the Spring, which he contradicts in poem No. 2 'Old yew . . . O not for thee the glow, the bloom, Who :hangest not in any gale'! Both these facts are noticed in the nterpolated poem :

> "Dark warder of these buried bones,
> And answering now my random stroke
> With fruitful cloud and living smoke."

And again :

> "To thee, too, comes the golden hour
> When flower is fading after flower."

. had the pleasure of telling Longfellow about this when I lined at his house in Harvard in 1878, and he asked me to write him the particulars, a commission which I regret to say I failed o fulfil."

The following letter, dated December 2, 1870, is pleasantly illustrative of the relations that prevailed between Grove and his contributors :—

[*To* Miss Paget]

"Not a word! It is a pleasure to put in a phrase or change a sentence where the matter (*Stoff*) is so good.

"I want to put in the 'Bull Fight'[1] in the January number. Would you look over Freeman's article on Field Sports in the December *Fortnightly* and see if there is anything for your father to notice? Get the number ready for him the next time he has a journey to take. I will send him a proof if he has not got one there. With regard to your own writing, at present it is a little stiff—a good fault but still a fault in papers of that sort. The aim should be to *write like talk* on such a subject. Now in talk one is as picturesque as one can be, and one does not care so very much for the form of sentences, for all the 'whiches' being carefully put in, or all the sentences being in such exact order

[1] An article signed "J. P." (Sir James Paget) which appeared in *Macmillan* for January, 1871. In the same number is a paper on a visit to France during the war, by Mr. J. Scott Russell, a friend of twenty years' standing.

that they can't be mistaken. In a grave treatise that's all right, but in a light paper it hinders freedom. I find (or found, for I don't write now) it a good plan to read a 'good author' before writing. Thackeray is a *model* for such things—in his best books—in *The Newcomes* or *Pendennis* or *Denis Duval*. . . . Also some of the *Saturday Review* papers, though I hate their *Stoff*, are charming for style."

Other contributors were not always so satisfactory, as may be gathered from the following reminiscence of 1897 :—

"During my editorship of *Macmillan's Magazine* I received a very well written account of a ghost story, or rather of immense and inexplicable noises in a house. The writer had held a curacy there, and he and his wife had been frightened out of their lives while drinking their tea on the first evening by a sudden explosion in the hall as if a load of coals had been discharged down stairs, and the same thing occurred again, varied by other curious demonstrations. The story was too good not to be entertained, but I could not do anything with it without some further certificate, and accordingly wrote to the author. His letter, however, did not reassure me, as there was a looseness of statement about it which was rather suspicious. Amongst other things I remember that he told me that the house was close to the church, and that from the sitting-room window there was a view of a splendid Saxon doorway. Now I knew that there were no Saxon doorways to be found either on the border of Shropshire or Wales, the neighbourhood in question, or anywhere else, and there were other evident inaccuracies. He wound up his letter by saying, 'If you know —— the present dean of —— you have only to ask him, for he succeeded me and the nuisance was so great that he had to pull down the parsonage and rebuild it. Oddly enough I saw the Dean, whom I happened to know, a week or two afterwards, but his answer was not reassuring. 'I remember the curacy perfectly well,' he said, 'and a very nice place it was, but I remember nothing of any ghosts; and as for pulling down the house, what we did was to build an additional room or two for the nurseries, as I had more children than it would accommodate.' I need not say that the article never appeared."

It appears from Grove's pocket-books that he began in this year the study of the characters on Chinese porcelain on which at a later date he seriously contemplated publishing a handbook. For the rest, the entries are of the usual miscellaneous character, ranging from notes of a visit to the Abbey with M. Gabriel Monod, with the Dean as cicerone, to transcripts of the quaint sayings of his children, and an American undertaker's advertisement: "No party who has used these coffins has ever used any others."

One of the earliest letters received in 1871 by Grove was from Gounod, then residing in London, indignantly denying a statement made in a Breslau paper to the effect that he (Gounod) had written to the Crown Prince of Prussia about his mother-in-law's house, and offering a million francs to any one who would produce such a letter. On February 27th, Grove was elected to the Athenæum,[1] and paid his first visit to the club as a member on March 1st. Frederick Lehmann, like many others, had been interested in his candidature, and, as throwing a pleasant side-light on Browning's relations with Lehmann and Grove, I am glad to be able to reprint the following note:—

"19, WARWICK CRESCENT,
"*February* 24, '71.

"MY DEAR LEHMANN,—I wish I could fairly promise to oblige you by voting for Mr. Grove, as your friend,—but it happens that I simply oblige myself in so doing, and that I have already signed his certificate in the rooms, as earnest of my purpose to do all in my power on Monday next. You must,—in justice to the extreme desire I cannot help feeling to make you some slight attempt at return for the manifold kindness you have shown myself,—you must tax your ingenuity to pick out, amongst your acquaintances, some really unpleasant and ineligible person; you

[1] His name had been entered, so I am informed by Mr. Henry Tedder, the Secretary of the Athenæum, on August 11th, 1858, proposed by the Dean of Westminster (Stanley) and seconded by Dr. (afterwards Sir) William Smith. He was elected at the ordinary ballot on February 27th, 1871, and on his certificate, which bears a very large number of signatures, he was described as "Honorary Secretary of the 'Palestine Exploration Fund,' and one of its originators. Author of most of the articles on Palestine in the 'Dictionary of the Bible.' Distinguished by extraordinary labour and research. Secretary of the Crystal Palace."

will have difficulty enough, I know,—but find him, and, for your sake, be assured he shall have the vote of,

"Yours ever truly,

"ROBERT BROWNING."

Grove's manner of life in 1871 is pretty clearly indicated by his social and literary engagements, of which we may transcribe a few typical specimens. "Feb 8 Sir. A. Grant on the Moral Principle. 15 'Passion' at Barnby's. March 6 Franklin Taylor at Monday Pop. 11 Joachim in Beethoven Concerto at C. P. 15 Sir M. Costa dinner. 29 Opening of Albert Hall. 30 Dine Macmillans. April 6 'Passion' music at Westminster. 11 Quartets (Straus, Wiener, Zerbini, Piatti). 13 Dine Madame Schumann. 20 Lecture on Petra. 'G' in chair. May 5 Dine Mr. Murray. 12th Huxley at R. I. 16th Froude on Evidence. 22 Philharmonic. Schubert in C."

By way of commentary on this list the testimony of J. R. Green[1] is worth citing. In a letter to Miss Olga von Glehn, written from San Remo on March 10, 1871, *à propos* of the intention of her sister to spend a year in Oxford, Green says :—

"As to studying, there are a thousandfold better lectures to be got in London than in Oxford, and the society of Peak Hill is of a healthier intellectual type, because of a far broader intellectual type, than that of the ——s. Deutsch is a greater scholar, Haweis a greater wit, and George Grove a more accomplished person than any three men she could meet in Oxford, barring Max Müller and one or two she isn't likely to have much to do with."

Green's testimony is all the more valuable from the fact that Grove had recently passed a discouraging judgment on the first chapter of the Short History. "His [Grove's] verdict is a very severe though a very kind one," and later on he speaks of Grove's comments as "very frank and valuable."

Immediately after the fall of the Commune—as a matter of fact it was by the first train that admitted the

[1] *Letters*, p. 290.

outside world—Grove, accompanied by Mr. William von Glehn, hurried off to Paris, where they were shortly afterwards joined by Arthur Sullivan. They were met by William Simpson, the well known artist and war correspondent, who had been in Paris for a good part of the siege and under the Commune, and who now proved a most helpful cicerone. Sullivan, in a letter quoted on p. 79 of Mr. Lawrence's "Life-story" says :—

"I found Grove and Willie Glehn and their surprise was only equalled by their delight. We hired a small open carriage, and drove all through the city to see the ruins—it is something too shocking to see the result of the uncontrolled, devilish spite of these ruffians of the Commune. The people all wear a miserable look, and this, added to the wet, nasty day, and the absence of the greater part of the population makes a very dismal effect."

During their visit Grove and his companions went to the Gymnase, where they saw the famous Aimée Desclée playing to a house of less than a hundred people. On June 5th Grove attended a Requiem service at the Madeleine and was much impressed by the spectacle—the catafalque in the middle, the soldiers ranged along the building, the priests in their black copes and the singing broken in upon by the discordant cries of soldiers carrying and grounding arms. On June 6 he went to Passy, on June 7 he was home again at Sydenham.

The month of July was marked—for Grove—by two or three musical events of more than usual significance. Jules Stockhausen[1] whose singing of Schubert's songs gave Grove the greatest possible delight, gave a Concert on July 5th and on July 7th Grove heard Brahms's *Requiem* for the first time. On August 17th he started for a month's much needed holiday on the continent beginning with the

[1] There is a note of Stockhausen's to Grove, undated, but obviously written in an earlier year, in which he says: "Pray let me know where and at what time I can find you? I must as soon as possible thank you for your kind letter, and I think the only way of doing it well is to sing for you the songs of Schubert you seem to be so fond of. Another reply to such a hearty compliment as yours there is not."

Bonn Festival (August 20-23), where he was principally interested in the performances of the C minor and 'Eroica' Symphonies. Monday night, August 28th, found him at Basle, and an evidence of his mood is found in the prayer written on that date in his pocket-book :—

"O God who hast given us the good gifts of moonlight and sunlight and shade and thick trees and rushing rivers and eyes and ears and hearts to see and hear and feel them—make us to see and hear and feel them to the utmost and Thee through them : soften us and purify us, and make us to love each other and Thee, and bring us to Thy eternal life where there shall be love without misunderstanding and without end, through Jesus Christ our Lord. Amen."

The entries in his almanac read "August 29 Lucerne. 30th Pilatus" and in his pocket-book under the latter date he notes the wealth of flowers, cowslips, and larkspur and the extreme beauty of the mountain ashes. On September 1st he was at Brünig and *à propos* of the view makes the curious comment, "I am not sure but when one is in these panic states one sees a great deal of beauty and gets a great deal of feeling out of scenes and things that would pass unnoticed in rude health.[1]"

Another entry dated Friday, September 11th, is headed "written on some pine logs opposite the waterfall below Brünig" and is in the nature of a commentary on Wordsworth's greatest ode :—

"I can understand Wordsworth's 'thoughts that do often lie, etc.' The sight of the bank of wild flowers where I am now sitting—like many a bit of turf or tree or other natural object at other times—has given me an unutterable feeling in my heart much too big for words, wanting a language which here I have not got. Now no brute or savage can have such feelings. They are certainly real ; there can be no doubt of that—they can be nurtured and increased. Are they then merely transient ? Will they die with our bodies ? I think not and for this amongst other reasons. They are between one's own soul and one's maker, or

[1] Compare Sir Walter Scott's *Journal*, June 22, 1827. "I think illness, if not too painful, unseals the mental eye, and renders the talents more acute, in the study of the fine arts at least."

some thing or person that is altogether above one. They can hardly be communicated though they may be sympathised in, but they have little direct influence on the world around us. They are not like the efforts and results of the intellect which go directly to improve and aid the world. Therefore if they don't survive what do they do, what are they? I know that this is no argument, but still taking into account the very strong piercing nature of these emotions there is perhaps some weight in it."

Later on he writes under the heading "Nach Mürren":—

"I wish I could describe the strange feeling that comes on me as I get higher and higher and more opposite the great mountains. For four hours this morning I have been climbing up and up the side of a valley on the other side of which stand three of these great giants. For the most part of the way the road goes through the most delicious pine-woods, varied every quarter of an hour or so by an opening when you come out into the sun, and then you see the three great creatures, each time as if a little closer than the last, and they are taller and get more definite shape and their features come out more sharply, and what when you looked at it from the valley was merely a distant romantic mass of snow and rock lifted up above one's reach altogether becomes really like a person. . ."

Nach Schmadribach.

"The spot where you gain the edge of a ravine and look down into it is one of great interest. Suddenly a depth is revealed to you that you did not dream of before. The mountains are so much taller, and as you look down you see their great 'roots' spreading out below—the round world itself which cannot be shaken. . . ."

Two further entries made during this tour, from which he returned on September 19th, are worth quoting. In the first he insists on the fact that "all great artists have addressed themselves to the great world of their fellow-men—the mass of sober unimaginative men, not the *élite*." In the second he dwells on two defects in the English language—the lack of a middle term between 'dear' and 'dearest,' and the fact that we have only "one word 'Love' to express the very different feelings towards friend, child, and lover." Other entries show that he was still working away on his life of David, and amassing biographical notes on Mendelssohn and illustrative details for his analyses of Beethoven's symphonies.

The earliest dated entry in Grove's pocket-book for 1872 refers to the account given him by Miss F. Mayow on February 4th of her having seen Napoleon at Torbay, and of the two occasions on which she saw Nelson. The particulars of these "links with the past" are embodied in a letter from Grove to the *Spectator* of February 3, 1894. Music and musicians loom large in his list of engagements—there was the presentation to Mr. Manns in January and the public testimonial to Sterndale Bennett in April; quartets at his own house; the Passion music at the Abbey; the Philharmonic concerts, Madame Schumann's recital, and so forth. Outside the Sydenham coterie he continued to see a good deal of Stanley, Tom Hughes, Vernon Lushington, and the Frederick Lehmanns, while his resignation of the secretaryship to the Crystal Palace Company in the following year is foreshadowed in the brief entry in his diary for July 27 "G. G. to leave C. P." On August 2nd he started for a holiday trip in Scotland, the successive stages of his journey being Glasgow, Oban, Banavie and Inverness, whence he proceeded by Dingwall and Strome Ferry to Loch Carron. On the 13th he crossed to Skye, returning to Loch Carron on the 16th and started for home on the 21st. Casual references in his private correspondence prove him to have been much in need of a holiday, and that he profited by the rest and change. A rough draft of a letter makes it clear that he had already conceived the idea afterwards carried out in his Geography Primer, while his continued interest in the poetry of Tennyson is shown by the following letters:—

[*To* Ernest von Glehn.]

"Lower Sydenham.
"[No month] 1872.

"'How fares it with the happy dead?
For here the man is more and more;
But he forgets the days before
God shut the doorways of his head.

The days have vanish'd, tone and tint,

"MY DEAR E.—I can see no crux in the above, nor anything to cause difficulty if you only supply the word 'there' (or some longer interpolation meaning 'in the next world') between 'but' and 'he' in line 3. What is the condition of the happy dead? *In this world* a man keeps on growing more and more, building always on the past, and recollecting what he *was* before he became what he *is*—but *there*, in that other state, he forgets all that happened to him before his senses were closed by death—the days of his earthly life have vanished, tone and tint. The whole purpose of the poem is to ask what will happen if in the midst of that obliviousness some faint memory—some dim touch of earthly things—should surprise him, and make him question his guardian angel as to what it means. A much harder passage is in XXVI—'Still onward winds.' The general meaning is that as soon as he ceases to live a real life, and only *exists* and Love turns into indifference he hopes Death may come and take him away. That is all clear enough, but why '*the*' indifference? Also in LVI—'Peace, come away.' Who speaks the first stanza? Who are the 'we'? Whose cheeks are pale? And who is it that leaves half his life behind? If his friend is richly shrined in *his* verse, how is it that his work (that is his verse) will fail—then what connexion have 3 and 4 with 1 and 2? I confess this beats me. I must go down to Blackdown and ask the seer unless you can tell me."

Grove did not visit Tennyson, but at the close of the year a letter enclosing a review by R. H. Hutton elicited the following very interesting letter from the poet :—

"ALDWORTH,
"*December 2nd*, 1872.

"MY DEAR GROVE,—Thanks for Hutton. I am not going to criticise the criticism though I may say that his calling the Idylls an Epic, which they are not, is to me a misnomer, and may set my foes blessing—but I wish to say that he had better have let that dictum of Coleridge alone. It is true that in the folly of youth I played some tricks with orthography and metre, but Coleridge ought—only old men get shut up in themselves—to have seen that it was from wantonness, not ignorance. Coleridge's dictum is that I began to write verse before I knew what metre was. Now I perfectly well remember that when I was 8 years old I was unwell one Sunday and could not go to church and my elder brother gave me a slate and said: 'see if you can write verse,' and a subject 'flowers,' and before he came back I had covered both sides of the slate (a large one) with very fair Thomsonian verse and perfectly metrical so that he said: 'you've done it.'[1] When I was 13 or 14 I wrote an Epic between 4 and 5000 lines in Scott's octosyllabic, mingled with heroics, perfectly metrical. I can still recollect portions of it—happily it has vanished from the face of the earth. . . and when about 14 or 15 I commenced a drama perfectly metrical which I have yet, and Hutton or any one may see it, but I shall make away with it before I pass.

"I say all this because my enemies were always quoting C. against me—my friend Hutton should not endorse the dictum. H. is utterly wrong about the Farmer and the Grandmother costing me more labour than other things, wrong too about Maud and the Vision of Sin. I said I would not criticise the criticism, but I see I am doing so—so I stop, saying merely that it is a kindly and reverential article and I am obliged to him for it.

"I am grieved to hear of your being so out of sorts—pray get away as soon as possible and get the fresh blood of leisure and mountain air into your veins. My wife sends her kindest remembrances. You should have come down here, it was my fault not to have asked you. Now we are going but another year you will come. Yours ever,

"A. TENNYSON."

The last entry in Grove's pocket-book for 1872 relates to a visit to Eastbourne some time in December, and contains, besides transcriptions of sundry epitaphs, the following curious speculation: "Surely Heaven will be nothing without regret and longing: perfect satisfaction can never be our lot here or there."

The Sydenham coterie sustained a serious loss in 1873, on May 12th, by the premature and tragic death of Emanuel Deutsch, the great Semitic scholar, author of the remarkable articles on the "Talmud" and "Islam" in the *Quarterly Review*, who had been associated with Grove as a valued contributor to the *Dictionary of the Bible*, and for many years afterwards had belonged to the inner circle of his friends. The bond with Sydenham seemed likely to be

[1] A shorter account of this incident, written by Tennyson in 1890, will be found in his son's *Memoir*, pp. 9 and 10 of the one volume edition of 1899.

drawn all the closer when Deutsch became engaged to one of its most brilliant and attractive residents. But on subsequently learning that he was suffering from an incurable complaint, he broke off the engagement, and travelling to Egypt in the despairing hope that change of scene and climate might arrest the mischief, died at the Prussian Deaconesses' house at Alexandria at the early age of forty-four. Grove, who was suffering from overwork as usual—he wrote on July 6th to his brother-in-law that the visit of the Shah had nearly killed him, adding, "Wildbad appears to be good for cripples . . . it's rather the legs of my mind than of my body that are broken"—started for a trip to the Continent on July 17th, and sent from Wildbad a short article which appeared in the September issue of *Macmillan's Magazine*, dealing with the depreciatory references to Deutsch in the current *Edinburgh Review*. What chiefly and justly provoked Grove's resentment was the epithet "superficial" as applied to Deutsch's "Talmud" article in the *Quarterly Review*. He was well qualified to speak on the subject, as Deutsch was living in lodgings in Sydenham when he wrote the article, and frequently consulted Grove while it was in progress:—

"No article was ever less 'got up.' No single page of it can have been written without knowing all about the matter, without that familiarity which years and years of incessant affectionate study, aided by a burning nationality, and guided by the genius and impulse of a true poet, can alone recall. How he laboured and selected and wrote and re-wrote, and destroyed and wrote again, those few only know who saw him in the process of composition. How he succeeded it is hardly necessary to recall. Perhaps it is not too much to say that no review-article was ever devoured by so large a number of readers—and competent readers. . . . It procured for its author the immediate acquaintance of the most eminent scholars of the day, and at once raised him to a high rank in London literary society. . . . No doubt so splendid an introduction should have been followed by an extended and systematic work—so glorious an overture by the entire Opera. And this was the steadfast purpose of my friend. It never forsook him; he struggled on with it through the terrible, long, wearing, painful disease which at length carried him off." But the materials left were too fragmentary to be of any practical value, and "there is nothing for it but to join with the Dean of Westminster and say, 'It is the greatest calamity of the kind that could have happened to me.'"

From Wildbad Grove went by way of Freudenstadt to Rippoldsau in the heart of the Black Forest, where he stayed for the best part of three weeks. Here he fell in with W. H. Thompson (the Master of Trinity), and H. E. Pellew, a club friend at the Athenæum, and has left copious notes of their conversations:—

"Thompson told me a curious story of coincidence or rather second sight. His sister was stopping with some friends at or near Hull. One morning she came down to breakfast and her hostess said, 'What is the matter, Miss Thompson, you don't look well this morning.' 'No,' she replied, 'I have had a very extraordinary dream. I dreamt that I came down to breakfast here as usual, and that in the middle of the meal the servant opened the door and said to me, "You are wanted to speak to somebody in the hall." I went into the hall and found there the servant of my brother (not the Master). He said "Miss Thompson, you are wanted at home, your brother has broken his leg and is in some danger."' While she was speaking the servant opened the door and said to her, 'Miss Thompson, you are wanted to speak to somebody in the hall.' It was her brother's servant with precisely the same message, and she went off at once to him. The Master said he had only very lately seen his sister and she had given him the details of the story exactly as he told me."

Another story related to a visit to Harrow which Thompson had made with Arthur Stanley, where they had to examine for a prize at the end of the term. They were late in finishing the examination and did not get done till between eleven and twelve o'clock. When they had finished, Vaughan came in to make some civil inquiries, and took them for a moonlight walk in the Master's garden. He then left them saying, "Well, now, I must go away and write a sermon to be preached to the boys to-morrow morning, and I hope you will come and hear it." Thompson did so in the morning, and a better sermon he never heard. He told Vaughan his opinion and Vaughan said, "It will probably be printed and I will send you a copy." The copy came in due time, and to his disappointment Thompson could not read it at all, it was so dull. "He told me this," adds Grove, "as an instance of the very careful way in which Vaughan brought out his sermons in delivering them. He said that the effect in reading them as compared to that in hearing them from Vaughan's own mouth was as nothing. I remember to have been struck with some of his manuscripts, which I have seen and in which the words were extraordinarily marked for his elocution."

Thompson also gave Grove Thackeray's impromptu on Spedding :—

> "There was a young party named Spedding,
> Who tore cigars up for his bedding.
> His head was so bare
> That you really might swear
> He had danced at his grandmother's wedding."

On August 1st Grove went over to visit Karl Mendelssohn at Freiburg, being now, as at all times, most anxious to obtain any first hand information about the composer. About the middle of August he moved on to Bonn for the Schumann Festival, and on the 23rd paid the Duke of Meiningen a visit at Liebenstein. From him, again, he gained some reminiscences of Mendelssohn, and was told the following story of William IV., who visited the Schloss Altenstein, while he was Duke of Clarence, on matrimonial plans intent :—

> "It was then the custom, which I believe is still maintained in the fine weather, to dine under a large tree on the terrace outside the house. The Duke was asked whether he would object to dining there and his answer left nothing to be desired. He said : 'Je n'aime pas partager mon dîner avec les mouches.'"

Grove, who returned home at the end of August, had been giving a great deal of attention to the study of Chinese porcelain, and his pocket-books for 1873-4 are full of hundreds of drawings of jars and vases and careful copies of their "marks." That he intended embodying his researches in permanent form is indicated pretty clearly in the following rough draft of a preface to a projected handbook on the subject. It runs as follows :—

"This little book is concerned with blue and white Oriental china only. It is little more than a translation of a portion of the great work of M. Stanislas Julien on China porcelain—itself chiefly a translation from a Chinese treatise—and was provoked by the pretension inaccuracy and incompetence of the existing works on the subject with which the writer came in contact. He has added to the information taken from M. S. J. some marks of his own collecting and some remarks on the appearance and characteristics of the porcelain of various dates, made from his own observations."

The scheme was never carried out—probably because the big book he was soon to undertake for Messrs. Macmillan left him no time to write "little books" always excepting the Geography Primer on which he was already engaged.

By September Grove was in a position to announce to his friends his resignation of the Secretaryship of the Crystal Palace in order to enter on his new duties with the firm of Macmillan. Of the letters congratulating him on the change two may here be given. Mr. John Murray wrote on September 18th :—

"DEAR BROTHER BIBLIOPOLE,—I will not congratulate you because the new Profession you have assumed involves very serious responsibilities ; but I will offer you my sincere wishes for your success in it. I am heartily glad also that you are freed from the trammels and drudgery of the C. P. It was like putting a racehorse to draw a diligence. . . . With all good wishes for your health and prospects I am, dear Grove, yours very sincerely,

"JOHN MURRAY."

The other was from the brilliant and indomitable J. R. Green, and tells its own story without any comment :—

"4, BEAUMONT STREET,
"*September* 19*th*, 1873.

"Many thanks, dear Grove, for all your kind offers. I am better now again—shaken and feverish, of course, and bothered at the breakdown of my hopes that I might be able to fight out the winter in England. But I am quite up to work again and somehow I find proofs and noises just the sort of mechanical drudgery which 'dulls' the mind and keeps one from useless regrets. I am immensely glad of your deliverance from the C. P. both for your own sake and for Macmillan's. What a fine fellow Mac. is, when one comes to know and understand him. It was one of my fixed fancies in life that I never could like a Scotchman: but I have got very fond of Macmillan in spite of it. It is just the work you can do better than almost any man; and I have an odd notion that just as we have got to learn what the capacities of Literature are as a profession, we have still to realize what Publishing may be, and what an immense power a Publisher might wield for good without the least neglect of business considerations. But it seems to me that all the good things in the world lie in a future I shall never see. Goodbye. Many *real* thanks. Yours ever,

"J. R. GREEN."

The close of 1873 was also marked by an event in which Grove took an especial interest—the laying of the foundation stone on December 18 of the National Training School of Music, the forerunner of the Royal College of Music, which was opened for study in 1876 with Arthur Sullivan as Principal, and John Stainer, Ernst Pauer, Franklin Taylor, J. F. Bridge, Ebenezer Prout and others as professors. The building, which was presented by Mr. C. J. Freake, subsequently served as the home of the Royal College of Music until its transference to the new buildings in Prince Consort Road.

Throughout the year Grove was as assiduous as ever in his attendance at the principal concerts. Indeed it may fairly be contended that inability to appreciate Wagner and Liszt's music was certainly not due to avoiding his opportunities of enlightenment. In 1873, for example, he went to three Wagner concerts, and two organized by Walter Bache. With regard to Wagner, as will be seen later on, these efforts continued till the end of his life, and he always refrained from advertising his antagonism. Brahms had already come to be added to his list of musical heroes, and his devotion to Schubert grew with every year. As he was walking along the streets in the City early in 1873 his eye was caught with the legend "Shoobert and Grove, wine bottlers," a collocation that at once tickled his fancy and pleased his sense of the fitness of things. The omen was duly entered in his pocket-book and was often laughingly referred to in after years.

Though Grove was not a whole-hearted admirer of Wagner, he sympathised with him entirely in the matter of dogs. One of the most favoured of all his fourfooted friends was a collie named "Help," various events in whose life are duly entered in Grove's diary. "May 4. 'Help' brought back" refers to the fortunate chance by which a friend recognized the dog, which had been stolen and sold, and purchased him from the new owner. "May 5. Saw 'Help' again first" needs no explanation.

CHAPTER VII

The Dictionary of Music: contributors and assistants—Grove's methods and enthusiasm—His multifarious interests—Visits Düsseldorf, May 1875—Hard at work on his Beethoven article—D.C.L. of Durham, June, 1875—Dean Stanley at Norwood—A letter from Robert Browning—Extracts from Grove's note-books—His views on the connection of Music and Morality—Reminiscences of Manning and Newman—Conversation with Rubinstein—Trollope's story of Bonteen—The Geography Primer—Meets Wagner in 1877—With Stanley at Alderley—Work on the Dictionary—Relations with the Firm of Macmillan.

In January 1874 the prospectus of the *Dictionary of Music and Musicians*, the editorship of which was entrusted to Grove, was issued by Messrs. Macmillan. The prospectus, after dwelling on the absence of a comprehensive English work on the subject, set forth the aim and scope of the projected work, which was originally intended to be completed in 2 volumes demy 8vo. of not more than 600 pages each :—

"There is no book in English from which an intelligent inquirer can learn, in small compass, and in language which he can understand, what is meant by a Symphony or Sonata, a Fugue, a Stretto, a Coda, or any other of the technical terms which necessarily occur in every description or analysis of a concert or a piece of music ; or from which he can gain a readable and succinct account of the history of the various branches of the art, or of the use and progress of the pianoforte and other instruments, or the main facts and characteristics of the lives of eminent musicians. Such questions are now constantly occurring to those who five-and-twenty years ago would never have thought of them. Within that period music in England has made immense progress and the number of persons who attend concerts and practise music has very largely increased. It is no longer regarded as a mere idle amusement, but has taken, or is taking, its right place beside the other arts, as an object of study and investigation."

The response from the musicians whom Grove sought to enlist under his banner was immediate and encouraging. Amongst the first to answer the appeal were Sullivan, Hullah, J. W. Davison, C. V. Stanford, Hubert Parry (who acted as his sub-editor in the early stages of the work), Dr. W. Pole, Ernst Pauer, Ebenezer Prout, Sir Frederick Gore-Ouseley, and E. Dannreuther, and in nearly every case the writers placed themselves unreservedly at the service of the editor. Others who followed suit with equal alacrity were William Chappell, A. J. Hipkins, W. H. Stone, Paul David, to mention only a few out of many. The friendly relations that Grove in his frequent visits to the Continent had already established with many foreign musicians stood him in excellent stead. C. F. Pohl, his devoted Viennese friend, was a tower of strength from the outset, not only offering to do all that was asked of him but securing the services of other competent writers. What Pohl did for Vienna, Gustave Chouquet did for Paris. Furthermore, while enlisting the aid of experts strong on the technical and scientific sides of the art, Grove did not neglect to call in, where necessary, the assistance of those who approached the subject from the historical or archæological standpoint. Thus we find amongst the contributors the names of C. A. Fyffe, the historian, H. Sutherland Edwards, E. H. Pember, Horatio F. Brown, Lionel Cust, Reginald Lane Poole, and Julian Marshall. But the printed list of contributors gives no idea of the number of authorities who indirectly assisted in the Dictionary. Thus early in 1874 we find Grove in communication with Mandell Creighton (the late Bishop of London) with reference to the portraits in the Music School at Oxford and early Italian Academies. In 1876 we find him repeatedly consulting Mr. Edward

Speyer on a variety of minute points connected with the Viennese currency in order to clear up certain difficulties involved in the question of Beethoven's pension, &c. The character for "extraordinary labour and research," with which Grove was credited on his certificate paper at the Athenæum, was fully maintained throughout his editorial labours in connection with the *Dictionary of Music.* Mr. Dannreuther, whom Grove was in the habit of consulting on technical matters, tells me that "letters came almost daily while 'G.' was working at his article on Beethoven." Mention already has been made of Pohl, his correspondence with whom alone would fill a volume.[1] Then there was Mr. A. Thayer, the author of the classical work on Beethoven, with whom he had begun to correspond as far back as 1864. Thayer was obliged to devote his entire energies to the *Life of Beethoven*, but though he never contributed directly to Grove's Dictionary, he was of the greatest indirect assistance in answering questions, verifying references, anecdotes, etc., and assisting Grove in following up any clues which he considered likely to enhance the personal interest of his narrative—witness his queries about the Lobkowitz, Lichnowsky and Esterhazy families. It was characteristic of Grove's method, again, that he was never content with getting merely secondhand information from books. He invariably relied where possible on the living links with the past, establishing communications by letter or personal interview with the family, descendants, and friends of those about whom he had to write. With all the members of the Mendelssohn family in particular he set up the most friendly relations, and visited them frequently on his trips to the Continent. His correspondence and scrap-books abound with evidences of his indefatigable curiosity—his enthusiastic importunity in

[1] Pohl's letters show that every detail of any musical interest in Vienna was at once communicated by him to Grove. They abound in quaint but charming instances of his devotion and gratitude. "How often I think on you," he writes in one, "when I read about the Crystal Palace. . . . You work like a giant. Your name will stand as long as the Palace stands and 5,000 years longer."

following up a trail. Thus Fräulein Geisler-Schubert tells me how he wrote begging her to ask her grandmother for any particulars she remembered about her brother-in-law the composer. And when his old friend Mr. C. A. Barry, whom, like Mr. Dannreuther and other experts he constantly consulted on technical points, was going to Munich a few years later, Grove wrote begging him to get all the information he could out of old Lachner, a contemporary and friend of Schubert's, adding "an unpublished letter or anecdote are always nuts to a biographer." It is not too much to say that he never missed an opportunity or threw away a chance of adding to his stock of materials. If he freely utilized the labours and the learning of others, he did not fail to acknowledge his indebtedness. Of the value of the *Dictionary of Music* and of Grove's contributions to it occasion will be found to speak later on; for the moment it is enough to say that no editor ever entered on his task with greater enthusiasm or carried it through with more laborious or conscientious industry.

Though Grove had resigned the Secretaryship of the Crystal Palace—his services were acknowledged by the presentation of a silver inkstand from the staff and a handsome set of plate from the Directors—his connection was maintained by his joining the board and above all by his continuing to edit the programmes for the Saturday Concerts, which he attended regularly. When Brahms's Variations on a theme by Haydn were given for the first time at the Crystal Palace in 1874, Grove sent a complimentary letter to the composer on behalf of the subscribers, expressing their admiration and hopes of favours to come in the shape of a symphony. Another famous German musician with whom he was in touch this year was Hans von Bülow, whose crisp incisive notes Grove carefully preserved.

After attending the Prize day, on July 28th, at Marlborough, where his two eldest sons were at school, Grove crossed to Paris on the 31st, and spent the best part of a month in Switzerland at Chamonix, Bel Alp, Andermatt, Lucerne and Basle. No records of this tour are available beyond a few notes in an almanac. Of the journey from Bel Alp to Brieg he writes, "horrid walk down (*quà* feet), but lovely views and good frame of mind," while his sojourn at Basle elicits the comment "always a good time at Basle."

Earlier in the year the date of a meeting of the Metaphysical Society is recorded in his almanac, but Mr. James Knowles, on referring to the Minutes of the Society, assures me that Grove's name never appears after December 19th, 1871, adding, "he never read a paper, and I rather think he never spoke in a debate. I fancy he only joined on account of Stanley." But though he was gradually concentrating his energies more and more on music, Grove was by no means inclined to abandon his other interests. As the columns of the *Times* for 1874 show, he continued his advocacy of the claims of the Palestine Exploration Fund, while his pocket-books are full of notes for his Geography Primer, memoranda on Chinese Porcelain and sketches of his projected Handbook to the Bible. One of his great points about the Bible was its essential unity, a view which he develops in the following passage: "These twenty-four books, though written by so many different writers and at such different ages, are yet one as much as the plays of Shakespeare. The ground of the unity is the strong nationality that inspires each one. 'Thou shalt see Jerusalem in prosperity all thy life long' is the keynote." He goes on to compare the Bible to an autobiography, as it gives you not only actions but the springs of action. Another witness to the freshness of his view is found in his contention that the writings of the Prophets were political. "There was then no distinction between religion and politics. Jehovah was the ruler of the nation. Righteousness, Justice and Truth were His law, and injustice and untruth were treason and disloyalty."

The last entry for 1874 is a quotation from Rogers: "Whenever you are angry with one you love, think that that dear one might die that moment. Your anger will vanish at once;" and for many years afterwards Grove repeated this sentiment on the first page of his pocket-books as a guiding maxim for the intercourse of friends. But, as I have already mentioned, everything that interested Grove was entered in these little books. He was always much amused by the quaint sayings of his own children, and two "Malaprops" of his daughter Millicent's—"Take a good whelp of it," and "Papa, why do we have three fires all at once? Why does not all the family congratulate itself in one room?"—belong to the opening weeks of 1875. Grove was already hard at work on Beethoven and immersed in correspondence with contributors; yet, like the busiest men, always found time to write letters of a non-obligatory nature. Thus after the memorial concert in honour of Sterndale Bennett at the Crystal Palace on March 6—Sterndale Bennett died on February 1st, 1875—we find him writing to the composer's son: "I never realized till yesterday what a difference death makes in such cases. I have always been fond of your father's music, but yesterday it was all lifted on to a higher plane." Grove's taste in music had some limitations but it may safely be said that he never waxed enthusiastic over what was unworthy. Brahms he admired from the very outset, and this year he was at pains to have a translation made of a notice by Hanslick, the Viennese critic, of a performance of the *Deutsches Requiem*, in February 1875, in which the writer notes the altered attitude of the public since the first performance of a part of the work in 1867.

In the spring of 1875 Grove paid a flying visit to Germany in order to attend the 52nd Lower Rhenish Festival at Düsseldorf on May 16th–18th. Joachim conducted, and the programme included Beethoven's *Missa Solennis* and Handel's *Hercules* as its chief choral features. Here are his rough notes on the performances as jotted down in his pocket-book:—

"Chorus and band not first rate. Fine singing by Henschel and Madame Joachim as Hercules and Deianira. Mozart's *Jupiter* a very rough, coarse performance, ditto *Meeresstille.* Schumann's Symphony, immense spirit, but might have been more refined. *Schicksalslied*—a most beautiful work. Songs very good. Concerto played with great delicacy and fire and well accompanied. But so severe a strain should not have been thrown on Joachim. Pauses between moments of symphony much too long. Applause excessive and quite absurd. *Tusches*, bouquets, &c. Garland on Joachim's head."

Though he found the standard of excellence in the performances inferior to that attained at Bonn in a previous year, it is evident that he enjoyed himself considerably and added to his stock of illustrative material for the biographies of Beethoven and Mendelssohn. He notes also the following dialogue between a friend of his and Brahms :

"X. Do you smoke much, Herr Brahms ?
B. No—I never smoke at night.
X. And perhaps you don't smoke at work ?
B. O, I'm a very lazy man. I never work."

Brahms was evidently a difficult nut for any interviewer to crack. Following hard on this entry is another of a grotesque epitaph, "Sacred to the memory of Methusaleh Perry, aged 12 months," followed in turn by a sheaf of French puns and these bizarre lines :

"So when the last shrill flageolet shall sound,
And call out dicky-birds from holy ground,
This little corpse again its wings shall prune
And sing eternally the self-same tune
From everlasting night to everlasting noon."

Before and after Düsseldorf Grove paid short visits to his brother Thomas at Penn, when he speaks of working twelve and thirteen hours a day at his Beethoven article, and complains of a "wearing and deepening sense" of his own "increasing inability," adding, however, "when I realise as I have done lately, how painfully and slowly Beethoven worked (the Choral Symphony took him eight years), I ought not to grumble." In the same letter—to his sister-in-law Miss Marian Bradley—he condemns his account of his visit to Vienna in 1867 as "fearfully gushing" but continues :—

"Still it's all real enough, I can tell you. Yes. I do love to think of it and of fifty other foolish things in my life besides, though on the whole a review of life makes me low. So much talk and fun and so little done. Oh I have one good thing to tell you of—a raw German pianoforte player whom I met at Düsseldorf came to me on Friday. When he went away he said 'Well, goodbye—*for review*,' wasn't it neat for *Auf wiedersehen?*"

In the previous December Professor A. S. Farrar of Durham University had, in a letter to the local press, suggested that an honorary degree should be conferred on the "illustrious geographer, Mr. Grove," adding "it is a disgrace that this learned and reverent writer remains without a degree." The suggestion evidently met with a cordial support, for on June 29th, 1875, a Convocation of Durham University conferred the honorary degree of Doctor of Civil Law on "George Grove, the eminent civil engineer, and the present editor of *Macmillan's Magazine*, for the great services rendered to literature by his writings." I offer no excuse in reproducing the speech in which Professor Farrar introduced the new doctor, as it contains a singularly just appreciation of the peculiar qualities and merits of Grove's work :—

"Professor Farrar said that the University conferred that degree to mark its sense of the value of Mr. Grove's writings in that branch of Biblical learning which related to historical geography. It might be permitted to him to testify to the startling impression which the perusal of Mr. Grove's first published papers on this subject created in Oxford about fifteen years ago. It was felt that a new writer had appeared who, without a special University training, and immersed in the engagements of life, had evinced such a knowledge of the Hebrew language, and such a ripeness of judgment, that placed him at once in the first rank in the department of theological study to which he had devoted himself. These writings, though they appeared in the modest form of articles in Smith's *Dictionary of the Bible*, were in many cases in reality little treatises, which must have made a name for their author if they had appeared in the learned periodicals of Germany, and were characterised by that combination of physical and historical inquiry which had marked the gifted German geographer Karl Ritter. Mr. Grove's literary work was not only thorough, but original; not merely a reproduction of materials collected from foreign sources, but was marked by that freshness which belonged to original inquiry. He was 'a voice and not an echo'; a voice, too, which gave forth tones of reverence and faith. They in Durham that day added their tribute of respect, and at the same time were able by that act to testify as a University their interest in the important work of exploration now being carried out in the Holy Land by the society, for conducting which Mr. Grove had liberally given his help as Honorary Secretary, and the success of which lay near to his heart. In adding Mr. Grove that day to the roll of their members they truly felt that the University was receiving an honour as well as conferring one."

Writing a few days later, Grove's brother-in-law, the Rev. J. C. Harrison, while congratulating him on the honour, very properly emphasized Grove's claim to recognition:—

"No one has done so much in one department of Biblical literature as you. No one has more zealously striven to make the Bible intelligible and attractive to all than you. This is very widely acknowledged by competent men. In the present instance you *give* far more honour than you receive; for your name is more than any degree, and Durham will be proud that it was on *her* roll you were first written 'D.C.L.'"

That Grove appreciated the distinction is abundantly clear from a letter, dated July 5th, 1875, to his sister-in-law, Miss Marian Bradley. "Of course," he says, "I wish it had been Oxford instead of Durham, but considering how entirely unsought it was, and how nicely it was proposed to me, and what a very warm reception I had, I should be a brute to be dissatisfied . . . The Cathedral is the finest Norman in England, all built in about fifty years, and not clumsy as Norman often is, but beautifully proportioned. Freeman was there and took me all over it." Yet though his mood was not ungrateful, he was far from being self-satisfied. Writing to the same correspondent on August 12th, he says :—

"Tomorrow I am 55 years old and what am I? As much a slave as I was at 35, as little near the attainment of any settled position of mind and spirit as I ever was. I am active and energetic and ready to do my best, but the day for *that* is gone. I ought now to be reaping the fruits, and feeling like Stanley or Jowett or other men of my own age that I am enjoying the harvest of my earlier years. You who know me well must feel how very far I am from that, and the thought presses on me very much. Of course you will say—no you won't say—but it might be said—'Shut up such grievances in your heart and don't confess them'—but to confess is with me a necessity : it does me good by the mere act and may get me useful advice. I ought not at my time of life to be a mere shuttlecock at the sport of all the people who employ me or have the least claim on me. I ought somehow to have more *weight* and leisure—but I can't get it. And yet I feel in myself plenty of capacity."

In the months of August and September Grove had for neighbours at Norwood Dean Stanley and Lady Augusta, whose health had already begun to fail, and in a letter to his daughter he describes a sermon preached by the Dean at St. Bartholomew's on August 29th :—

"MY DEAREST MILL,—Thank you very much for your nice long letter. We had a day of excitements yesterday. I will tell you all. The Dean preached at St. Bartholomew's, but it was not certain he would be able to leave Lady Augusta, and at any rate he would not come till the beginning of the Communion service, so till he appeared I was not easy in my mind. However, at last I saw his dear white head, and heard his clear loud voice reading the Commandments. Then he preached. It was about sacrifice. He gave a picture of the old Temple, with hundreds of oxen, sheep and goats, lowing and bleating—blood running about as they were killed, thick smoke ascending from the altar, and a revolting smell of burning meat all around—and then contrasted that with Christian worship, and with the *sacrifice* which we make when we give up a darling wish because it is not right, or because it may hurt some one else, or because we think God will not like it. It was a long sermon, but every one listened to the end. . . . Persian is not at all well. She cries so loud and so much and yet purrs; and is always in my cupboard."

Among the names that appear for the first time in his lists of social engagements in 1874 and 1875 are those of Sir Henry Taylor, Sir Frederick Goldsmid, the Orientalist, Frederick Leighton, and Lieut. Kitchener R.E., now Lord Kitchener, then doing good work for the Palestine Exploration Fund; while on the 1st of December he received the following charming letter from his friend Robert Browning, in reply to one in which Grove had acknowledged and expressed his admiration of *The Inn Album*:—

"19, WARWICK CRESCENT W.,
"*November* 30*th*, '75.

"MY DEAR GROVE,—How very good you are, and how grateful ought I to be! Your copy went to you by a dozen rights—Grove, the Orientalist, the Schubertian, the Literate in ordinary and extraordinary, and the old valued acquaintance (I won't presume farther) into the bargain. Do I forget the day, dinner and all, when Rubinstein broke your piano in the rush of his inspiration? But your liking my book is not so absolutely a matter of course as your receiving it—and I am very glad indeed that it interests you. If anybody considers it 'unnatural and revolting,' as I see a critic does, from whom better judgment was presumable, you may tell them the story is true, except in the infinitely less revolting circumstances which I have softened away—to their disappearance indeed. So, take my true thanks, and best wishes in return for your own, and believe me ever, truly yours,

"ROBERT BROWNING.'

Grove's pocket-books for the close of 1875 are mainly filled with notes connected with the *Dictionary of Music*—lists of subjects, and names, &c. There is, however, an interesting memorandum of a conversation with his old friend, J. W. Davison, on the stupidity and insolence of the Philharmonic Directors in their treatment of Mendelssohn, and an amazing examination paper answer to the question, Give a general description of Mozart—"Mozart was an Egyptian by extraction. He lived through the last century, and his habitat was Central Europe." Grove delighted in these "howlers," another of which, recorded at the same time, is the translation of *odor immundus* by "an unearthly smell;" while, *à propos* of the story of the German governess who found a prayer for herself in the petition "for all women labouring of child," he adds, "this was told by S. Oxon [Wilberforce] to Ouseley as having been said to himself." One can easily imagine with what delight Grove retailed these and other favourite anecdotes at his "Smoky Evenings," an informal sort of entertainment for his friends which he instituted about this time, and at which Sir Henry Thompson, Hubert Parry, Dr. Pole, and Prinsep were to be found among the guests.

Grove's ability to find time to answer letters, no matter how busy he was, and no matter what the subject might be, has already been noticed. And though—or perhaps because—these letters were often dashed off without any pretence at style or completeness, they always had something characteristic in them: as you read them you saw him before you speaking, laughing, gesticulating. The following letter to his sister-in-law Mrs. Bull, dated January 28th, is interesting, not only because it sets forth his views on the meaning of Music and its relation to morals and culture, but because it reveals the fact that he was himself the author of the ingenious "Phaethon" programme for the last movement of Schubert's C major Symphony:—

"It is an abysmal subject—that of the meaning of music and its power to cultivate. As to the latter, anything that obliges you to think, and observe, and compare, is a cultivating agent, and this music evidently does, *if you look at it in that way;* but you may choose not to take that trouble, but just let it go through your senses, and please, or rouse and lull them—but even that is a cultivation. And that is one reason why I did my C. P. programmes, because it added so much to my own pleasure in listening to observe how the subjects came back and were treated, and were related to one another, or were like those in other pieces, &c. As to the *meaning* I have always been puzzled. Mendelssohn insists (in a letter to Souchay) that it has a meaning *far more definite* than words. That I *can't* understand, though I have tried over and over. There must be something vague and undefined in the word 'meaning,' and at the best it is a meaning for *him*, and may be (but need not necessarily be) the same meaning for others. As to Miss —— [a lady who had submitted a paper to 'G' with a view to its appearing in *Macmillan's Magazine*] I really hardly know what to advise. Her paper at present I feel sure no editor would take, and yet a woman who has thought so much about the subject ought to be able to write something that would do us all good. If I were writing it I think I should begin by defining what I meant by culture. If culture is outside of morals, then music may be a cultivator, but I can't see that it has anything to do with morals. A particular piece of music may have made some one say 'Entbehren sollst du, sollst entbehren,' but it is more than a chance that it conveyed quite an opposite idea to his neighbour. *I* have a definite story connected with the Finale of Schubert's great Symphony, and because I have written it down probably some hundreds of people have the same—but only because of that—probably no one else would ever have thought of the Fall of Phaethon in common with it. So too in the *Hebrides* overture, in the working-out, I am always transported from Staffa to the bay of Naples and see the nymphs floating across the bay, and everything bright and sunny, and Triton's shells blowing far and near, and deep coves in the depths of the sea, &c. but I can't believe—at least I can't be certain—that F. M. B. meant that. In fact judging by two stories of his (too long to tell here) he did not mean it at all.

"Will you please tell me who Miss —— is, and if there is any chance of my meeting her? I am sorry to be so discouraging to her. If culture means refinement of mind, or of morals, thoughtfulness, unselfishness, power to divine the feelings of others—or of manners, then I am bound to say some of the best musicians are the most uncultivated. It is an absolute mystery to me.

"How I did want all those people to go away and leave us alone. I had such a lot to tell you, but I could only get it out bit by bit. If only some one would only give me a small Deanery!"

Grove's diary for 1876 has the entry "Manning to Concert," opposite the date February 5th, which may serve as an excuse for the insertion of the following reminiscences dictated in 1897:—

"I was sitting in my office at the Crystal Palace one afternoon —I forget the year—when I heard a knock at the door. I said 'Come in' and to my astonishment Cardinal Manning opened the door. He said 'I have been taking the chair at our annual Temperance meeting, but my duties are now over, and I have come to see you: we have many friends in common and I have often heard of you. Why not have a walk together and become better acquainted?' 'O certainly,' I said; 'I shall be delighted and proud, but let us make an agreement not to talk of ecclesiastical matters, because I cannot agree with you, and yet you will not convince me.' 'Certainly,' he said. 'I want to show you the town and gardens which the Oratorians have on Sydenham Hill'; and we walked to that delightful spot. It is about a mile from the Palace on the upper part of the Hill. I found it charming—a plain house to which the Fathers of the Oratory come when they are not well and want a day or two's rest. It was then in charge of the gardener, an excellent Irishman named O'Brien, and his wife, and the Cardinal introduced me to them, and gave them his orders to admit me with any of my friends whenever I presented myself there. We walked about the delightful garden and at last found our way to the burial ground. It is a plot of a quarter of an acre or so surrounded by monthly roses in full bloom. There were then only some half a dozen graves, among which I remember those of Faber, Gloag and Hutchinson—particularly interesting to me on account of his controversy with Stanley (*Sinai and Palestine*, edition of 1881, p. 446 note). After this Manning and I met not infrequently. We were members of the same club and often met there. I also breakfasted with him once or twice at his house in Westminster. One point we discussed more than once was the florid music of the Mass, to which he had a rooted objection. He very much preferred merely vocal services without accompaniment—such as those of Palestrina, Vittoria, &c., and if he had lived I cannot but think he would have taken a more decided step in that direction. His intercourse with me on this and any other subject was marked by the utmost kindness. Of another great ecclesiast of the day, Newman, I saw but little, but that little was characteristic. I went to hear one of his lectures ('Anglicans under Difficulties') very soon after he went over. It was held in the then chapel of the Oratorians which afterwards became Toole's Theatre, when the Oratorians moved to their new chapel at Brompton. I do not remember the exact subject of the lecture, but the part which much interested me was his reference to men who were certainly good men, and yet were quite in error in their attitude towards the Church—for instance 'What are we to say with respect to such people as Bunyan or Wesley, or to that remarkable man who doubted the efficacy of sacramental grace at night and'—in the most solemn tone—'died in the morning,' evidently referring to Arnold and his conversation with Lake reported in Stanley's *Life*, then only recently published (vol. ii. p. 329), which struck me then and always since as most unjust criticism. It produced an indescribable effect on his audience. The same sermon afforded an extraordinary instance of Newman's absolute indifference to passing circumstances. He became hoarse, and suddenly interrupting himself in the flow of his discourse he began to clear his throat, louder and louder each time, beating himself on the breast as if no one were present, but he were absolutely alone, and then, having overcome the difficulty, went on entirely unmoved. It produced a great impression on me, which I have never forgotten. I saw him again, I think on a railway platform, and last of all at a Birmingham Festival, where I sat behind him in the President's Gallery at one of the morning concerts, and had a good look at his face as he passed me in going out. He had a bright colour, but had aged greatly since I saw him before."

Grove's pocket-book for the spring and summer of 1876, which has on its inner leaf Matthew Arnold's lines "Calm Soul of all things, make it mine, &c.," is full of interesting memoranda. To begin with there is a grim entry headed, "Mr. Greg's Story," which may be commended to any modern novelist in search of a gruesome plot:—

"A beautiful English lady had had two husbands who had each died not suspiciously but suddenly. A gentleman, friend of the second, was much piqued at this, and at last married her in order to find out the secret. She was fond of him and he became fond of her. On one occasion he observed her extreme horror of a man who had taken too much to drink, and (always thinking of the secret) he resolved to feign the same. He did and irritated her extremely. He did so again and then found out that she got out of bed, got a phial, and was just about to pour something into his ear when he opened his eyes and caught her arm. He then collected the evidence of the deaths of the former husbands and—hanged her."

Under date May 27th we find the following fragmentary notes of a conversation with Rubinstein, which foreshadows a good deal of the *brochure* which Rubinstein published a good many years later on *Music and its Representatives* :—

"Bach very much first.
Then Beethoven.
Schubert.
Chopin.

and then one of our [composers] Glinka.

"Haydn is not in my line. I do not like a man to have made a Symphony every Sunday for his patron's dinner and a quartet for the evening. No doubt he was very great. But he he is not in my line.

"I do not like to see the sketches of Beethoven. I like to think of his things as they are and not of all the process by which they became so. No one else ever wrote like that [opening the Schubert Symphony]. This is all [word illegible], but Beethoven would have written this bar fourteen times over and that sixteen.

"People with a great deal of national music will not be great in the art. They have enough without it. The Germans have no national music (except the Chorales for sacred music) nor the Italians of the North. In Naples and Sicily they have. In England you have very little, mostly $\frac{6}{8}$, but in Ireland and Scotland "—— [ends.]

In the movement which led to the establishment of the Bach Choir in 1876, Grove took a keen interest. He attended the final rehearsal as well as the inaugural performance, given under the direction of Mr. Otto Goldschmidt, of Bach's Mass in B minor, on April 26th, and has left on record his impressions in the following letter to Sir Hubert Parry :—

"*April 29th*, 1876.

". . . . I was rather tired on Wednesday before getting to St. James's Hall, and by the end of the first part I had heard enough : I mean that I could not take in more. The *Gloria*, the *Cum Sancto*, the *Et Resurrexit*, and the *Et Exspecto* form such a chain of wonders, that even the *Sanctus* and *Hosanna* seemed *de trop* after them. It is a very wonderful thing certainly, so much more forcible and direct than I ever imagined Bach could be. Still, I should like to reserve my opinion as to its being 'the most gigantic work in music' till I knew it better, and till I could hear the *Messiah* or *Israel* done as well as this has been. I fancy if one heard either of those for the first time, it would seem very tremendous. . . ."

Of his life in the summer of 1876, with its various calls and claims and alternating moods of sunshine and seriousness, a good picture is to be found in the following letter to Miss Marian Bradley, dated June 15th :—

"I went with the Glehns to an evening party where the Hungarian Band played. It was very interesting—gipsy—full of Schubert, but the real delight was the coming home. It was 2 when we left, the dawn had already begun, and as we came to each cross street there were the 'black fronts long withdrawn' and the 'light blue lane of early dawn' between them. I never saw it before and it sank *for ever* into my mind. Then in crossing Westminster Bridge you can't think what an effect it was. It was still dark enough to give everything a magic look: for instance, the huge Charing Cross station looked *exactly* like a distant hill with a castle and church on the top —all in sombre purple ; and the river was covered with glancing light and might have been a noble Italian lake. And then all the way home the sights and the beauty grew, till after I left the carriage and walked down the hill, the red sun burst flaming out from behind my own house. These are things to recollect . . . . I was joking old Trollope about the name *Bonteen* (the man who is murdered in *Phineas Redux*), and telling him what a creep it had given me to be asked to take a Mrs. Bonteen down to dinner ; and then I said I always fancied the name was his invention. 'Oh no,' said Trollope, 'I knew a Bonteen once, and a very droll thing he did. We were going along the Strand together, years ago, when he said "Trollope, just come here for a moment, I want to go into a shop," and we went into Holloway's —Holloway's Pills. No sooner were we in than Bonteen jumps on the counter and dances like a madman, waving his hat round his head. There were five men behind the counter making pills, and one of them said "Sir you mustn't do that. Come down, or we must call Mr. Holloway." "Call Mr. Holloway," says he : "do you know who I am? Look at me, my name is Peters. Three weeks ago I was a confirmed cripple. I've only taken one barrow-load of your pills and look at me now."' What a curious freak to have entered into a man's head! Adieu and excuse a shabby letter, but there's much love behind it. P.S. This is one of my great anniversaries: Lucy's death. I dare not think about it much—it still knocks me quite over, but I like to remember it and to say a word thereon to one or two (not more)."

Though oppressed at times by the burden of his work, he writes of himself this summer as being "wonderfully well and hearty," and in a letter to the same correspondent on July 6th, gives an amusing description of a night visit to the Crystal Palace:—

"On Monday the moon was lovely, and so after Prayers I scuttled up to the Peak, hooked out two of the boys and went all round the *top* of Sydenham Hill into the C.P., caught a policeman and a dark lanthorn and went all through the stables and dens or the horses and wild beastesses of the Circus, got nearly killed by a Helephant, and arrived at home about 1. It was so jolly being with those nice boys."

All this time Grove was hard at work on his Geography Primer, copious notes on which alternate with Beethoven memoranda, questions for Thayer, &c., throughout the remainder of the autumn pocket-book. An entry in his almanac for 1876 shows that he finished the Primer, which formed one of a series issued by Messrs. Macmillan, on September 30th, and it was published in January, 1877. The scope of the work was modest, and the style simple, but it is one of the most genial and illuminating primers that were ever written. As soon as it was finished, he at once projected another handbook or "Class Book," which, to judge from his notes, was to be devoted to an account of the commercial development of Great Britain; and almost simultaneously he seems to have contemplated making a collection—for an article or book—of *jeux d'esprit*. "A.P.S. or Liddell for Oxford Squibs: Thompson [of Trinity] for Mansel's: Manning for his brother's collection," are amongst the entries relating to this project, which was never carried out, though Thompson sent him several of Mansel's epigrams, and there is a larger proportion than usual of jokes in his pocket-books for the next few months. Amongst these were Theodore Hook's famous Impromptu on Sennacherib and Jehoshaphat; and a brace of riddles:—

> "Why are novelists the most wonderful people?
> Because their tales grow out of their heads.
> Why was Scott the most wonderful of all?
> Because his grandfather's tales grew out of his head.'

Of the musical events of the year that chiefly appealed to Grove one may specially mention a concert at the Crystal Palace referred to in a letter to Miss Marian Bradley, dated February 29th, 1876:—

> "Saturday is a great day with us in our small way. Joachim plays (the Beethoven Concerto) but, even more, we have a new symphony by Schubert, *first time*—one he wrote for the P.F. and Joachim has scored. It is too beautiful and grand, and the whole thing is an event you know—like one of our good old days when we brought out a Reformation Symphony or *Rosamunde* music every two or three months and all was electric and the air full of Schubert . . . . Here is a good story of von Bülow's wit. At St. Louis, where he gave a concert, a dreadful screaming soprano sang before his solo. On which, as a little prelude before beginning, he played the recitative from the Choral Symphony 'O Freunde, nicht diese Töne'! Just like him."

He also attended the performance of Brahms's First Symphony by the Cambridge University Musical Society in the spring, and the concert given on June 23rd by Miss Sophie Löwe, who, after a short but brilliant career, quitted the concert platform on her marriage with William von Glehn in the following year. "Smoky Evenings" or "Smoking Bees" were kept up at home and among the friends of whom he saw most, outside the Sydenham set, during the year were the Frederick Lehmanns, the Pembers, Sir Henry Thompson and his wife, Alfred Ainger, the Macmillans, and the Acworths. He did not go abroad this year, contenting himself with an occasional run into the country, to Penn or Brighton, and in July paid a short visit to Tennyson, whose *Queen Mary* he had seen on April 18th.

Throughout 1877 Grove worked without intermission at the dictionary, and made such progress that by the end of the year we find him well on in the letter F. Indeed, he was so absorbed in his work that his pocket-books contain little else besides notes and suggestions, lists and references. They contain hints, however, of yet another unfulfilled project—a Primer on Beethoven in collaboration with Thayer. At the end of August he enlisted another most valuable contributor to the Dictionary in Mr. W. Barclay Squire, F.S.A., then an undergraduate at Cambridge. Grove was anxious to give some account of the Fitzwilliam collection in the Dictionary, and a common friend at Cambridge had recommended Mr. Squire as knowing more about it than anything else. The acquaintance soon ripened into an intimate and unbroken friendship fraught with a profit to Grove which he never tired of acknowledging, while Mr. Squire writes—and the compiler of this memoir can re-echo the sentiment as regards himself—"I owe him more than I can say, and his warm friendship and encouragement is sacred to my memory."

1877 was the year of Wagner's visit to London, and Grove not only attended some at least of the tremendous concerts given under Wagner's own direction in the Albert Hall—he writes to Miss Marian Bradley on May 17, "I went to the Wagner Concert last night. It was *delightful*, and the funeral music in the *Götterdämmerung* was like the crack of doom"—but had two short interviews with him in Orme Square, where Wagner stayed with Mr. Dannreuther during his stay in London, besides assisting to entertain him at the Athenæum.

"The first interview (writes Mr. Dannreuther) took place in the morning, when 'G.' wanted the master to appear at the Crystal Palace, the second late at night after one of the Albert Hall concerts, when 'G.' tried to 'draw' Wagner about Brahms. This false move at once put a stop to the talk. On the following day when Wagner dined with 'G.' and Doctors Pole and Siemens (the late Sir William Siemens) at the Athenæum Club, he was again catechised on the Brahms question, and his indignation was most comical. 'These gentlemen stumble about in my musical precincts like donkeys in a cabbage garden (*wie Esel im Kraut-garten*).'"

That Grove was greatly impressed by Wagner is abundantly clear from his subsequent allusions to him, but to the end of the chapter he remained in imperfect sympathy with the spirit of the music-drama. It was far otherwise with Brahms, whose *Liebeslieder* he heard with delight at the Monday "Pops." in March, and at Lady Thompson's in May, while the First Symphony was given twice at the Crystal Palace Saturday Concerts in March, Grove contributing to the programme an eloquent analysis, in which he hailed Brahms as the lineal descendant of the great classical masters. His impressions of Rubinstein, who also visited London this summer, are vividly summarized in an interesting letter to his sister-in-law, Miss Marian Bradley, dated May 15th :—

"I can sympathize with you fully about Rubinstein and the Erl-King: when I hear him play it I always think how far better it is than singing—than the singing of 99 out of a 100 singers at any rate. Instrumentalists have a great advantage over vocalists. Their gifts are not so obvious—are less those of nature than of hard conscientious work; and in consequence they are not amenable to flattery and conceit to the same degree as singers. Of course they get plenty, but then when you praise Joachim or Rubinstein, you are praising a man who has worked like a slave to reach the point he has attained, whereas when you praise Signora A. or Herr B., the chances are that nature has given them a lovely organ and they have done very little to improve it. And thus in most cases they are people of more intellect and judgment than singers and think less of themselves and more of the composer whose music they play. They can give you an 'interpretation' which few singers can. Where Rubinstein fails I think in playing is in a thing which nevertheless impresses you very much—in the tremendous noise he sometimes makes: pedal down—utmost force of hands—utmost speed of execution: the result being a mass of confusion, and confused music is simple absurdity. But you are quite right; he certainly does make an almost *terrible* impression on one, like a storm or a great fire or any other thing where you feel that it is all beyond one's control, and that if it comes near you you must be overwhelmed. Still I like his tenderness best, it is *so* very tender."

From a note, dated September 21st, 1877, it appears that he paid a visit to his brother Edmund at Saltburn where, always interested in links with the past, he mentions meeting "Mr. Ayrton of Saltburn, who recollected seeing the hay made in St. James's Park, and carted away by oxen, and being told that it was 'King George's hay.'" Another note, evidently intended for the Press, states that *Macmillan's Magazine*, for November 1877, "would contain an article on M. Thiers, founded on information given to the writer by Thiers himself during the last three years of his life, with a view to publication. The author is Mrs. Crawford, of Paris." *À propos* of *Macmillan's Magazine*, it is worthy of note as an instance of Grove's encouragement of beginners, that in the September number of this year Mr. J. St. Loe Strachey, the Editor of the *Spectator*, made his literary *début*, being then seventeen, with a poem, "Love's Arrows," while on the other hand the October issue contained a Homeric study by Mr. Gladstone. The record of the year may be closed with a letter to Mrs. Bull in reply to one written by her after having heard Schubert's variations on the *Death and the Maiden* theme, begging him to interpret them, and giving her own impressions :—

"LOWER SYDENHAM,
"*December 26th*, 1877.

"I can't do much more than a hasty word of hearty blessing for your dear precious letter. (Illegible! I like that, when everyone knows I write a regular copperplate.) But I must say how heartily and thoroughly rejoiced I am at what you tell me about those variations; I don't think that anything could have been better chosen for you. The most poetical, the most mournful, the most *musical* thing in the world. Know them? I should think I did, and I can tell you something of the secret of them, and you'll be delighted to find how near your instinct has led you.

"The theme (which I scratched down for you last night) is

from Schubert's own song of 'Der Tod und das Mädchen,' a poem of Claudius, in which a young girl says: 'Oh don't take me yet. I am so young and love the world so much'; and Death says, 'Give me your hand and come along.' It is Death's part that he has taken for the theme. I am glad to send you the theme, because it is too delightfully mournful to play, and the last three notes (mind you make the turn and catch the B natural) are like an escape into heaven."

One of the last things that occupied Grove in 1877 outside the Dictionary was the drawing up of one of the periodical statements in connection with the Palestine Exploration Fund, summarizing the results achieved in the last five years, pointing to the help received from America, and insisting on the representative and entirely unsectarian character of the General Committee. One passage, as it occurs in the rough draft in his pocket-book, emphasizes a point on which he never wearied of insisting:—

"If we look on the Bible as a charm or a talisman, we need not try to understand its contents. But if we believe the book which is thus put into our hands is a book which speaks as no other book speaks, then we shall try all we can to understand its contents, to enter into its remotest meaning, to vindicate its authority and genuineness."

One of the earliest entries in Grove's pocket-books for 1878 comes home with peculiar force to his biographer. It is dated January 27th, and sets forth how "A. P. S. [Stanley], on re-reading Newman's *Apologia*, and Mill's Autobiography, urges me to write to N. and press him to write an autobiography. It is impossible that any one else can adequately enter into the mind of another. The facts may be got, but the animation and interpenetration, and all the real life of the person can only be got in an autobiography." Besides his general editorial work on the Dictionary, Grove undertook in succession the three great monographs on Beethoven, Mendelssohn and Schubert, which formed his chief contribution to its pages, and was already busily engaged in collecting materials for the life of Mendelssohn. The names of his musical friends and associates—Parry, Dannreuther, Joachim, Stanford—occur with increasing frequency in his diary, and music undoubtedly absorbed the greater part of his time and attention henceforth, but he thoroughly sympathized with Sir Walter Scott when he wrote, "I have no temptation to be idle, but the greatest temptation when one thing is wanted of me to go and do something else." This engaging habit, the outcome of an inexhaustible interest in all fields of endeavour, no doubt has its drawbacks, but in Grove's case, as in Sir Walter's, it never interfered with his industry, while it prevented him from getting stale and served as an anodyne against anxieties and troubles. Of these 1878 was by no means devoid, since on March 6th the Sydenham coterie was thrown into gloom and mourning by the death from consumption of the beautiful and gifted Miss Louise Scott Russell, while in the summer Grove's eldest son Walter, who had developed chest delicacy, was, on the advice of Sir Andrew Clark, hurriedly shipped off in quest of health to Australia, where a prolonged residence happily gave him a new lease of life.

From the faithful Pohl, who wrote on March 8th, Grove obtained a most satisfactory report of Brahms's Second Symphony together with other interesting musical gossip from Vienna, while his memoranda of conversations with Stanley at Alderley—where their visit to America was doubtless discussed and arranged—contain two entries worth preserving. One relates to Stanley at Rugby, and describes how he saved time in doing his themes by putting in all the short words he could: the other runs: "Angeli told A. P. S. that the whole time he was painting Disraeli he never once saw his real face—always a mask."

Grove had now been closely associated for upwards of ten years with the firm of Macmillan, as editor of the magazine since 1868 and since 1873 as literary adviser and as editor of the *Dictionary of Music*. For a sketch of his relations with the firm both during and after this period I am glad to be able to avail myself of the following paper of reminiscences kindly contributed by Mr. George A. Macmillan :—

"As in the nature of the case not many letters pass between men who are in daily contact, and as I was thrown into specially close relations with Grove in the early days of his connexion with our firm, I welcome the opportunity of putting on record some impressions of my old friend as he went in and out among us. I do not know when he and my father first became acquainted, though I fancy it was through Tom Hughes, but the acquaintance soon ripened into a life-long friendship. Grove had been editor of *Macmillan's Magazine* since 1868, and it was in 1873 that he regularly joined our staff. The first letter I ever had from him was written to me at Eton in December of that year, when it was still uncertain whether I should go on to Cambridge or not. It was characteristically kind and sympathetic, and speaking from his own experience urged the advantages of the University training which he himself had missed. Circumstances prevented my following his advice, but it was a delight to me when I began my business career not many weeks later to find myself closely associated with its giver. For the first two years we shared the same room and all who knew him can imagine what a stimulating effect the daily intercourse with a man of Grove's vivacity and versatility must have had upon a boy fresh from school. Some of the keenest pleasures I have since enjoyed, especially in the fields of music and literature, owe their origin or encouragement to his infectious enthusiasm. He was just then planning the *Dictionary of Music*, and much of my time was spent in drawing up lists of subjects and authors under his guidance. It was most instructive to note the zeal and thoroughness with which he threw himself into his task. No detail was too small for his notice, and the hours of labour were agreeably lightened by the quip or the story which so readily suggested themselves to his fertile brain. It was characteristic of the almost boyish exuberance of his nature that he would now and then tempt me out to a neighbouring pastry-cook's to partake of certain three-cornered jam tarts for which he had a weakness. On Saturday afternoons I constantly accompanied him to the Crystal Palace Concerts.

"Grove's previous training in connexion with the *Dictionary of the Bible*, and his enthusiasm for music, made him an ideal Editor for the *Dictionary of Music*, and it is no wonder that as its successive numbers appeared, it quickly won, and has so long maintained, its high reputation. When Grove joined our staff it was hoped that other books, especially dealing with his two other favourite subjects, Geography and the Bible, might come from his pen or be produced under his guidance. But the work on the Dictionary, added to the monthly demands of the Magazine, and of his large correspondence, gradually absorbed his energies, and in the end nothing else was produced except the little Primer of Geography. But after all the *Dictionary of Music* remains as a splendid monument of his work with us, and apart from actual product it was of no small advantage to a publisher to have at hand a man of his keen literary sense and varied knowledge. Needless to say that his unfailing vivacity and humour made him a delightful companion, and that his eager face, and his inimitable laugh, were ever welcome at our daily luncheon hour. I remember that for some reason his memory, usually so good, could never retain the name of one of our clerks, Charlton, whom he would call after Lewisham, Penge, or any other station on the South Eastern Railway, until at last he was obliged to write the name on the wall of his room. The courtesy and consideration which always marked his treatment of subordinates endeared him I am sure to every member of our staff, and no one was more welcome at the annual summer gatherings which then took place at my father's house at Upper Tooting. The mention of that house brings back to my mind many other occasions when Grove was present there, and usually the life and soul of the party; and particularly the All Fools' Dinners which for many years my father gave there, and at which he was a frequent guest. Of dear old G's unvarying kindness to myself I shall ever retain a grateful recollection, and among my most cherished possessions is the complete set of Schubert's Songs which he gave me as a wedding present.

"After he left us to take up at the College of Music a post which fitted him more perfectly than any he had previously held our meetings were necessarily few, but our cordial relations were maintained, and the staunchness of his friendship was shown by the fact of his attending my father's funeral at Bramshott in January 1896, though by that time he was already in failing health. Two members of the firm attended his own funeral four years later. We used often to urge him to put together his reminiscences or at any rate to set down some of his inexhaustible fund of good stories. He seemed to shrink from the task, but fortunately his biographer found that he had acted upon the suggestion so far as to dictate in 1897 the contents of several note-books of which effective use has been made in the present volume. I am only sorry that another favourite project, the expansion and separate publication of his brilliant lives of Beethoven, Schubert and Mendelssohn from the *Dictionary of Music*, was never realised."

CHAPTER VIII

Trip to America with Stanley in 1878—At Boston, Baltimore, and Washington—Visits the Bradleys in Virginia—Niagara, Toronto, Montreal, Quebec—With Emerson at Concord—Dr. Harper's reminiscences—Grove's article on Mendelssohn: special visits to Berlin and Leipzig in 1879—Renan and Stanley at the Abbey—Rev. William Addis's reminiscences—Trip to Germany in 1880—Completion of the Mendelssohn article: testimony of Jenny Lind—Testimonial to Grove, July, 1880: his autobiographical speech—Two ghost stories—Trip to Vienna to obtain biographical material for the Schubert article.

GROVE's trip to America in September—the great event of the year 1878—was due to the realisation of a long-deferred scheme on the part of Stanley. Many years earlier the Dean had contemplated the journey in the life-time of Lady Augusta and of her brother Sir Frederick Bruce, the British Minister at Washington, but on the death of his brother-in-law in 1867 had abandoned his intention indefinitely. Recommended a complete change in 1878 he decided, not without serious misgivings, to cross the Atlantic, but the effort was undoubtedly greatly lightened in advance by the fortunate circumstance that Grove—himself sorely in need of a holiday—was able to be his travelling companion. In a letter to the Queen, dated August 31st, 1878, Stanley writes: "My old and tried friend, Mr. George Grove, goes with me and also a young medical man, Mr. Gerald Harper, a friend of my sister, Mrs. Vaughan, who is much in favour of my going."

At 7.30 a.m. on the morning of September 5th he left London and sailed from Liverpool at 4 p.m. on the *Siberia*. They had a fine day down the Channel, and on the 6th he wrote from Queenstown to his daughter

Millicent to say that so far all had been perfect. "We sit on red velvet and feed on the fat of the land." The next four days are described in his almanac as "rough and bad" after which the weather improved, the 12th and 13th being both "lovely quiet days." The voyage was spent by Stanley and Grove in a continuation of their preparatory study of the literature and history of America varied by conversation with the passengers, amongst whom was the Bishop of Western New York (Cleveland Coxe). It was from the latter that Grove heard the witty misapplication of the historic saying "Fils de St. Louis, montez au ciel" to the Louisiana man about to ascend in a lift. His pocket-book during the voyage also contains copious notes on Beethoven's *Eroica* Symphony and the following story told him by Stanley :—

"A Scotch friend of A. P. S. being at Valparaiso and walking on the sea-shore, meets a Spaniard, who walks up to him and says, in good English, 'On her white breast a sparkling cross she bore, which Jews might kiss and infidels adore.' The Scotchman says, 'I am delighted to meet you. How do you come to speak English so perfectly?' The Spaniard, 'On her white breast—' (all over again). And this was literally the only English the man knew, and as Stanley's friend could speak no Spanish, the thing stopped there."

They landed at Boston at 4 p.m. on the 16th, and spent the night at the Brunswick Hotel, Grove being at once struck by "the foreign appearance of men in light blue blouses." Here they saw Longfellow, Eliot, Oliver Wendell Holmes, Rice, Governor of Massachusetts, Winthrop, and other worthies. Grove's impressions of Harvard are limited in his note-book to notes on the Musical Society and the College tune, "Believe me, if all those endearing young charms"; but a visit to Mr. John Quincey Adams, formerly Minister at St. James's, on September 20th, is recorded at length with full particulars of the Adams family, their portraits and books, together with a characteristic anecdote of a serious Bostonian, "a very grave slow-speaking man, who was met by a friend in the street and congratulated on his recent marriage. 'Yes, sir,' he rejoined, 'I have been married, and I have now nothing to look forward to but the grave.'" On Sunday Stanley preached for Phillips Brooks in Trinity Church, and Grove has left rough but copious notes on the church, service, music, sermon and congregation. He was pleased by the excellent singing of the solo-quartet, but disconcerted by a "grotesque Japanese fan in our pew." The congregation struck him as very rich and well-behaved rather than devotional, and he adds "A. P. S. *most distinguished looking:* not too audible, though he spoke very loudly. Sermon very noble and in his best manner, and the peroration very touching." Phillips Brooks preached at the 4 o'clock service, but Grove was disappointed in his first impressions, finding the preacher's extreme rapidity of utterance most trying, though he was struck by the excellence of the matter. In the evening Grove went to the Congregational Church, where Brooks also took the service, and preached, which Grove remarks was "an unusual thing." Next day he went with Dr. Harper to see Wellesley—the American Girton—and came away with the intention of sending them "Photo of A. T. (Tennyson); *Dictionary of Music:* and Facsimile of first Folio of Shakspere." At Newport, on the 24th, they were the guests of the venerable but evergreen Bancroft, the historian. The 25th saw them at Hartford, the 26th at Newhaven, where they were entertained by Professor Fisher, and met Porter, the President of Yale, and other Professors. The most interesting contribution to the conversation at this gathering, to judge from Grove's pocket-book, was the following extremely characteristic anecdote told by Stanley:—

"Lunching at some public entertainment to ministers, he sat next Mr. Gladstone. It was shortly after Gladstone had gone out and Disraeli come in. After the luncheon was over Disraeli came round to where they were standing and said: 'Why have you left Parliament? We *must* have you back; we *must* have you back '—in the most playful way. On which Gladstone said: 'There are some things which are possible, and some which are impossible, and what you have asked me belongs to the impossible.' On which, turning to A. P. S., Disraeli said: 'You see, it is the wrath of Achilles.'"

On leaving Newhaven the travellers paid a flying visit to New York to enable Stanley to meet and address the American Revisers, and on the 28th reached Philadelphia, which, in Grove's view, "seems to unite the advantages of both Boston and New York. Solid, good, intellectual people. Great activity of business, very fine long broad streets, with picturesque houses, and fine shops." At Philadelphia, where they were the guests of G. W. Childs, Stanley preached in St. James's Church on Sunday, September 29th. Shorthand writers were present and Grove corrected the proofs, in which the reporters had managed to confuse Richard Hooker with Joe Hooker—"fighting Joe" of 1862. Dr. Harper recalls the difficulty that arose over the phrase from John Bright's speech on the Crimean war quoted by the Dean. Stanley had used the incorrect expression "flapping" of the angel's wings. Grove suggested "rustling," but neither could hit upon the right word "beating." In the evening they attended service in the negro Methodist meeting-house. The sermon was pronounced by Stanley to be a "hideous exhibition"; and Grove has recorded one sentence, in which the preacher observed that, "Not all the Deans, sceptics or Tom Paines in the world shall make me believe that there is no Hell." Grove also notices the violent bursts of *forte* and *piano*, without any reference to the text, which characterised the singing of the coloured congregation. The next stage in their journey was Baltimore, where Stanley addressed the students at the Johns Hopkins University. Of their hospitable host, President Gilman, Grove has left the following reminiscences, dictated in 1897:—

"When I was at Baltimore with Arthur Stanley and Harper, we saw a good deal of Gilman, the principal of the Johns Hopkins

University, and his charming wife, who had been a Miss Coolidge, with a great reputation for writing children's books and poetry. One day we dined at the Gilmans, and had a new experience. There were, I think, four guests, Mr. and Mrs. Gilman at the two ends of the table, and the guests two and two on each side. I sat on Gilman's left hand, and the conversation was lively; but to our surprise and pleasure when the dinner was half-way through, Mr. Gilman rose, Mrs. Gilman did the same, and they changed places, which put an entirely new face on everything.

"One thing which struck us very much, was that each department of the University was carried out in practice; thus the department of engineering and mechanics had a complete workshop attached to it in which locomotives and other machinery were made, and, I believe, contracted for and sold.

"A few years after our visit I happened, to my delight, to meet Mr. Gilman one day in the Westminster Palace Hotel, and on my asking him whether anything had happened to the University since our visit, 'O, yes,' he said; 'we have now got a hospital added to our medical department.' 'Indeed!' said I; 'and how did you manage that?' 'Well,' he said, 'one day I was sitting in my room, and a gentleman and two lads of fourteen or thereabouts were announced. The gentleman went to business at once and said: 'Well, Mr. Gilman, is there anything that you particularly want?' 'Yes,' I answered; 'I particularly want a hospital to complete our medical department.' 'And how much do you think it will cost?' said the visitor. 'I don't know exactly,' said I, 'but should think a million and a half dollars.' 'Well,' was the reply, 'I have given several small sums, half a million here, and half a million there, and I should now like to do something bigger. Will you kindly have the plans and estimates prepared and let me know the amount? As soon as you tell me I am ready.' The result was the hospital of which he was so proud. When it was completed, Mr. Gilman said to him at the opening dinner: 'I should like to know, sir, what was the motive which prompted this splendid act of generosity?' 'Well,' said the other, 'you remember those boys who called with me on my first visit. Now I thought that when they grew up I should like them to come around and see what their father had done, and then they would say, 'This is pretty, and Poppa did it.'"

Neither Grove, who was deeply interested in all that concerned Napoleon, nor Stanley saw old Madame Bonaparte-Patterson, then living in Baltimore. The Dean called upon her, but she declined to see him and sent down a message, "All my feelings are dead, except hatred of mankind." Another characteristic saying of hers is recorded in Grove's pocket-book: "God," said old Madame Bonaparte of Baltimore "has given me three passions: love, ambition and avarice. My love is slighted, my ambition is thwarted, and I exist upon my avarice." She died in the following year at the age of ninety-four.

The 6th of October found the travellers at Washington. On the road from Baltimore Grove noticed that "directly you leave for Washington the scenery becomes more southern—torrent beds and sandy cuttings. N.B. remember a lovely bushy green beech tree growing out of a torrent bed. 'His roots are wrapped about a spring.'" At Washington they visited the Capitol and the Admiralty Museum, in connection with which an incident occurred that Grove was very fond of narrating in after years. On their voyage out, an American clergyman had told them that they would never hear an "h" mispronounced:—

"Accordingly we listened diligently, but never succeeded until our visit to Washington. There we were shown over the Admiralty Museum by an intelligent person—half clerk, half porter—who came to us with a flag in his hand, saying, 'Gentlemen, this flag ought to interest you. It was taken on board the *H*alabama.' 'Hallo, my man,' I said, 'Where do you come from?' thinking that I had got the real Simon Pure at last. His answer was: '*H*alfreton in Derbyshire, sir.'"

The events of the next fortnight are told in a letter to Miss M. E. von Glehn dated Quebec, October 18th:—

". . . I have too much to do to get time for writing here. Stanley stands the journey wonderfully, and I must not complain, but we have had some severe bouts. I think my last to you was from Philadelphia, but I can give you only a mere catalogue of the places. Baltimore, where there was a new university to see and professors in crowds to dine with, and a splendid little address from Stanley to the students, quite extempore; then Washington, with visits to President, and English ministers, and all the public buildings to see, and Washington's house at Mount Vernon: an ideal thing and an ideal day. From Washington we went on together into the south to Richmond, capital of Virginia, and there we parted; Stanley and Harper stayed there, and I went on 120 miles further to 25 miles below Lynchberg to see the Bradley Colony.[1] It was quite an adventure. I had to sleep at a roadside store and be driven about 13 miles next morning through lovely woods (like Kent) and over the most amusingly and incredibly bad roads to the lonely happy valley in which they live—a beautiful place, with fields and farms and woods, and a great river and the Blue Ridge Mountains filling in all the background. They had no idea I was coming (for not a line of mine had reached them), but were delighted, and gave me a most enjoyable time, Friday to Monday. We had two long horseback rides and a charming picnic up a high mountain, and on Monday morning I said adieu to these young farmers with real pangs . . . I came right back to New York at one go, travelling twenty-seven hours, and then after one day at Albany [we went] to Niagara, and that was splendid—no words are enough. Quite different from what I fancied; much lower and much more widespread, but in the end far surpassing everything one could imagine beforehand. We were there three days, and saw not only three but 300 different aspects. By the full moon in the very dead of night; in a splendid calm day; and in high wind. I can't describe it; it would take sheets, and then would be absurd. I can only say it was the climax of the journey (or of any journey), and that if I had seen it every day for a week, I should still have longed to see more. It remained to me an immense, wonderful, overpowering thing, quite outside of me, and I was truly sorry to come away. It would be worth any one's while to come to America simply to see it[2] . . . We stay here till to-morrow; on Sunday Stanley preaches, and on Monday we go to Montreal (said to be a 'second Paris'), and then through some historical country (Lake George and Lake Champlain, seat of much of the old wars), then to Concord to see Emerson, then to a place in the 'Berkshire Hills' for the foliage, and about Monday the 28th to New York

[1] Dean Bradley's son, Mr. A. G. Bradley, was then settled in Virginia. A married and an unmarried daughter of the Dean's were also there at the time.

[2] Grove used to tell a story of a Miss Porter, to whose family Goat Island belonged. While on a visit to England she was asked if she had ever seen Niagara. "It belongs to me," was her crushing answer. Another of his Niagara stories was that of an Irishman who when a visitor remarked, "What a fall! what a fall!" replied, "What's to hinder it?"

for a tremendous ten days' grind till the 6th, when we leave in the *Bothnia*, the newest and fastest Cunarder."

Stanley in the meantime had been at Richmond, had preached for Dr. Washburn in the Calvary Church, New York, on Sunday, October 6th, and on the 7th was the guest of Cyrus Field at Irvington on the Hudson. It was here, while Stanley was at dinner, that the following formidable list of questions, transcribed at the time by Grove, was sent in to him by a representative of a New York paper :—

(1) The necessity for a New Revelation?

(2) His views (*a*) on the Christianity of the present day; (*b*) on the religious tendencies of the age.

(3) Is the present spirit of inquiry earnest, or is it a retrogression?

(4) What does he think of the condition and growth (present and prospective) of the entire Protestant Church, of all divisions, in America?

From Niagara the travellers went on to Toronto on October 16th, thence *viâ* Kingston to Montreal, where they met Lord Dufferin, travelling all night to Quebec in his company. Of this journey Grove dictated an interesting reminiscence in 1897 :—

"Stanley rode with Lord Dufferin, and I went to bed in a Pullman car. I could not sleep, however, and soon asked the conductor to come and talk to me, which he did. He was an extremely intelligent American, who told me that his father had been a clergyman in one of the two Carolinas. One day the father called all the children together and said: 'I have just heard that General Grant's army has come into the State. Our house will very soon be destroyed, and therefore we must part immediately, and all do the best we can.' Then he questioned each as to what they would do. This son said: 'I know what I shall do. I have had some practice in acting, and I think I can get together a tolerably good company, and we will go through the West Indian islands in one of the steamers, and no doubt make some money by acting.' This he actually did, and some years afterwards while he was at Havana an incident occurred which he related to me as an instance of the care which the English consuls took of the interests of their countrymen in the Spanish and French islands. Havana at that time, as it too often was, was under martial law. There was a street row in which a Spaniard was killed. Everybody in the crowd flew at once except an Englishman, who did what he could to help the wounded man. The soldiers came up, however, and the Englishman was arrested, accused by somebody of having committed the crime, marched off to the citadel, and condemned by a sort of court-martial to be shot next morning. He managed to let the English consul, Mr. Crawford, know the exact hour fixed for the execution, and accordingly next morning Crawford drove up in full dress as the Englishman was being blind-folded and a shooting party drawn up with loaded rifles. Crawford made a formal demand for the life of his fellow-countryman, but the officer in command produced the written authority of his government, and said he could only obey orders. 'Then,' said Crawford, 'at least let me shake hands with my countryman before he dies.' The officer consented and Crawford walked up to the man, pulled a Union Jack from his pocket, and threw it over the prisoner, crying 'There now, fire if you dare. It will be a declaration of war.' The officer was staggered, the question was referred back to the Governor, and the Englishman was saved. More than that, it was actually found that the man who had accused him of the crime was the real murderer himself."

Grove's notes and memoranda, while mainly referring to the places he saw and people he met during his journey, contain many references to his "beloved Dean." It was during this tour, *e.g.*, that Stanley told him several excellent stories, and Grove more than once observed that when Stanley told you a story you could rely upon its absolute correctness. I give one as it was jotted down in Grove's pocket-book at Quebec while fresh in his memory :—

"The Emperor Nicholas—with whom, according to Gladstone, no man could ever compare for majesty and beauty—was made a Knight of the Garter, and the Marquis of Hertford was sent to invest him with it. The process is to buckle the garter round the knee in public. This the Emperor absolutely refused to submit to. He always wore uniform and high boots, and this because the calf of his leg was so poor that he would not expose it. Lord Hertford of course was unable to agree to leave the

Garter without buckling it on, and at last, after an enormous amount of debating and bad temper, it was arranged that it should be put on in strict privacy, no one being present but Lord Hertford. It was the occasion of innumerable heart-burnings, and when Lord Hertford left, he found out the price of the diamond box which had been given him, and paid the sum to a charitable institution at St. Petersburg."

From Quebec they went to Montreal, and thence, on October 22nd, to Ticonderoga, where Stanley was particularly anxious to track out the legend of Inverawe :—

[*To* Miss Millicent Grove.]

"Ticonderoga,
"*October 22nd.*

"... To-day from 9 till 4 p.m. was occupied in driving about Montreal, and we have just now, 11.30 p.m., reached this remote spot—this 'lodge in a garden of cucumbers'—where we are to start exploring battle-fields at 8 to-morrow morning. The bad weather fled as rapidly as it came, and yesterday and to-day have been cloudless and truly heavenly. The colours of the woods no one can imagine who has not seen them—whole rows of large maple trees of lovely yellow, set off with deep tones of red and contrasted with the fresh spring green of the pines—all this in the bright sun is too lovely ... I should have been photographed in Montreal, but I could not get my hair cut and I am too ragged a spectacle as I am—no scissors has touched it since your fairy fingers played with my locks. ..."

They travelled to Saratoga on the 23rd, and on the 25th to Concord, where they were the guests of Emerson. On the same evening Grove wrote to Miss M. E. von Glehn :—

"I am writing to you from Emerson's house at the end of a delightful day which I shall not easily forget. What is left of him is quite charming, and there is much left, though very much has gone. His memory has almost entirely fled, and he has to speak very slowly and to appeal to his daughter, not only for names of people and places, but for very ordinary words; but, on the other hand, his face is one of the most expressive and lovable ones I ever saw, his voice is very sweet, and his manner the kindest possible. He has been reading to us for more than an hour, his own poems and things of Wordsworth's and others. This morning he drove us about in a pony chaise through delicious meadows and woods. He says nothing worth remembering, but it is impossible not to carry away the image of the greatest goodness and sweetness. I have got a photograph of him for you, with his autograph, but it really gives no idea of the beauty of his face. His eldest daughter—who is unmarried and devoted to him—is well worthy of such a father."

Under the heading "Concord" there are a few notes in Grove's pocket-book of a conversation with Emerson which turned a good deal on Carlyle and Goethe, but contains nothing of special moment. One is glad, however, of the excuse to give Emerson's memorable lines on the Concord Monument, which Grove transcribed on the spot:—

> "By the rude bridge that arched the flood,
> Their flag to April's breeze unfurled,
> Here once the embattled farmers stood
> And fired the shot heard round the world."

From Concord they went on to Stockbridge, where Stanley preached his fifth sermon, and the 28th found them back again at Boston, where they saw a good deal of Phillips Brooks and Dr. Ellis, from whom Grove gleaned two additions to his copious store of anecdotes. One was of an enthusiastic fruit grower, who, speaking at a meeting of an Agricultural Society observed: "I would found my hopes of a gracious reception, of a lenient view of my imperfections, and of my future happiness, on the introduction of that pear." The second took the form of a dialogue: "Do you believe in the Doctrine of Personal Election, Mrs. ——?" "Aye, do I, and firmly too, and it's my greatest comfort, for I fear that if the Lord had not chosen me before I was born, He would never have chosen me afterwards." Another good story was told him by Dr. Emmans of Franklin, near Plymouth, whose little grandchild once said to him: "Oh grandpapa, that foolish John! He wants me to believe that the moon was made of green cheese. But I know it isn't, it's the moon." Dr. Emmans replied, "How do you know? Never say you know anything till you can prove it." Next day the child returned to the subject, "Oh, grandpapa, I *can* prove it from the Bible. I began at the first chapter of Genesis, and I found that it could not be, because the moon was made before the cows."

On the 29th they travelled back to New York, where the last week was spent in one continuous rush of receptions. On October 31st Stanley preached at All Saints, and on November 1st at Grace Church. On November 2nd the Century Club entertained the Dean and his companions at breakfast. Stanley made a memorable speech, in the course of which he said that without the devoted care of his two friends, Mr. Grove and Dr. Harper, his visit never could have been accomplished, adding :—

> "When in after years you read at the end of some elaborate essay on the history of music or on Biblical geography the name of George Grove, you will recall with pleasure the incessant questionings, the eager desire for knowledge, the wide and varied capacity for all manner of instruction, which you experienced in your conversation with him here."[1]

Amongst the scores of distinguished Americans whom Grove met during this last week in New York were Henry Ward Beecher, Dr. Hitchcock, the American representative of the Palestine Exploration Fund, and Theodore Thomas, the famous conductor.

On November 6th, at 2 p.m., the travellers sailed in the *Bothnia*, and landed at Liverpool on the 14th. Grove's entries in his note-book during the voyage were as variegated as usual. On one page we find a list of the general characteristics of America—the foreign look of the towns, the wide streets with trees planted in them, the excellent hotels, great plenty of water, and cleanness of the houses. On another he enters the names of a number of possible contributors to *Macmillan's Magazine*—G. W. Curtis,

[1] In December, 1879, the Dean, during a visit to the late Bishop of Limerick, spoke of the way in which Grove "devoured the Americans."

E. L. Godkin, Colonel Anderson, F. Grant White. Then he turns to Nottebohm's *Beethoveniana* or adds to his store of "Limericks":—

> "There was a musician at Rio
> Who attempted to play Hummel's Trio;
> But his skill was so scanty,
> He played it Andante,
> Instead of Allegro con Brio.
>
> "There once was a fellow of Trinity
> Who raised *xyz* to infinity;
> And then the old brute
> Extracted the root—
> He afterwards took to Divinity."

The best day in the log of the *Bothnia* was 335 miles—an insignificant performance compared with modern records—and Grove's last entry refers to the weather on their trip: "As if we had left the fogs and damp of England behind, we arrived at Boston in lovely sunshine which never withdrew its brilliant brightness during the whole of our stay till we plunged at once into the mists and winds of the Atlantic."

Altogether the visit to America was an immense success. He was intensely interested in all he saw; he met nearly all the leaders of thought in the States; visited most of the great Eastern cities; had a glimpse of the South and a run through Canada, and proved himself throughout a most devoted and helpful travelling companion to Stanley.

"During the visit to America," writes Dr. Harper, "Grove effaced himself so much on all public, and even private occasions, sitting as it were at the feet of the Dean, that it is not easy to recall anything of particular interest in what he said and did. He was often absurdly impatient with people who did not appear to have a proper appreciation of the Dean, and now and then let himself go with what he described in a letter to me as a 'horrid ferocity,' so that the Dean used to say, 'I must keep him in order.' I never saw him so easily managed by any one else. As a fellow traveller he was all that could be wished for, and more, as nothing would prevent him from undertaking most of the trouble

R 2

of arranging the details of our journeys, and we had no servant with us. Then there was his inexhaustible fund of good stories, his vivacity and sympathetic interest in all that concerned his friends, and his delightful candour in all discussions."

On his return to England Grove was at once immersed in his labours on the *Dictionary of Music*. The year 1879 was for him pre-eminently a Mendelssohn year.[1] His note-books are full of memoranda on the subject as well as conversations with those who had known "F. M. B."—Jenny Lind and Charles Hallé, Joachim, Piatti, Horsley, H. J. Lincoln, Dr. Turle, &c. Indeed it might be said that his correspondence and note-books show less evidence of his versatility and wide range of interest in this year than at any previous stage of his life. Most of his notes were worked up in his articles, but occasionally one encounters a reflection which belongs to a different category as, for example, the distinction drawn between Music and Painting. "In the former all second-rate composers fall into oblivion ; in the latter the second-raters are all preserved to be the will o' the wisp of critics and amateurs for ever and ever." Grove thought the great painters ought to swallow up the smaller fry, as the Mozarts and Beethovens swallowed up the Dusseks, &c., adding, "and a very good thing too." Another entry refers to a scheme which he never carried out. "April 23rd, 1879. The idea of a Beethoven Dictionary entered my mind as I was walking down from the station after being to Kneller Hall and reading Thayer's vol. iii."

In the early months of the year he took his recreation chiefly by going to concerts, visiting Cambridge twice to attend performances of the C.U.M.S., but otherwise kept pretty close to his work in London until the dog days. A visit to his sister, Miss Eleanor Grove, at Sevenoaks, on July 24 is probably to be associated with an anecdote

[1] It may be noted that Grove had served on the committee of the Mendelssohn Scholarship Fund from the institution of the Scholarship in 1856, when Arthur Sullivan was elected.

which he was very fond of telling, and finally dictated in 1897:—

"I once went down to Sevenoaks to see my sister Ellen, who was unwell, and stopping there. After lunch we went into Knole Park, which had a good many excursionists in it. There was a wooden platform there from which you could see several counties; it was then in the possession of an orator who was abusing the family, and I heard him make the following remark: 'There they have been for centuries a-sitting there like spiders sucking the blood of the people, marrying in and in, cousins and I don't know how much nearer, and they will never be right until they get some of the *pelebium blood* mixed up with them again.'"

On September 29th Grove crossed to Flushing in company with the J. R. Greens and the Lauder Bruntons, travelling *viâ* Cologne to Hanover, where he witnessed a performance of *Fidelio* on October 1st, and journeying on to Berlin on the following day. The week that followed was almost entirely devoted to Mendelssohn—visits to his family and friends (Paul and Ernst Mendelssohn, Hensel and Joachim), examination of scores, documents, letters and portraits—with an occasional night at the opera or the play. On the 8th he moved on to Leipzig to continue his researches with the assistance of the Wachs, Mrs. Moscheles, Schleinitz and others. Leaving Leipzig on the 14th he spent a night at Magdeburg and another at Cologne, reaching home on October 16th. Mendelssohn still continued to dominate all other interests, and, apart from biographical details, little else occurs in his note-books. As an instance of his habit of acquiring information outside the ranks of musicians, one may note the striking remark made by Mrs. Grote to Stanley and by him communicated to Grove: "I have during the last thirty years felt poignant sorrow through the death of friends, and for four individuals above all—Catherine Stanley, Felix Mendelssohn, Alexis de Tocqueville and J. S. Mill."

With the exception of references to Stanley and Franks, all the names and entries in Grove's diary for the early months of 1880[1] are connected with music until we come to April, when he met Renan, then on a visit to London, on several occasions. The most notable of these was a visit to the Abbey, which Grove has described in the following letter to Miss M. E. von Glehn :—

" *Thursday Afternoon.*" [2]

". . . The visit to the Abbey yesterday was really delightful—the party was quite small. Renan, A. P. Stanley, Matthew Arnold and I were all the men, and there were about six women. We began at the West door, and Stanley talked French hard for two and a half hours till we finished in the Chapel of the Pyx, which, by good fortune, being under repair, could be entered (a most rare occurrence). For the political and literary persons in the nave, I don't think Renan cared much, but with the building itself he was quite in ecstasies, and the Royal tombs with all their wonderful histories and stories and extraordinary associations and connections with France, &c. delighted him. The Chapter House in particular he was quite wild about. He is an odd creature to look at—short and very thick, with an *immense* head and most plebeian features, the whole supported on the most useless legs and little infirm feet. The contrast to Stanley—every line of face and hands so delicate and refined and so full of fire and action and expression—was most curious. I can't pretend to recollect, much less to tell, a thousandth part of all the lovely and interesting things Stanley told us. . . . It was really a thing to recollect to one's death. I kept close to Renan and Stanley and was in delight, as you may imagine. At lunch, Lecky and his wife came in, and one or two more. Renan recollected me perfectly, and asked me about Palestine, and talked of Clermont-Ganneau."

To the same period—the early part of 1880—must be referred the beginning of one of the closest friendships formed by Grove in his later life—that with the Rev. William Addis, now of Mansfield College, Oxford, who has kindly furnished the following reminiscences :—

"It was, I think, in the early spring of 1880 that I first

[1] The old motto from Rogers is still repeated in his pocket-book, with the addition "Tout comprendre c'est tout pardonner."

[2] No date is given, but reference to Grove's diary shows that it must have been either April 7th or 14th, 1880.

became acquainted with Sir George Grove. How well I remember our first meeting! One cold evening in early spring I was walking up the Sydenham Road, and just opposite the old Greyhound inn we met, and he introduced himself to me, claiming acquaintance on the ground of our common friendship with Father Dalgairns[1] who had been an elder contemporary of mine at the London Oratory. At the time of our meeting, Father Dalgairns had been dead for several years and I was a very near neighbour of Mr. Grove's, leading then a rather solitary life as priest of the little Roman Catholic chapel in Sydenham. I told him how much I owed to his work in Smith's Dictionary: indeed I had, as it happened, been busy with one of his articles within half an hour of this our earliest conversation. That at once aroused his interest: he asked me to dine with him next day, and so a friendship began which I have good cause to reckon among the chief blessings of my life. I was constantly in his house, dining there, as a rule, every week, while he used to come constantly to me. I cannot look back without gratitude and wonder at the extraordinary kindness which I received from Lady Grove and from himself, nor shall I cease to cherish the memory of it while I live. In those days his vigour was unabated, and I have never known his like for energy of mind. He was then immersed in anxious business connected with the Royal College of Music, which was just beginning to be: he was editing the huge musical dictionary, and he still held his place as editor of *Macmillan's Magazine.* Notwithstanding all this weight of distracting work his interest was as keen as ever in his old Biblical studies. Many a time he has spoken to me of the happy days when he was working for Smith's *Bible Dictionary* and described the trepidation with which he entered on the longer and more ambitious articles, and the enthusiasm which woke him from his sleep at three or four o'clock in the morning and drove him down stairs to his work. Sometimes he would sigh for lost opportunities and regret that he could not give himself once more to the serious study of the Bible. Every new discovery, every change in criticism arrested his attention, and he had a singular gift for seeing the point of new theories and testing them by their relation to the facts. But his interest was universal: *quicquid agunt homines*, all that men did or thought supplied him with his theme. He had a great fund of anecdote. It was drawn from his boyhood at Clapham, from his youthful experiences as an engineer in Glasgow and the West Indies, from

[1] Father Dalgairns had been, like Grove, one of the original members of the Metaphysical Society.

the great part he took in establishing the Crystal Palace, from his recollections of distinguished men (and probably there are few who have known more distinguished men than he). He told stories inimitably, with the keenest sense of humour and without a word too much. There was another feature in his conversation scarcely less remarkable, I mean its unfailing kindness and good humour. He saw what was best in everybody, and always dwelt on that. Above all he welcomed any sign of talent or of thirst for knowledge: a young clergyman especially who studied the Bible with some measure of intelligence, was sure to find a way to his heart. I used to feel almost with pain the need of discounting his kindly judgments of his fellow men, and I never could persuade him that to me at least he attributed knowledge and talent which I was very far from possessing. Nor was his kindness merely one of sentiment. He was ingenious in devising means of helping others: he would lend them books, give wise advice, and help them in their difficulties with ready sympathy. I used often to meet the pupils from the Royal College, whom he invited to his house for the Sunday, and he was never weary of discussing their prospects and the best ways of improving their general education and giving them knowledge of the world. To me he was ever the staunchest of friends, and when in 1888 I left the Church of Rome, and had to quit Sydenham, he did more for me than almost any one else. He interested others in my behalf: he kept up a regular correspondence with me in Australia, and when I came home again, my comfortable settlement was chiefly due to him. Only once again were we to live close to each other. That was during the summer of 1896 in Scotland, where he, like myself, had gone for a few weeks' holiday. We were together as of old, meeting twice every day. The only difference was that we sat side by side in church, and that he now extended to my wife and daughter his old affection for me. He was full as ever of schemes for helping every one who was capable of being helped. I remember an admirable address which he once gave to the children of the National School at Sydenham. The burden of it was 'Get all the education you can, and then never miss a chance of helping others.' It was a lesson which he, if ever man did, faithfully practised throughout his long life."

In the spring of 1880 it was arranged that his daughter Millicent should spend some months studying in Germany, and an undated letter to Dr. Bradley written somewhere about April 20th, shows how keenly he felt the severance :—

"I take Milly over to Wiesbaden at the end of next week. Nobody knows what a pang it is to part from her, or how I dread the change that may take place in her before she comes back, but God is merciful."

On April 29th Grove crossed *viâ* Flushing to attend the Schumann Festival at Bonn, breaking the journey at Cologne to call on Ferdinand Hiller. At Bonn (May 2–3) he saw Joachim and learned from him the welcome intelligence that Brahms had completed his 3rd Symphony. From Joachim also he had the following pleasing anecdote of Brahms's modesty :—

"Brahms was at W——'s house in Coblentz. W—— is a great amateur of wine, and brought up some of a very special vintage and set it before Brahms, saying, 'Now, Herr Brahms, this wine must be drunk with great consideration. It is the same thing among wines that you are among composers.' On which Brahms at once remarked : 'Do you happen to have Bach in your cellar ? If so, bring him up at once.'"

On May 4th he slept at Rolandseck, reached Wiesbaden on the 5th, and went over to Frankfurt on the 6th to visit Madame Schumann, Raff, and his old friend Stockhausen, starting home from Wiesbaden on the 8th. Contrary to his wont the notes of what he saw and heard during the last few days of his stay abroad are extremely brief, but he records one strikingly epigrammatic criticism by von Bülow on Mendelssohn :—"Mendelssohn began by being a genius and ended by being a talent : so did Schumann, but with this difference, that Mendelssohn was perfect in both phases, Schumann imperfect in both." It should be added that the pleasure of Grove's trip was immensely enhanced by the companionship of his daughter. As he put it in a letter to his sister-in-law, Miss Bradley, on May 20, "it was a regular honeymoon."

The first volume of the Dictionary containing Parts I—VI, had been published in 1879, and the Part containing Grove's Life of Mendelssohn in February, 1880. The latter met with instant recognition of its happy combination of zeal and research—amongst the congratulatory letters which he received being one from Mr. Frederic Harrison, dated February 1, 1880. "I think the Mendelssohn admirable," wrote Mr. Harrison, "full of life and solid learning. It shows immense industry and enthusiasm"; and he went on to suggest that on the completion of the Dictionary Grove should bring out a volume on "The Great Masters in Music," a reduced reprint of 10 or 12 of the principal lives, shorn of technical and antiquarian details—"something that mere outsiders like myself can quite understand. As notes or appendices to each life, give us some of the admirable bits of enthusiastic criticism by '[G]' in the Crystal Palace band books." Even more striking was the testimony contained in the following letter from Jenny Lind bearing the same date :—

"Let me . . . congratulate you on the finishing of the article on Mendelssohn. It has been a labour of *love*; that one clearly sees all through, and it touches me deeply to see how you speak of that exquisite spirit as if you had really seen and known him. Of course to one who, like myself, have had a nearer insight into his loftiness of soul—(and I believe that no one after his sister Fanny ever had that artistic intimacy with him which I had), it is impossible not to confess that he was one of those beings whose real character can never be fully described by a human pen. Yet one must feel that all justice has been done to him, and that you have tried, *contre cœur*, as it seems to me, to describe *some* of his few faults. I have read your article with deep interest, and thank you most heartily as one of his best friends, and one who, besides, was honoured by his friendship, and to whom his death was a blank never to be filled. . . ."

". . . You are such an unselfish man that I daresay you will never get anything like what you deserve in this dark, blind, foggy world of ours. But there must be treasure laid up for a nature like yours where no sorrow, no toil, no sickness, no death will reach you, and so God bless you and guide you thither, says your affectionate friend,

JENNY LIND GOLDSCHMIDT."

That Grove keenly valued Jenny Lind's testimony is evident from a letter to Mr. Otto Goldschmidt, in which he says, "These great spirits, like Madame Goldschmidt, are like suns who warm and vivify all who come near them." The year 1880, however, was marked by a more tangible recognition of Grove's services than the written testimony of friends and critics. The original idea of Mr. Ernest von Glehn, who acted as one of the honorary secretaries to the Fund, was that of a present to Grove from the personal friends who had sat with him in the gallery at the Saturday concerts for so many years. This, however, was taken up so warmly that it grew into a more extensive scheme, upwards of £1000 was contributed in a very short time, and a testimonal, in the shape of a handsome gold chronometer, and a purse of 1000 guineas, was presented to Grove in the banqueting room of St. James's Hall on the afternoon of July 19th, 1880. The address ran as follows :—

[*To George Grove, Esq.*]

"We the undersigned ask you to accept the accompanying purse of one thousand guineas and gold chronometer, which we offer you as a token of our appreciation of the great services which you have rendered, in the first place, to Biblical History and Geography, by your valuable contributions to the *Dictionary of the Bible*, and by your labours in connection with the foundation of the Palestine Exploration Fund; in the second place, to Music and Musical Literature, during your long association with the Crystal Palace Saturday Concerts, and more recently by the production of the *Dictionary of Music and Musicians*.

"In these and many other fields of research in art and literature you have earned the gratitude of your countrymen at large, and the high esteem and friendship of all those associated with you in your labours, and we welcome this opportunity of testifying in a manner however inadequate our gratitude, friendship and esteem."

The list of subscribers—upwards of 300 in all—contained the names of Alfred Tennyson, the Archbishops of York and Canterbury (Thomson and Tait) Dean Stanley, John Millais, Frederick Leighton, Frederic Harrison, Arthur

Balfour, Tom Hughes, Sir James Paget, Sir Henry Thompson, Sir Frederick Goldsmid, Norman Lockyer, Alfred Ainger, Sir Austen Layard, Sir George Dasent, Frederic Greenwood, Tom Taylor (who died just a week before the presentation), James Fergusson, Cyrus Field of New York, Dr. William Smith, Sidney Colvin, William Black, E. H. Pember, George Granville Bradley, Godfrey and Vernon Lushington, Spencer Lyttelton, John Murray and Alexander Macmillan ; while music was worthily represented by Sir Julius Benedict, Arthur, Thomas, and W. Chappell, W. H. Cummings, J. W. Davison (the musical critic of the *Times*), Jenny Lind and Otto Goldschmidt, A. J. Hipkins, Francis Hueffer, John Hullah, Joseph Joachim, Henry Littleton (of Novello's), George Macfarren, August Manns, Julian Marshall, Mrs. Moscheles, the Rev. Sir F. A. Gore-Ouseley, Hubert Parry, Dr. W. Pole, Alberto Randegger, Sims Reeves, Carl Rosa, John Stainer, C. Villiers Stanford, Arthur Sullivan, Franklin Taylor, and Miss Agnes Zimmermann. The Archbishop of Canterbury occupied the chair and Dean Stanley, in a speech marked by deep personal feeling, spoke of Grove's splendid services to Biblical research, of the invaluable aid given him in the preparation of his own works, of Grove's contributions to the *Dictionary of the Bible*, and finally of their long and intimate friendship, culminating in their recent tour to America. Sullivan followed, dealing with Grove's services to musical art and literature, laying special stress on the unfailing encouragement he had always extended to young and aspiring musicians—himself among the number—and his labours, in conjunction with Mr. August Manns, in securing recognition for the works of Schubert and Schumann. The Archbishop of Canterbury then presented the testimonial, endorsing what the previous speakers had said in a few generous words of his own, and Grove replied in the charming autobiographical speech from which I have already so frequently levied contributions in the foregoing narrative.

A verbatim report was published in the *Musical World*

of July 31, 1880, then edited by his friend, J. W. Davison, from which the opening and concluding passages may now be taken :—

"Mr Grove said :—My Lord Archbishop, Ladies and Gentlemen,—You will hardly be surprised at my being somewhat overcome, for this is an occasion which only happens to a man once in his life, and however much one may have anticipated it, yet when it actually arrives it must be overpowering. The amount of the gitt that you have put into my hand is in itself serious. To a poor man, whose income is precarious, is limited to what he is able to earn with his hands, a thousand guineas is a great sum. I do not remember ever to have handled so large an amount of my own before, and I need not tell you that I am very glad to possess it. But still the money is not what is most valuable to me ; indeed it is the least of all. This list of names—250 or 300 of the best men in the theology, art, and literature of England ; the terms in which you, Mr Dean, and you, Arthur Sullivan, who have known me so long and so intimately, have been speaking of me ; the dear faces of my beloved friends before me in the room ; the people by whom this testimonial was originated, a family[1] to whom I have been bound by the closest ties for many years, and who of all others I should have chosen to do it ; and the manner in which it was done—these, these are the gratifying things to me, infinitely more valuable than any sum of money can possibly be. I think there never was a testimonial in which the chief person concerned had so little to do with the getting up of it. My friends have done it all, and with such tact and delicacy that it was not till long after it was started that I became at all aware of it, and only a few days since that I knew more than that general fact. It is this list, inscribed with so many names dear to me, that I shall hand down with pride to my children. The money is valuable, and gratifying, and useful, but *this* is the prize."

The greater part of the speech resolved itself into a series of illustrations of the statement that "few men ever had more or better friends, kept them longer, or were more proud of them"—Granville Bradley, Robert Stephenson, Brunel, Charles Barry, Scott Russell, Manns, James Fergusson, Arthur Stanley, William Smith, John

[1] The von Glehns. Mr. Ernest von Glehn tells me that he kept as a memorial of his secretarial connection with the Grove Fund a postcard from Stanley, which no one was ever able to read.

Murray, Aldis Wright, "and half a hundred other good men and true." Then he went on:—

"And don't suppose that because I have laid down these tasks and occupied myself lately with music, I have therefore forgotten my old love. Quite the contrary. The Bible is as fascinating to me as ever; and with all the attractions of Beethoven and Mendelssohn I am always ready to turn back to the lists in Chronicles and Joshua, to the Hittite warriors, and the Edomite kings, with the same enthusiasm as ever. Well, out of the dictionary, somehow, came the Palestine Exploration Fund; and that I could never have worked if it had not been for Captain Wilson[1] of the Engineers, one of the best and staunchest friends a man ever had.

"One dictionary led to another, and now I am in the middle of the Dictionary of Music, with which I am doing my best. And here let me mention two delightful things. First the devotion and enthusiasm of my contributors. They not only answer, they exceed, any wish I can form, and they more than second all my best efforts. The work is full of drudgery and has to be done in a hurry, but they are always equal to it, always ready; and I can point to their work as really first-rate—Rockstro, and Squire, and Mrs Carr, and Husk, and Parry, and many more—too many to name. That is one thing; the other is the liberality and generosity of my friend Mr Macmillan throughout this long and difficult undertaking. It is only of a piece with my experience all through our connexion, now existing for more than twenty years, during which he has always shown himself a generous and sympathising friend. So that you see I was quite right when I said at starting that I have owed almost every opportunity in my career to my friends.

"As I look back through the long corridor of my life it is studded with dear faces and figures, with every one of whom I have a pleasant and profitable association. A little distance back stand Cyrus Field, and Phillips Brooks, and Childs, and the Gilmans, and all the others who made America so welcome and pleasant to me; and in the very foreground stand Ernest Glehn, and Charlie Stanford, and Arthur Chappell, and Hughes, and the Dean of Westminster, and Arthur Sullivan, and the others by whose tact and pains this last kind action has been so splendidly carried out. Alas that some of the dearest and most familiar faces who once shone in that corridor are there no longer. The three[2] whom I

[1] Sir Charles Wilson. [2] Stephenson, Brunel and Barry.

spoke of at first are gone, and Paxton (dear old Paxton), and Farquhar, and Bowley, and nearly all the old Crystal Palace set to a man—Bicknell and Tom Taylor only the other day. And there are others whom I can only dare to touch upon, who were bound up with one's inmost joys and griefs, three or four who were snatched away before their time, and have left an irreparable void—an irreparable void behind them. But I will not throw any gloom over these happy proceedings by such thoughts. If I do refer to those three or four, whom I can never forget, it is rather to look forward to the time when we may all meet again and be fonder friends than ever.

"And O blithe breeze, and O great seas,
Though ne'er, those earliest partings past,
On your wide plain we join again,
Together bring us home at last.

"One port, methought, alike we sought,
One impulse hold where'er we fare;
O bounding breeze, O rushing seas,
At last, at last, unite us there!"[1]

In the evening there was a dinner at which Stanley presided over a large gathering of Grove's friends, and some excellent speeches were made. Dean Bradley, who was present, told me of the surprise felt by Grove's various colleagues on this occasion at his achievements in unfamiliar departments of mental activity. It came almost as a revelation to those who had associated him chiefly with Biblical research to find him appropriated by the musicians, and *vice versâ*.

Grove's note-books for some time had been almost exclusively musical in their contents, but in the summer of 1880 we come across a couple of ghost stories—narratives of which Grove was particularly fond. The first is headed "Fisher Rowe's Story," and runs as follows:—

"Lord —— has a place for shooting in Ireland, a tower with the rooms above each other and a spiral staircase. He was there with his wife and her sister and one or two men. They had gone to bed and the sister wanted a book. She came down one flight, and on the landing was aware of a face poked over her shoulder trying to blow out the candle. She shielded the candle and

[1] Adapted from Clough.

hurried on down the next flight. On the next landing it occurred again. She then got seriously angry and went into the drawing room slamming the door behind her. She found the book and after waiting a moment or two went out, and on going upstairs the same thing occurred, and then she saw it was only a hand with no body at all. She was terribly frightened and rushed into Lord ——'s room (above the drawing room). Lord and Lady —— were both there. She told them what had happened on which Lord —— got very pale and very much excited and said 'I won't hear it. Don't describe it. I will never have you mention it again.'"

The other story recounts the alarming experience of a Foreign Office clerk who came down for a ball at Bisham Abbey, the seat of the Vansittarts—now Vansittart-Neales—near Marlow :—

"He arrived the day before and Vansittart told him that he was to be put up at the inn. He begged for a room in the house. 'Only the green room.' 'Well, what is the green room?' 'Well, it's an old room that is never slept in; indeed, they say it's haunted.' 'Oh I don't mind that if you'll let me have my retriever.' A high room with a very tall old bed and immense fireplace. He came into the room and there was a great bright fire and the bed newly made. He got into bed and went to sleep but woke and found the fire died down and only glimmering—heard a drop and then another and another—a thick sort of sound not like water. The drops came nearer. Then he saw a great black shadow, but that was the dog whom he heard going all round the room. At last it leapt on the bed—then the drops came nearer and he heard them on a strip of carpet at the foot of the bed and then *on* the bed. Then the dog came right up and lay on his breast quivering. At last some sort of cold mist came over him and he fainted. In the morning he woke and was so ashamed that he got off to the inn and away to town. No sign of drops in the room."

But his interest in the supernatural did not impair his love of Nature in her normal aspects. Writing on August 16, 1880, to one of his friends he says :—

"I find nature more to me every year—not only the philosophic Wordsworthian view of it—*that* I am not ignorant of—but the mere beauty and quiet, and the forms and colours—I find I know the things better and divine them more deeply every year, and I think it one of the great compensations of advancing life to do so."

A letter, bearing the same date, to his sister-in-law, Miss Marian Bradley, gives us a pleasant picture of other compensations :—

"LOWER SYDENHAM :
"*August* 16, 1880.

" . . . [My visit to] Vienna is of course for Schubert. I must do him myself. Schumann I have been obliged to give away. He was too complex, and also (what a come-down !) the materials are too much in MS., which is such a despairing grind to me, so I resigned him to a man recommended strongly to me by Joachim and Madame Schumann, who will do it as well as it can be done. . . .

"I can tell you that Testimonial day was a jolly day. It was so delightful to see one's dearest friends (and with the exception of you and one or two more the dearest were there) all before one, and to hear one's praises and not to feel embarrassed, but to be able to say just what one wanted. . . . There were only one or two small drawbacks. One, that I felt that what both Stanley and Sullivan said was exaggerated. It was laid on too thickly, and (as it happened) unjustly with regard to two people in the room. No 2 was that I was not nearly strong enough in thanking Ernest. Somehow he came off with very little praise when he ought to have had very much. . . .

"Thanks for mentioning Milly—dear thing. I should think I *do* miss her. I hope it is all right with her. I sometimes fancy it's a terrible risk leaving her alone like that. It may make her plucky, but will it make her too self-reliant ? She has done very well hitherto as far as one can judge by letters, &c. . . . *my* time with her I shall never forget. It was one of the happiest weeks of my life. . . .

"A wonderful treat of music at the Peak yesterday. Blume[1] came and brought a pupil, a very good baritone, who sang lots of fine things including *Gruppe aus dem Tartarus* of Schubert, also *Rückblick* (Winterreise) a song I had never heard and which

[1] Alfred Blume, subsequently Professor of Singing at the Royal College of Music, who returned to Germany in the "nineties," was appointed a "Royal Professor," and to the great grief of his many friends in both countries, died at Berlin, December 30th, 1902.

was *quite beautiful* :—Each new one is more characteristic and more impressive than the last, isn't it so ? . . .

"How about your story ? What is Blackwood doing with it ? Have you ever read *Irene MacGillycuddy* by L. Oliphant ? or *Dolly and the two Smiths* ? The first is much the best, and is really first-rate. I have read no good novel lately except Trollope's *Duke's Children* which I thought very good, though I am not at all sure if you'd care for it. Not elevating, not exciting, but a thorough good piece of painting of character and manners. Have you found out Susan Phillips yet ? She's there at Whitby somewhere, Crescent Terrace, I think—a long woman in black with large eyes and a brown face. You'd get on excellently with her and be amused beyond belief, and you'd hear all her attacks on me for not writing (and perhaps defend me a bit). Do find her out. I should like you to know her. She is Yorkshire to the backbone and friends with all the fishermen and pilots, &c. . . ."

Grove never allowed his work to detach him from his intimates. On the contrary, he had a happy knack of utilising it to keep in touch with his friends, old and new. Thus he had sent Tennyson a part of the *Dictionary of Music*, containing a reference to the Laureate under the heading "Bugle," and this elicited the following answer, dated September 6 :—

"Very good of you to send me your great work and to mention me in it, though I cannot see how I can 'immortalize' the Bugle, which will go on blowing till the last trumpet blares it down without any help of mine."

On September 20 Grove left for the continent, crossing by the Flushing route, meeting his daughter Millicent at Frankfurt and reaching Vienna on the 23rd. He was already hard at work on his life of Schubert for the Dictionary. The motive of this visit, as we have seen, was exclusively Schubertian, and his pocket-books overflow with elaborate notes on the MSS. of his favourite composer, and the houses in which he was born and died. The devoted Pohl as usual placed himself and the treasures of the Musikverein entirely at Grove's disposal, and much effective assistance was also lent by Herr Heilpern and others. On the 27th he dined with Brahms at the Igel, and on the 29th, after a visit to the graves of Beethoven and Schubert, which he found in much better condition than on the occasion of his last visit, he called on Brahms at his apartment. In some notes hastily jotted down the same day he describes the three rooms and their contents: "a pianoforte in the middle one, very bright and clean-looking; delightful disorder but no untidiness. A long bookcase in the third room with shelves partly filled. Books well used, *e.g.* Schubert's Thematic Catalogue, all bent and worn, and a German Shakespeare." He also describes the various valuable autographs and scores shown him by Brahms, "including the score of one of Wagner's operas with an inscription."

A second visit was paid on October 1st, and devoted mainly to the study of Schubert MSS., but on this, or the previous occasion, as will be seen from a letter given below, Brahms played some of his own compositions to his visitor. After a busy ten days spent in copying MSS., interviewing the few surviving contemporaries of Schubert and certain members of his family, and visiting the composer's favourite haunts, Grove left Vienna on the night of October 3rd and travelled home by Nuremberg, Frankfurt and Wiesbaden. The indefatigable industry he showed in following up any trail that was likely to throw any light on the subject of Schubert is shown by the accompanying letters written on his return to Miss Geisler-Schubert:—

"*Oct.* 17, 1880.

". . . I am very glad to know the exact room in which Schubert was born, which is not stated in any of the biographies . . . . Mr. Heilpern tells me that you have found a letter of Franz Schubert's and that it is an interesting one. Are you anxious to publish it at once or do you propose to allow me to print it in my biography for the first time? . . . . You told me that Professor Door had a mazurka of Schubert's. Could you get him to give you leave to copy it? If so and you would take the trouble, copy every word that there is on the paper, date and signature (if any) and everything else. Mr. Brahms has a most interesting manuscript —an oblong sheet with a song by Beethoven on one side, and a p.f. piece by your uncle on the other. Then, the sheet was torn in half: half was given to Mr. Brahms by some one in Gratz and the other half he bought years after by chance in Vienna."

[*To the Same.*]

"*Oct.* 26, 1880.

"The photograph of the letter has arrived and is most delightful and I am immensely grateful to you for such a treasure. One thing in it is really important—that it fixes the *Trauermesse* as his [Franz Schubert's] which before was considered as Ferdinand's (see Kreissle p. 618). The affection for Ferdinand and all the family, and for Vienna, is quite remarkable, and this last part of the letter is just like a fervent *arioso* bursting out after a *recitative*—nicht wahr? . . . . [see Dict: of Mus: vol. iii. p. 330 a]. I have asked Herr Heilpern to speak to you about making a *Stammbaum* [pedigree] of the Schubert family, beginning with your great-grandfather Franz, and including all the descendants. When I am writing about the family of Franz (der Grosse) I ought to know everything about it."

[*To the Same.*]

"*Nov.* 8, 1880.

". . . Any letters you can get me from your uncle Rudolph or anyone else bearing on Franz Schubert's music or transactions are sure to be of great value to me . . . The story you tell me on your grandmother's authority about Franz Schubert's last moments is new and *most interesting*. Her memory for dates and for the order of facts may be confused, but she is sure to remember many of *the facts themselves*, and as these will be very important to me, I venture to urge you to get all such as you can. [See Dict: of Mus: vol. iii, p. 353 b.]"

[*To the Same.*]

"*Nov.* 8, 1880.

". . . I am very glad you liked the two Rhapsodies. I also found them extremely interesting—It was the first of the two that he [Brahms] played to me when I called upon him, but I had heard them before from Madame Schumann in April. I shall send you the new Hungarian Dances in a few days—I think you will like them extremely."

Any new work from Brahms's pen was a matter of genuine interest to Grove, and almost the last entry in his pocket-book for 1880 is a note of a letter from Hausmann—the 'cellist—about Brahms's visit to Breslau and the success of the "Tragic" and "Academic" overtures (*opp.* 80, 81). On December 10th he describes the sonatas by Schubert which Franklin Taylor played for him at his house. Mention may be also made of a note inspired by a visit to the National Portrait Gallery: "Shakespeare wore ear-rings—little gold ones. Had a very curious mouth and a *Welsh* look"; and of an Irish Bull, which is perhaps worth preserving: "A man defending marriage with the deceased wife's sister said, 'I am not myself a marrying man, but if I were, my wife should certainly be one of them.'"

CHAPTER IX

Tour in Italy in 1881—Impressions of Venice—Death of Dean Stanley—Grove chosen to be his biographer—Reminiscences and anecdotes—Appointment of Dean Bradley—Grove's article on Schubert—Theory of the "Gastein" symphony—Royal College of Music scheme: Grove's exertions in its behalf—Campaign in the Provinces—Appointed Director in the autumn of 1882—Choice of his staff—Formal opening of the Royal College, May, 1883—Knighthood conferred on Grove—His conception of his duties—The *Edinburgh Review* on Schubert—Visits to Northumberland and Norfolk—Contributions to the Press—His Activity in 1884—Impression of Wagner's *Tristan*—Progress of the College—Literary and theological interests.

THE year 1881, which opened sadly for Grove and his Sydenham friends with the death, on January 14th, of Mrs. von Glehn, derived a melancholy significance from the removal in August of the man whom of all his intimates he admired and revered the most—Dean Stanley. This same year signed the death-warrant of another great friend and neighbour—Miss Mimi von Glehn—on whom Sir Andrew Clark in May passed a verdict so unfavourable that Grove speaks of it as "the beginning of the end." The effect of these sorrows, deep as it was, was mitigated in Grove's case by the anodyne of ceaseless work, a still inexhaustible interest in life, and a faculty that never left him of making new friends. In an autobiographical fragment in one of his note-books for this year he says:—"It is not exactly that I can't feel as acutely as I used, but that I am so crushed down with work and things that nothing else can properly get into my head." To argue that because his pocket-books are unusually full of humorous anecdotes this year he was insincere or callous would be to misinterpret his character entirely. No matter how worried or troubled he was himself he could always sympathise with the troubles of others, and show that sympathy not merely by word of mouth but by writing and visiting them, though it must be admitted—and he would probably have been the first to admit it—that he had not the "ministering angel" quality in the face of suffering, but instinctively shrank from the sight of the ravages of ill-health. Yet, as we have seen, he had many friends amongst doctors—Sir James Paget, Sir Henry Thompson, Dr. Gerald Harper, to mention no more; and it was from a doctor—Dr. Waring—in this month of January 1881 that he got the charming story of the grateful housemaid. The poor woman, whom Dr. Waring had attended in St. Giles's workhouse, said to him: "Oh, sir, when I'm in heaven I shall watch for you every day, and when I hear you are coming, I shall ask God *to let me go and open the door for you*"!

The Dictionary was meantime steadily progressing, Grove's pocket-books being full of lists of subjects in the letter R, and notes on Schubert's early symphonies, prefaced by an admirable quotation from de la Place: "Let us beware of condemning irrevocably what our grandchildren are not unlikely one day to applaud"—an excellent maxim for an editor and critic, and one which Grove certainly never disregarded, for even where he could not appreciate, he was always careful to abstain from public condemnation.

By April he had begun to feel the strain of his work to an extent that threatened a breakdown, and accordingly set off for a short holiday in Italy on April 9th, in company with his old friend, Mr. J. S. Forbes, the well-known railway magnate. He attended one of Pasdeloup's concerts in Paris on the 10th, and travelled *viâ* Turin to Milan, whence he wrote to his wife on the evening of the 13th:—

"My DEAREST WIFE,—We have travelled so fast and done so much that I have been quite unable to write before. Sunday Paris:

Monday night Turin: yesterday evening here, and to-day a halt. Turin I had seen before but not Milan. Both are very fine modern cities. *This* I think the most imposing place I ever saw, the streets so long, so broad, so high, and such good architecture, and the cathedral!—astonishing. Tennyson in the *Daisy*, in the same volume with *Maud*, has hit it wonderfully— the height, the space, the gloom—a mount of marble—a thousand spires—the beautiful delicacy and symmetry, and the bright white marble colour are really quite astonishing. We went to the opera last night.[1] The Theatre, La Scala, is one of the finest in Europe. I had often heard of it and written its name, but never seen it. There are six tiers of boxes, eighteen on each side of the Royal Box. The opera was not very much—noisy, and not well sung—but after her great air Mlle. Angeri the *Prima Donna* had six bouquets and a sort of banner carried on to the stage by the footmen of the theatre. The smallest took one man to carry it. Others took two men, and there was one literally the size of a cart-wheel. How foolish! and this to a little second-rate singer who could not act a bit, and in the most tremendous emotion had always a pleasant smile. The band was very fine.

"To-day we stay here I am thankful to say, as I am very tired. I left completely exhausted, and have not yet recovered. What we are going to do I cannot tell. I firmly believe we shall go to Rome. If so I shall be sorry, and it will put me into a rare difficulty, as I ought to be back in a fortnight. I will let you know. We are four: Mr. Forbes the Chief, Captain Godbold the Continental manager of the Chatham and Dover, Mr. Quilter, and G. I have to stick pretty close to the Chief who is very good . . . In Paris I only managed to get a quarter of an hour to call on the Lehmanns. Mimi [Miss von Glehn] was there; better, but not like herself. I don't feel as thankful for the whole expedition as I ought, but I am so horridly tired. . . .

"Your loving husband
"G. GROVE."

On the same evening Grove attended a performance of *Mignon* at the Teatro Manzoni, and left the next day for Verona, where he spent Good Friday. His pocket-book records a visit to the Giusti Gardens; "so wild, and yet the cypresses give it a look of refinement and dignity.

[1] The opera performed was the revived version of Verdi's *Simon Boccanegra*.

These old cypresses every now and then come in like a text from the Bible." Venice was reached on Saturday afternoon, and he notes, "My first impression of Venice was in the gondola, when I was carried back to the wherry in which my father and I used to go to town from Vauxhall to Whitehall Stairs." On the following day he writes to his daughter Millicent :—

"Florence has been given up, and we have come through Verona (stopping there two days) to here, which we reached yesterday afternoon. Verona was charming, but everything fades before Venice, which is more beautiful and strange and different from anything else that you can conceive, besides containing in it two buildings—St. Mark's and the Doge's Palace—which are of themselves quite enough to upset one. The result of this our first day has just been to bewilder me completely. I can really give you no description. I am at last beginning to feel not tired and to enjoy myself. I shall be here till Saturday and then shall go home, arriving I hope about Wednesday morning. Write me a letter (not a card) to Hotel S. Romain, Rue S. Roch, Paris.

"*Verona* has a nice sound, hasn't it? They show the house of the Capulets, but it is very doubtful; but even without that the very name is enchanting. So is Padua which I fear I shall not see. How I long for a chance of bringing you to these lovely spots! Some day may we not hope to come! Read all you can and fill your mind so as to be able to enjoy them when the time arrives. . . ."

On the 18th he saw *Faust* at the Malibran theatre, and writing to his wife on the 19th waxes enthusiastic over the work of Tintoretto :—

". . . I never saw such wonderful things. There was one great Crucifixion, at least 70 feet long and 20 feet high, with certainly 150 figures on it, which for extraordinary incidents and reality beats everything I could imagine—the wildest life all through it, and the most curious and natural things going on; and yet nothing, either in the actions or the circumstances or attitudes, that could be called extravagant. It really transported me into the noise and horror of the dreadful story. . . I really think he is the greatest genius I ever saw or heard of; and if the pictures could be properly seen they would attract millions. As it is they are in very dark rooms, covered with dust, the windows choked with cobwebs and dirt, and the keepers refuse all offers to have them cleaned. . ."

On the 21st, "a lovely hot day," he wrote to Miss Olga von Glehn the following summary of his impressions :—

"VENICE,
"*Thursday, April* 21, 1881.

"It has been an astonishing journey, too quick . . . . but with many great pleasures, of which Venice will abide for long. I have never felt more inadequate to describe a place and I shall not try—but certainly of all the great cities I have seen, it is the most strangely beautiful and attractive and penetrating. Outside and inside alike—when you are on the gondola moving along so fast and so silently and easily through such beautiful strange scenes, you think that is the only thing to do ; and then when you stop at a church and go in and see lovely Carpaccios or splendid Paul Veroneses and Tintorettos or the most beautiful capitals and reliefs on none of which has anyone laid a finger to harm them, you forget the outside completely. The curious state in which things are preserved strikes me very much. The most delicate leaves, birds' beaks, heads of 14–1500 are there quite safe. The pictures are often dirty enough, but they have not been repainted, sometimes not even varnished. On the whole though as yet the outside is *the* thing. It is just wonderful—every day a new light and a new aspect of things—the water such a constant charm, the air so perfectly delicious. Really hot but not too hot, and we have gone up and down the Grand Canal and side canals and out into the sea and then back again into the dark narrow canals with their strange echoes and then suddenly out again into glory and brightness and yet never had enough. If you had only even been here so that you might know what I am talking about ! This is my 5th day and I feel as if I had seen nothing—oh for five more ! but I *must* come back. I begin already to feel the shadow of the dreadful work creeping on like an eclipse."

Friday, "a bad, cold day," was spent in sightseeing, and on Saturday morning Grove travelled through to Botzen : "a most lovely, peaceful afternoon, up beautiful mountain gorges and valleys—*Kennst du das Land, &c.*" He left Botzen early next morning, slept at Munich, and travelled home *viâ* Paris, reaching Sydenham on Wednesday, the 27th, as he had planned.

Grove's relaxations from his labours while at home were now generally in the direction of concert going or musical parties. He attended the performance of Parry's *Prometheus Unbound* at Cambridge on May 17th, and his diary records engagements to attend musical evenings at the Lehmanns' and Moscheles' houses. At one or the other it may well have been that he heard the curious remark of Rubinstein on "the first creation" noted in his pocket-book for June: "Under the Emperor Nicholas, it was dark, all dark; then came Alexander, and he said, 'I will have light,' and he gave them candles, little candles, and the people want not candles but gas." Another amusing saying noted about the same time is that of Costa at a rehearsal of *Lohengrin*: "Bring back the man with the goose."

On June 15th he dined for the last time with Stanley, and there is a curious entry in his pocket-book which from the context points to this meeting: "A.P.S. Gambetta told Père Hyacinthe that Mr. Gladstone was endeavouring to make a combination of the Presbyterian Churches with the Greek Church against the Pope." The story of the next month as it affected Grove is best told in the laconic entries in his almanac: "July 7th, A. P. S.'s flower show. July 9th, Stanley's last sermon. July 13, A.P.S. corrected proof of article on West[minster] Confession of Faith and wrote to S. J. Gazette. July 18th, A.P.S. died 11.40 p.m. July 25th, A.P.S. buried 4 p.m." A week later he wrote to Miss M. E. von Glehn, who had gone to Mulhouse for change:—

"LOWER SYDENHAM, S.E.,

"*Monday, Aug.* 1, 1881.

". . . I fear my letter will not be an enlivening one, but I trust the sweet air is so reviving you that you may be able to bear up against any sorrows. . . . You went away the Wednesday after he died. Well, all that week there were constant visits to be made at the Deanery; questions to be answered and papers to be looked at and memorandums written and the poor women-folk all in a flutter and Lady Fanny, who had nursed him too closely, herself sickening and then getting worse, and at last lying in the greatest danger. Then there was my doubt about the magazine: the desire to write something about him: the feeling of utter incompetency and dried-up-ness. However, at last, I did it, the thoughts and words came into my mind, and with the tears flowing from my eyes I dashed off a page, which quite expressed my own feelings and which others seem to like. Then there was the thought of the funeral ahead, and the will and what terrible duties might be thrust on me. . . . That Monday was a wonderful day. There was everyone in the abbey, all the great and eminent men of all parties and schools in England round his coffin. It was all very orderly and impressive and just as he would have had it. And then by degrees I began to feel what I had lost and to realise how much I had lived on him and how I had unconsciously referred to him on all kinds of points, and how many difficulties vanished when I thought 'Oh, I shall see Stanley next week and then I will ask him.' It is quite curious that since his death hardly a day has passed, but something has turned up in the paper, or the Bible, or a book, to make me say, before I recollected he was gone, 'Oh, I will ask Stanley about this.' I have not got a copy of the words of his will relating to me yet. We are to have a meeting at the Deanery to-morrow and then the lawyers will give it me. Meantime I know simply that all his letters and papers and books are left to three literary executors, Hugh Pearson his oldest and closest friend, Walrond and myself; and of course a Life will have to be written; and I suppose that will fall on me, but *how* am I to do it? Putting aside the *utter incompetency* that I feel on more than half of Stanley's life—all the early part up to 1854, of which I know nothing—all the Court and semi-political part which is absolutely foreign and distasteful to me—putting aside all that, in which of course I should get all possible help, *how* am I to find time? I am bound to finish the Dictionary for Macmillan and until that is done, can undertake nothing that will seriously interfere with it. That is certain, and yet it is equally certain that Stanley's Life ought to be done soon. The mass of letters to be gone through is *perfectly enormous* and I should say that it would take a year's hard work at least, *to collect and arrange the materials*, and yet for a year, I shall not be able to do anything serious at it! Half the success of his own Life of Arnold came from its being out in less than a year after Arnold's death. But in addition to these difficulties, there is that of the Royal College of Music and my possible connection with that. . . .

"One of your sentences is *very* true. The feeling of regret that I was not more to him [Stanley], that in so many directions there were walls between us—has distressed me so much that sometimes I can hardly bear it. I accuse myself terribly, there are so many things on which I might have come down to him and shared his *perfect simplicity* and unselfishness. You have no idea what he was —in one thing, the curiously simple way in which he trusted one. You told him a thing and he never seemed to question it for a moment; that you, his trusted friend, had told him, was quite enough. You can understand how afraid that made one to say anything not strictly correct and how different it is from the usual way one is treated. I could go on talking about him for hours, he was such a wonderful person in some things: no doubt he had littlenesses somewhere, but I never saw them.

"And now he is gone clean out of our reach—that's the most wonderful thing of all. When his breath actually stopped and one knew that he was gone my first thought was one of intense curiosity and longing—where is he? what is he doing or saying or feeling? can he feel or speak? and then the dreadful blank of the answer "you *can* know *nothing*."

As a commentary on and supplement to the foregoing letter, the following from Phillips Brooks will be read with interest:—

"233 CLARENDON STREET,
"BOSTON,
"*August* 6, 1881.

"MY DEAR GROVE,—Ever since the news came of the dear Dean's death I have thought very much of you, for you and he belong together in my recollection, and always will. I think that he can never have really known what a bright spot in the life of many of us was his little visit here. We loved him and we loved America and we had the feeling which everybody has, the wish that the two whom we loved should love each other. And when he came it was so perfectly satisfactory. He and America took instantly to one another. And somehow it all seemed to bring him still nearer and make him still more intelligible to those of us who had loved and understood him before. It was like reading a book, which had been very much to you in a foreign tongue, translated into your own and finding that it stood the translation perfectly and was all the more rich. Do you remember the

Benediction that he pronounced in Trinity Church the morning that he preached there? I never shall forget its impressiveness—I could almost hear it again as I stood on the same spot and talked about him the Sunday morning after he died, while he was still lying unburied in the Deanery.

"You cannot think how different it makes England look now that he is gone. I shall go there with dread and fear if I ever go again. One will have to look about in so many places for what one used to find concentrated and summed up in him. And it is hard to think of anybody else being Dean of Westminster.

"Who will write the story of his life and do for him what he did for Arnold?

"To the Church his loss is one of those which are never supplied. There will come times when, out of mere force of habit, we shall listen for his voice and find always with a new surprise and sorrow that he is silent and that there is no one left to say exactly what he would have said.

"I am sorry for you with all my heart for I know how dear he was to you.

"Ever sincerely your friend,
"PHILLIPS BROOKS."

Apart from the revelation of his constant reliance on Stanley, Grove's letter to Miss von Glehn is interesting first as indicating the reasons which ultimately induced Grove to abandon a task which Stanley himself had wished him to undertake,[1] and second as foreshadowing his connection with the Royal College of Music. The "page" which he "dashed off" is the prefatory note to Stanley's paper on "the Westminster Confession of Faith,"—the proofs of which were actually corrected by the Dean during his fatal illness—and will be found in *Macmillan's Magazine* for August 1881 (Vol. XLIV. p. 282). In addition to this printed tribute to his "beloved Dean" Grove has left a good many interesting notes and reminiscences, mostly anecdotic, in the pages of his pocket-books. "No one," he begins, "is now left to stand up for justice and freedom and goodness in whatever shape it appeared." And again,

[1] Dean Bradley told me that Stanley in his lifetime more than once made this clear, and that it was on this account that he was so anxious for his companionship on their American tour.

"His Church was more the Church of the future than the Broad Church." Of the anecdotes one may note two curiously illustrative of Stanley's artistic and physical limitations—his lack of musical ear and smell :—

"On hearing a new organ given to some church, after the first service he said in reply to a query how he liked it : 'Well, I don't think the sound was so unpleasant as I expected it to be.' When given a very fine rose at Oxford A.P.S. said, 'It is no use giving it me ; I can't smell it any more than I can taste this food.'"

Another entry is headed "Stanley's Dream" :—

"He was on the terrace at Windsor Castle and there saw James I. by himself. The King beckoned to him and said he wished to be read to and gave him the *Fortunes of Nigel* to read, but Stanley broke down in the Scotch and suggested that the Archbishop should be sent for."

To these reminiscences, noted down in August and September 1881, may be added the curious story dictated by Grove in 1897 of the Emperor of Brazil's visit to the monument of Dr. Blow, to which a passing reference is made in Mr. Prothero's *Life of Stanley* (vol. ii. p. 305) :—

"The Emperor of Brazil was an indefatigable sightseer while he was in London. He had promised Stanley to go and see the Abbey before he left for America, but unfortunately he put off his visit almost too long. He arrived at the Deanery unexpectedly about two o'clock one Sunday afternoon, and said that this was his last opportunity before leaving ; could Stanley come and show him anything ? It was extremely inconvenient, the matting and the benches were down for the service in the nave, and it was only possible here and there to clear the way enough to show him some of the chief brasses on the floor. After Stanley had done his utmost to satisfy his curiosity the Emperor said most unexpectedly, 'Now I want to see the tomb of Dr. Blow, a famous organist, do you know where it is ?' Yes, Stanley knew, and took the Emperor to the tomb which is in the north aisle behind the organ. Standing before the monument, the Dean read the inscription to the Emperor, and it is said—though I will not vouch for this—that the Emperor hummed the upper line of the music which is engraved on the monument. The most jealous belief in the English school of music could never have conceived that Dr. Blow's fame could have reached as far as Brazil."

In spite of what he said himself elsewhere as to the blunting of his feelings by the stress of overwork, it is plain that Grove felt Stanley's loss acutely, and was keenly interested in the appointment of his successor. It may easily be imagined, then, how deep and unfeigned was his satisfaction when the choice fell on his brother-in-law and life-long friend George Granville Bradley, the Master of University College, Oxford, and formerly headmaster of Marlborough.

On August 30th he wrote to Mr. W. Barclay Squire :—

"I have been plodding along with Schubert for eight mortal hours (not very successfully) and am so tired that I feel I must stop a bit and thank you for your nice note which came last night. . . . This has been a week of dreadful excitement, culminating in the appointment of my wife's brother to the Deanery of Westminster. I am very satisfied with the appointment quite apart from the fact that he is my brother-in-law. He has not made himself known to the world by any startling books or deeds, but he is widely known, was a pupil of Arnold and of Stanley himself, and will carry on the Abbey on Stanley's lines. . . . It would have been a dreadful calamity if the Abbey had been thrown into the hands of either of the two great sects—High Church or Low Church—and it is a great gain to get a man who without being at all tame or commonplace will hold the scales evenly, keep up the broad national character of the Abbey and excommunicate no one.

"I steadily defer all the Stanley work till the Dictionary is done, but still about six letters a day *do* have to be written about it, and it is rather hard, I can tell you. Schubert I have got down to 1825, leaving '26 '27 '28 and all the wind-up still to do. Last week I could only get one day, but this week I shall get four, and ought to make a great hole in it. . . . Richter is coming for October, but only for London, not the Provinces. Brahms has written a p.f. concerto—that's all the news I have got. In fact my poor brain is rapidly softening, and I can only just bleat out how much I love you."

"Miss von Glehn was in a bad accident the other night—was awoke at 1 A.M. between Basle and Paris by a collision. Fortunately she was not even scratched, but the next carriage was smashed all to atoms, and in another a man stood at the window covered with blood and shouting, 'Je me meurs dans mon sang, et je suis père de famille.' God preserve you and yours from such accidents and also—let me remark before closing—from such a detestable pen as this is. Still I am, now and always,

"Yours affectionately,
"G. GROVE."

It is hardly too much to say that the chief consolation which Grove found in this year of bereavement and anxiety was in his biography of Schubert. It was in this autumn that his theory of the lost "Gastein" symphony took shape, and the untiring importunity which he displayed in seeking for corroborative evidence is touchingly shown in a series of letters addressed to his friend Sir Charles Stanford, then on a visit to Vienna. The first, dated September 13th, begins: "Your letter is a regular Godsend. I am so glad to think of you in Vienna. Here's the letter to dear old Pohl. He's *such* a good old fellow, so old and broken down and infirm and overworked and oppressed, and yet such an angel through it all." Then follow minute instructions as to a variety of Schubert MSS. which Stanford was to examine and report upon, and a string of questions about Schubert's early life, winding up with the *cri du cœur*. "Oh, *why* am I not there with you? It is too hard. It would not only be such a dear delight to be with you and J., but such an advantage to my article." Another letter follows on the 15th with questions as to the value of the *Gulden* in Vienna in 1827—8, the motive being supplied by the following passage:—

"I have been writing the account of poor Schubert's death-bed and it has nearly killed me. Fancy his having corrected the proofs of the second part of the *Winterreise* less than a week before his death! As he went through the *Wegweiser*, *Letzte Hoffnung*,

Wirthshaus, *Nebensonnen*, *Leiermann*, it must have been like his own fate before him :

> "'*Und sein kleiner Teller*
> *Bleibt ihm immer leer*'—

when he had got twenty gulden, 35*s*., only a week or two before, for his E♭ trio!

"I am so sorry to bully you with all these questions, but you are at the fountain head and I am thirsting in the desert."

A third letter broaches the theory of the missing Gastein symphony of 1826. Stanford replied on the 17th adducing evidence that conflicted with Grove's view, and the latter begins his rejoinder dated September 20th, "Yours of the 17th at first gave me profound disappointment. I nearly wept at having to give up the 10th symphony. But on looking again at the entry in Pohl's book I have a little revived," and he forthwith gives reasons for adhering to his original view as to the independent existence of the Gastein symphony. A second letter, written the same night at 11 P.M., adds further arguments drawn from Ferdinand Schubert's article in the *Neue Zeitschrift für Musik* of April 30th, 1839. Lastly, a final *questionnaire* on a postcard followed on the 21st prefaced with the words "What a *horrible* bore you must think me, but Schubert is *my existence*."

The result of these researches, as the sequel showed, was not to make Grove surrender his cherished theory but rather to confirm him therein, and the *Athenæum* for November 19th, 1881, contains on p. 675 a paper signed George Grove and headed "Schubert's Gastein Symphony," in which he marshals his evidence and draws the following conclusions :—

> "That in 1824 Schubert began to contemplate writing a grand symphony, and spoke of it in his correspondence; that in 1825 he wrote it, either wholly or in part, at Gastein; that in October 1826, he dedicated it to the Society and sent it in; that eighteen months after, in March 1828, he wrote another symphony—his last; and that a few months after his death the two were known and mentioned as separate and distinct works."

The objection that the two works were identical—that Schubert may have recalled the symphony sent in in October 1826, revised and returned it in March 1828, is met by Grove with the argument that in that case Schubert must have torn off the first page and substituted a new one with a new date—an unprecedented thing with him—also that the corrections in the MS. of the symphony of 1828 are few and unimportant. The adoption of the theory involved, as its corollary, the renumbering of the great C major Symphony No. 10, and those who attended the Crystal Palace Saturday concerts during the last twenty years of Grove's lifetime will remember that this course was invariably followed in the programme books. As "G" put it, until the chain of evidence adduced in the *Athenæum* of November 19th, 1881, is disproved, we are justified in assuming that there was a separate Gastein symphony, and that the C major of 1828 should be regarded as No. 10. It was of course open to sceptics to urge that the entire disappearance of the score and the continued failure of all efforts to discover it prevented Grove's theory from emerging from the category of an ingenious hypothesis, but his confidence in the accuracy of his deductions was never shaken. Perhaps the best comment on this whole episode was that of the late Henry Bradshaw, the distinguished Cambridge librarian. A friend had alluded to Grove's belief in the existence of the Gastein symphony with some irritation as a mere hallucination, whereupon Bradshaw rejoined, "No. If he doesn't find the symphony he'll stir up people to find other things just as good."

Schubert may have been, and in a sense was, Grove's "existence" at this time, but he did not altogether forget his other interests. Thus we find him contributing a paper on "Western Palestine" to the *Pall Mall Gazette* of October 25th, 1881, on the occasion of the issue by the Palestine Exploration Fund of their map—a reduction of the larger one published eighteen months earlier—of the country west of the Jordan. Grove quotes Pusey's remark that the connection of the Bible with the Hol Land could never be fully understood without "a ordnance map" of the country, and continues :—

"This the present publication is in a double sense. It is no only the reduction of an inch-scale map, made with all the minut care and accuracy of an 'Ordnance map,' but the survey wa actually executed from first to last by Ordnance Surveyors. I embodies the measurements and observations of Sir Charles W Wilson, Colonel Anderson (now, alas! no more), Colone Warren, Lieutenants Conder and Kitchener, with their abl subordinate sergeants and corporals, all belonging to the corps c the Royal Engineers. Excellent as were the maps of Van d Velde, Palmer, Petermann and Kiepert—and considering th imperfect materials at their command, they were marvels c accuracy and intelligence—they are for ever extinguished by th present map. Even that of Messrs. Grove and Saunders, in D W. Smith's Classical Atlas, which contained the results of th Exploration up to that date, is now superseded." Grove goes o to emphasize the superiority of the new map in regard to th representation of the country and the number of names. "In th first respect it is really a picture, for the accuracy of which th names of the surveyors are a guarantee—and a beautiful picture i is. The long slopes gradually rising from the Mediterranean t the high lands, and then again the more sudden, rugged and fa deeper descent to the Jordan valley and the Dead Sea; the lon defile through the hills north-west from Nablus, and the transvers valleys opening on the traveller's right as he advances along tha most interesting and curious road; the fortress-like character o the ridge of Jerusalem and of the high ground north and south o it; the sudden protrusion of the long saddle-back of Carmel; an on the other hand the plains which contrast so delightfully wit these heights—Esdraelon and Beisan, the Buttauf, the soft park like glades below Carmel and the seaside stretch above Akka; th flat beach north of Sebbeh—all these things are so finely brough out as to form a real picture, which, partly from the nature of th country, partly from the manner in which it is rendered, is no les striking than interesting. In the number of names the new ma is equally satisfactory. The large inch-scale map contains abou 10,000 names. Of these there is only room on the smaller on for between 3,000 and 4,000. But even these are more tha double those in the previous maps."

Here we have Grove in his serious vein. A mont

ater (November 29th, 1881) he sends one of his ntimates the following extract from the letter of a German friend who always insisted on writing to him n English :—

"The little boy —— is very content in the happy season of nilk; his mother is already walked out and much occupied with he new Spielzeug. . . . Moved trough occasion and vanity I ave we allowed the innocent childly pleasure to let make the ld visage in a new photo, which I have the arrogance to send ou."

Meantime the movement for the establishment of the Royal College of Music was rapidly maturing. This cheme was originally mooted as far back as July 13th, 878, when a meeting was held at Marlborough House nder the presidency of the Prince of Wales "for the urpose of taking into consideration the advancement of he art of music in the United Kingdom by establishing a College of Music on a more permanent and extended basis han any existing institution." To this end it was uggested that an amalgamation should be effected with he Royal Academy of Music and the National Training School of Music. An executive committee, with Prince Christian as chairman, was accordingly appointed to carry ut this proposal, but after protracted negotiations the Royal Academy decided in favour of maintaining their eparate existence. The Training School, on the other and, which had only been started in 1876, cordially ccepted the proposal, and the next stage in the history of he undertaking was the completion, in 1880, of the draft harter for which the Prince of Wales undertook to ecome petitioner to the Privy Council. The purposes f the scheme as set forth in the original draft of the harter are :—

"The advancement of the art of Music by means of a central epresentative body, charged with the duty of providing musical nstruction of the highest class, and having a capacity to exercise a owerful influence on the cultivation, practice, and regulation of the art and science of music, and, further, having in view the promotion and supervision of musical instruction, as may be thought most conducive to the cultivation and dissemination of the art of Music in the United Kingdom."

Furthermore, and this constituted a special feature of the new institution, the charter contemplated the institution of a fund to provide not only for the gratuitous education but in certain cases for the maintenance of those who, having shown themselves by competition worthy of such advantages, were unable to maintain and educate themselves. On the other hand, the Royal College of Music would open its doors to paying students desirous of obtaining the advantages of a serious collegiate course of musical training. The interest shown in the scheme by the members of the Royal Family from the outset has been keen, continuous, and practical. The King—then Prince of Wales—in addition to the services already mentioned, accepted the Presidency of the Council, and it is generally understood that it was at his recommendation that the large sum, ultimately collected by subscriptions throughout the country and capitalised, was permanently invested, so that the institution should not be dependent on the fluctuating support of annual subscriptions to meet the expenses of scholarships and so forth, but should rest on the solid basis of endowment. In the campaign which was initiated with a view to enlist the interest and support of wealthy and enlightened amateurs in the provinces as well as London, the late Dukes of Coburg (then Edinburgh) and Albany took an active part, and on December 12th, 1881, they attended a public meeting at the Free Trade Hall, Manchester, in support of the movement. The Duke of Albany delivered an admirable address on the influence exerted by music on mankind together with a history of its development in England, while his brother confined himself to a consideration of the difficulties and expense of musical education and the need of its being fostered by public aid, while Prince Christian described the progress of the negotiations during the past three years. Grove, who had been closely in touch with the movement from the outset, had placed his pen at the disposal of the speakers, with what excellent results may be gathered from the concluding passage of the Duke of Albany's address. After speaking of the wide and deep love of music in England, he continues :—

"True, as I said at the outset, far too much of it is done by foreigners. The old traditions of the Italian Opera are too strong upon us, and we sit down quietly and think that because we *do* not make our own music for ourselves, therefore we *cannot* do it—*could* not do it, however much we tried. But, ladies and gentlemen, we will not allow that this is the case. Englishmen are in all essential qualities the same that they were in the sixteenth and seventeenth centuries, and I am convinced that if proper means and methods were afforded them they would become a musical nation in the best sense of the word. It only wants the use of the same means and the patient expenditure of the same time that have been so successful in Germany, to enable us to rival the Germans.

"Recollect the state of things in Germany exactly one hundred years ago. The same struggle was then going on in Mannheim, Dresden, and Vienna, between the native and the foreign element in music, as is now going on in London and Manchester. Mozart's great operas, *Idomeneo*, *Don Giovanni*, *Le Nozze di Figaro*, *Così fan Tutte*, *La Clemenza di Tito*, were all Italian operas. Anfossi, Salieri, and a host of other composers from the southern side of the Alps, held the ground against the Germans, just as Frenchmen, Germans, and Italians now hold it against the English. Mozart wrote but two German operas—the *Entführung aus dem Serail* (1782), and *Die Zauberflöte*. Rossini expelled Beethoven from the field, even in Vienna. It is curious to read in Mozart's and Schubert's letters the same lamentations over the prevalence of Italian works at the theatre, and the neglect of German ones, that we still hear so frequently in regard to our own English operas. The failure of Schubert's many operas and the long delay in the appreciation of such masterpieces as the *Zauberflöte* and *Fidelio* were in a great measure due to the fact that they were native and not Italian works. Their time was not then come. But the national cause is always sure to triumph in the end. For look at what has happened since, and remember that the immense fabric of German dramatic music, the great national school of the theatre, to which Weber and Spohr,

Marschner and Kreutzer did so much, and on which Wagner has now placed so mighty a cupola, has all been reared in one hundred years."

The Duke of Edinburgh addressed himself to the practical side of musical education, the arduousness of the preparation for a musical career, and its peculiar exigencies in regard to accommodation, literature, instruments, and teachers—arriving at the logical conclusion that if music was to be promoted in its highest and best form, external aid must be afforded to a considerable amount, and that, failing the state subvention provided in other countries, such aid must come from the public. Prince Christian finally described the practical steps that had been taken and were still being taken to carry into effect these aims. Grove had already—in July 1881—been invited to become a member of the Council and of the Executive Committee of the proposed College, and in March 1882 at the special request of the Prince of Wales he undertook the task of organising the subscriptions for a period of six months. This was the outcome of a conference of Mayors[1] and distinguished representatives of religious and educational bodies convened by the Prince of Wales and held early in 1882, and led in turn to the successful movement for the establishment of local and colonial scholarships. Into this campaign Grove threw himself with the same energy that had characterised his exertions on behalf of the Palestine Exploration Fund. Speeches had to be made, journeys undertaken and circulars drafted so that no section of the community might escape the appeal. In his eloquent advocacy of the claims of the proposed institution Grove laid special stress on the fact that it was not a musical but an educational movement; he appealed to wealthy colonials on the ground of the essentially national character of the College, and forestalled the objections of utilitarians who might contend that "music did not pay" by the argument that it *did* pay to

[1] There was also a banquet, at which Grove suggested, when the toast of the Mayors was proposed, that it should be drunk in koumiss!

have people happy, and their minds occupied. Apart from this financial campaign in which he had a most efficient lieutenant in Mr. George Watson, afterwards Registrar of the Royal College of Music, the question of securing a teaching staff was already occupying a great deal of his attention and time. Amongst those whom he originally hoped to secure were Joachim, Sullivan and Piatti ; and his

failure was certainly due to no lack of persuasion on his part or of goodwill on theirs.

On March 7th the Cambridge University Musical Society gave an orchestral concert at which Joachim played Brahms's violin concerto and his own Variations, and Stanford's "Elegiac" Symphony was produced under the direction of the composer. Grove managed to run down for the concert and at a gathering of friends in the evening Hubert Herkomer took his silhouette which, by the kind permission of the artist, is here reproduced.

Meantime Grove was still hard at work on his Schubert

article—how hard may be gathered from the following letter to Mrs. Edmond Wodehouse :—

"LOWER SYDENHAM, S.E.,
"*March* 18*th*, 1882.
"7 A.M.

"It is a poor return for your long charming letter to leave it unanswered all this time, but I have had so very much to do. I only wish I could get on with my Schubert as you are doing with your article on "Song"—I have got it all done except the wind-up—characterising his music, etc., and there I stick. I have done it at least four times over, each time quite differently. Each time I think now I have got it, and then the next morning I find that it won't do. I want to bring out the fact that in listening to Schubert one never thinks of the cleverness or the contrivance, as one often does even in Beethoven, but simply of the music itself—the emotions it raises in you and the strong personal feeling it excites towards the composer. Easy enough to put it in that way, but hitherto impossible to work it out in proper terms. It's quite curious how innocent he is of innovation or experiment or of trying æsthetic contrivances as Schumann, Mendelssohn, Spohr, even Beethoven himself do. His symphonies and sonatas are just in the old form as far as arrangement of movements go, etc., and in the construction of each movement, if he wanders from the form, it is not from any intention of neglecting it and setting up something fresh, but just because he goes on pouring out what he has to say and so gets into all kinds of irregular keys and excrescences.

"I really don't believe that such questions as form or calculation, or doing a thing in a new way, because it would produce a better effect, ever entered his head. And as to counterpoint he is very innocent of it. You find a canon here and there (E flat Trio, Scherzo of No. 10 Symphony) but very rarely, and his working-out suffers very much from a want of science.

"The matter always seems to have overpowered the manner, and that the manner was so fine and so touching was owing to the gift of God—well, to his wonderful genius.

"All so far good, but then to say this is very amateurish, and it may be very easily exaggerated, because his skill and power of writing are immense. Remember the splendid effects, the beautiful instrumentation, &c., and then recollect that every piece was written without note or sketch as hard as his pen would go, and you form some idea of the skill and technical ability of the man with all his want of learning.

"I am talking now of his instrumental works. His songs are quite apart. What do you think of it all? Can you give me some hints or help? Just see what you can say, as if we were talking. . . .

"Glad you liked the songs. Look at *Der Einsame* (iv. 74 in your book), and see what a delightful air of domesticity is got by the little quaver figure that comes over and over again: the very picture of a man at his fireside.

"Do you know *Ganymed*, ii. 51, and the *Fahrt zum Hades*, xvi. 50? There's a wonderful long phrase at the end of *Ganymed* (recalling something in the *Junge Nonne*) which is like the pure blue ether. *Auflösung* (xix. 2) is a very fine song, but the *Waldesnacht* is a *King!*"

In this context it is worth noting that Madame Schumann, with whom he was in constant correspondence this year on the subject of Spitta's article on her husband for the *Dictionary of Music*, writes on May 16, "You are right. *Waldesnacht* is splendid. I once heard it wonderfully sung by Stockhausen, but have more often heard it played."

The bulk of Grove's voluminous correspondence in 1882, was occupied with the College and the Dictionary. A letter to his brother-in-law, Mr. Wilkes, on May 24, is interesting as affording evidence of his literary likes and dislikes:—

"What a good fellow you are! I do think you're the nicest brother-in-law a man ever had. I've often heard of the *Oxford Sausage*, but never saw it till now—and what a nice copy! The cleverest thing that I have seen in it yet is the set of parodies, which are really extremely good. As to the epigrams and many of the other pieces, I do think we do better now, and that there is more wit and fun in a couple of numbers of *Punch* than in the whole of this volume.

"I am sure you are right about the old authors. There are two books which always lie on the stool beside my bed, and of which I never tire—Spence's *Anecdotes* and Johnson's *Lives of the Poets*. My Boswell would be there too if he were not too big to be handy in bed, for bed is the only place where I can read. I do not however care so much for the *fun* of those times; *Tom Jones*, for instance, which one hears so much praised, is to me a coarse, tiresome book, and far inferior to *Vanity Fair* or *Esmond*, which I think almost the best reading in novels."

For the rest, Stanley was still constantly in his thoughts. Phillips Brooks, writing on March 27, sent him a list of American subscribers to the memorial, and alludes to the Life which Grove still hoped to be able to undertake:—

"You will know many of the names—Emerson, Longfellow, Holmes, Bancroft, Whittier, Parkman, Gray, Winthrop, Ellis, Field: I am sure they will recall something of how glad they were, all of them, to see him when he was here. East and west, north and south, rich and poor, orthodox and heretic, bishop, priest, and deacon, high churchman and low churchman, scholar and merchant, and quiet reader of his books, they are all here, and all here because they counted it a privilege to say thus that they owed him much and honoured him truly.

"I wonder whether you are at work yet on his Life? It must be a delightful work. For a life so thoroughly free from bad spots, a life of which you can tell everything, is rare enough."

As for Grove's own feelings they are shown in a letter from him to Dr. Harper a few months later:—

"LOWER SYDENHAM,
"*Monday Night, July* 17, 1882.

"I can't let this anniversary go without a few lines to you. A sort of cloud has settled on me during these last few days, and my thoughts are constantly with you and our dear lost friend, and all the terrible scenes of last July 18. That fatal Monday—how well I recollect it. I can account to myself for nearly every minute of it, up to the time when we finally lost hope—up to the moment when his dear heart ceased to beat.

"I wish I could see you to-morrow: words are no use—a good clasp of the hand is the only thing. But I am so busy that I don't see how I can come to you. I wrote to the Drummonds this evening, and will send a line to Lady Frances and Mrs. Vaughan to-morrow. Adieu, my dear fellow! What a loss he was! and how one connects him with everything! Even now, hardly a day goes by that I don't actually feel his absence in some way or other."

Throughout the year, though his occupation was for the most part thoroughly congenial, he often complains of the ceaseless pressure and strain of his work. "What a *furnace* life is on the whole!" he exclaims in a letter to an intimate friend in October. "I have neither time nor fingers to write," and he reproaches himself bitterly for his irritability. "If one could only always keep one's temper! but I do get so cross sometimes, and yet really I am not a bad-tempered man." Grove's explosions were nearly always like summer lightning and no one regretted them more than himself—"but I am so driven sometimes that the nasty things comes doubly nasty. . . You say one has too much to do to think. No, that's just what one has *not*. My botherations often won't let me work." Grove was by temperament incapable of acting on Stanley's golden rule, which he records elsewhere: "Never to worry over a misfortune which does not proceed from one's own fault." Happily for him these fits of depression never impaired his sense of humour, and his pocket-books for 1882 are unusually full of entries contrasting oddly with the tone of his letters. One records the experience of Sir George Macfarren, who, when examining for the Mus. Bac. at Cambridge, asked a candidate, "Will you be kind enough to give me some account of the Ecclesiastical Modes?" "Forgive me, sir," was the unexpected answer, "but I am a Dissenter." Another preserves a dialogue between a friend of his and a German professor on their meeting near Vienna: "What are you doing here?"—"I am on my wedding tour."—"Oh, indeed, but where's your wife? Let me pay my respects."—"Oh, we are too poor to travel together, so I have left her at home." Lastly, we may quote the Devonshire girl's enumeration of the first books of the Bible: "Devonshire, Exeter, Liticus, Numbers, Astronomy, Jupiter, Judges, Ruth."

Grove's tenure of the editorship of *Macmillan's Magazine* was now drawing to a close. The list of contributors to the last volume which appeared under his control—November 1882 to April 1883—includes the names of Matthew Arnold, E. A. Freeman, Mrs. Oliphant, Christina Rossetti, Mrs. Humphry Ward, J. H. Shorthouse, J. R. Seeley, Thomas Hodgkin, and affords sufficient evidence of the high standard of excellence maintained throughout his occupancy of the post, which he resigned on his appointment to the Directorship of the Royal College. To the December number Matthew Arnold contributed the charming elegy on a canary, "Poor Matthias," in reference to which he wrote Grove the following note on November 10, 1882:—

"I was in hopes you would like the verses. The *genre* is a light one, but being a musician, you know that not the *genre* in itself, but the treatment is what matters; and you know too the great importance of a good *motif*, and in this case the *motif* I feel sure is good. I think the public will take kindly to the thing; so many keep canaries!"

The final stage of the movement which resulted in the opening of the Royal College of Music began, as we have seen, with the meeting convened by the Prince of Wales, and held at St. James's Palace on February 28, 1882, when the proposition was first formally launched on the country. In response to the appeal then made to the lord lieutenants, mayors, town clerks, and other leading representatives of the counties, cities, and towns of England, meetings were speedily organised throughout the provinces. In the period of 14 months that elapsed before the opening of the College, 44 meetings in all were held—from Exeter, Plymouth, and Hastings in the South, to Newcastle in the North, from Swansea and Shrewsbury on the one hand, to Lincoln and Norwich on the other. Several meetings were also held at the Mansion House, at one of which, presided over by Sir J. Whittaker Ellis, then Lord Mayor, the Prince of Wales again urged the claims of the proposed College. As a result of this movement, in which Grove took an energetic part as the chief official organiser, a very considerable sum was raised, and the promoters were able to realise a considerable instalment of their plan, by founding 50 scholarships for tuition, several of which included maintenance. It is difficult to ascertain the precise date at which Grove was formally offered the Directorship of the College, but it is clear that at an early stage of the movement his fitness for the post had been recognised by the Prince of Wales, and that the confirmation of the appointment rested solely on the reception of the Prince's appeal to the country. Anyhow it was a tolerably open secret amongst his friends by the summer of 1882, and in the *Times* of October 20th he is for the first time publicly described as Director. In the selection of his staff, Grove's inability to secure some of the most famous singers and instrumentalists was not due to any lack of endeavour on his part. But he did succeed in inducing Madame Lind-Goldschmidt to emerge from her retirement, in order to further the interests of an art of which she had been so bright an ornament. For the rest the staff with very few exceptions was composed of musicians whose antecedents justified their appointment, or whose subsequent careers vindicated the confidence and prescience of the Director. Above all it was in his securing the co-operation of men of wide culture and accomplishments, apart from their musical achievements, that Grove rendered the College a peculiar service. Many of the professors were already old friends. Madame Arabella Goddard was the wife of J. W. Davison, the musical critic of the *Times*, whom Grove had known intimately for nearly thirty years. His close friendship with Franklin Taylor dated back from 1862; Ernst Pauer and John Francis Barnett were also old allies; while the universities were brilliantly represented by Walter Parratt, Charles Villiers Stanford and Hubert Parry. John Frederick Bridge, Signor Visetti, Frederick Cliffe, Algernon Ashton, to mention no others, were also associated with the College almost from the outset, while the services of Mrs. Kendal and Mrs. Arthur Stirling were secured as teachers of declamation.

That the foundation of the College supplied a real need was sufficiently indicated by the fact that 1588 persons from the United Kingdon and Ireland sent in their names as candidates for the scholarships. Of these 480 were selected by the local examiners and sent up for the final examinations by the Board of Professors, which resulted in the election of 17 scholars for the pianoforte, 13 for singing, 8 for the violin, 6 for composition, 2 for the violoncello, and one each for the organ, clarinet, flute and harp. Of the 50, London supplied 12, 28 came from 14 different counties in England, 2 from Scotland, 6 from Ireland, 1 from Wales, and 1 from Jersey. Lastly, as a welcome evidence of the application of the principle *la carrière ouverte aux talents*, the fifty successful candidates included a mill girl, the daughter of a brickmaker, the harmonious son of a blacksmith and the son of a farm labourer.

The formal opening of the college by the Prince of Wales, the President and Founder of the institution, took place on May 7th, 1883, and in an autograph letter dated Downing Street, May 3rd, Mr. Gladstone wrote to express his pleasure at having her Majesty's permission to offer Grove the honour of Knighthood in acknowledgment of the services which he had rendered to the Art of Music in England, wishing him at the same time every success in the work which he had undertaken at the Royal College of Music. The announcement of the honour, however, was not made until the opening ceremony, when the Prince of Wales alluded to the newly appointed Director as one who, "eminent in general literature, has specially devoted himself to the preparation and publication of a *Dictionary of Music*, and has earned our gratitude by the skill and success with which he has worked in the difficult task of organising the Royal College." The ceremony took place in the building previously occupied by the National Training School of Music, and presented to the Prince of Wales for the purposes of the Royal College of Music by Sir Charles Freake.[1] The proceedings were opened with a special prayer from the Archbishop of Canterbury, on which Grove gave a concise account of the movement

[1] The building faces the west side of the Albert Hall. "G's" room was on the ground floor on the right hand side, where he did a great deal of his work at a standing desk in the window.

which had resulted in the foundation of the College and of the competition for the open scholarships. He was able to announce that in addition to the 50 scholars, 42 persons had entered their names as paying students on the College books, and referred to the various acts of private generosity by which the College had benefited—notably the gift of the valuable library of the late Sacred Harmonic Society. The Prince of Wales in his reply, commenting on the open scholarships, stated his belief that they were really calculated to discover latent musical ability and that the College was designed to assist in "bridging over the gulf between different classes, which it is the tendency of increased wealth and increased civilization to widen." He further claimed for music "the distinction which is awarded to it by Addison—that it is the only sensual pleasure in which excess cannot be injurious."

The report of the proceedings, which were attended by Mr. Gladstone, and made the subject of an extremely sympathetic leading article in the *Times*, brought Grove a great budget of congratulatory letters from his friends, colleagues and collaborators. Foremost amongst these was Dr. William Smith, who in the course of a most affectionate letter declares, "No one knows better than I do, how hard you have worked for many a long year, and how fully you have deserved this public recognition of your great merits." The tribute from Mr. August Manns, who had been already intimately associated with Grove for nearly 30 years, was equally generous, and amongst the letters which must have given him special satisfaction on this occasion, were those of Canon Ainger (in verse), of his old friend Lady Paget, of Tennyson, and of Gustave Chouquet, his valued French contributor. Perhaps the most striking letter, in view of subsequent events, was that sent by a friend who has since attained high rank as a scholar and orientalist. After congratulating Grove on his appointment, he continues :—

"Though I dare say you do not know my ruling passion, if the Royal College of Music had been founded fifteen years ago, I should there have found the professional training which I could not get when I wanted to devote myself to an art which in my mind has no rival. Perhaps by being fifteen years too late, you have spoiled a budding musician and created a second-rate 'literator.'"

The spirit in which Grove entered on his duties as Director did not belie the confidence of his friends, or run counter to the principles which had guided his career up to this point. First and foremost, he always regarded himself as the head of a family, and while singularly accessible, sympathethic, and unsparing of time and trouble in encouraging serious effort and high aspirations, he strongly resented any disrespect or neglect of rules and regulations as disloyal to the institution of which he was the head. Holding, as he firmly did, that the arts reacted on each other, and that the more a musician read, the better would be his work in music, he did everything in his power to widen the interests of the students, and to extricate them from a merely musical groove. In conversation, in his terminal addresses, in his letters, in the choice of his staff, he never failed to exemplify his belief in the abiding value of culture. Whenever he got a chance he urged his "children" to read poetry,—Tennyson, Matthew Arnold, Wordsworth—recommended, lent, or gave them books, and insisted on the vital importance of cultivating an interest in intellectual pursuits as a resource in later life. He was a great believer in travel as an instrument of education, and always made a point of telling his pupils in his terminal addresses when and how he had spent his holiday trips. Along with these great qualities were combined certain obvious defects. He came to the work with an immense fund of enthusiasm, goodwill, and a deep sense of his responsibilities as the head of an institution for the cultivation of an art peculiarly exciting in its influence on ill-balanced or highly-strung natures, but he came after thirty years of chronic overwork. He was in consequence often irritated by trifles, worried by details, and inclined to exhibit his impatience at the frivolity, unpunctuality, or disregard of rules shown by the more Philistine pupils with an explosiveness not always consonant with the dignity desirable in his position. His lack of sympathy with athleticism and field sports was also a drawback in his relations with young men. Again he was not always able to conceal his very intelligible preference for instrumentalists over singers. But when all deductions are made, the fact remains that throughout his tenure of office he exercised a great and salutary influence on the *élite* of the students, and that, without exception, the most distinguished *alumni* of the College who studied there during his directorship are unanimous in their testimony as to the stimulating influence of his enthusiastic personality, his unfailing appreciation of good work, his high conception of the musician's calling, his sympathy and sagacity as an adviser, his loyalty and generosity as a friend. Mere ability, however, was no passport to his favour, and his memory is still reverently cherished by many former pupils of very ordinary endowments in whom he recognised the sterling qualities of character without which he reckoned the highest talents of little account. Of the 92 pupils with whom the College started in May 1883, no fewer than 50 were scholars, many of whom have since risen to distinction in various walks of their profession, or subsequently joined the teaching staff. Amongst them it may be enough to mention Dr. Charles Wood, Fellow of Caius College, Cambridge; Mr. Sidney P. Waddington, (afterwards Mendelssohn scholar); Mr. W. H. Squire, the admirable 'cellist; Mr. Emil Kreuz, the viola-player and composer; Dr. A. H. Brewer, now organist of Gloucester Cathedral; Mr. Jasper Sutcliffe, and Mr. Arthur Bent, violinists; Messrs Barton and Waddington Cook, pianists. The list also includes the names of Miss Annie Grimson, the first of a gifted family long and honourably associated with the College, Miss Edith Oldham, now of the Dublin Academy, Miss Margaret Jenkins, Miss Emily Daymond, and Miss Louisa Kellett, an Irish pianoforte scholar of remarkable promise, in whom Grove took especial interest, and whose untimely death from consumption caused him deep grief. And his interest in all these and many other gifted young people was by no means restricted to his official relations. Grove very soon started the practice, which he maintained throughout his directorship, of organising parties of pupils for the Crystal Palace concerts, where he might be seen Saturday after Saturday throughout the season, in his seat at the back of the Gallery, the centre of a group of his "children," with a full score in his lap, pointing out his favourite passages, and leading the applause. When the concert was over, there was generally a tea-party at a special table, where "G" was at his best, discussing the concert, telling anecdotes, and generally radiating sunshine. Another practical way in which he befriended his young charges was by enlisting the help of generous friends, so that if a deserving pupil was in need of rest or change, he was generally able to secure an invitation to the country or the seaside.

Grove had relinquished the editorship of *Macmillan's Magazine*, but was still hard at work on the Dictionary—at the end of letter S and the beginning of letter T. His article on Schubert—perhaps his most remarkable contribution to the Dictionary—had appeared in 1882 and elicited many notable tributes to its excellence, including a wonderful rhapsody from John Addington Symonds. But the chorus of praise was broken in upon by a jarring note struck in an article in the October number of the *Edinburgh*. Grove had no cause for complaint against the references to his work, but he was so deeply wounded by the reviewer's disparagement of Schubert's genius that he addressed a vigorous remonstrance to the editor, the late Mr. Henry Reeve, who replied in the following letter on October 26th :—

"In fairness to the authors I must say that it exactly expresses my own opinion ; indeed as you may perceive I contributed several passages to it. It is quite impossible that any one should feel personal animosity against Schubert. No one admires his astonishing natural genius and vocal power more than I do, but as your biography proves, it was genius growing in a Vienna beer-shop, with a slender amount of education, a low social standard, and more facility than application. Wonderful but incomplete. Such at least is my opinion; but your biography of him is one of the most interesting articles in the dictionary. I think you should have made more of Chopin. . . ."

The author, Mr. H. H. Statham, also remained impenitent, for he reprinted the article with its sneers at Schubert's bourgeois habits and "the creed of Sydenham" in a volume published in 1892, in which Wagner is described as "the most remarkable charlatan who has ever appeared in art."

Grove did not visit the continent in 1883 and was not able to get away for his holiday until the second week in August, when he went to Saltburn to spend a fortnight with his brother Edmund. Writing on the eve of his departure, on August 9th, to his brother-in-law the Dean of Westminster, he complains bitterly of the perpetual strain of his life:—

"How cruel life is! I declare to you I lead the life of a slave. From the moment I wake till the moment I close my eyes it is one fight to do what it is impossible to get through. Hard work is a delight, but when it comes to giving up everything that you care for, and being always in anxiety, always in difficulty, never to have a quiet or a good time undisturbed by the thought of masses of duty left undone, then really life is not worth having. I am off on Saturday to Saltburn, but I fear I shall not get more than a fortnight, and then the shadow of the 24th September, when my College opens again, will begin to deepen and deepen as every day passes. . . . I am taking down A. P. S.'s letters to H. P. [Hugh Pearson], which Victor Williamson has put in order for me. I read a score or so in the train yesterday, and how good they are! The *utter* unreserve in discussing every one is new to me, and very interesting. Of course of such *dicta* nothing can be made, but interspersed with these are delightful traits. His distress, for instance, on returning to Canterbury from Oxford only a few months after he left it, to find out how *entirely* all interest in the place had vanished! That is a real trait of character, and no one could put it better than he does in half a page of note-paper."

In illustration of Grove's mercurial temperament it may be noted that on the very same day, August 9th, he wrote to his sister-in-law, Miss Marian Bradley, and at the end of a despondent letter he suddenly exclaims, "Dear me, as I write I declare life begins to look pleasant again, and the grim appearance that everything has worn to me for the last two years actually gets brighter and the possibility of sunshine again enters my mind. Who shall say we are destructible? Never—perish the thought." After leaving Saltburn, Grove paid a short visit to the Creightons in Northumberland and writes on August 26th to his daughter Millicent from Embleton Vicarage :—

"There is no post *from* here to-day, but I must write you one line to thank you for your little notelet with the two scraps, but with no cutting. However, I do not mind, and am as glad of your intended thoughtfulness as if I had got a hundred newspapers. I am on the move to-morrow. . . . The service to-day was one of the nicest I ever took part in. There was communion to about twelve people, so simple and quiet that it was most impressive. Then the church is a beauty, not large—three arches on each side of the nave—but of fine solid stone, and good proportions, and of a very good date—1320—which was when Norman had just given place to fine Early English. This house is nice—part of it an old Peel-tower, square and massive, and with a most attractive garden. But I must get on to Ripon and then to Cromer, and then home, I hope, by Friday."

Of this Norfolk visit the only record I can find relates to Whitlingham, between Norwich and Cromer, which Grove describes in his pocket-book under date August 30th as "a most lovely little village, one of the most attractive I ever beheld in England or out of it."

In spite of these complaints of over-pressure, Grove found time in the latter half of 1883 to contribute freely to the columns of the daily Press on a variety of topics. There is a letter from him in the *Times* of September 14th on the imagery of the Psalms with special reference to the word *Tsinnor* translated "gutter" in 2 Samuel v. 8

and "waterspout" in Psalm xlii. 7. In the *St. James's Gazette* of October 6th he has a long note on the origin and meaning of the name "Phœnix Park," while in the *Pall Mall Gazette* for October 8th he writes on Dean Stanley's handwriting, recalls the famous misreading of his MS. "the remarkable view of Jones [Jerusalem], and adds,

"I well remember the glee with which he pointed out to me, in one of his proofs, an error by which the printer had transformed 'practical sermons' into 'penitent sinners,' a result which he thought highly satisfactory."

In the same journal (October 16th) he takes up the cudgels on behalf of the artistic merit of Sullivan's operas and (November 30th) announces that a complete edition of Schubert's music has been projected in Vienna on the initiative of Herr Dumba, a public-spirited and wealthy Viennese, the owner of a vast collection of Schubert autographs, and taken up by Breitkopf and Härtel. Grove also refers to Max Friedländer's labours in collating Schubert's songs with the autographs for Peters, and urges on the Vienna Committee that "their edition of the songs should be chronological, arranged in order of the composition, not the publication of these immortal productions." Finally to the *Pall Mall Gazette* for December 4th he sends a note on the true rendering of Solomon's proverb about the net and the bird. His note-books, too, show that his appreciation of good stories remained unimpaired and that he constantly acted on the admirable maxim of Gray: "Half a word fixed in or near the spot is worth a cartload of recollections." One of the best stories recorded in 1883 was told him by the Archbishop of York and may be given in Grove's own words:—

"Wilberforce after a hard day's work went to a country house where there was a large party to dinner, including a local squire full of politics and poor law. After dinner the squire buttonholed Wilberforce, and began to harangue him. Wilberforce fell asleep for a moment and dreamed he saw a ship trying to get round a dangerous headland. He woke up exclaiming, 'She'll never weather the point,' whereon the squire observed: 'I don't see the force of that remark.' 'Oh, don't you?' said Wilberforce, and walked off."

Another takes the form of a dialogue between a high church stranger and a low church verger:—

"H. C.: Do you have matins?
L. C.: No, sir. We have Kamptulicon."

The year 1884 was one of the most crowded of Grove's long and busy life. The record of his extraneous activities outside his multifarious duties as Director, and editor of the Dictionary, is almost bewildering in its variety, and is difficult to reconcile with his complaint that he was "obliged to surrender all that made life worth having." It was a year rich in musical experiences. To begin with he had already embarked on his "History of a Phrase," subsequently published in the form of a series of articles in the *Musical World* under the editorship of the late Dr. Hueffer, and was constantly accumulating new materials and illustrations for his "Symphony Book." One of the most interesting of these is recorded in a letter to Mrs. Wodehouse at the close of the year:—

"ROYAL COLLEGE OF MUSIC,
"*Nov.* 11, 1884.

"I have made a discovery. Every movement of the Choral Symphony ends with a 𝄐 except the slow movement, which has the necessary rests in the bar after the last note and then goes on to the *Presto*. The inference is obvious, that Beethoven intended the lovely dream of the Adagio to be broken in upon by that horrible clamour *as suddenly as possible*. In England the singers *generally come on at that place*! so that there is an interval of three or four minutes, utterly destructive of all *il proposito effetto*.

"I remember pointing this out to Manns years ago, but without effect. I have now written to Richter in the hope that he may try it to-night. The horns change from E♭ to D, which may make a difficulty. But I am convinced that Beethoven meant it."

Again the record of his attendances at concerts, etc., is of unusual interest. On March 13th he ran down to Cambridge for the Joachim concert.[1] On March 19th he went to hear Parry's Quintet at one of Mr. Dannreuther's Chamber concerts. On April 23rd he attended the performance of Stanford's *Canterbury Pilgrims* at Drury Lane. On July 2nd he heard Wagner's *Tristan und Isolde* for the first time and recorded his impressions in the following interesting letter to Mrs. Wodehouse:—

"LOWER SYDENHAM,
"*July* 11, 1884.

"In spite of immense monotony and diffuseness, *Tristan* takes in spite of yourself an immense hold of you. The first act ought to be very much shorter; the dialogues between Isolde and Brangäne are interminable. The love scene (second act) is too realistic. . . . How different from the way in which Shakespeare touches all those hazardous scenes! Romeo and Juliet and even Wagner can't lengthen out such raptures for half an hour, without one's feeling the monotony. The gem of all to me is the third act; the dialogue between Tristan and Kurwenal goes to my heart, but even that is much too long for the stage. It is the old story of 'better half a loaf than no bread.' You must idealise, you must compress, you must show things in a diminishing glass rather, and I do think that, instead of such an exact, literal reproduction of the scene, it should be shortened and idealised a little for its own advantage. (The shepherd's pipe, on the other hand, is too ideal, it is not a tune, or *Weise*, it is a mere rambling succession of phrases which no peasant but a first-rate

[1] Grove was obliged to return to London after the concert. The next day he received a document in Joachim's handwriting beginning:— "G. G.

whose health was drunk, and who was awfully missed by all present who signed this document in Nevile's Court, Trinity College, March 13th, 1884." Then follow twenty-one signatures headed by "J. J." and including the names of Stanford, Parry, Francis Darwin, J. Ludwig, Robert Hausmann, Harry Cust, Sedley Taylor, F. J. H. Jenkinson, etc.

musician could or even would play, with transitions, etc., impossible in a Volkslied.) The opera seems to me to try to do what the pre-Raphaelites did—to transfer nature exactly to the scene—and that is, I think, to misunderstand the relations between Nature and Art."

September found him at the Worcester Festival, where he heard Dvorák's *Stabat Mater*, and on October 25th, "a day to be remembered," there was the annual performance of Schubert's C major symphony. Grove contributed a notice of this concert to the *Pall Mall Gazette* of October 28th in which he writes:—

"Mr. Manns took the finale a shade slower than usual, and it was possibly due to this fact that its impetuosity and enormous force were shaded with an awful supernatural cast, never before apparent. It was as if the tremendous conflict or drama depicted by the music were taking place somewhere outside the world, and as if the inhabitants of the earth were regarding it awe-struck, longing, but powerless to help."

He also attended many other concerts and recitals, not to mention the fortnightly pupils' concerts at the College—then held in the West Theatre of the Albert Hall—which, so long as health and strength remained, he never missed.

In 1884, again, he took three short holiday trips. The first was in the second week of March, when he made a little tour in Sussex and examined six churches in three days. Early in June he spent a week in Paris with his daughter Millicent, where he saw the Salon, went to the opera, and paid two visits to the Louvre. Finally in the middle of August he left England for a fortnight in the Engadine, travelling *viâ* Bâle and Chur to Pontresina and San Moritz, and thence to Davos, returning to Bâle on September 1st and reaching home on the night of the following day.

Another instance of his energy and many-sidedness in 1884 is to be found in the wide range of subjects treated by him in his numerous contributions to the *Pall Mall Gazette* and *St. James's Gazette*. These comprise Charity

Concert programmes: assaults in the streets: the mutilation of figures in the Abbey: two-eyed rifle shooting: the superiority of Australian mutton: von Bülow's concerts: Mendelssohn's alleged "New Symphony": and a humorous note in the *Pall Mall Gazette* for October 14th on Sir Julius Benedict's experiences in teaching the London Scottish volunteers singing. It answered for a while, but the "singing corps" was ultimately chaffed out of existence. "And yet," says Grove, "we call ourselves a musical nation. A musical nation we may be, in one sense, since we pay any amount of German musicians to play and sing their music to us, but a musical nation in the sense in which Germany and Italy are musical nations, that we most assuredly are not."

His pocket-books as usual are full of interesting *obiter dicta* and notes. The ethics of railway travelling was a subject which exercised him greatly at this time and he writes: "It is as if when a man takes his seat in a railway carriage he left behind him all the virtues of private life." Then we have a list of the minor miseries of life amongst which he gives prominence to the gumming up of envelopes and the shouting of newspaper boys. On September 4th he notes a charming saying of Mr. Manns that the horn was "the instrument of hope," and the visit of the Roman Catholics to the Abbey provokes the remark that it would have delighted the hearts of our two great liberal Churchmen—Arnold and Stanley: "Would God either of them could have witnessed it!" Lastly I find two interesting entries, probably intended for use in his addresses to the pupils:—

"Music should be in sympathy with the age in which it is composed, but this relates to the spirit and not the form."

"Suppose we had no literature but translations from German—no manufactures, but what came from the workshops of Berlin or Vienna. We should go on in life, but oh! how we should struggle and strive to get rid of it and have our own English things. We don't realise this in music and therefore we don't struggle for it."

That he still found or made time to keep in touch with the best contemporary literature may be gathered from the two following letters to Mrs. Wodehouse :—

"LOWER SYDENHAM, S.E.,
"*Oct.* 24, 1884.

"I have been—well, not comforted, but encouraged by two letters of Mazzini's in the 1st volume of Froude's new book on Carlyle—so noble, so tender, and so truly religious, on the subject of resignation and the continued existence of our loved ones after death, that they have given me quite a new start. They form a wonderful and refreshing contrast to the rest of the book, which is a sad and humiliating record of selfish and unavailing complaints over evils which might have been easily avoided—a most painful picture."

"ROYAL COLLEGE OF MUSIC,
"*Nov.* 19, 1884.

"Do you get books from Mudie's? If so, get the Bishop of Exeter's Bampton Lectures on Science and Religion. They are worth reading even though you don't agree with them. I am afraid he has not solved the difficulty, but I find them very interesting and quite fair. The drawback is, no advocate of Religion—no 'believer'—knows science accurately enough to argue adequately, just as no scientific man is religious enough (by real conviction I mean) to appreciate the religious difficulty."

As for Grove's work at the College during the year the best summary is to be found in the speech which he delivered at a public meeting held on October 22nd at Portsmouth in connection with the recently-founded Whitcombe (Portsmouth) scholarship. He was happy to be able to say that they were going on extremely well at the College[1] :—

"They would remember that it was opened in May of last year by the Prince of Wales, and while they began with 50

[1] An interview headed, "Half an hour at the College of Music," appeared in November in the *Pall Mall Gazette*, in which Grove is represented as saying: "I feel like the father of a large family. I try to rule by kindness and confidence, and to know each of the pupils personally, and enter into their successes and difficulties." He further defines his wants as, "fifty more open scholarships, which means £100,000 more from the public, a much better building, with concert room and lecture rooms within our own walls and houses near at hand to lodge our country scholars and students."

scholars and 45 paying students, they now had increased the latter to 125. The conduct of the pupils, too, had throughout that period been all that they could desire. It must be remembered that they had come from all classes and ranks of life, and many of them had been previously under very little discipline, but these had now become more civilised, and were working hard, and every term witnessed an improvement in manner and cultivation—it testified in fact to the humanising and civilising effect of music—an effect which he trusted it would in time exercise in all parts of the country."

He further dwelt on the sound financial basis on which the College had been established, thanks to the common sense and practical genius of the Prince of Wales, and the good work done by the Finance Committee, mentioning amongst others Lord Charles Bruce, in whom he found a friend whose devotion to the interests of the College and chivalrous support of Grove himself never flagged throughout twelve years of intimate association. Lord Charles often alluded in his letters to the great happiness he derived from their friendship, and his gracious gentle nature was never more admirably displayed than in the most difficult and delicate task that fell to his lot—that of urging Grove to retire from the Directorship in 1894. Of the impression created by Lord Charles's extreme courtesy, Grove has left on record a curious and entertaining instance in the reminiscences dictated in 1897 :—

"Bell, the headmaster of Marlborough, told me how after an election in which Lord Charles had been defeated but had given much satisfaction to the electors, one of the farmers in the neighbourhood said to him, 'An extraordinary nice man, Lord Charles. Now do you think, Mr. Bell, if anything was to happen to the Queen, would he have any chance?'"

Grove's work at the College brought him anxiety, worry, and occasional friction, but it also brought him many compensating advantages, and for the moment he ceased to complain of the burden of overwork. The entries in his pocket-book for 1884 close on a note of contentment. "One of the great blessings of advancing life," he writes, "is that it teaches one to be thankful. I am far more thankful now than I ever was for Nature, the sun, poetry, music, all the things of life," and then follow two sayings which specially appealed to Grove: "there is no such thing as a trifle," and "Tous les grands hommes ont toujours du caprice—quelque petit grain de folie mêlé à leur science."

The new interests and friendships created by Grove's association with the College were all the more helpful in that without replacing they formed a substitute for what he had lost, and was losing, at Sydenham. For time had made many gaps in that bright coterie which had its focus at Peak Hill. Mr. von Glehn had since his wife's death sunk into a state of profound melancholy, and his daughter Mimi, who for the last four years had been obliged to winter at Cannes or Davos, was literally dying by inches of consumption. The delightful Sunday afternoons, with Mimi von Glehn at the piano and Stockhausen, with unwearied voice and unflagging enthusiasm, singing Schubert, Schumann, Bach, and Brahms, or with Canon Ainger or Grove reading poetry aloud in the garden in summer, or round the fire in winter, were already a thing of the past. Still, Grove was a frequent visitor at "the Peak" till the end, and one of the earliest entries in his 1885 pocket-book records an excellent ghost story told him there on January 18th. It is headed "Miss Yeatman's Story," and runs as follows:—

"S—— Park, now Lord R. G.'s, belonged to Lord A——. They lent it to Mrs. B——, who lived in it for 6 or 7 weeks. One day she gave a tea to the school children in the great staircase hall. The children had gone and 5 o'clock struck. She was standing opposite the foot of the staircase when suddenly she heard a door slam in the corridor above, and a lady rushed out with her dress all in flames and ran into another door crying out 'She has done it.' She [Mrs. B——] ran upstairs, but there was no one there. Next evening she saw the same thing and then the housekeeper told her the story. Some generations back a young man of the family lived there with the grandmother who had entire command of the property. One day he said to her that 'True love was master of all' and he wanted to marry the keeper's daughter. She forbade him, on which he told her that he *had* married the girl that morning. On this she cast him out and away he went and lived elsewhere with his wife. In two years he came back and said that his wife was so ignorant it was wretched living alone with her. She accordingly invited them to live with her, and said as they had come back she would not do things by halves, gave the wife a lot of clothes and the family diamonds, and gave a great ball. Before the ball she asked the wife to come into her room and she would put the diamonds on her. As she was doing so she set her alight with the candle and the girl rushed along the balcony [? corridor] to her husband's dressing-room. She died and he married again, and on her death-bed the old lady told the story."

Grove's delight in ecclesiastical architecture has already been mentioned. Early this spring he again devoted a week to an excursion among village churches, making his headquarters at Salisbury with his sister, Mrs. Wilkes, whence he wrote to Mrs. Wodehouse on March 7th :—

"I have seen 5 village churches all restored, but well restored, and all most interesting. What a wonderful thing it is that every hamlet of this blessed country has a little work of real art set down in it—and not of art alone, but how they teem with historical and personal associations! Not one but has at least its windows, piers and mouldings to tell you all the transitions it has witnessed, and almost always an inscription or a brass with some suggestive date. . . . *Du reste*, I have got the score of Beethoven's no. 4 with me—almost as inexhaustible as the churches. They do it at the Crystal Palace on Saturday, and I want to enlarge my analysis for the occasion."

Grove's views on the most important literary ethical and theological questions of the hour are set forth by the first and second of the following three letters to the same correspondent. The third shows a poetic imagination which enables one to understand his regret that he had been denied the gift of expressing himself in verse :—

"I am just reading Mark Pattison's memoirs, which interest me very much. They also throw a light on my conversation with —— on Sunday, when she avowed such a strong admiration for Pater's new book, with which I never shall or can sympathise . . . . I have never gone much into the controversy of the Humanists and the Religious people, but I have no doubt as to which is right—no doubt that life without *Duty* is no life at all, and how are you to have Duty without Religion? A life which consists in nurturing your love of the beautiful, and your sensations of pleasure is a poor civilisation, and a poor preparation for this world and the next. And to find —— of all people on that side shocked me terribly."

"ROYAL COLLEGE OF MUSIC,
"*May* 26, 1885.

". . . Have you seen the new Bible? and would it interest you if you had? To me, of course, it is keenly interesting, but my first impression is that they have been far too Conservative. To have retained such words as *ouches*, *astonied*, *tabering*, *chapiter*, (for *capital*), *daysman* (for *umpire*), *harness* (for *armour*), can serve no purpose. In fact, the difficulty in reading the new book is to persuade one's self that one is not reading the old. No doubt there are many corrections of translations but there too, I think, they might have been more [? exact]. Even the geographical words, hill, valley, etc., do not seem to have been set right. I had hoped that the word 'brook' would have gone for ever. It denotes a broad, dry torrent bed, which in winter is a rushing stream, and in summer often has no water at all. 'Brook' certainly can't be the right word for that! But I must read a great deal more before I can form any adequate judgment. . . .

"Forgive a dry letter, but I am as arid as a bit of tinder."

"LOWER SYDENHAM,
"*May* 30, 1885.

". . . What a beautiful experience your morning watch must have been! I love those times and have had many of them. I have often watched the dawn, till I realised so strongly the motion of the earth—heaving round towards the sun, and gradually discovering his light and warmth—that I felt myself, as it were, the only human being standing on the shoulder of the great round world, as it whirled round—and almost seemed to feel my hair being blown back by the breeze caused by the motion. And the gradual awakening that you describe is so wonderful. Once experience a thing of that kind and one never forgets it."

After this letter one is not surprised to hear of his getting hold of Clough's poems " in the dead hours of the night," and re-reading many of them with the greatest delight. As he says in another letter written a few weeks later, "I have always had the greatest admiration for (no, sympathy with) them: the feeling is too much a part of myself to be admiration." Another book which he read this summer with much interest was Amiel's Journal, transcribing in one of his pocket-books the description of an autumn morning, and the admirable appreciation of Mozart's music, in which the writer speaks of its exquisite and aristrocratic beauty, its healthiness and serenity, and the fact that it showed as much talent as genius.

For his summer holiday spent in Switzerland, Grove had his daughter Millicent as a travelling companion. They left London on August the 12th, and returned on the last day of the month. I can find no record of the tour in the shape of letters or notes, but from the brief entries in his almanac, it appears that Lucerne and Interlaken were successively their headquarters, and that at the latter place they met Stockhausen and the Henschels. Of his interests and occupations in the autumn a good picture may be found in the following highly characteristic letter to Mrs. Wodehouse :—

"LOWER SYDENHAM,
"*Oct.* 23, 1885.

". . . I have just been looking over and adding to my account [1] of the Pastoral Symphony for the Crystal Palace Concert to-morrow, and have put a lot of new and interesting things in about Beethoven's love of the country, etc. I shall soon have done all that I can to the whole of the nine and then will come the question of publishing them. I know that I am too fastidious to consent to this, while I live, and after I am gone, who will care? However, we shall see. Amongst other things I have been lately reading Wagner's cool proposal to re-instrument a large part of the ninth Symphony with the insulting and ridiculous comments of his adherent Mr. ——. Such audacity and such horribly bad taste!

[1] Grove greatly appreciated the action of the Birmingham Festival Committee in printing his analysis—specially revised for the occasion—of Beethoven's Choral Symphony in their programme this autumn.

I keep getting up and walking about my room roaring out the most injurious words at them both. What an age it is since I told you any College news, and there is plenty to tell. We are going most likely to have a real new proper College before long. We have found a great vacant plot of ground belonging to the Commissioners of 1851, just behind our present house—and we believe that they will give it us for the purpose. The land once ours, it will be easy to get £50,000 or so to build with. Meantime we are preparing for the renewal of the Scholarships in April next, settling who are worth keeping and who are to go away, etc.—a process involving no end of 'considerations.' We have had one Pupils' Concert at which Kellett and Sutcliffe played the Sonata in G (op. 31 No. 3) very nicely indeed. K. has also run through the first movement of the E♭ Concerto at Rehearsal in a very splendid manner. But she is beginning the troubles of life. Her extraordinary simplicity and unconsciousness is beginning to be disturbed. She finds that she does not get on as she did, that she is nervous and thinks about herself, and is beginning to be anxious and to feel how little she knows and how much there is to learn. It is *most* interesting but also most afflicting, lest one should not say the right thing, or be too sympathizing, or make any other mistake. It is just now that a real good lady friend would be such a boon to her. The child *is* so nice—such a fine nature *au fond*, and is much improved. She of course will stay at College."

CHAPTER X

Letter to Millais—Deaths of Mr. and Miss von Glehn—Grove as Director—Impressions of Liszt—Brahms's Fourth Symphony—The "Dream of St. Jerome"—Last visit to Peak Hill—At Saltburn, Chatham and Penn—Views on librettos—The musical knowledge of George Eliot and G. H. Lewes—Death of Grove's daughter Millicent—Miss Coleridge's reminiscences—Opening of the Alexandra House—Death of C. F. Pohl: letter from Brahms—At the Natural History Museum—Performance at Windsor—Address on English organists—Napoleon, Wellington and Beethoven—Views on the art of resting—"Coleridge Notes" in *Athenæum*, 1888—At the Birmingham Festival—Sussex churches—Enthusiasm for Tennyson—Views on the equipment of a musical critic—Tour to Bayreuth and Vienna, August and September, 1889—Leeds Festival—Dr. Walford Davies's reminiscences—Grove's generosity—His addresses to his pupils.

Grove had now been nearly three years at the Royal College where his work, though thoroughly congenial in the main, was not without rubs. His staff were, with hardly an exception, thoroughly loyal to him and conscientious in the discharge of their duties. But the results, as tested by the reports of external examiners, were not always satisfactory, and it was Grove's painful duty this year to have to communicate a most serious criticism of inadequate preparation to a member of the teaching staff who was not only an old friend but had occupied a most distinguished position as an artist for many years. Such a conflict between personal goodwill and the duties of his position was peculiarly distasteful to a man of Grove's temperament. As he once said to the present writer, "I should have been a much more *successful* man if I could have trampled on people now and then." Grove certainly did not excel in trampling. He greatly preferred the attitude illustrated in the letter written to Millais on New Year's Day, with reference to the exhibition of Millais's pictures in the Grosvenor Gallery :—

"*Jan.* 1, 1886.

"MY DEAR MILLAIS,—I went to the Grosvenor yesterday and I cannot help trying to communicate to you a little bit of the great pleasure which I received from those lovely rooms. It was so delightful to see so many dear old friends, all as familiar and as well-remembered as if one had seen them only yesterday, and all so sweet and kind, not a snarl, not an angry word among the lot. Each one as harmonious and comforting as a bit of Mozart! And then when I came to look again at the 'Carpenter's Shop' and the 'Huguenots,' and the dear old knight in the river—all which I saw the first time you exhibited—I was struck with the magical way in which they brought back those early days—the astonishment, the enthusiasm, the half fear, which all came into my mind again as if I were there seeing them for the first time. It is out and out the most interesting exhibition I have ever seen, and what's more, there isn't a drawback to it. God bless you, my dear friend, I feel proud to have ever pressed your hand,

"Yours affectionately,

"G. GROVE."

Nor were personal troubles and bereavements lacking to cloud his natural cheerfulness. Mr. von Glehn died in July, 1885, in November the news reached him of the death of his daughter-in-law in Australia, and the year 1886 opened sadly with the deaths of Miss Mimi von Glehn, perhaps the most gifted and attractive of a family with whom he had lived on terms of the closest intimacy for nearly thirty years, and of James Fergusson.

[*To* C. L. GRAVES]

"LOWER SYDENHAM,

"*Friday, Jan.* 15, 1886.

". . . I have had a *dreadful* time since you went. I have not been able to get one hour's holiday, but that was nothing. My dear friend of twenty years' standing, Miss Mimi von Glehn, died after prolonged suffering on Friday night, and we buried her on Wednesday; and on Saturday departed another still older friend

James Fergusson, who had a very large share in my intellectual life. Added to this, I am terribly overworked and near to give up the ghost. . . ."

[*To* W. Barclay Squire]

"Sunday, *Jan.* 17, 1886.

". . . We buried dear Miss Mimi on Wednesday. It was a terrible day for those who loved her, but it was a beautiful service, and we all owe a deep debt to Stanford, who came and played the organ. . . ."

I have already endeavoured to convey an impression of Grove's conception of the responsibilities of his office, and it is interesting to see how his efforts to carry out that conception appealed to those pupils who were resolved to make the most of their opportunities. For this purpose I cannot do better than avail myself of the testimony of Miss Zoë Pyne (now Mrs. Oliver Madox-Hueffer), who entered the College as a violin pupil in 1883, and has kindly furnished the following reminiscences of her relations with its first Director :—

"In recalling my memories of Sir George Grove, I find a difficulty in choosing amongst so many those which represent him as I know him best. Though his mind was so many-sided, his personality never varied—on the first occasion (in 1883 at the opening of the Royal College of Music) as on the last (after his resignation as Director) there was the same energy of manner and keenness about his own and his friends' affairs.

"It would be difficult for me to explain sufficiently my sense of indebtedness to him for the many opportunities he gave me of talking to him during ten or twelve years. Such keen intuitive sympathy, wide knowledge of men and things, and free giving out of himself to a young and very ignorant girl seem to me now very unusual. In these talks there was never any suggestion of a pedestal or talking from an altitude: simplicity, sympathy, and a curious personal humility were his strong characteristics.

"I rarely came away without feeling I had been in the presence of a great mind, and one always at the service of one's own doubts and difficulties. His wide view of life and tactfulness never failed one. His accessibility was wonderful. If alone, he seldom refused to see students—the most I ever heard him say was, 'What is it, my dear? I am very busy to-day.' He was somewhat hasty in temper, but on looking back, I can see that the qualities which irritated him most in a student were—a casual manner, a slovenly style and want of reverence for great men. The last of these qualities was almost pathetically developed in him. I can never forget hearing him speak of Beethoven and Schubert. This impression is still so strong that when a couple of years ago I was in the room where Beethoven was born (in Bonn) I found myself thinking almost as much of Sir George as of Beethoven. His worship of Beethoven was indeed a religion, and one out of many proofs of this occurs to me at this moment. It was at the Leeds Festival Rehearsal in St. James's Hall. The ninth Symphony was being rehearsed by the band and Sir George and I were sharing a score, when an unhappy relative of mine seated himself behind us and in a moment of intense appreciation gave vent to his feelings in a somewhat prominent 'Bravo.' 'Hush,' said Sir George, turning round, but with such a deadly white heat of fury that the unfortunate gentleman scorched and shrivelled in the sight of the whole audience.

"His mind was an extraordinarily healthy one. Art was always to him a strenuous soul-compelling thing which admitted of no effeminacy or self-indulgence. Yet his emotions were easily touched and his sense of beauty admitted quite as much of colour as of form."

Mrs. Oliver Madox-Hueffer's remark about Beethoven is pointedly illustrated by a letter of Grove's in the *Times* of March 22, 1886, suggested by a remark in a leading article of a previous issue and advocating the extension of non-congregational Sunday music by the more frequent performance of oratorios and even symphonies at afternoon services. Grove puts forward suggestions for the organisation of such a scheme, raising of funds, drawing up of a special form of service, etc., but discountenances efforts to "dodge" the legal provisions against performances by payment. There are, further, two notable points in the letter. One the remark that "to those who believe in the cultivating powers of music—morals, I, for one, think it has nothing to do with, unless in a very indirect way—it must always seem cruel that on the only leisure day in the week, concerts are not legal," and the other the *obiter dictum* that Beethoven's symphonies are "as truly religious as any oratorio." It is interesting to note how the suggestions contained in this letter have since been realised in our churches and by the inclusion of symphonies in the programmes performed in cathedrals at our provincial festivals.

Though, as we shall see, Grove's contributions to the Press on a variety of topics were more numerous than ever in 1886, the College absorbed his best energies, and was never absent from his thoughts. In January Lord Charles Bruce addressed a friendly remonstrance to him not to overwork: "If you would only go to bed and take proper and regular nourishment as a Christian, then *la force ne vous manquerait pas*." The impending withdrawal, owing to failing health, of Madam Goldschmidt from the regular teaching staff was a matter of serious concern to him, but he was able, in writing to Mrs. Wodehouse on April 10, to give a most encouraging report of the progress of the pupils as tested by the external examiners:—

"ROYAL COLLEGE OF MUSIC,
"*April* 10, 1886.

". . . Our exams. are going on well. The p.f. has been very good. All have made great improvement, but "the red-haired girl"[1] is far above all. She really *astonished* us all with her performance of Schumann's Études Symphoniques. Dannreuther said it was the finest performance he had ever heard in a school, and that she was ready to go before the public at once. . . . He also said that the average standard was far higher than at any other school he was acquainted with, and that the result was certainly above that of any place in England or the Continent."

In this spring Liszt paid his last visit to England, and Grove records his impressions in the same letter:—

"I went to Liszt's reception on Thursday and was delighted (1) by his playing, so calm, clear, correct, refined—so entirely unlike the style of the so-called 'Liszt School'—(2) by his face. Directly he sat down he dismissed that very artificial smile, which

[1] Miss Kellett.

he always wears, and his face assumed the most beautiful serene look with enormous power and repose in it. It was quite a wonderful sight."

Another musical event of 1886 which appealed even more strongly to Grove was the production of Brahms's Fourth Symphony. He writes to the *St. James's Gazette* of May 10 calling attention to the adoption of the *chaconne* form in the last movement of the new work, which was to be given that evening by Richter, and in the issue of May 12 he has a note full of enthusiasm for the "enormous power of Brahms's genius."[1] He is like Carlyle's Indian, "who had fire enough in his belly to burn up every one else." Grove has a grievance, however: that no chance is given to hear a great work like this again soon after its first performance. It would, he urges, be a real boon to amateurs, and professional musicians too, if in the case of new works of the calibre of Brahms's symphony a second performance could be given within a few days of the first.

The *St. James's Gazette* for June contained no fewer than eight contributions from Grove's pen, including a characteristic outburst, *à propos* of the discomforts of suburban railway travelling—"Issachar is a strong ass, crouching down between two burdens might well be our motto in a hundred cases of annoyance"—and a note on a personal trait of Stanley's which he shared with Tennyson, viz., his liking for Tauchnitz editions. Grove concludes:—

"The Dean, however, never attained to a Tauchnitz edition of any of his most popular works, not even 'Sinai and Palestine.' He was too proud to complain of this; but he would confess his disappointment in a very characteristic way by expressing his envy of Robertson of Brighton, one of whose volumes was included in the Tauchnitz series."

[1] Grove was constantly kept advised by his Viennese friends and others of Brahms's progress. Only a month before this Max Friedländer had written to him to say that he hoped to go to Vienna to see Brahms and Pohl, and to Trieste to see Thayer and hunt for traces of Schubert's "Gastein" symphony.

To the *Times* of June 16th, he contributed a full account of that strange fraud known as "The Dream of St. Jerome," a piece for pianoforte purporting to be by Beethoven, which was "faked" by an enterprising publisher in response to a demand created by a reference in Thackeray's *Philip*. The story, it should be added, was told Grove by J. W. Davison, and it prompted Grove in a further letter to the *Times* (June 28th), to suggest that it would be an interesting subject of inquiry to ascertain "why a fraud should be successful in music which in literature would be unmasked and denounced in a moment." He always vigorously resented this treatment of Music as the Cinderella of the arts, and in one of his contributions to the *St. James's Gazette* (June 15th), we find him commenting on a ceremony mentioned in the *Times* itself, at which a new organ was opened, but nothing was said of either organ or organist. The "Dream of St. Jerome" letter had an amusing sequel. In tracing the history of the piece, which was founded on Moore's setting, in song form, of a mutilated version of the theme of the variations in Beethoven's A flat sonata (Op. 26), Grove wounded the patriotic susceptibilities of a writer in the *Irish Times*. But he made the *amende* in a graceful letter to that journal (July 16th, 1886) in which, after explaining that nothing was further from his thoughts than to say anything derogatory to Moore or Ireland, he continues :—

"As to Ireland, were my sentiments different from what they are, I am not likely to have any feeling towards her but gratitude and affection as long as she sends me such clever, hard-working, good pupils as those who form the Irish brigade in the Royal College of Music, London, of which I have the honour to be Director."

Grove had special reason to be proud of his young people at the moment, for they had recently acquitted themselves with great credit in a performance of Cherubini's "Water Carrier" (*Les Deux Journées*), on June 23rd—one of the earliest of the long and interesting series so admirably directed by Sir Charles Stanford.

But music did not entirely absorb all Grove's energies. Though the secretarial connection had ceased long since, his interest in the Palestine Exploration Fund was as keen as ever. He attended the meeting on June 22nd this year, and made a speech in which he defined the purpose of the work on which they were all engaged as "the investigation of the greatest document which the world contains—the Bible."

On July 5th the dinner to Dr. Charles Pritchard, Grove's old schoolmaster, took place at the Albion Tavern with Dean Bradley in the chair; but Grove was, much to his regret, unable to attend. On the 18th there is a brief entry in his almanac which closes a separate chapter in Grove's life: "My last visit to the Peak [Peak Hill]. Went all round with Olga. The most lovely day." Entries in his pocket-books show that he was busily occupied on his "History of a Phrase," and on August 5th there is an amusing note from his pen in the *St. James's Gazette* on a ludicrous musical blunder in the previous issue of the *Spectator*, where a Heidelberg professor is said to have attired himself in the dress of a street musician and amused an evening party with his "improvised [*sic*] organ-grinding." His pocket-books also show that he was reading Landor's poems and Conversations, and Hamerton's *Painter's Camp*. From the latter he copied out the following extract: "They say in Burgundy that when the English believe in you they buy blindly, whereas until you get them to that point they are most difficult to deal with, because they have no judgment of their own to which you may appeal," adding as his own comment, "What a parallel to their judgment in music!"

Grove was too busy to manage a trip to the Continent in his holidays, contenting himself with a visit to his brother Edmund at Saltburn. Thence it was that he wrote to the *Times* of September 6th, calling attention to the new and important musical publications undertaken "by the great publishing firm of Leipzig" (Breitkopf and Härtel), viz. the supplemental volume of Beethoven's work, the progress made with the monumental Schubert edition, and the centenary edition of Frederick the Great's compositions for the flute—an enterprise which he notes as happily characteristic of the German's *Pietät* towards their great men. By the second week in September he was back at the Royal College, whence he wrote to the compiler of this memoir a letter pleasantly illustrative of his many-sided interest in life, art, and literature :—

"I came back from Saltburn ten days ago, and have been here ever since except Wednesday, when I had a most *delightful* day at Chatham Dockyard, seeing Ironclads, Turret ships, and Torpedos, and filling myself with wonder and pleasure. Also I got hold of a boatswain, who told me that before the new regulation was made some twenty years ago, the song for heaving the lead was

so that my recollection of the man-of-war in Porto Rico in 1841 was correct! . . . . I don't know how you will approve of a letter which I am writing to the *Times* in the character of a Gloucester man to protest against the novelties in the programmes of the Festivals. I hope they will put it in.[1] I have for long thought that some such protest was wanted in the interests of quiet, ordinary, musical, country people, and I shall try to introduce a few digs against the 'critics' who are so anxious for the English school and then directly a piece appears give it no quarter, and slaughter wholesale instead of picking out equally the bad and the good points. . . . I have been reading again Mérimée's *Lettres à une inconnue.* Wonderfully clever, wise and pleasant, but deformed by constant lapses of taste."

A visit to his brother Thomas at Penn led to a descriptive paper, "A Country Church," in the *St. James's Gazette* for September 27th—"so spoiled by the editor that I hardly care to own it," he has written on the margin

[1] The letter, signed G. Grove, appeared in the *Times* of September 23, 1886.

of his scrap-book—from which I quote the following passage :—

"A little Buckinghamshire village which has been practically unchanged for the last two hundred years, Penn stands in a triangle between Beaconsfield, Amersham and High Wycombe; and as its name implies, it is the highest land in that part of the country. One part of it is still called Beacon Hill; and the fires anciently lighted thereon are said to have been visible at sea. It is its height that has been its safeguard against innovation. The railway station is Loudwater; and from that it is a steepish gradient of some three miles to the village. Penn proper consists of a street about half a mile long, a school, a chapel, a few houses and cottages on each side, and, at the further or eastern end, the church, the blacksmith's shop, and the institute, which is almost the only modern thing in the place. On either side of the street are some of the most delightful fields in England, and thence you may have unrivalled views."

On a clear day, as Grove mentions, Windsor Castle is easily distinguishable. The chancel has been burned down and rebuilt, but the tower and nave of the church is "fourteenth century at latest," and in the parsonage garden stands a grand old yew-tree, which he had on more than one occasion seen smoking like an altar, and thus learned the meaning of Tennyson's lines.

The London rehearsals for the Leeds Festival held in the first week of October prompted another contribution to the same journal (October 8th), in connexion with Sullivan's *Golden Legend.* After praising the music, "the greatest thing he has written," Grove goes on to say that "the chief lesson of the rehearsal was the advantage of a good libretto." Handel, he notes, "sank and revived" according as he had the platitudes of Morell and Humphreys, or the words of Milton or the Bible to set. He appeals accordingly to the good minor poets to come to the rescue of the composers. "Cannot something be done to ally these two natural friends, music and poetry? Cannot some of our numerous poets turn their attention to the making of opera books?" The case of Mr. Gilbert, he adds, seems to show that the occupation, besides being new and not unattractive, would be far from unprofitable as well. He reverts to the same subject in a letter to Mrs. Wodehouse a couple of days later :—

"LOWER SYDENHAM,
"*Oct.* 10.

" . . . I am going down to Leeds on Wednesday so as to get there in time for the evening concert (Mackenzie's Persian Story), and shall stay till after the *Golden Legend* on Saturday. I heard the *G. L.* rehearsal and liked it very much indeed. It is far beyond anything he has yet done and *beautiful* to hear. It is curious how much Wagner there is in it. I don't mean in Leit-motives, etc., but in spirit and declamation. It is a capital book and made me think what a good thing it would be if the young poets would turn their attention that way. I also heard the orchestral part of Stanford's 'Revenge,' which I thought very good too. Dvorák's new work I did not hear, but I was very pleased that he came up and spoke to me. I never thought that he would have remembered me again."

Grove's interest in music outside his immediate official surroundings is pleasantly shown by his contributions to the Press during the next two months. Thus the announcement of the discovery of some early works of Wagner, encouraged him to draw the inference in a note in the *Musical World* that Schubert's "Gastein" symphony might be unearthed some day. Then he has an excellent letter in the *St. James's Gazette* on November 2nd, exposing the ignorance and ineptitude of the musical critic of the *Daily Telegraph* in advising Brahms "not to write so much in his study," but "to go into the largeness of the world ; let the generous sights and sounds of nature work upon him as upon Beethoven, and let him catch their spirit." Grove retorts by asking what largeness of the world did Beethoven enjoy, deaf, absent-minded, working six or seven hours daily in his room, with little social recreation. He certainly spent his holidays in the country, but "it is notorious that Brahms is an insatiable lover of the open air. This very year the beautiful country on the lake of Thun was his summer resting place for months. In conversation, too, he is one of the most genial and humorous of men." Even better reading is furnished by another note in the *Musical World* (November 6th) *à propos* of a paper in the *Monthly Musical Record*, on passages in George Eliot's works relating to music :—

"We hope that they will not omit the delightful one in the third volume of *The Mill on the Floss*, in which the praises are sung of the 'perfect accord of descending thirds and fifths' with a transition to 'linnet-throated sopranos and full-toned basses.' This has all the false air of learning, which is the great defect of this truly charming writer, and which so ruins the effect of many of her best performances, especially in her later works, when she wanders off her own ground, where she is so delightfully sure. The writer knew her, and has sat next her at more than one performance of chamber music. She listened absolutely with the air of knowing everything beforehand; but it was evident from her remarks afterwards that she looked on music, not as a pleasure in itself, but as a branch of knowledge interesting from its effect on the human mind."

G. H. Lewes, Grove says, was much the same, but there was more *pose* about his attitude, and he gives a ludicrous account of him at the first rehearsal of Brahms's First Symphony in London, ostentatiously beating time all wrong. Mention may be also made of Grove's letter to the *Times* of Dec. 7th on "The Performance of Oratorios," advocating a more rational disposition of the performers on the platform and the employment of a certain amount of gesture—not acting, but a "certain sufficient recognition of the situation implied in the words." The letter was suggested by a performance of the *Golden Legend* at the Crystal Palace, at which the anomalies inherent in oratorio performances were brought home to Grove with peculiar force.

On the 10th of November, Grove met with a serious accident, being run over in Knightsbridge by a cab, but fortunately without permanent injury. A week later he wrote to Mr. Edward Speyer, then at Frankfurt :—

". . . I was thrown down and run over and shaken and dirtied, but here I am again just as before—and always your great admirer and friend. I was in bed for three days, and then I got up again and became myself. You seem to be having a pleasant life. If you see Madame Schumann, give my kindest warmest love to her and tell her she has not a more devoted friend in the world than I am, and that I wish her all health and happiness and never to be run over by a cab in the dirt! . . . Henschel begins his concerts to-night and my doctor won't let me go, which I am very sorry for. Henschel and Blume are now both professors in the College and I like them extremely. If I had leisure, I think I should devote it to hearing Brahms's two last symphonies and his PF concerto, till I knew them; but alas, I have none. . . ."

This accident led to a charming letter from an Indian pupil at the College:—

"Kind Lát Sahib Salamat.—I was so very sad when our darling Miss Sahiba [Miss Campbell] told me that a cab had run over you, but we hope that you are quite well now, and we think that God must have sent flying down His shining angels to guard and take care of you from getting more hurt! We often think of your kind words to us and of your smiles the first day we saw you, and we pray that God may let us see your kind face again. Now I must say Salám noble Lát Sahib. May God put a garland of love round your neck.

"I remain your grateful little Indian friend,

"Háfizán."

The year 1886 which opened so sadly with the death of two of his most intimate friends closed in even deeper gloom. His daughter Millicent, who had for some time past been in failing health, was ordered abroad in November, and on the 22nd of that month she started for Alassio. A fortnight later she developed such serious symptoms that her parents hurried out to join her. The sequel is told in the sadly laconic entries in his almanac. "December 15 Milly sinking. December 16 3 a.m. dear Milly died. December 17th 2.30 p.m. buried her in the Protestant cemetery, Alassio." What this bereavement meant to her father and mother may perhaps best be understood from the letters written to his friends on his return to London.

[*To* George Lillie Craik]

"Lower Sydenham,
"*Jan.* 4, 1887.

"I have just got back your dear note and the *Locksley Hall* from Italy. It is extremely touching to me, as it was written when there was still hope, and brings back to me so strongly the state of mind in which I passed the last few days, catching at hope, exaggerating any little turn for the better, and at last sinking into blank despair when the truth could no longer be resisted. It has been a terrible blow to us. My wife is stronger and more self-controlled, but I confess that it has been sometimes more than I could bear. I know that work is the great refuge, but hitherto work is so distasteful, and I can only sit and mope. She was so much my companion and friend—we enjoyed nothing so much as when we enjoyed it together, and our journeys were like lovers' journeys. And yet I am not sure whether there is not almost a drawback to the happiness of this recollection in the thought of how much there must always be *un*felt and *un*said between a girl's mind, and that of a man so much older—and the pang keeps continually intruding 'might I not have been more to her, have known more of her?'

"Well, she's gone—Oh! if one had but some grain of knowledge as to her state, and as to the future.

"*Locksley Hall* was a great pleasure to me, and I thank you sincerely for it. These later poems of Tennyson are wonderfully interesting to me. . . Of course the man is old and sad, but what *glows* of faith burst through the gloom! And what a far stronger appeal to our hearts (at least to mine) there is in the 'fuller day than our poor twilight here on earth,' and in the 'for ever since our dying race began—Ever, ever, and for ever was the leading light of man,' and the 'sacred passion of the second life' than there would be in more detailed and less real utterances. Well, goodbye, dear friend. May you never have such a blow."

[*To* C. L. Graves]

"Lower Sydenham,
"*Jan. 5th.*

". . . I have begun work but it is gall and wormwood—even the College has no interest to me, and I would fain do nothing all day but sit and mope. . . . We were so fond of each other and enjoyed so very much being together; and that relation between an old man and a young woman has always in it something special. Then she took great care of my papers, knew the place of everything and had a particular knack about it all, and I looked forward to her for the last 10 years of my life in a way which is difficult to describe and terrible to recollect. . . . She died at 3 in the morning; at 7 I went in to look at her once more, and the look of the face and head was the most ideal thing you ever saw. It was as I knew her, but so raised and idealised as it might be at the Resurrection. I have not had much experience with the dead, but this was an astonishing change. I don't say *glorified*—because the prevailing air was naturalness but perfectly idealised. There was also a half air of humour. It was to me as if some one were saying to her, 'What sins have you to answer for?' and she were replying, 'I don't know the meaning of the word.' I have been very much touched by reading a number of letters of her friends, of whom she had two or three very close ones—mostly on literary subjects. She was a great student of Shelley, and had just completed a concordance to one of his longer poems, and I was much gratified to receive a letter from Ellis, the editor, to say that though many had undertaken concordances, she was almost the only one who had carried through her work properly."

[*To* MRS. WODEHOUSE]

"ROYAL COLLEGE OF MUSIC,
"*Jan.* 7, 1887.

". . . One curious likeness I find between her and myself—the curiously backward condition in which our minds are compared to our age. I was always 10 years behind my boy friends, and when Bradley came home from Rugby and Oxford, and used to talk to me about poetry and the Oxford Movement, I listened, but it was all Hebrew to me, and it was not till years afterwards that I found myself really caring for the things which he had then told me about. Even now I am continually discovering the worth of principles or modes of life which most men assimilate at 25. And so with her: her letters display a great vigour of mind, sympathy, interest in books, in pictures, in people—and yet all combined with a curious freshness and childishness and immaturity. It's quite astonishing how good people are, and now I get letters from men and women whom I looked upon from quite a different point of view and have even despised, but whose letters well over with soft tenderness. . . ."

The distaste for work happily soon passed away and he found in his labours at the College the best anodyne for his grief, the relations that prevailed between him and the pupils at this period being pleasantly sketched in the following reminiscences furnished me by Miss Florence Coleridge, then a student at the College :—

"Early in the term (Easter, 1887), the whole College was summoned to the West Theatre one day at 1.30; no explanation being given, we were mystified and inclined to expect a scolding. It was a long and impressive speech from Sir George, lasting about 40 minutes. He began with a scolding for a very whimsical set of crimes. There had been rowdy behaviour among the boys, they had torn down inscriptions in the dining-room, one of them had even danced a hornpipe on the landing before a select audience of girls. Sir George could not endure to make rules, and he appealed to the good feeling of the College to enable him to do without them. He reminded them of the first time that he had addressed them, just after the election of the 50 original scholars, of how little either he or they knew of their duties then, of how much they had all learnt since. He spoke beautifully of the daughter he had so lately lost, and went on to the relations existing between him and us: he said he hoped that all his children would write to him *at least* once a year when they left College, to let him know of their welfare. Then came a goodly list of the appointments, etc., won by old Collegers, to cheer us up at the end. . . .

"I left the College with the firm conviction that there was no such place in the world. There were certainly various drawbacks, but in spite of these there was a beautiful feeling in the place, due, I believe, chiefly to Sir George, but greatly to the masters, too, that held us all together in a wonderful way, and will continue so to hold us, I trust, as long as the College stands, and long may that be! It seemed to me that there was about it something of that ideal community where 'all feel what befalls any, and are all solaced with the same joys, and all languish in the same sorrows and all unite in the same ends, and all bear the weaknesses, and supply the needs, and seek the good and pleasure of each other, as they do their own.' I saw it all through rose-coloured glasses, some people will say: if so, it did the College no harm, and me much good."

The gradual recovery of his spirits is traceable in the resumption of his contributions to the *St. James's Gazette*. In the issue of February 8th, he notes that "Schubert scored another triumph at the Popular Concert last night," when Mr. Thorndike sang *Waldesnacht*, though he adds that the song wants a much better accompanist than was provided on this occasion—this was before the days of Mr. Henry Bird. A few days later Mr. Henschel sang the same composer's *Ganymed* at his recital and elicited a fresh transport of enthusiasm from Grove (*St. James's Gazette*, February 12, 1887). To the same journal (February 21st) he sent an amusing letter on "Persian Hyperbole," giving extracts from a book written by some Persian Princes who visited England about fifty years earlier. They spoke of the Thames Tunnel, "with inimitable *naïveté*, as a contrivance 'for making ships pass over the heads of the people.'" In regard to figures they practised throughout a precise and colossal exaggeration. Some phrases are delightful. Astley's is called "the opera of the horse" and we read that at the entertainment of Mr. R.—the "beautiful circle of the family," had "fine arms of jasmine colour, hair of ambergris odour, eyes of the gazelle, and conversations sweet as sugar-candy."

Hitherto the pupils' concerts had been held in the West Theatre of the Albert Hall, but after March 14th, 1887, when the Alexandra House was formally opened, they were held in the hall of that building. The first concert held in the new room was remarkable for a most admirable performance of Brahms's Pianoforte Quartet in A, by Miss Kellett and Messrs. Sutcliffe, Kreuz and Squire, which gave Grove the utmost pleasure. But his championship of Brahms never degenerated into mere partisanship. About this time the *Daily Telegraph* had noticed a new opera produced at Pesth and *more suo* praised the composer for not being influenced by Wagner—"he seems to his credit to have forgotten Wagner's very existence." Grove immediately wrote to point out that this is incredible. Whatever Wagner's faults, "that he has made a revolution in the form and structure of opera is admitted by nine-tenths of the musical world." Another of his contributions to the *St. James's Gazette* (April 23rd, 1887) grew out of the performance of Sullivan's *Golden Legend* at Berlin. Grove ascribes the hostile reception with which the work met to Sullivan's policy of an "all British orchestra"—as carried out in the Philharmonic Band. "Whether he [A. S.] is right or wrong is not the question, but it is certain that the unfair and absurd judgment passed on the *Golden Legend* in Berlin, was the mode which the persons who do the musical criticism for the German papers have taken to show their sense of his opinions. The only wonder is that with his extraordinary mixture of cleverness and common sense he did not see what was sure to happen."

The *Times* of March 31st contained an interesting letter from him in support of the aims of the People's Concert Society, and to the issue of May 11th he contributed the obituary notice of his faithful friend C. F. Pohl, who died at Vienna on April 28th. The notice concludes with this admirable summary of Pohl's character:—

"... He died lamented by a large circle of friends in this country, Germany and Austria, including Brahms, Mr. Pauer, Sir George Grove and many others, who esteemed him as much for his remarkably simple and amiable nature as for his unselfish devotion to his subject and to all to whom he could be of any benefit therein. Pohl was one of a class of men like Otto Jahn, Nottebohm, and Thayer, to whom no labour or patience is too great, and who never seem to think of pecuniary profit when any point of fact can be cleared up by their exertion. His memory was extraordinary and always at the service of those who wanted it. . . ."

Pohl's death prompted Grove to write to Brahms, from whom he received the following interesting letter a couple of months later:—

"THUN, SWITZERLAND,
"*July* 6, 1887.

"DEAR AND HONOURED SIR!—Once again I hope you will accept my friendly greetings and thanks. As far as we are concerned the length of time that has elapsed makes no difference. Both of us still sincerely mourn our friend, and that your feelings impelled you to write to me about his loss gratifies me now just as much as it would have then. I often saw our friend during his illness in the winter and never without his alluding affectionately to you. He did not lack sympathy nor tender care—indeed the excellent people with whom he lived were all that could be desired in this respect. I left for Italy a few days before his death, and found your letter had arrived here when I got to Thun a few days ago. To read your words and know that they were addressed to me gave me a peculiarly pleasant sensation. Late though it is to send you my thanks, they come from the heart, as does everything connected with the memory of our friend, the kindest and dearest friend in the world. With heartiest greetings,

"Yours very sincerely,

"J. BRAHMS."

At the College most of the first generation of pupils had now gone. What this meant to Grove may be learned from a note to Miss Florence Coleridge after the close of the Easter term :—

"LOWER SYDENHAM, S.E.,

"*April* 23, 1887.

"Thank you for your note. I did not know that you were going, and am heartily sorry for it. It was not till after the Associate Examination that I realised what it would be not to see the old faces any more—to miss Macdonald and Edith Oldham and little Kate Boundy and all the rest. It made me feel very desolate, and now here you come to swell the crowd of the parting ones. Well, there is one alleviation—that you who go should feel as strongly to the College as you do and say as nice words about it and me! I shall always prize such letters far more than you who write them may think. They, and the occasional visits of the writers, will be my real reward. But you are wrong in thinking my life so hard. It *is* hard: but there is a background of warm colour, a heaven of affection and feeling permeating all the difficulties—always ready to brighten up and to come into prominence and to give me encouragement such as nothing else could do—and of such elements your letter has been one of the strongest and most gratifying. I have been for a long time intending to devise some plan by which the pupils could keep their names 'on the books' of the College, and I will at once see what can be done. . . ."

The preparations for the annual operatic performance and for a special concert at Windsor, gave Grove a good deal of trouble and worry in the month of June, but there was nearly always some humorous or instructive side to his experiences. Thus the tedium of a rehearsal was enlivened by his overhearing an eminent actress remark, "Those musicians are stuck-up devils," and at the very time when he describes himself as utterly fagged and depressed, he is yet able to record in dramatic form a delightful dialogue with a little boy whom he met crying on Sydenham hill:—

"G. Cheer up, old man; what's the matter?
"Boy. It's that other boy: he pulled my nose and said I had no business to have it.
"G. Oh, never mind; don't cry and the pain'll soon go away.
"Boy. I shall never like him again. *'E's howed me a happle for four months.*" [Exit.

The opera chosen for performance was *Der Freischütz*, and this led indirectly to a visit to the Natural History Museum recorded in a letter to Mrs. Wodehouse:—

"*June* 18, 1887.

"I snatch a moment to have a little talk with you. I am very much occupied and very faint of heart but there is an end to all things, and Monday week will, I hope, see the last of our troubles. . . . I went to the Natural History Museum on Thursday. What to do, do you think? To borrow the skin of an eagle for the opera! and there I found my old friend Flower the keeper, and made him take me round and show me some things. There is a large glass case as you enter, containing the *original* pigeons (rocks) and all the various kinds which domestication has brought out of them; some in which the tail, others the beak, others the crop, others the leg-feathers, etc., are exaggerated out of all proportion. It is a complete illustration of Development and matches well the statue of Darwin at the other end of the hall. They are beautifully done—flying, feeding, complimenting one another, etc. Then he showed me a beautiful flat case in which it was shown how *ornament grows*. There was a small plain feather, next that one with a mark, then a greater mark, and so on through seventy, till we arrived at the perfect peacock's feather. . . . . I could see no more as Mrs. Kendal was waiting for the eagle, and I had to run. . . .

"The two volumes of Schubert's Masses in the complete Edition arrived yesterday. How differently the next generation will be placed as to the possession of things from what I was! In my early days nothing was published and everything had to be copied. It was not bad discipline—the copying—but it was long and cumbrous; one knew little but well, now one knows much but imperfectly. I was writing a little paper last night for the *St. James's Gazette*[1] on the difference between the life of an English composer and a German one. Perhaps I stretched it too far, but Brahms's life *e.g.* must be very much quieter and more favourable for thought than ——'s; no pupils, no cabs, no railway journeys, no society. If they print it, I will send you a copy, but there's really nothing in it more than I have said above."

Writing twelve days later to the same correspondent he was able to give a good account of both events:—

"LOWER SYDENHAM, S.E.,
"*June* 30, 1887.

". . . My life for the last ten days has been one of great turmoil and I am now quite collapsed and feel like a perfect rag. Fortunately everything was very successful. At Windsor it was splendid! The Queen had us put into the Waterloo Room which is magnificent for music. My young heroes rose to the occasion and I really do not think that the overture to *Ruy Blas* has been often better played. Russell sang Wood's two songs very well indeed. The mass of the room talked loud, but the Queen was very attentive and very intelligent. I and Charles Morley were taken to her afterwards by the Prince of Wales, and I understood her to say that she was very much pleased, and that she was astonished to find them playing so well. She also asked questions about the performers, but her voice was so low that I missed much of her words. It was a splendid night. Two kings at least, and lots of beautiful women of the highest rank. The most interesting thing to me was to see an Infanta of Spain for the first time in the flesh! Another very interesting thing was the transformation that occurred when the Queen said that we were not to play in the Tapestry Room but to go into the Waterloo Gallery. Just as in an Arabian Night, when you stamp your foot everything is carried away, etc., so here, on the instant (as it seemed to me), thirty or forty men appeared, carried off all the desks, seats, music, etc. at once and the change was made within five minutes.

"Our opera was really a great success—of course judged by its

[1] It eventually appeared in the issue for December 18th, 1887.

own standard. The house was full and everyone much delighted. The best account is in the *Daily News*. I don't mean the most laudatory one, but the one which, while admitting the shortcomings of these young creatures, yet also did justice to their merits, which indeed were very great. . . . I have been looking at Princess Christian's translation of the memoirs of Frederick the Great's sister. Very curious—but it's difficult to read page after page of such monotonous details of cruelty and bad manners. I have taken a few doses of Kinglake's Crimea—Balaklava and Inkermann. The sight of the Infanta made me feel warlike towards the whole world. It did indeed! . . .

"P.S. I have been too dry about our opera. It was really very good judged by *any* standard and did the pupils infinite credit. What is to be the next? Stanford says *Fidelio*, but that *is* a mountain to climb."[1]

Business connected with the preparation of the Appendix to the *Dictionary of Music* and the *Life of Stanley* prevented Grove from getting away for a proper holiday after the end of the term, and at the end of August, to use his own words, he was still "loafing away and bemoaning his sad fate." A letter from one of his Irish pupils suddenly inspired him with a desire to visit the West coast of Ireland, and he proposed himself as a guest to his friend the Bishop of Limerick, then at his country place in Kerry. The proposition was hailed with enthusiasm, but the visit never came off, as Grove found it necessary to go down to Cuckfield and discuss plans for Stanley's Life with his brother-in-law Dean Bradley, who at that time had undertaken to write the memoir.

[*To* C. L. GRAVES.]

"CUCKFIELD,
"*Sept.* 10, 1887.

"I don't know what you will say to such vacillation on my part, especially after such solemn promises from me, but I find that I must give up my dear, delightful, paradisaical Irish trip. The business on which I have come here turns out bigger and more exacting than I thought, and the Appendix to the Dictionary is plaguing me a good deal; and though the difficulties are not

[1] The mountain, however, was successfully climbed in December, 1902.

serious yet they want my *presence*. Besides this, I must be back at College by Monday week the 19th, and it would be such a hurry and scurry that I feel bound to give it up. You'll forgive me, won't you, old man? Just think for a moment how great the *miss* is to me compared to that to *you*, and your heart will be softened; I know you want to have me, but then I want to come to you; and I really do require the change. I certainly have managed very badly this time, and yet I am very well in health. My worst symptom is a sort of craven feeling at meeting my work again—almost a fear; but that flies when I come really to the encounter.

"I have just been reading *The Mill on the Floss*. I never read it but once before, and the remembrance of the deep tragedy of it has always kept me away from it since. It's wonderfully true to nature and in parts wonderfully fetching; and certainly the tragedy is as great as I recollected it. But Tom, true to life as he is, is to me very repulsive—and yet what a fine character for conflict with the world! Two things annoy me; the constant epigrammatic turns, and the stupid priggishness put into Maggie's speech and behaviour. However, to talk like this of a book published 27 years ago is indeed kicking a dead horse. Beethoven's music is the only thing which will bear commenting on so long after its date. . . . Miss Kellett has been very seriously ill. Mrs. Franklin Taylor has got her down at Herne Bay. I fear she won't do much this term."

In the *Musical World* of the same date, September 10, there is a full report of the address delivered by Grove at the annual dinner of the College of Organists. Grove dwells on the "separate independent mission" filled by every organist in England—there were at that time about 12,000.

"The organist" he continues, "is not an ordinary musician who is able to put his instrument into a green bag at the end of service to leave the church and think of nothing else till the next time; he has got a church, an organ, an organ stool, a house somewhere near the church; he is a definite individual, he has a position, he is almost as necessary to the church as the clergyman is, and all these responsibilities and privileges add to the serious nature of his employment. Moreover, organists are not only a strong body, and a good body, but they are also a very important body from a musical point of view. Now I confess to be a very great admirer of the parish churches of England.[1] They form the school in which I have learnt the little knowledge of architecture which I possess. In the most remote village of the country you find a building, which is, as it were, a little gem around which has crystallised the historical associations and the traditions of the many-sided character of English institutions, in their most prominent side, the English Church. Every arch, every window, every moulding, tells of a definite date with its struggles, its movement, its changes, its part in that singular mixture of progress and permanence which distinguishes England, and has made us what we are. These things are always to be found if you know how to look for them, and they give a dignity and an interest to the smallest parish church in the country. And, gentlemen, I have always had a similar idea in my mind about the organist. The principal person in the church is of course the clergyman. He addresses the reason and the understanding of his hearers, tells them their duties, what to do, and what not to do—a most serious function. But the organist is not less important, for if the clergyman's business be with the duty and the moral sense, the organist's deals with the imagination. It is he who gives wings to the old poetry of Psalms, Canticles, and Litanies, and sends the soul heavenward on the more modern strains of the Hymns. A most important mission, if you look at your calling in this light; if you reflect what public worship would be without the 'sweetness and light' which you, and you alone, can impart to it! It is a mission which at once gives dignity and importance to the organists of England. One cannot help thinking, that when you have twelve thousand of them, they form a great, solid, musical influence, which somehow or other ought to be made the most of. It seems to me that while you are going on in your business-like way, you are influencing in a remarkable and definite manner the whole fabric of society. Of course all these advantages are not without risks or unaccompanied by corresponding dangers. Nothing is more remarked on by the German musicians who visit England than the prevalence of organists. They say it has coloured our national music. So it may have done, but I do not see that the colour need necessarily be an unpleasant one. Sebastian Bach was an organist. We cannot all be Sebastian Bachs, but we can look to his example, and do what we have to do to the best of our powers. For it is a very great thing to be a good organist, and surely any monotony or any sameness which

[1] In his pocket-book this same month Grove entered a saying of Sir Walter Scott's: "If a man has half an hour to spare on a journey he can't do better than go into the Parish Church."

devotion to a single instrument gives is largely counterbalanced by the status of the organ as a kingly instrument."

In conclusion, he asserts that an organist is a centre of musical life capable of any amount of useful expansion, that our organists furnish more eminent musicians than any other branch of the art, and that "no one can help more than they to pull down that wonderful musical ignorance which still besets this country"; in illustration of which he refers to an article in a great London daily advocating the claims of the Crystal Palace and saying nothing of the splendid services of Manns and his band, or the honourable record of the Saturday Concerts.

Grove's interest in Napoleon may have partly grown out of the personal history of the "Eroica" symphony, but his admiration for Wellington was directly inspired, as we see from the following letter to Mrs. Wodehouse:—

"LOWER SYDENHAM,
"*Sept.* 25, 1887.

". . . I have been reading a new book about Waterloo—not a new book, tho' new to me, by a certain G. Hooper. It wants close attention and might have had more anecdotes and traits, and be better written, but it is well worth reading. The whole of the Prussian side is particularly well told, and their share in the battle shown to have been premeditated and arranged. Everything I read about Wellington raises my opinion of him. He is emphatically an Englishman, and it is no wonder that he was never valued or understood abroad, or that to the French soldiers, or the Belgian, Dutch, Hanoverians, etc., he was nothing by the side of Napoleon's marshals; but the record of the battle is an astonishing tribute to his foresight and self-possession. Do you care much about him? If so, you should read Croker's memoirs, published last year: they contain many excellent new anecdotes. . . . Every now and then, I get terribly impatient to begin on the 2nd edition of my article on Beethoven in the Dictionary as a separate volume. I look forward greatly to it. I will have all the portraits, views of spots, houses, etc., facsimiles of writing and music. By degrees, perhaps, I may do the same with Mendelssohn and Schubert . . . . I send you the note which Addis wrote me after reading my article on Beethoven. It pleased me very much, because what I wanted was to get the ear of non-musicians."

Grove, however, contrived to establish parallelisms even between Beethoven and the Iron Duke, for I find in his pocket-book a few months later a note of an anecdote which his informant had from the Duke's cook. It is headed "Beethoven" and runs: "Duke of Wellington endeavouring to show the servants that he only required *one* egg at breakfast and when he failed to do so, calling up the kitchenmaid and *shying* them at her." The entries are as diversified as ever in 1887 and towards the end of the year there are a good number of amusing stories and sayings, *e.g.* that of the butcher who, when some one complimented him on his boy's appearance replied, "Yes, sir, his face is the best joint about him." But most of them relate to business matters, or are of a serious turn. On September 18, there is a long entry beginning:—

"The idea of the next world must depend on the intellectual and spiritual condition of the race . . . In 1987 when our intellect has gone still further into the understanding of Nature and the laws of the world it will be very different and probably quite unintelligible to us of 1887."

Very interesting, again, as a piece of autobiography is the draft of a letter—I have not been able to trace it in print—prompted by an article in the *Daily Telegraph*:—

"I agree with much in your admirable leader on the way to rest one's self, but I think you have omitted one very efficacious mode. Lying in bed rests one's body, but it too often does not rest one's mind. If I lie in bed on a Sunday morning, I am [sure] to keep thinking over and over about all my worries, the letters I have not answered, the difficulties I have ahead, etc. I find that visiting on a Sunday afternoon is one of the surest and most effectual modes of dissipation. You see fresh faces, you talk of other things than those which occupy you on working days so incessantly and on Monday morning you rise refreshed you know not how. So too with dining out."

With this may be contrasted part of a letter written some time in 1888 to his brother-in-law the Dean of Westminster in a mood of depression :—

"I feel every day how bad it is to be obliged to move in a *rut*, and yet I can see that, for me, I am fixed in the rut till the end of my life. I am getting *ossified*, and now really quite hate society. The fact is, I am so beaten by the end of the day that I am fit for nothing, and I begin to find myself often longing for the end. I hope that wherever we may go we shall get some rest, and yet as long as we are intelligent and sentient beings, surely we must strive."

Sometimes the two moods are combined in the same letter, as in that dated March 22nd, 1888, and addressed to Miss Lucy Stone, who was then visiting Australia for her health :—

"I was very glad to get your two letters, and felt very proud at being so much distinguished by you ; and it was so very nice to find you improving so much and writing quite like a person of consideration who has nothing to do but enjoy herself and be condescending and sweet to her friends. Bless you ! may it continue to do you good, and may you always be as sweet to me. You are in the middle of summer—my boy in upper New South Wales in his last letter says that he must leave off writing because of the crowd of creatures which have rushed into the lamp on the table. We on the contrary are in the midst of the most fearful winter. Such east-winds, such snow, such general misery of feeling have never, I think, been known. It will get worn out at last, but meantime here it is. But this is only the beginning of my sad story. My poor dear Kellett has gone at last. We got her moved ten weeks ago to the Consumption Hospital at Ventnor—a *lovely* place, beautifully situated and managed in an ideal manner. After a great deal of delay caused partly by College business, partly by my being in bed for a fortnight, I got down to see her on Saturday the 10th, and stayed over the Sunday. She was horribly weak and fallen away, and oh, so thin ! The Saturday was her twenty-second birthday.

"On Wednesday I had news from the Doctor that she was more cheerful and had even wanted to get out of bed, which she had not left for four or five weeks. On Wednesday, however, a great change came, and on Thursday she gradually sank and departed at 1 o'clock. Her sister was with her. Her mother arrived just too late. I went down on Sunday last and we laid her in her grave at 3 o'clock. And so ends what was the beginning of a very fine career . . . She was as you know a very sincere Catholic. She left no messages, but our last talks were very nice. We made endless plans for the future and were to travel together, and hear and see everything in the world.

"College is doing very well. The exams began yesterday, and go on all next week. I am now writing amid scales and solfeggi and shrieks more easily conceived than described. We have had some good scholarship exams and elected 3 singers, 1 P.F., 1 violin, 1 'cello, 1 double-bass—some of them very promising. But dear me, why do I go on describing these things? What can a young person sitting in a bower of gum trees and wooed by persistent Australian swains care about our little triumphs, hopes, and fears? Besides, you have no doubt heard it all from someone who knows these things better than the poor Director! So I must leave off, for Parratt is looking over my shoulder with a horrid expression of countenance (you know how fiendish he can look when he chooses) . . ."

Ten days later we find him writing to another favourite pupil, Mr. (now Doctor) Charles Wood, on the subject of the singing pupils :—

"*April* 2, 1888.

"It is one of the few things that gives me anxiety at College. I cannot but feel painfully that it is not taught in the same systematic and thorough way that the piano or the violin are. Everything seems against it; the pupils in most cases seem to acquire a conceit and a want of interest in their study that is not possessed by the instrumental pupils—then their throats are so easily put out of order; and there is the constant temptation to sing things which will get them applause instead of the ineffective solfeggi and studies which are necessary for forming the voice; and then the most effective ways are so often the worst music. Altogether the path of a singer seems beset with difficulties. . . ."

Grove in early life had been an assiduous student of Coleridge, and the *Athenæum* of April 14, 1888, contains a paper of his headed "Coleridge Notes" based on materials collected nearly half a century earlier. He begins :—

"When I was in Jamaica in the year 1841, I met with a young general practitioner of the name of Porter, who was as eager a student of Coleridge as I was myself. He had been a pupil of Mr. Gilman's at Highgate, and was full of anecdotes of the poet. He had wonderful stories of the *marginalia* written by Coleridge on the pages of the circulating library books, and returned all unbeknown. There were also a few pieces of verse by him. Of these I have one or two which have not been printed, and I give them as I copied them."

These consist of (*a*) six short sets of verses, epitaphs, album pieces, etc. (*b*) a satirical answer to Rogers's Poem "The Wish" (*c*) two MS. notes by Coleridge in a volume of "Omniana" by Southey and Coleridge published in 1812, and lent to Grove by the late Mr. Pickering of Piccadilly in 1844 (*d*) the story of Lamb and the pudding told Grove by Mr. Porter (*e*) a short set of verses by S. T. C. printed in the *Keepsake* for 1829 or 30.

Hans von Bülow visited London this summer—he gave a recital on June 12—and Grove has preserved notes of a conversation which they had on the subject of the love of nature shown by certain great musicians. Von Bülow noted that in this respect Brahms was like Beethoven, but he denied the quality to either Liszt or Rubinstein. Rubinstein, he added, after his last recital invited a party of friends to Richmond for Sunday. It was a lovely sunny summer's day, but Rubinstein insisted on playing whist. The landlord remonstrated, and at last they had to go to a garret where they played from 2 till 8.[1]

Constant references to the Building Committee and the Commissioners of 1851 with regard to the proposed site of the new buildings of the Royal College of Music show that the question of a move into more commodious premises had already begun to assume a more practical shape. The College, which opened with 92 pupils, had

[1] I have heard the late Sir Charles Hallé, who was one of the party, tell this story in substantially the same terms.

now 228, and the accommodation was in many respects quite inadequate. Mr. Samson Fox had already placed a large sum (£30,000) at the disposal of the College, but Grove was evidently of opinion that it would be dangerous policy to commit themselves at once to the erection of a large and costly building, as the annual charges of all sorts would *ex ipso facto* be very much increased. It was his opinion in consequence that they ought to see how far these could be met by the increase of paying pupils before venturing further. The College opera this summer was Nicolai's *Merry Wives of Windsor* and, *à propos* of opera, it may be mentioned that Grove had recently joined the Board of the Carl Rosa Opera Company, and was a regular attendant at their meetings.

To this year, so far as I can make out, belongs a letter to Dr. Charles Wood describing one of Grove's brief but stimulating country visits :—

" *August* 11*th* [no year].

"I only came back last night from a few days in Wilts and Dorset, where I saw most beautiful and interesting old houses, churches, barns, etc., and a truly lovely country. I had no idea of the wide extent of the views over these great chalk downs ; and owing to the harvest-fields—to the extreme greenness of the hedges and trees (of which there is profusion)—and the clearness of the air—the colours and distances are most beautiful. To me, too, in the barrows, the old stones and druidical remains, there is something extremely touching—it seems to bring one nearer the cradle of one's race than any other part. Of course there are no *mountains* like the beautiful ones you have been going through. I hope that they have pleased you, and given you good feelings to use now and to remember in future. Half my recollections are those of moods of mind caused by the afternoon shadows, or some effect of light, or of the moon, and so on. . . .

"'The splendour falls on castle walls' (*Princess*) is said to have been suggested by Killarney, but there must be much mixed up with it. . . . There are no 'snowy summits old in story' at K., are there ? or castle walls ?"

In August he again contemplated a trip to Kerry and had got so far as to write to me on the 10th, "The great question is must I bring a tall hat? Please wire about this." But on the very day on which he had decided to start, he was disabled by a swelled knee, while a few days later his brother Edmund's wife was taken so dangerously ill that all hope of realising a long cherished desire vanished. On August 22nd he attended the orchestral rehearsal of the Birmingham Festival in London and has recorded his impressions in an interesting passage under the heading "Beethoven" in his pocket-book:—

"Such men cannot be judged by the standard of ordinary men—of Englishmen particularly. They are free from conventions which bind us, they are all nerves, they indulge in strange gestures and utter odd noises and say strange words, and make everyone laugh till we find that the gestures and looks and words are the absolute expression of their inmost feeling, and that that inmost feeling is inherent in the music and must be expressed in the performance. And they get what they want. Those who have seen Grieg conduct will know what I am attempting to describe."

A week later he wrote to me from Birmingham:—

"QUEEN'S HOTEL, BIRMINGHAM,
"*August* 30, 1888.

"On Friday last I was called down to Worthing, where my poor brother's wife is dying. I came on here on Tuesday, out of duty to Parry and Bridge, and I go back to Worthing to-morrow morning early. On Monday week is our Building Committee meeting at the College, so that I need hardly tell you all hope of Ireland is over. Will you please tell your father so with my most sincere regret?

"I don't know what the papers will say about Parry's *Judith*—damn it with faint praise after their vile fashion, I suppose. But *I* was immensely surprised and pleased with it. It is full of spirit and continuity, and abounds with melody and sentiment . . . A very interesting thing was Grieg's overture last night and his conducting of it. How he managed to inspire the band as he did and get such nervous thrilling bursts and such charming sentiment out of them I don't know. He looks very like Beethoven in face, I thought, and though he is not so extravagant in his ways of conducting yet it is not unlike."

A fortnight later he was settled in town for the winter.

[*To* C. L. GRAVES.]

"LOWER SYDENHAM,
"*Sept.* 13.

"I ought to have told you that my poor brother's wife died on the 1st. I got there in the afternoon and have remained with him off and on ever since . . .

"I saw *such* an interesting church on Sunday—Bosham on the shore of Sussex. Here are three historical facts about it. It was a basilica built by *Vespasian* and he must often have judged in it. Some of the original Roman pillars are still there. *Canute* had a palace hard by and his daughter is buried there, and is now in her coffin under the pavement. *Harold* heard Mass there with his hawk on his fist before the battle of Hastings! Fancy! It is *lovely* too—with a noble Saxon tower and the most beautiful early English Chancel. How very touching your brother's Irish ballads are! I found them at my son's at Brighton.

"'And there in the gloom of the groaning mast
We kissed our first and we kissed our last.'

Oh! oh! the blood of sixty-eight is stirred by that."

On the same date (September 13th, 1888) Grove began a new pocket-book with the entries:—

"*ἐχθίστη ὀδύνη τῶν ἐν ἀνθρώποισι πολλὰ φρονέοντα μηδενὸς κρατέειν* ('And that worst woe which baffled souls endure To see the evil that they may not cure').

"These striking expressions are the property of all poets, in all ages, and however different in general traits. Who were more unlike than Moses and Dr. Johnson? And yet compare 'Thou hast set our iniquities before Thee, our secret sins *in the light of thy countenance*,' with 'He left *the name at which the world grew pale*.'"

On this follow the drafts of two letters, both of them highly characteristic of the writer. The first was addressed to Lord Tennyson, who had been ailing, and who (so a friend had told Grove) had been saying that people thought Browning a greater poet than himself. "Don't you believe it," protests Grove, and goes on to give his reasons for believing Tennyson to be the greatest poet since Shakespeare. The second is an ebullition of delight provoked by a review of Ewald's *Biblical Theology* in the *Spectator* of October 6th, written by his friend the Rev. William Addis :—

"Oh my dear A. what a lovely article! It has made me so happy. It is all, and more than all, that I ever hoped for. Generally speaking I begin my *Spectator* at the beginning directly I sit down in the train and go steadily through, but this time I fastened on you and could read nothing else with any attention. Bless you, my dear friend, go on and make a vow never to write less than four columns. *Himmlische Länge* says Schumann of Schubert's great symphony, and so say I here."

Another event in the same month which appealed to him was the Jubilee of his old friend Madame Schumann, celebrated at Frankfurt on October 26, while among other entries in his almanac I note "Macmillan's birthday" (October 3) and "Max Friedländer's marriage" (October 24th). It was characteristic of Grove that he rarely failed to record not only the landmarks of his own but of his friends' lives.

The Life of Stanley, which Grove had abandoned in 1883 on his appointment to the Royal College of Music, and had then been undertaken by the late Theodore Walrond, was, as we have seen, subsequently taken over by Dean Bradley, and it is to the progress which the Dean was making with this task that Grove refers in the following letter :—

"LOWER SYDENHAM,

"*Dec.* 3, 1888.

"There's no question as to your being 'literary man' enough! Who *could* be better? But it is only a question of opinion as to whether a certain section of the life should be longer or shorter. It will solve itself as you go on, and I hope you won't bother about it. How much more you must have to worry you! Bright's burial of course will be a difficulty. But I should hope that as he was a Quaker his people would not wish for the Abbey. I was looking over a note-book of 1863 yesterday, and found a story of

Fergusson's told him by some great personage. 'What is the difference between an accident and a misfortune?'—'If Bright were to tumble into the river it would be an accident; if he were to be picked out it would be a misfortune.' How curiously the feeling has altered now!

"I am worried about the site proposed for my new building. It is just like a box, with no room or air and no possibility of future extension. I *can't* take it. . . ."

The severe weather, overwork, and a bad cough combined to make Grove's outlook for the New Year somewhat gloomy. Yet he never failed to preach the duty of cheerfulness. "How much better," he writes in his pocket-book, "life would go on, for instance, if when one met a friend one showed one's gladness and was not only glad to see him but showed it unmistakably. It adds, as I know by experience, immensely to happiness, and there would not be the least exaggeration about it. Many people seem to think that expression of our feelings is wrong. I am sure it need not be." These were no doubt notes for one of his addresses to his pupils, for he certainly did not need the advice himself.

Another characteristic means of influencing his young charges that occurred to him about this time was that of having placards with "rules and hints of great musicians," *i.e.* extracts from the letters of Beethoven, Mendelssohn, Weber and Schubert. Schubert was especially in his mind just now owing to the statement of a certain Mr. F. J. Crowest that he (Schubert) "drank himself to death," a statement which, as he said of the *Edinburgh* article on Schubert, was "enough to make one's teeth gnash of themselves." "I have got to write to the *Times* about Crowest," he wrote to me on December 29th, and the *Times* itself was in his black books a couple of days later for "giving in its annual obituary a long list of painters, etc., under the heading of Art, but cramming music into the 'miscellaneous characters.'"

One of the earliest indications of his consciousness that he could not go on indefinitely bearing the burden of his office is to be found in a letter to Dean Bradley early this year :—

"Lower Sydenham,
"*Jan.* 21, 1889.

"I have much to answer for to you, but not with *blame.* I have been dreadfully busy, and lately really ill with a terrible cold and cough which drove me to my bed last Monday and has nearly killed me. . . . Age and partings are dreadful and the old order of the world is too strong for us; I feel it sadly. I am much perplexed about my work. It is too much for me, and I ought either to get a 'sub.' or give it up. You will say, 'all this is coloured by your bad state of health.' True; but my body won't get more vigorous—and next January (please God I see it) will be worse than this."

Yet his own anxieties never weighed with him when it came to be a question of assisting or advising others. At this time, owing to the death of Dr. Hueffer, the post of musical critic to the *Times* was vacant, and two of his friends were standing for the post. As an example of his honesty and modesty, and as evidence of the extent of his musical equipment the following letter to the deservedly unsuccessful competitor is worthy of reproduction :—

"Royal College,
"*Jan.* 29, 1889.

"I did not actually know that you were standing but I fancied you would. . . . In taste, feeling, historical and biographical knowledge and literary power, you have every qualification. . . . But then you are not a musician; and how a man is to report adequately for the *Times* without being one, I really do not know. I have always thought of you (if you will forgive the comparison) as about on a par with myself as to musicianship—and I know that nothing could induce *me* to take such a post. If I had a new Symphony or quartet to report upon, I should be all abroad; and then should have to refer to others more qualified in that respect though perhaps beneath me in taste and literary ability."

To Mr. J. A. Fuller-Maitland, with whom as contributor and editor of the Appendix to the Dictionary of Music and Musicians he had long been closely associated,

Grove wrote a fortnight later on learning that he was to be Hueffer's successor :—

"*February* 15, 1889.

"What I should feel if it were my case, would be the difficulty of not being biassed, and the risk of being narrow and *smart*, and not judicial and at the same time sweet enough. I have often thought with pain of the way some of the writers fall tooth and nail on a new work, and give all their blame but no praise; when there is probably as much to praise as to find fault with."

If Grove began the year in rather low spirits he was quite himself by the middle of March, when he attended a dinner given at Caius College, Cambridge, at which Joachim was the principal guest. In the course of an after-dinner speech he made a humorous reference to a member of the common-room who played the side drum, a fact which gave him an opening to mention what use Beethoven and Spohr and Brahms had made of that instrument. But instrumentalists always interested him more than singers, and I find, in reference to the examinations being held this month at the College, the following notes in his pocket-book :—

"Is it not waste of time to teach such pupils as —— counterpoint or even higher grade of harmony?

"Should not singers be taught singing only and the branches connected, excluding anything belonging to the mind?"

On April 4th Grove had another serious accident, being run over by a cab in the fog while crossing Piccadilly near Apsley House, and was laid up in bed for ten days. But after a few days in the country he was able to resume work and assure Dean Bradley on the 24th that "no permanent harm had been done." April also removed an old friend in Sir Frederick Gore-Ouseley, who died on the 6th, and an efficient colleague—both as a member of the Council of the Royal College and examiner—in Carl Rosa, who died in Paris on the 30th. But though the old friends were passing away, the old interests remained, obscured for a time by the pressure of immediate occupation, yet reviving in all their keenness when anything occurred to bring them uppermost. Thus when a review appeared in the *Spectator* for May 11th, 1889, of Renan's *History of the People of Israel*, Grove drafted a long letter to the editor expressing his dissent from Renan's estimate of David's treatment of Uriah. The letter never appeared—perhaps was never sent—but the central passage is worth quoting :—

"The lesson of the Bathsheba intrigue does not seem to me to be any general one of the wickedness of adultery, but the lesson of the fearful power which a passion can have over a man in the full strength of his life with his feelings as keen as those of early manhood, while he has all the force of mature age. The chivalrous knight, the darling of his people, the very man after God's own heart, is driven to depths of meanness to which the story of Lancelot and Guinevere gives no parallel. The Moabite massacres and cruelties which followed show how completely his mind was unhinged."

Some years had now elapsed since Grove had left England in the autumn. He indemnified himself for the enforced abstinence by a long and thoroughly successful trip to the Continent in August 1889. Leaving London on the morning of August 7th with his old friend Mr. Manns, he crossed to Calais in lovely weather, his first stopping place being Cologne, where he visited the Conservatorium on the morning of the 8th, pushing on to Frankfurt in the afternoon. Madame Schumann was away, and at midday on the 9th he was on the road to Nuremberg, where he spent the night, reaching Bayreuth on the 10th. Though not written until the 28th, from Interlaken, the subjoined letter to Mrs. Wodehouse may be inserted here as summarising his impressions of *Tristan* and his view of the Music-Drama generally :—

". . . I should probably agree with Manns about the *Meistersinger*, but as to *Tristan*, never! To it I have a distinct and strong moral objection which with me will always strongly affect my judgment about art. Art exercised on an immoral subject may be the finest art, but I want it not: the world must not be corrupted, however fine the music or the painting or the writing in which the corruption is conveyed, and therefore I never can or will admit such creators as Wagner or Gustave Flaubert, or many of the great French painters to the first rank. I am sure I am right. If art must be immoral then let it perish; but it need not be so. See Dic: vol. i. 196 b for my sentiments. Also I do think that the tendency to make music so long and ultra-earnest is wrong. If everything is to take the same road what amusements will the world have in the end? Music is turned from a relaxation into a study, but no other relaxation is put in its place. Surely this is wrong. It is one of the main arguments for me against what they call 'women's rights.' Who is to amuse and soothe us and help us along on this dull road if women are themselves pulling the cart as hard as we are? However, this is all very dull. Fancy how odd! I began to talk to a man who sat next me last night, and found him a great collector of Saxon antiquities of all sorts, living close to us and the owner of a huge museum. I was able to tell him, however, of one or two fine Saxon church towers in Sussex which he knew nothing of."

Along with this may be given the letter on *Parsifal* written on September 15th to Dr. Charles Wood:—

". . . I had a very good time abroad. The first point was Bayreuth, where I and Manns heard Parsifal. Well, of course one hearing of such a work is nothing—and of this *less* than nothing. The circumstances of the dark theatre, the hidden orchestra, the very prominent and brilliant stage, and the *extraordinary* stage effects and machinery—are all so new that of themselves they throw you off your balance: and then the piece is so unusual in its form, and the necessity of knowing it beforehand so essential, that all goes against a first hearing, especially in one so slow of taking things up as I am. I confess I was disappointed and very wearied. . . . But this I have not said to any one but you, and don't wish it repeated, because I should probably have said much the same after first hearing the 9th Symphony. . . ."

But the real objective of his tour was not Bayreuth but Vienna, and thither he made his way *viâ* Regensburg, where he sketched the church and was delighted by the "lovely glass," and Passau, noting *en route* "the tameness of the creatures on the Austrian railways—horses feeding close to the line, birds sitting on the telegraph wires, goats and cows never looking up." He reached Vienna on the evening of his birthday, August 13th, and devoted the next morning to a critical examination of the new white marble statue of Schubert in the Stadtpark, which he found as regards drapery, attitude and general spirit most inept and inappropriate.[1] In the evening he saw *Le Prophète* at the opera, and began the next day that campaign of exploration, which was the prime motive of his visit, amongst the villages in the environs of Vienna which Beethoven frequented in the summers of the later years of his life. He spent the 15th at Döbling where, though some of the streets, etc., were named after Beethoven, he notes that "two girls (well bred) knew nothing about his connection with the village." Two notes made on the same day are also interesting. First there is the query: "Did Beethoven wish his works played with that staccato and emphatic precision that the Austrian bands now play with? Was it *then* a characteristic of the Austrians' playing?" And second there is the characteristic reminder, "N.B. Mention in my Beethoven strongly in the Preface that it is not a book for musicians" —a reminder which he faithfully acted upon when the book ultimately appeared in 1896. On Friday the 16th he paid a visit to the Musikverein, making notes of the size of the rooms, the number of pupils, the arrangements of the theatre, etc., and afterwards made an excursion with his friend Mandyczewski to Schönbrunn, and thence on foot to Hetzendorf on the track of Beethoven's rambles. On Saturday, with Mandyczewski again as a companion, Grove went by the electric railway through lovely scenery to Vorderbrühl. The modernity of the surroundings did not distress him, for as he writes in his pocket-book, "it is easy to dismiss the intruded novelties and imagine the dear man revelling in the heavenly Nature so abundant and beautiful." They dined at the "Zwei Raben" at

[1] He embodied his criticism in a letter which appeared in the *Times* of October 2nd, 1889.

Vorderbrühl, and then took an *Einspänner* and drove into Modling "along a beautiful road with an almost Alpine hill before us, clothed to the top with pines." They went first to visit the rooms where Beethoven wrote the Credo of the Mass in 1820 and thence to Hauptstrasse No. 79, which has a tablet "Ludwig van Beethoven wohnte hier im Sommer 1818, 1819, 1820." Of this house Grove made a most careful examination, taking measurements, etc., and adding: "He must have been lonely in this room; but loneliness is the condition of great works such as he was then composing."

This was perhaps the red-letter-day of Grove's Beethoven pilgrimage, but the following Monday, Tuesday and Wednesday were also rich in interesting experiences. On the Monday, he paid a visit to old Artaria, the publisher (born in 1807), who regaled him with reminiscences of Beethoven and Schumann and showed him his autographs, and on the same day he went by omnibus to Heiligenstadt and Nussdorf to inspect the Beethoven Denkmal. Tuesday he explored the Schwarzspanierhaus, where Beethoven died, called on the Richters, and had another interview with Artaria, who took him to his house in the *Gasse* off the shop and showed him room after room full of treasures—old engravings, autographs and pictures. Finally on Wednesday, leaving Vienna at 7.14, he made an expedition to Krems and Gneixendorf. Reaching the former village at about 11 he took a *Zweispänner* up the steep winding road through the vineyards, where he met "a little cart drawn by two large panting dogs, with a brake! and a man on top" to Gneixendorf, a "small but charming village," with a straight street and clean whitewashed houses. He has recorded his impressions of Johann van Beethoven's house, "evidently *the* house of the town," with great minuteness. There are notes on the vicissitudes of the property, on Beethoven's room, the garden, trees, skittle-alley and view of the surrounding fields. It was "quite a gentleman's house, and at the time I saw it was most charming." Frau von Schweitzer, the owner, received him most amiably, and as her uncle Baron Schönstein had been a famous singer of Schubert's songs, there was an extra bond between them. He tells also how when Frau von Schweitzer walked out in the fields with him, "all the people, young and old, came up to her, stooped, took her hand and kissed it—a very pretty sight." Thursday, his last day at Vienna, he spent studying the maps of the city in the Museum and paid a final visit to Artaria, starting on the following morning August 23rd and travelling *viâ* Linz, Salzburg, Innsbruck, Zürich, to Interlaken, which was his headquarters till the end of the month. His second son met him at Lucerne on the 28th, and on the 30th he paid a most enjoyable visit to the Wachs at Ringgenburg. Mrs. Wach (Mendelssohn's daughter) and her husband greeted him with great cordiality; he was delighted with their children and came away with a goodly stock of fresh Mendelssohniana relating to the composer's visit to Ringgenburg in 1847. On September 2nd he travelled by Berne and Lausanne to Martigny, thence by carriage to Chamonix on the 3rd, and by diligence on the 5th to Geneva. The 6th and 7th were spent at Prangins, in the company of his old friend J. S. Forbes, and on the night of the 7th he travelled through to Paris. There he spent a couple of days, renewing old friendships with Clermont-Ganneau, "a dear fellow and bursting with knowledge," de Vogüé, and Renan, whom he found fatter than ever,—talking constantly and laboriously in French, but with "wretched results." He also inspected the musical exhibits at the Exhibition before crossing on the 10th, and reached home the same night.

A fortnight later the College opened, and in October Grove went down to Leeds for the Festival. The especia significance to him of this meeting was revealed in his letter to the *Times* of October 28th, in which he calls attention to the innovation in the performance of the Choral Symphony under Sir Arthur Sullivan, by which the customary pause at the end of the slow movement was omitted. "On the present occasion," writes Grove, "for the first time, to the best of my knowledge, Beethoven's intention was strictly carried out; no pause was made, and the effect was new, extremely dramatic, and to my mind convincing."

It will be remembered that some time previously he had endeavoured to convert Dr. Richter to this view, but Dr. Richter, relying on the unbroken Viennese tradition, remained unconvinced. The record of 1889 may be closed by an interesting autobiographical touch in a letter to Dean Bradley on October 30th:—

"Curious that you are so *wuthend* against proof sheets! To me they are *bliss*. I love correcting them and always put the plums into them. . . . I have been fearfully busy of late. Being a camel is all very well up to 68, but after that the flesh (what is left of it) will rise."

It may be added that his engagements in one fortnight in December included four concerts either given by old pupils or at which they took a prominent part. On the other hand, against the premature exploitation of their talents by pupils, however gifted, he always vigorously set his face. "Teaching power," as he wrote to Lord Charles Bruce, "and quiet unobtrusive solid ability of that kind is quite as essential if not more so to a position in the country as brilliancy of execution." Thus he would caution new scholars to remember that education was their prime aim, not performance or engagements while they were still at the College. As to his general influence on his pupils in the later years of his Directorship, I cannot do better than quote the testimony of Dr. Walford Davies, the organist of the Temple, who studied at the College from 1890 to 1894. He writes:—

"He was loved by his students at the College for his unfailing personal interest in their art, and for his enthusiasm for Beethoven and other great musicians. His smallest piece of advice to a student was seasoned with what some great man did or said.[1] I

[1] Canon Ainger tells me that when he informed Grove of his promotion to a canonry, "G." at once burst out: "*Now* you'll be able to afford to buy the great edition of Schubert!" Again when he had been reassured that two pupils, in whom he was much interested, were not

remember once he followed me from an exam. room, and seizing both my shoulders besought me to improve my handwriting, after the splendid example of some composer—probably Bach—and I am not sure that he did not add something about Beethoven even then. I think he hoped that the College would produce a musical saviour. When enumerating our achievements at a terminal address, I remember his saying: "We have not produced a Beethoven *yet*." His faithfulness to hasty promises was remarkable. Once in conversation he found that I had never read Nottebohm, and said, casually, 'I'll send it to you.' Some days later the 'Zweite Beethoveniana' arrived, to be one of my life-long treasures. I remember, too, his keeping a casual promise to come out to Hampstead to a concert at which many of his students were to play, though in his own words 'Hampstead seemed as far off as the Sahara.' Sir George taught one to think of him as pre-eminently an *amateur*. It is curious if this pre-eminence, together with his human kindness, formed his best qualification for a great professional post. I think this must have been so. And I believe most of us who had the good fortune to come under his influence would gratefully acknowledge that our own musical fires were kindled and fed by the Director's unique, unfailing enthusiasms for our great Art."

Along with his sympathy with young people must be reckoned his unabated interest in young writers and contemporary literature, though here he confessed to very human limitations. "Theological novels and novels of misery," he wrote to Dean Bradley on January 27th, 1890, "I *cannot* read—the first because they seem so poor, the second because they make me so unhappy." He had no liking for the creators of gratuitous gloom when there was so much real distress in real life. That was another matter and constantly gave him his opportunity. Thus in the *Times* of March 4th, 1890, he appeals eloquently for funds on behalf of Madame Arabella Goddard, now in ill-health and reduced circumstances, for whose benefit a concert was to be given on March 11th, and lays special stress on her

contemplating immediate matrimony he wrote to his informant: "It will do them good to be apart and test the reality of their affection. You remember that Mendelssohn went away from his *fiancée* voluntarily and deliberately to test the strength of his love."

pioneer work in the "fifties" as interpreter of Beethoven's later pianoforte music. Of course the College now had the first claim on his energies, his sympathy and his purse, and instances of his practical generosity to pupils might be multiplied to any extent. As he said himself, "I know what it is to want a stray pound." For the moment I will confine myself to three such instances. Meeting one of his most gifted pupils abroad, when the latter was shabby, moody, and generally in low water, he thrust a couple of sovereigns into his hand and literally bolted before the recipient had time to thank him. There was "G" in his impulsive mood. On another occasion he insisted on defraying the charge for copying the parts of an important composition by the same student. Last and most delicate of all, was his gift to him of tickets to attend the Bayreuth Festival. What Grove himself thought of Wagner has already been shown, but that did not in the least affect his judgment of the educational value of such an experience to one who he knew would turn it to the best advantage. But besides these tangible proofs of his solicitude Grove had all sorts of characteristic ways of encouraging and helping his "children." On one occasion, for example, one of them had to play at a College Concert for the first time and was looking forward to the ordeal with something approaching consternation. Being aware of the girl's anxiety, and discovering her in the course of the afternoon at work at harmony, he at once prescribed a half-holiday, and carried her off there and then for a walk in Kensington Gardens, talking the whole time in his usual stimulating way of music and culture and making his companion realise—I quote her own words—that "if there would be one sympathetic listener that evening it would be the Director, besides giving a solid hour of his valuable time in practical demonstration of the fact."

It was Grove's practice, as has been already mentioned, to address the pupils every term. These speeches were not hastily or perfunctorily composed, but much of the material was accumulated in advance, and the important passages carefully written out at length. That delivered on May 1st, 1890, opens with an appropriate and topical contrast : "You know what is going on outside to-day. Well, this is *our* 'Labour Demonstration,' not for strikes and conflicts but for progress and improvement." He speaks of the gratifying advance made in the previous term, the testimony of examiners, the higher average of attendance, going on, however, with a characteristic ebullition to condemn the *rudeness* of those who stopped away from the examination of the choral class : "It is an insult to the College and myself, who am so careful not to insult you." Then there was the list of achievements to be read —the successes of MacCunn and Duncan, of Charles Wood and Waddington, and the various posts to which old pupils had been appointed. The last term, again, had been rendered memorable by the first practical results of the establishment of the Associated Board of the Royal Academy of Music and the Royal College of Music, an organisation founded in co-operation with the sister institution in Tenterden Street, to provide a *bonâ fide* system of local examinations in music. The first series of Local Examinations had been held, and the outlook was most encouraging. "I hear," he continues, "that there were some curious instances of ignorance—but indeed I have long ceased to be surprised at any cases of ignorance in regard to music. When one of the greatest modern writers of English (who always professes to understand music too), in describing a duet, speaks of the 'sweet cadence of descending fifths,' one can hardly go further."

The summer of 1890 was also rendered memorable, so far as the College was concerned, by the final settlement of the plans relating to the structure and site of the new buildings, the foundation stone of which was duly laid on July 8th. The College, which opened in May, 1883, with 94 pupils, now had 285 on the roll, of whom no fewer than 60 were free scholars.

CHAPTER XI

Von zur Mühlen and Leonard Borwick—Letters on *In Memoriam*, Renan, and the Celtic feeling—Holiday trip to Norway in 1890—Attachment to his brother Edmund—Letter to his grandchild—Views on Handel and Scott's *Journal*—Visit to Paris, Easter, 1891—Views on musical critics and the Registration of Teachers—Schubert's Sketch Symphony—Letters on pens, Dvorák's symphony, the love of beauty in Italian musicians, and Matthew Arnold's poems—Trip to Riffel Alp, August 1891—Advocates the publication in facsimile of Beethoven's Symphonies—Interest in Bible study—Trip to South of France, Easter, 1892—Article on "The Birds in the Pastoral Symphony."

For Grove's interest outside the College at this period one turns to his correspondence or his pocket-books. That containing the entries in the early months of 1890 was lost—he notes the fact himself—but the pocket-book which starts on May 16 abounds in kaleidoscopic evidences of his mental versatility. On one page he quotes a passage from Walter Scott on Lord Nelson and compares Lady Hamilton with Bathsheba. On another he writes: "N.B. Byron took pistols in his carriage when he went down to Sydenham to see Campbell." On a third occurs the draft of a little sermon on manners addressed to the male pupils at the College:—

"Because you produce a good tone from your instruments and write good counterpoint, you need not therefore forget to wash, or smoke such bad tobacco or in such quantities that your examiners wish you out of the room. When I think of some of our old scholars, I can't say we have improved."

July 10th brought him a rare pleasure in the shape of a concert given by von zur Mühlen, a singer who both by his choice of songs and his fine intelligence—Grove says he seemed to be improvising as he went along—appealed to him perhaps more than any other since Stockhausen. Another great musical treat was furnished by Mr. Leonard Borwick, who paid the College a visit at the end of June. "Borwick came here to see me," he writes to Mr. Edward Speyer on July 4th, "and did us the honour to play a movement of the Schumann Concerto with our band. I liked his playing very much, and I liked him himself almost more. I shall cultivate his friendship all I can." But in spite of these occasional relaxations, he was feeling the strain of his work a good deal, and after the College Opera—*Cosi fan tutte*—on the 16th, and the usual rush at the end of term, he was, on his own showing, sorely in need of rest and change of air. As he puts it in a letter to his brother Edmund, "I strive to imagine to myself that *terra incognita*, the mind of a man who has nothing that he need absolutely do. I envy, but I fail to conceive it." I have already endeavoured to give some notion of his relations with his pupils at the College: of the way in which he interested himself in those who had already left the following letter, written before he started on his holiday, may serve as a characteristic example :—

[*To* MISS L. HEATH.]

"LOWER SYDENHAM, S.E.,
"*Aug.* 5, 1890.

". . . I have no doubt you enjoy being at home again : to get back to the rooms and the tables and chairs and books that are associated with one's early times is to me always in itself a pleasure. And how your people must enjoy having you! That's quite a distinct pleasure from tables and chairs and even books.

"Fine weather seems to have set in here. The evening yesterday, as I sat on the lawn and watched the light gradually fade, and the trees all around grow black—with not a breath to stir a branch or to mar the outline of the various leaves against the sky—was wonderfully touching and lovely.

"'To-night we lingered on the lawn
For underfoot the herb was dry,
And genial warmth, and o'er the sky,
The silvery haze of summer drawn'

"I was wrought up to such a pitch of feeling that I might well have had all the sequel which Tennyson describes. 'The others' had gone to the fireworks, and I was quite alone. *À propos*, just look at that section of *In Memoriam*. I doubt if you ever read it as I mean. (The numbers I give refer to the 1st edition. Afterwards 2 poems were inserted making the numbers 2 later.)

"After lxxxvii—'Witch-elms'—a portrait of Hallam in private life—comes a section of 6 poems on the subject of his possible reappearance—how it might happen, and how it did happen.

"lxxxviii. 'The meeting of the dead and the living.' The dead will be as loving and as much loved, if they come back, as they were when here.

"lxxxix. May he return, not in the dark, or as a ghost, but more beautiful even than he was.

"xc. No possibility of any revelation of form.

"xci. He will not be seen but felt;—

"xcii. And that only if everything is at peace.

"xciii. How he actually did come.

"If you have not got an *In M.* I will lend you one.

"As to your reading I think you will enjoy Renan's *Vie de Jésus*, if you don't think of it as a theological work, with theories to support, but as a mere attempt to set forth the life in the Eastern surroundings. There are one or two terrible faults of taste . . . but a great part of it is delightful. But there is a book that I do want you to read and that is *Christian Institutions*, A. P. Stanley's last book. See if your father has got it. If not I will send you one. Let me. It consists of essays in which such subjects as the Sacraments, the Trinity, the Lord's Prayer, are treated as they never were before.

"I go off to-day to Marlborough, where I have belongings, bu[t] I only stay a day and come back on Thursday. . ."

[*To the Same.*]

"*Aug.* 10, 1890.

"I have been re-reading Renan's *Vie de Jésus*, and with all th[e] charm of style I confess I don't like it. Perhaps it is that I a[m] old, but from whatever cause it be, I don't like to see the Divinit[y] so very much taken off the pedestal. He is really lowered to th[e] level of an agitator and sometimes not a very honest agitator to[o]. No, I don't like it, and I resist continually as I go along. Do le[t] me send you Stanley, it is not a costly book and I should love t[o] give it you.

"How do you find life down there? I am sadly weak an[d] tired. I can't get up my strength at all, and every now and the[n] have such very bad times—fits of unhappiness and low spirits—of no real significance but dreadful to bear: times when I seem to myself more useless and contemptible than my worst enemy could think me."

After a visit to Penn, August 14–16, he wrote in a more cheerful strain on the 17th to Mrs. Wodehouse:—

"LOWER SYDENHAM,
"*Aug.* 17, 1890.

". . . What a lovely day it has been to-day. I do hope you have had the same. I went to a church where I had only been once before and heard a *Te Deum*. Such fine music, and so well sung and so devotional, that as it finished I said to myself, what more *does* one want? What a noble hymn it is—the tears were in my eyes more than once; so they were during the Creed too.

"I am so glad that you like your Wordsworth. It is a great mixture—such exquisite moments and so much dreary didactic commonplace.[1] I like best the 'Daffodils' and the poems on Lucy, and of all others the Highland Reaper who was filling the vale with sound, and on whom there is that exquisite simile about the cuckoo-bird—

"'Breaking the silence of the seas
Among the furthest Hebrides—'

with the next stanza:—

"'Old, unhappy far-off things
And battles long ago.'

"These two passages are so *full* of that Celtic feeling which Matthew Arnold discovered in the exquisite conversation between Jessica and her lover in the end of the 'Merchant of Venice'—

"'On such a night as this—'

'and of which the following verse of Walter Scott's (Legend of Montrose):—

"'The orphan by the oak was set,
Her arms, her feet were bare:
The haildrops had not melted yet
Amid her raven hair.'

seems to me a beautiful example.

[1] With this may be compared a passage from a letter to his brother written about a year earlier:—

"I have an immense admiration for a few things of Wordsworth's, but I cannot be called a Wordsworthian. The set ponderousness and even commonplace style of the majority of the poems repels me; and the entire absence of the *passion* of love robs them of one of the main elements of poetry."

"*À propos*, just read that scene in the 'Merchant of Venice,' and see what an ideal conversation it is, changing from serious to gay in such a natural way. Isn't it?"

On the 19th he started for Norway with his second son, Mr. J. C. Grove. "I have left it too long," he writes to Miss Heath on the 18th, "but now I mean to try and *saturate* myself with mountain air." On the way down to Hull, where he embarked, he was busy reading Wordsworth, and after leaving Doncaster jotted down in his pocket-book a remark which confirms Dr. Walford Davies's observation above:—

> "'While not an English mountain we behold
> By the celestial Muses glorified.'

"So said Wordsworth (*Pelion and Ossa*), and so we might say o English music, too. The giants Bach and Beethoven an Schubert have taken away all our praise from us, but Wordswort himself altered the fact as to the mountains, and some one is sur to come and alter it as to music."

A week later he wrote to Mrs. Wodehouse fron Odde:—

"ODDE (NORWAY),
"*Aug.* 26, 1890.

"It has been impossible to write sooner. We crossed o Wednesday, landed Thursday morning; Friday and Saturda were incessantly on the move. Sunday I was too tired to d anything, and yesterday was taken up with a long ride to se waterfalls. The weather has been very bad so far, but to-day oper bright. The road hither has lain along narrow gorges betwee mountains—the gorges mostly filled with water (lakes), and le often passes for which one has little 1 horse gigs. This seems t me the characteristic of the whole of Norway. I had no ide how very much it is cut up with lakes (fiords), and how the interpenetrate and permeate the whole land. The journey w monotonous, only varied by the sunset on Wednesday—one the most lovely and romantic and singular things these ey ever beheld. When one could catch the point of view one ha before one a golden shore sloping up inwards for miles from th sea-line—and covered with forests, hedge-rows, plantations, farm fields—all perfectly delineated on it by grey purple clouds—th most singular and life-like delusion possible.

"The landing at 5 a.m. on Thursday in Stavanger harbour was most lovely: the delicious cool gleaming light over everything—water, mountains, houses, quays, all as bright as if they were just 'out of the egg' (F.M.B.). This is a little town with 2 hotels and a dozen houses at the end of a beautiful narrow long lake. On Thursday we shall go up that lake to Eide, our next point. Meantime I have found very nice old friends here. The country is more like Scotland than Switzerland, though all on a larger scale. It has not got the Eternal Snow, nor the frequent contrasts of Switzerland nor the indefinable charm which will always make Switzerland the dearest country to me. The people are Scotch, with more mildness and innocence, and less *pawky* than the Scotch. We mean to work northwards for a few days, and then, turning to the left, get to the sea-coast at Bergen and cross on Monday, 7th Sept. While at Bergen I shall certainly call on Grieg—I wish I had brought a symphony with me. The nearest approach I have to it is the first 50 bars of the slow movement of the Pastoral, which I copied in a sort of shorthand into my note-book, and in which I have found one or two things I did not notice before. Also here I find *Elijah* and *St. Paul*—not bad companions. For books I have *In Memoriam*, Wordsworth (one of the green ones like yours), and 3 plays of Shakespeare's, also a vol. of J. B. Mozley's Sermons which I can't get on with. I have been reading Wordsworth a good deal, and am much struck with the superiority and spontaneity of the early poems up to 1815 or so, to the later ones. To me they are like handfuls of ore with a fragment or two of solid gold embedded in a mass of inferior material. The Leech-gatherer has more gold than rock, but in many of the others I find a terrible amount of stone and clay; still the little nuggets are splendid and redeem any amount of the other. I find the notes at the head of the poems (W's own) very interesting. For the mixture of fine and base, look at a poem written at Milan (in 1820, I think) on the eclipse, which beginning with 'Sol' and 'science from her speculative tower' goes on to 2 or 3 most characteristic and noble stanzas, 'Angels she sees,'—'the uplifted palms, the silent marble lips, all bathed in that stupendous light, all suffering dim eclipse' (splendid: and compare Tennyson's stanza in his Daisy, splendid too). . ."

As a traveller Grove confessed that he belonged "to that class which looks about in all directions, fascinated not only with the grand sights above, but also with some humble prospect of nature at their feet." But then he beheld these "humble prospects" with a poet's eye: and a "field of standing shocks" which he saw a few days later called up to him the vision of "an army of trolls." For the rest his pocket-book shows that his College "children" were constantly in his thoughts. In the rough draft of his next term's speech he urges upon them to cultivate a taste for literature, church architecture and history. He protests against the tyranny of athletics: "Any one can handle a bat, but it is not every one who can realise an ancient scene . . . Athletics came in after I was grown up, and the interest I take in them did not grow with my growth. The things I was brought up to were literary matters and (please don't laugh) they can really be very interesting." Finally he recommends etymology, architecture and travelling as potent instruments of that culture which would make them better musicians as well as more interesting and self-sufficing men and women.

That he enjoyed and profited by his trip to Norway there is no reason to doubt, yet there is no enthusiasm in his references to the country. Writing to Mr. Speyer shortly after his return, he says, "Norway doesn't do after Switzerland." On September 8th he landed at Hull, on the 10th he was present at the marriage of his youngest son, and before the reopening of the College on the 25th he spent a day at Worcester, during the festival week, and paid a short visit to his brother Edmund at Preston Park, near Brighton. They had always been great friends, but their paths in life had widely diverged. Now, however, on Mr. Edmund Grove's retirement from business, the bond was drawn closer than ever, and in the last ten years of his life George Grove frequently visited and constantly corresponded with his brother, in whom he found, as so many others have found, the most charming and considerate of hosts, the most sympathetic of companions, the most intelligent of listeners. "I can't exclaim to you (as Milly used to say)," he writes about this time, "how fond I am of you, or what a pleasure—no excitement bu comfort and *real* pleasure—your society is to me. You deserve everything that a brother and sister-in-law can wish you, for if ever there was a good brother on earth it is you. May you live to be 150 and be as nice to the end as you are now." And again, in another undated letter, "How can I thank you for all your goodness? Golden hospitality I must call it. . . . I have told them to send you Roget's *Thesaurus*. The index is the part to use. Look out, for instance, 'generous,' and there you will find 'hospitable, liberal, Edmund Grove, Esq., of Norlington, Preston, Brighton, &c.'"

The secret of Edmund Grove's success in looking after his more mercurial and excitable brother is very well described by the latter when he speaks on another occasion of his improvement in health being "all due to your way of leaving one alone, unless when you are feeding one's body or one's mind. Long may you be spared to keep on doing it!"

The *Spectator* of October 4th, 1890, has a letter signed George Grove on "The Cat's Toilette," mentioning that the Sanskrit name of the cat means the animal that is always cleaning itself, and the mention of cats and the *Spectator* may be a sufficient excuse for inserting the following characteristic undated letter to his brother Edmund:—

"LOWER SYDENHAM,
"*Friday*, 7 A.M.

"DEAR NED,—It may interest you to see the handwriting of the man [R. H. Hutton] who gives, or causes to be given to us, so much pleasure and profit every Saturday. Last Saturday's *Spectator* pleased me so much that I could not help firing off a note of gratitude to him, and here's his reply. What a lovely day again! I have just had a good beginning to the day. As I was drinking my tea in my bedroom at 6.15 or so, I spied down below me in the orchard a cat under one of the trees, cleaning and enjoying herself in great peace and happiness—the orchard is a perfect resort of the feline race, who are a deadly source of enmity to Russ. Accordingly, I opened the window quietly and lifted Russ up till he got sight of his enemy. At last the whole thing came into his mind, and he got much excited and whimpered and struggled. Then I took him down stairs and put him on his feet at the entrance to the orchard, thirty feet from where the cat was! But 'position,' or 'orientation,' or 'locality,' or whatever you like to call it, was nothing to *him*, and off he went to the right in quite another direction—the cat, too, regarding him with apparent unconcern, and not moving till fate brought him within ten or twelve feet of her, when she rushed off, and he realized what he had missed! It was quite amusing."

Links with the past always interested Grove, and under date October 21st, 1890, I find in his pocket-book the following reminiscences furnished him by his friend and neighbour, Mr. Mayow Adams :—

"In 1812 or 1813 he was at Eastbourne, and being out with his nurse was terribly frightened by a loud explosion: it was the guns in the fort firing at a French ship which had come too close to shore. He remembers the balls ricochetting along the top of the waves, also his fear for two men who were sitting down under the fort.

"He had talked to a man born in Queen Anne's reign. He was an old sailor named Andrew —— who used to come round with matches . . . he said he was born in 1712, and had helped to fire the guns at the coronations of George II. and III."

On October 30th he wrote to Dean Bradley :—

" . . . My mind has been much exercised about Newman lately. Interesting he certainly was, and deeply so as an individual; but as a leader of religion, I don't think we have to thank him for much beyond the revival of interest and vigour in the Church. To him, and to the stronger men who took the reins out of his hands, we owe the flood of ritualism and material worship and magic that now fills the Church, and I for one don't feel very grateful. . . . Our Church is fast becoming, from the reasonable Service which was the pride of the country, a mere magic mill for the production of Sacraments which are to act as charms."

Grove was an excellent correspondent—apart from the rapidity with which he answered every letter he received —in that he had the gift of accommodating himself to persons of all ages and seizing their point of view. He was perhaps never happier than when writing to young people, as the following letters may suffice to show. The first is to his eldest grand-child, then a little girl of five, the second to a former pupil of the College, then engaged as music mistress at a girls' school :—

"ROYAL COLLEGE OF MUSIC,

"*Nov.* 13, 1890.

"MY DEAR GLADYS,—I send you a picture of a soldier which I think you will like; ask Mama to read you what is written on the back!

"I miss you dreadfully, and only wish you would pop in some morning at breakfast, or before dinner, when the drawing-room is nice and dark. We should make a hullaballoo, and I promise you Rusty would bark. He is much better than he was, and had a famous romp with me round and round, and in and out, under the piano and round the table, and under the sofa and over the chairs, till Grannie said, 'Now, enough of this; go out into the hall. I wonder what Gladys would say if she was here!'

"I think I shall find Papa down here to-night, and Uncle Arthur and Aunt Emily, but *you* won't be there or Mama. Oh dear, oh dear! boo hoo, boo hoo! The leaves have come down so fast lately that Jacobs is quite tired of sweeping them up. We shall have a bonfire soon to burn them all up. Talking of burning I saw such a great fire last night near Buckingham Palace: the flames were so red, and went up so high into the sky, and the smoke rolled in great volumes! It was a part of the barracks, where the soldiers' families lived; and all the wives and little children were being carried out wrapped up in blankets, and the soldiers rushing in and out of the burning houses to save them; and the engines were galloping up and down the street spouting out fire and steam out of their chimneys. It was such a sight! There was another house on fire close by this one when I arrived this morning. Smoke was pouring out of the top windows (answering to your nursery), but happily they put it out, happily indeed, for it was close enough to this house to make one afraid.

"Now it is coming near the time for me to go and catch the train, so I must stop. How I wish I could clasp you in my arms, and give you a kiss! but we must wait. Grannie sends her best love to you; and so do I, and Rusty and the Cat. I am your fondly loving Grattypa."

[*To* Miss Louie Heath.]

"Lower Sydenham,
"*Nov.* 18, 1890.

" . . . I have seen the news of your explosion in last night's paper! I hope you are not hurt, or at any rate only a *small piece* blown off you. Perhaps the head mistress is killed and you will be put in her place! Who knows? Quick and assuage my heated indignation. This is all nonsense and comes of having been reading Dickens's Letters. But really I should be glad to know something. . . . I am glad you were made much of at the ——'s, but for *me* (strictly between our two selves) I don't care for that sort of people; so grand, so *shiny*, and so empty. Still they help one on up the ladder and mustn't be despised. And also I am wrong; for though they are not cut out to our pattern, there's a lot of kindness about these shiny people. . . . I don't remember *Literature and Dogma*—to distinguish it from M. A.'s other books, but they are all full of meat, a little dressed up now and then, and made into ragout and sauce—but meat all the same. I remember one book in which there is an astonishing passage about the difference between morality (in the Old Testament) and religion or faith—I forget the word—(in the New); a beautiful piece. Another (in another book) about the *Celtic* spirit in Literature, exemplified by Shakespeare's 'Dido with a willow in her hand.' There's a deal of that spirit in Arnold's own *poems*. Can you borrow them? If not I would lend you a volume. Tell me."

The recently published volume of the *Dictionary of National Biography* [Vol. xxiv, Hailes to Harriott] contained a somewhat iconoclastic article on Handel by his friends, Messrs. Fuller-Maitland and Barclay Squire. Handel was not one of Grove's special divinities, but he could not endorse the new verdict, and in a note in his pocket-book justifies his dissent on the following grounds:—

"I cannot agree with the estimate formed of Handel by my friends M. and S. Handel may have given rise to no school, or influenced the subsequent form of his art little if at all, but he wrote works two of which at least are as fresh as ever in the minds and the taste of English people. Did Shakspeare do more?"

Notes on "non-musical England" also abound in his pocket-book at the same time (November 1890). In these he comments on the inadequateness of general rehearsals, the absence of subsidies, and observes that not only are there few really musical people, but those few at once give up music for society or money, or any of the many other things which supersede it. One of the last entries for the year records an inimitable example of mixed arithmetic perpetrated by an old soldier, reduced to beggary, who carried a placard with the legend :—

Actions	7
Wounds	9
Children	8
Total	24

December 1890 and January 1891 were bad months for Grove. But ill-health, as the following letter shows, was unable to affect his interest in his pupils, past and present, or his enthusiasm for his heroes in music and letters. The reference to Walter Scott is interesting as it indicates that Grove was amongst those who are inclined to think that the 'Journal' is at least as immortal a monument as the novels :—

[*To* MISS LOUIE HEATH.]

"LOWER SYDENHAM,
"*Jan.* 18, 1891.

" . . . What will you be thinking of me? What must I think of myself, when I remember that I have never yet written 1891 to you! And yet you must have mercy, for I have been laid up and sadly busy all through our short holiday. I had an attack on Dec. 10 which obliged me to miss the concert at St. James's Hall. I was able to get up to the Exams. for four days. Then I absurdly exposed myself to the east wind and got knocked up again, and then the doctor said I must not go out. So I actually missed the Entrance Exam. and the first day of the term! However last Monday I went up to town, and have been there ever since. We have had three rooms lent us off Oxford Street, and Lady Grove went with me and we found it quite comfy, and I think we shall do that as long as the cold weather lasts—come here [Lower Sydenham] for Friday to Monday, and the rest in town. The winter is as hard as ever.

"We began College Concerts last Thursday. . . . Did you hear that we gave a Vocal Recital (nothing but songs, duets, trios, &c.), last term? It was such a success that we shall repeat the thing this term. It encouraged me about the singing very much.

"Have you ever noticed what I call the 'appoggiatura of expression' in Beethoven? I send you three examples. . . . They are wonderfully interesting to me—as indeed everything in Beethoven is—and more so from day to day. Can you give me any others in his sonatas, &c.?

". . . Have you read Walter Scott's 'Journal.'[1] It may not interest you so much, as it is old-fashioned, and deals with the things of 70 years ago, and in an antique style, but I am sure your father will like it, and I do immensely. I really put it with the Bible and Shakspeare. Don't laugh!"

By 1891 Grove was already exercised about the appointment of his successor. Under date February 1st, 1891, there is a memorandum in his note-book: 'N.B. write to the Prince and tell him about the qualifications of C.H.H.P. [Sir Hubert Parry] to succeed me.' Three years were, however, yet to elapse before this recommendation was to be acted upon—years almost if not quite as crowded as any that had gone before.

In Februrary he was again disabled by one of his cab accidents, fortunately without serious consequences, though he suffered considerable pain at the time:—

[*To* MISS LOUIE HEATH.]

"LOWER SYDENHAM,
"*Sunday, March* 1, 1891.

". . . You are a good friend and your letter was quite to my mind, and charming. But I fear *I* am a poor one, though not all to blame. On the day after I got it I was unhappy enough to *charge* a cab in the fog, and to get run over again. The cab

[1] From a correspondence with Mr. David Douglas, of Edinburgh, the publisher of the "Journal," it appears that Grove forwarded a list of queries and corrections, one of the former referring to Scott's visit to Sydenham. Mr. Douglas believed the Sydenham mentioned in one passage to be a house of that name near Kelso. But undoubtedly in 1806 Scott, Campbell, and Richardson met at "Campbell's modest little cottage" at Sydenham, London.

wheel stood on my left foot ever so long. However it was considerate enough not to break anything, but it bruised me badly, and ground my ankle bone (left leg) so hard into the ground that it made a nasty wound. I did not see the importance of this, nor did the doctor; and as I did not lie in bed or keep the foot up enough, it has not yet begun to heal properly. I was lodging in town with Lady Grove which was *à propos*: but last night got home here. *En route* I went to College and closed the Scholarship Exam., and had them all, successful and unsuccessful, into the Concert room and 'speeched' them. Poor things, there were 159 candidates (for the Final) and twelve elected! . . .

"I know the feeling you describe too well—the temptation to mourn over one's drawbacks instead of conquering them. Recollect half of them are imaginary, or much exaggerated. Sensitive people like you and I always distrust and depreciate themselves too much, and if our friends think too much of us, we think too little. . . . At one time I was troubled by what you describe to a morbid extent, and even now I often have to deplore a want of self-confidence. . . .

"I dined with Joachim (quite a small party) lately and had plenty of talk. He is as nice as ever. I was so vexed to miss him in the Beethoven Concerto at the Crystal Palace yesterday. But I heard him in the E minor quartet; in Brahms's Horn trio; the Septet and other things at two Monday Pops. and never heard him play more finely. . . ."

It was some time before he recovered from the effects of his accident, but he turned his enforced inactivity to good account, as may be seen from the following long letter to Mrs. Wodehouse:—

"LOWER SYDENHAM,
"*Easter Monday*, [*March* 29, 1891.]

"At last I have got free, and am at home for a few days, without the necessity of rushing up to town, and with some power of resting my foot. It is much better; indeed the wound is, I think, quite well, but I find that walking though not painful is very tiring. College finished with Stanford's orchestral concert on Wednesday night—a great success every one says—I was there Thursday; to-morrow I begin here the pupils' reports, which will take me four days. On the 8th, 9th and 10th are the Associate Examinations, and then I can get away. I think of a week in Paris, if I can find a congenial soul to go with me. Monod has given me a note to the sub-librarian of the Conservatoire; as one of my great objects is to see the autographs of the *Sonata Appassionata*, and be able to look it through and through and copy, &c. Monod is to dine here on Wednesday to meet the Dean of Westminster. He was here last Sunday, and was very pleased and full of information. And now after all this torrent of *nothings*, how are you? I fear it's no use asking: and that till the weather changes, you cannot be really better. I think it would be nice *now*, if the bitter north-easters would go. But go they will at last, and then you will obey the soft beckoning wing of the delicious Spring airs, and come out of your long retirement—'Rest and change.' I heard of a poor man who had gone to Harrogate and left this record behind him in the hotel book. 'I was sent here for rest and change. The waiter took the change and the landlord the rest.' Very witty.

"I asked Joachim the other day if it could be translated into German. He was patriotic enough not to say no, but he could not do it himself.

"Oh, I must tell you of an amusing thing I said to him on Thursday. 'Did you ever see the autograph of the 9th Symphony at Berlin, in which the trio of the Scherzo is written in 2–4 and not in 4–4?'—'2–4, my dear Grove, impossible, nonsense—don't think of such a foolish idea.' Well, I came and searched my note-book of 1879 (the last visit I made to Berlin) and there sure enough I found it! The trio was written in 2–4; and Beethoven had turned it into 4–4 by numbering each alternate bar, thus:—

all through up to the 119th bar.

"I also found a fugue of Handel's scored by Beethoven, and 'non nobis, Domine' written out in the key of F. It all gave me a keen wish to go off to Berlin at once. It also gave me a strong revived interest in my note-books. I found those containing all my Mendelssohn memoranda. Long conversations with Madame Goldschmidt, Charles Hallé, Joachim, Schleinitz, Ehrlich, Piatti and others containing the most interesting stories and traits of Mendelssohn; for instance here is one. He's talking about a certain Prelude of Chopin, and he says, 'It is so perfectly beautiful that I could go on for ever, playing it over and over; all the more because by no possibility could I have written it' (very characteristic, I think). Then I find a catalogue of all the MSS., letters and compositions in the possession of Ernst Mendelssohn in Berlin—an enormous list. . . ."

At Easter he carried out his intention and paid a short visit to Paris, one of his motives being to inspect the school at the Conservatoire and obtain information at first hand as to the methods of teaching employed. He also had a field day in the library of the Conservatoire on April 13th, and saw a good deal of his old friend Clermont-Ganneau and of Wekerlin, the Librarian of the Conservatoire, embodying some of his experiences in a letter to Mrs. Wodehouse written on the following day.

"Hotel St. Romain,
"*April* 14, 1891.

"Your card came last night and sent my mercury up several inches. By the way, where do you get the singularly clear *pencil*? Is it specially made for you? and who cuts it? or does it cut itself? You know one of Beethoven's great difficulties was to get his pens cut and mended, and there are the most piteous and angry and absurd notes to a friend of his who was in a public office, begging for fresh ones. The one with which he wrote the Appassionata (or began it) was beautifully mended, the tails are so fine and curving, and the heads so round and well made; and the writing never loses this character, but even in the rapidest parts is graceful and clear. He never wore his pen to the stump as Schubert did. I was led over the Library of the Conservatoire by the Librarian, M. Wekerlin, and saw most interesting things, and such a *heap*. I should say that there must be 50,000 volumes. A beautiful long room with the timber beams showing, ancient style, though only some forty years old. Two rows of fine marble busts, about ten on each side, looking across at each other. By a curious coincidence Beethoven and Le Sueur are vis-à-vis, and I at once thought of an amusing story of Berlioz's of his having got Le Sueur to hear the C minor, and of his rage and confusion after it—not able to get his hat on, and spluttering out that such music was *wrong* and ought to be prevented. But of course their being there was a mere chance. Then over I went into Wekerlin's room (a most delightful, impulsive old creature) and sat down to examine the things in the Appassionata, which Taylor and Dannreuther had set down for me, and there I stayed till nearly three, when I was quite starved and bent double. It is dreadfully cold here, and I long for the sun so. . . . I have just read an interesting, lively book 'Journal d'un Officier d'Ordonnance" during the siege of Paris. He knew German and therefore saw a good deal of Bismarck and describes things very well—a little too much of himself and his own grievances, but worth reading—nice clear print and a small book. Alas! I forgot your hatred of war. Good-bye, O Quaker! . . .

"P.S. Did you know that the French spell quaker 'Couacre'?"

A letter to the same correspondent on his return is interesting as exhibiting his impatience at the reticence of musical critics:—

"LOWER SYDENHAM, S.E.,
"*April*, 1891.

". . . How infinite are the gradations of feeling! so very near to each other and yet so different—I thought this when I listened to those two wonderful movements of Schubert's B Minor Symphony. What *miles* they are above F.M.B., in some particulars even above ———. Please forgive me! you know my feeling for him (B.), and yet, if one judges by the transport that is in it, one cannot doubt. It is not that it is *greater*. It is dearer, nearer. Isn't it strange how critics can hear those sweet, great things, and (I suppose) enter into them, and yet never show it by a word in their wretched accounts? *Could you* write down an account of the performance of the B Minor and not by ten words just let the world know that it had fetched, transported you, tho' you had no room for more than ten lines?"

In his address to his pupils on April 30th, Grove was able to point with satisfaction to the steady growth in their numbers, from 94 in 1883 to 320 at the opening of the ninth year. If they had produced no prodigies who had taken the world by storm, no one ever did take the world by storm—certainly not Beethoven, Schubert or Wagner. But the record of their achievements was most gratifying: Waddington had won the Mendelssohn scholarship, and 'our old scholars and students are beginning to spread well over the kingdom and take a real share in the musical education of the country.' The results of the examinations held by the Associated Board were most satisfying to the Royal College, and they could point to the excellent work done by the Musical Guild 'a thing which is in every sense our own.' Then, addressing himself to the new pupils, who had just joined, Grove made an earnest appeal to them to realise the responsibilities of their positions :—

"Every one has some gift, some ability; and every one can cultivate that as far as possible. Every one can be in earnest—can be thoughtful, can be correct, can do everything he has to do as well as he possibly can: and every one can be good, and unselfish, and think of others before he thinks of himself. Do this, and you will advance and improve, and make the world better than it is."

He further impressed on them that they were to be—

"missionaries, to carry the faith of music, as you learnt it here, into the world—to impart to others the good things which you will learn here. You will often have to *fight* as well as teach—to fight against ignorance, inattention, carelessness. I hope you will fight hard and win the battle."

In another passage he emphasises the value of living for an ideal :—

"'Live in an ideal.' I don't find fault with your enthusiasm and onesidedness, for your devotions to Liszt and Wagner. You are young, and unless you have the faults and virtues of youth (faults are exaggerated virtues), you would not be natural boys and girls."

Finally he exhorts them earnestly to avoid the dangers of overwork and overstrain.

The proposed measure for the Registration of Teachers, then occupying a good deal of public attention, exercised Grove a good deal at this time, and he writes with considerable heat to Mrs. Wodehouse to express his indignation at the mode in which the projected Bill, if placed on the Statute Book, would interfere with the liberty of action of the Royal College :—

"LOWER SYDENHAM,
"*May* 24, 1891.

". . . . There is a bill in Parliament for the Registration and Organisation of teachers which has occupied and excited us all very much. It proposes to exercise an absolute command over all teachers and examinations of music. We, the Royal College of Music—whose charter gives us all but perfect command over the teaching and examination of music throughout England—are to be subject to the ignorance and caprice of a great random Board composed of university men, and heads of colleges and presidents of learned societies, no one of whom has any knowledge of the most intricate and peculiar subject in the world: who are to have power to walk into our House, and question me and tell me that we are all wrong and that our certificates are inaccurate, &c. . . . Two years ago, we joined the Academy and formed an Associated Board of Examination for the purpose of starting a system of exams. on a proper basis, and with a proper band of competent examiners so as to put an end to the wretched system which has sprung up and is gradually substituting the possession of a certificate for the fact of being a good player. Already we have begun to exercise considerable influence in the right direction, not by examining teachers but by examining their pupils. And now all this 'promising beginning' is to be put a stop to. Each of our three bodies has sent in a remonstrance, and the whole matter is now before a Select Committee. All we want is to be let alone. But you can imagine the endless meetings and the weary conversations and debates before the whole thing came clearly to one's mind. *Our* manifesto of course came on me; and with my usual slowness it took me a good deal of trouble.

"I am busy 'redacting' my analysis of No. 7 Symphony for the Richter Concerts. It was very *à propos* of Stanford to make a little discovery last week. You know the queer subject of the Finale? It exists in an Irish song called 'Nora Creina,'[1] which Beethoven was setting with an accompaniment at that very time. How good for one it is to take those great works—and the same thing with poetry—sufficiently into one's memory to be able to ponder and *chew* (Schumann's word) them over and over! You too, have had your pleasures! And that dear old Sonata Pathétique, too! Isn't it—isn't Beethoven—*inexhaustible* . . . .? I too heard it last Sunday tumbled through by a new Australian scholar, and yet I seemed to enjoy it as much as if Madame Schumann herself had played it. That sonata is one of my *magic* things. Thirty years ago, I was walking up to the train from here and I heard the introduction being played behind the blinds of an open window. It was *grand*. 'What *can* that be?' said I, 'so noble, so peculiar, *so new*.' It was not till hours afterwards that what

[1] See the final symphony of the song, B. and H., Serie 24, No. 258, p. 27.

it was flashed on me; and since then I have always felt it peculiarly fine.

"So, too, one night wandering about through the dark streets of Basle after dinner, I heard a piano and pulled up underneath a house, on the first floor of which some one was playing finely with an open window, and *what* music! What could it be? It was familiar, but I could not give it a name! It was as modern and new as possible, and yet so dignified and classical. No, I could not recall the name; at last it flashed on me, Beethoven's Concerto in E flat, first movement. Oh, my dear, what things there are to happen to one and to wake up one's imagination!"

On June 9th Grove's friend and colleague, Mr. John Francis Barnett, read a paper at the Musical Association relating to the completion of Schubert's Sketch Symphony in E, the story of which can best be told in his own words:—

"Some years ago I was walking with Sir George Grove, then Mr. Grove, after a Crystal Palace Concert, towards his residence in Sydenham, when in course of conversation he told me that he had in his possession a very curious sketch of a Symphony by Schubert that had never been completed.

He gave me many interesting particulars concerning it; he described how the Introduction and a portion of the *Allegro* of the first movement were quite complete and fully instrumented, but that as the second subject was reached, it broke off into a mere sketch, as though Schubert's ideas came too rapidly for him to instrument.

He likewise told me that the sketch, which bears the date of August, 1821, was given by Ferdinand Schubert to Felix Mendelssohn, who, it is said, intended to have completed it, an intention which, unfortunately, he was prevented from carrying out by his premature death. It then came into the possession of Paul Mendelssohn, who some years later gave it to its present owner.

That Schubert would have completed this Symphony if his life had been prolonged, there is little doubt, but the sketch in itself being so complete, he probably felt that there was no danger of his forgetting the ideas and their intended treatment; he therefore must have put it aside for more pressing work. But, alas! a sad fate prevented him completing this work or the still more important unfinished Symphony in B minor.

When I undertook the completion of the sketch Symphony I told Sir George that I would in the first instance make a sketch of the first movement sufficiently advanced so as to be able to play it over to him on the pianoforte, and give him an idea of the manner in which I would carry out my task. When I was ready it was arranged that I should dine with him at Lower Sydenham and play over to him what I had done. The original score of Schubert had meanwhile been lent to Mr. Rockstro in order for him to give a description of it in Grove's Dictionary. Mr. Rockstro was to meet me at Mr. Grove's and was to bring this score with him. When I arrived at Mr. Grove's on the evening arranged, I found he had not come in, but a few minutes after he arrived with Mr. Rockstro in cheerful conversation. I noticed that neither of them had anything with them that looked like a score, so I ventured to ask Mr. Rockstro whether he had brought it with him. It turned out that they had left it in the train, and they at once returned to the station to make inquiries. Telegrams were sent up and down the line, but nothing was heard of the lost MS. that evening. This threw a gloom over the dinner, as the chances of recovering the MS. seemed very remote, there being no address on the wrapper in which it was contained. I, nevertheless, played over my version of the first movement with which Mr. Grove was, I am glad to say, very pleased. The next morning I received a telegram from Mr. Grove saying that the MS. had been discovered and was lying at Norwood Junction. I felt very much relieved at hearing this good news, as having taken very great interest in the work I had undertaken, and having even then bestowed a large amount of thought and time on working out the sketch of the first movement. If the MS. had not been discovered all that I had done would have been in vain; as for Mr. Grove he would have felt the loss of this unique MS. most keenly, as he prized it more highly than any original MS. that he possessed. The Symphony in its completed form was first performed at the Crystal Palace Concerts on May 5th, 1883, and was so successful that it was again performed the next season in 1884."

Grove's complaints of the miseries he suffered from bad pens are already familiar to the reader. He returns to the charge in the first of the subjoined letters written in the summer of 1891:—

[*To* MRS. WODEHOUSE.]

"LOWER SYDENHAM, S.E.,
"*June* 18, 1891.

" . . . . Can't some one be stirred up to invent a real pencil which shall take the place of pens and do away with those tedious incessant dips, with all the miseries which attend on writing with a liquid and put us on a solid, sensible *British* foundation. In the operation which so many millions of Britons suffer from, there would be seen the spectacle—but I won't go on: I only got into the vein from having been reading Macaulay for hours in bed. But seriously, one of my first paragraphs in the *old* 'Pall Mall' was to make a moving picture of the miseries incidental on ink (Macaulay again), and say how much a pencil was wanted. Have you not among your many admirers an engineer or inventor who can do this great change as thoroughly as William the III. accomplished the Revolution I have been reading about? . . . .

"I had a hard day on Monday, though full of pleasure, at Cambridge, where I heard Dvórak's new Symphony,[1] and was greatly pleased with it, and filled with an earnest longing to hear it again—a sure test, and one which rarely if ever fills me after anything by less inspired writers. It was full of feeling and beautiful tune, reminiscent of Schubert here and there—(Trio strongly so), but distinctly a master work and delightful. The *Stabat Mater* made little impression on me."

[*To the Same.*]

"LOWER SYDENHAM, S.E.,
"*July* 11, 1891.

" . . . Yes, indeed, there has been a whirl of life in London. I have kept out of it as much as possible, but was obliged to go to the Garden Party. Indeed it was very pleasant. It is always such a pretty scene, and such numbers of interesting people and beautiful women. . . .

"The only slight drawback to the Prince's party was the fact (discovered too late) that I had not a *frock* coat, as all the rest seemed to have, but these sort of things do not trouble me much. I am always prepared to answer such a charge as Dr. Johnson did—'Ignorance, my dear Madam, sheer ignorance.' I like the account of the quiet of your place. Ours is quiet too—so far—but a high road close in front, and cottages crowded round somewhat militate against more than a *degree* of it. I have just been sitting there under a tree with my body in the sun and my head in the shade, a cat on my lap, a dear dog at my feet, two children flitting about on the lawn, a number of *Nature* in my hand, and such tiredness pervading my bones and body as even you can hardly have felt—at any rate you can't have exceeded it. I *do* get so done up. A walk of a mile, though I may enjoy it at the time—as I did yesterday when I walked from the Athenæum to Victoria with a very

[1] The beautiful work in G major.

intelligent, amusing man, called Sutherland Edwards—tells on me terribly afterwards; and also talking in an animated way exhausts me sadly; and as, after I left Edwards, I had an hour's hard talk with the Bishop of Ripon, I got home more dead than alive. The Bishop of Ripon is a very interesting person, full of literature—and still young and fresh, and very tolerant and easy to talk to. There's a girl of his at the college, and he and I are quite friends . . . .

"I looked in at Esposito's recital three or four days ago. He is the chief piano-teacher at Dublin—an Italian, and I must say he pleased me very much. I heard him play a sonata of his own for violin and P., and the first 2 of the Symphonic Études of Schumann's. The sonata was full of reminiscences, but very nice to hear, and somehow the Italians have (if not the tremendous technique of Paderewski and other Germans or allies of Germans) a grace and love of beauty *and care for their hearers*, that is very dear to me, and that seems to be fast going out of the piano-playing world. It is very like the difference between Tolstoi and Tourguénieff. Tolstoi may be more terribly in earnest, but Tourguénieff is the greater and sweeter artist. . . .

"I have been reading a good deal of Matthew Arnold of late. How very difficult his poetry is to learn! It gives me greater trouble than any other. I have been *committing to memory* (Macaulay's favourite word) one of his mystic poems, and will write it out here first to see if I know it, and secondly because you will like it. It is a sort of comparison of life to a multitude of islands scattered over a vast ocean:—

"'Yes! in the sea of life enisled,
With echoing straits between us thrown,
Dotting the shoreless watery wild,
We mortal millions live *alone*.
The islands feel the enclasping flow,
And then their endless bounds they know.

"'But when the moon their hollows lights,
And they are swept with balms of spring,
And in their glens on starry nights
The nightingales divinely sing;
And lovely notes from shore to shore
Across the sounds and channels pour—

"'Oh! then, a longing like despair
Is to their farthest caverns sent;
For surely once, they feel, we were
Parts of a single continent!
Now round us spreads the watery plain—
Oh might our marges meet again!

"'Who order'd, that their longing's fire
Should be, as soon as kindled, cool'd?
Who renders vain their deep desire?—
A God, a God their severance ruled!
And bade betwixt their shores to be
The unplumb'd, salt, estranging sea.'

"The last stanza is clumsy—(except the last lines of all, which are superb), and the 'nights' and 'nightingales' come perilously close in verse 2—but it's a beautiful poem, isn't it? It's so full of what he himself calls the *Celtic* feeling (the type of which is Dido with the willow in her hand beckoning her love to Carthage). There are two others of the same cast (only my poor fingers *refuse* to copy them out); one called 'The Future' on a river as the image of Time, ending thus:—

"'As the pale waste widens around him,
As the banks fade dimmer away,
As the stars come out, and the night wind
Brings up the stream
Murmurs and scents of the infinite sea.'

"(Don't cry as you read it—but I am hardly able to help it.) And yet another called 'Morality' ending—

"'I knew not yet the gauge of time,
Nor wore the manacles of space;
I felt it in some other clime,
I saw it in some other place.
'Twas when the heavenly house I trod,
And lay upon the breast of God.'

"These things touch me in the most extraordinary way, and I think they will touch you—*me*, because I am old, *you* because you are of such a fine clay, and so sensitive. Tell me if they do.

"People are beginning to rush off to Bayreuth. I shall not go there: it doesn't please me, but on the contrary makes me angry and fierce. But I want to look carefully through (did I tell you?) the MSS. of B.'s Symphonies 4. 5. 6. 7, which the Mendelssohns have (with the Egmont music, the 3 great quartets, &c.) at Berlin."

[*To* MISS LOUIE HEATH.]

"ROYAL COLLEGE OF MUSIC,
"*July* 25, 1891.

". . . The change from Archangel and Revel to Criccieth (such a name!) rather amused me, and made me think of a good story.

W. S. Ralston, a great Russian scholar, an old friend of mine, met me one day. 'My dear Ralston,' I said, 'how ill you look!' 'Yes,' he answered, 'I'm very bad; but I'm off on Monday to Astrakhan, to drink koumiss, and live a Russian life: the fine air of the steppes will soon set me up.' Ten days afterwards I meet him again. 'What, not gone? I thought you were at the Caspian Sea by this time.' 'No, I've changed my mind, and I'm going to Godesberg on the Rhine instead.' 'Well, good-bye once more.' Another ten days or so and I see him again. 'Why, you don't mean to say you are here still?' 'Yes, I've given up Godesberg, and shall go down to my old father's vicarage in Somersetshire.' . . ."

On his seventy-first birthday, August 13th, 1891, Grove started for his holiday, travelling straight through *viâ* Paris and Lausanne to the Riffel Alp Hotel. Thence, after a most enjoyable fortnight, he moved on to Berlin. On August 31st, he went once more to visit the graves of the Mendelssohn family in the Old Trinity churchyard, and on the same day devoted some hours to an inspection of the autographs in the Imperial Library. As a result of his examination of the MS. of the Ninth Symphony, Grove was confirmed in his conclusion that Beethoven deliberately intended that there should be no pause between the third and last movements. The object and results of his journey are summarised in a letter to Miss Heath on his return:—

"LOWER SYDENHAM,

"*Sept.* 18, 1891.

". . . I went straight off to the Riffel Alp—a place with a hotel 7,500 feet high in the air, standing right in front of the famous Matterhorn. There, with 250 more of my fellow creatures, I revelled in the splendid air, the lovely views and beautiful weather, till a day or two before your letter was written, and then I fled off to Berlin, arriving there the very day of your letter itself. Then I had three full days looking over the autographs of five of Beethoven's Symphonies, 4, 5, 7, 8, 9; the three first are in the possession of Mendelssohn, and the other two at the Bibliothek. I had never before seen a real first-rate, large Beethoven autograph, and this fascinated me. Not only the sentiment of his having touched the paper and made the writing himself, and all that, but the beauty of the pages, and the interest of the way in which it is all done. Such rare and evident intention to let there be no mistake in putting down his exact meaning. And then the idea seized me, not to rest until I had got them published in a photograph facsimile edition, so that before long every one of us may have the actual writing of Beethoven in his own hands, and judge for himself on the many points which there are to be judged about in every symphony. I lost no time; but as soon as I came home, wrote a letter to the *Times*, and on last Tuesday it was in. Mackenzie has backed it up—very nice of him and very useful to me. I have written to Breitkopf and Härtel about it. They are the great publishers, known more widely than any other. They are on the spot; the collectors are familiar with their names, and know them to be trustworthy. Now do you think me foolish or not? What delight there is in the mind! What rapture it can give you! No one (I think) loves scenery or nature more than I do, and yet nature does not give me such keen, passionate delight as the products of one's inner mind and heart do.

"(I must go back a little, for after I got back, on September 6th, I went off to Hereford to hear Parry's beautiful Psalm *De Profundis*). His music does not always touch me as it ought, but this time it did, and I don't think I am far wrong in saying that it is the best thing in the English school so far.

"I am very well, but of course the gilt will soon be rubbed off. Already it's beginning—but never mind; one must *wear*, not *rust* out, as the proverb says. And you, my friend, are you down-hearted at beginning work again! . . . I will try to send you a telegram to-morrow to encourage you, and let you know that *one* friend at any rate is thinking of you. Forgive this scrawl. It's so imperfect, but I have several others to write. I read two of Rhoda Broughton's novels—*Nancy* and *Belinda*—too tragical (like Othello), but very powerful."

The letter to the *Times*, referred to above, appeared in the issue of September 15th. In it Grove states that he had recently had an opportunity, through the kindness of his friend, Ernst Mendelssohn-Bartholdy, the composer's nephew, and head of the well-known banking house in Berlin, of examining the autographs of the 4th, 5th, and 7th of Beethoven's Symphonies, which are in Ernst Mendelssohn's possession, and advocates the issue of a facsimile edition of these MSS. His own attitude in the matter is clearly shown in an undated letter to Dean Bradley :—

"A. P. Stanley is to you what Beethoven is to me—every additional trait or expression is a gem, and gives me the keenest pleasure. Those facsimiles I proposed in my letter to the *Times* will be an inestimable boon to musical people all over the world, and I hope to get them carried out. Suppose one could have a facsimile of the MS. of St. Matthew's Gospel, or of St. Paul's Epistle to the Galatians, so that instead of having to go to Rome or Petersburg to see it, one could have it in one's own house, and handle it, and mark it, and have it always at hand, eh? And the parallel is rather close, because the Symphonies, like the Epistles, have many places in them where the original must have been mistaken by the editor."

The address to his pupils, delivered on October 1, 1891, is one of the most interesting of the whole series. After the usual formal announcements—distinctions, posts, compositions, marriages of old pupils, etc.—he says: "And now, I suppose, you will wish me to tell you something about my journey"; and goes on to describe his stay at the Riffel Alp, and his pilgrimage to Berlin to examine the Beethoven autographs in the possession of his old friend, Ernst Mendelssohn, the nephew of the composer. That in turn serves him as an excuse to give a sketch of the rise of the Mendelssohn family, to applaud the indomitable perseverance that enabled them to emerge from the forlorn and depressed condition in which the Jews were for the most part sunk at the middle and end of the eighteenth century, and to allude in terms of just indignation to the reactionary tactics of the anti-Semites. From this he returns to the Beethoven MSS., and shows his young hearers wherein the value and interest of a musical autograph, especially a Beethoven autograph, resides, because it proves the composer's amazing faculty for taking pains, and shows those "patient touches of unwearied art."

In conclusion he dwells on the evidences that constantly accumulate of the solidarity of the Royal College, such as letters from old pupils showing how ardently they desire to come back themselves or to send up others. This he attributes in great measure to the interest which is taken in the pupils by their teachers—not merely a musical, but a personal interest. Science, he continues, is not everything; "life is more than efficiency"; and "accurate execution (necessary as it is) may be combined with a personal feeling of affection for your music and your piano." The "sweet human qualities, which made Beethoven, Mozart, Mendelssohn, Schumann, great men as well as great musicians, have a very large influence on performances which affect the great mass of unscientific men and women." So whatever their success as musicians, they will be on the right road so long as they have this feeling. However parted they may be—in St. Andrews, Cornwall, Vienna, Australia, Canada—they were all tending towards the same goal.

A few days later he was at Birmingham for the Festival, and on his return recorded his impressions in a letter to Mrs. Wodehouse:—

"LOWER SYDENHAM,
"*Oct.* 1891.

". . . The great delights of the Birmingham Festival *to me* were—

"Parry's 'Blest Pair'—a *noble* work, which improves every time.

"Brahms's Symphony in F. (the Beethoven no 7, I could not stop for).

"Joachim's 3 performances (the best perhaps his own Hungarian Concerto, which I liked better than ever), 2 overtures, 'Anacreon' and 'Euryanthe.' Richter's conducting is something wonderful. Stanford's 'Eden' has a great deal in it, and I desire to hear it again, as I hope to do on the 28th. It would be very much helped and improved by scenery.

"I saw a good deal of Joachim, went to the train with him yesterday, and he called on me at the College. I like him better and better. Both he and Richter applauded my facsimile plan very much. I had a very nice letter too from Breitkopf and Härtel praising the idea of it, and saying that if I would give my name at the head, they would form a committee and place the edition on the same general footing as the Bachgesellschaft."

On the 22nd of December Grove was able to make the gratifying announcement in the *Times* that Messrs. Breitkopf and Härtel had decided to issue a series of collotype facsimiles of Beethoven's works, as suggested by himself three months earlier.

It must not be supposed from the predominance of Beethoven in his thoughts that Grove was in any way forgetful of or disloyal to Schubert. It only needed that he should hear some of Schubert's music for the old enthusiasm to revive in all its fervour :—

[*To* MRS. WODEHOUSE.]

"LOWER SYDENHAM,
"*Nov.* 1, 1891.

". . . A good selection of *Rosamunde* was played yesterday at the Crystal Palace, which touched me extremely. It nearly broke me down, it was so beautiful, so tender, so absolutely inspired. Do you remember the happy expression of Joubert's that the 'lyre is a winged instrument and must transport"? If ever there were wings in music it is in Schubert's, and especially in those lovely entr'actes and pieces. They played also Mendelssohn's 'Walpurgisnacht,' but it does not move me.

". . . How good it is to have one's mind alive to nature. I fear you can't get a glimpse—but there must be beautiful tints and forms to be seen out of your window. I remember it so well, not that I could ever write poetry about it—my lyre would *have no wing*."

The following two letters show how unabated was his interest in the Bible :—

[*To* MISS LOUIE HEATH.]

"LOWER SYDENHAM,
"*Nov.* 4, '91.

". . . I am very glad of your rose-coloured account of yourself; only aren't you over-working? I know *I* am—my days are very hard, but I mustn't grumble. . . . I am glad to hear about Mr. Moulton's Bible Lectures. Are they printed, or will they be? It [the Bible] is a wonderful book in every regard; not least in its literary one. Compare it with the Koran or Vedas, for instance, and see how much more form, and breadth, and beauty, and art there is in it! And then the wonderful force of the meaning. Think of such an image as 'Thou hast set our misdeeds before Thee, *our secret sins in the light of Thy countenance*,' as if the mere face of God had a brightness able to illuminate every *cranny*. Then think, too, of the depth contained in this description of a hero (applied to our Lord)—the depth and also the modern cast of the sentiment—'A bruised reed shall he not break, and the smoking flax shall he not quench'—in modern language He sha'n't carelessly tear a twig of a tree as He passes by, or put His foot on a cast away lucifer burning on the pavement, or crush a beetle as He passes! Why, it gives a guarantee for any amount of sentiment towards the inanimate or lower creation, doesn't it? . . ."

[*To* MRS. WODEHOUSE.]

"LOWER SYDENHAM, S.E.,
"*Nov.* 11, 1891.

" . . . I don't know the book on the Bible that you speak of; but I read the lessons last Sunday, to my infinite pleasure, and hope to do so again next Sunday. I should like Micah vi better than iv and v, because of that most interesting fragment of Moabite history between wise old Balaam and Balak. Fancy that old prophet whom we are brought up to despise so, being the first promoter of the doctrine that practical goodness is better than theology! 'What doth the Lord require of thee, but to do justice, and to love mercy, and to walk humbly with God.' Balaam has always been a friend of mine, but I sha'n't have the privilege of reading his words on Sunday, nor shall I (as I should like) have the xith of Hebrews to read. I was so gratified after church, when dear old Mrs. Mayow Adams came up to me and thanked me so warmly for 'reading so that she understood every word.' As to the Revised Version, it never should and never will supersede the old Authorised Version—never—but it is a valuable commentary. But I sometimes ask myself if the Bible will ever again be the book it has been to England. It seems to be growing more and more out of harmony with the rush of the age, and with the form that life is taking."

As he had himself predicted on his return from the Continent in September, the gilt—in the shape of renewed vigour—wore off all too rapidly, and by Easter-time he was obliged to take a month's holiday. On the eve of his departure he wrote a letter to Sir William

Smith, which I reproduce because of the affectionate reference to their old association :—

"*April* 14*th*, 1892.

"MY DEAR OLD FRIEND,—I was much disappointed not to be able to come to dear John Murray's funeral. It was my full intention, but I was prevented at the last moment. I should then have seen you, which I so seldom do. How are you? The new number of the *Quarterly* shows that you have got all your old vigour, and that you drive your team as well as ever. . . . I am going off to-morrow to Paris, and perhaps Biarritz for a few days, but shall be back before long. . . ."

Crossing with his son and Joachim on April 15th, he spent a few days in Paris before moving southwards. On the 17th he heard *Mireille* and *Cavalleria Rusticana* at the Opera Comique. The former he found monotonous and artificial. "I never thought so much of *Fidelio* as after hearing *Mireille*." His impressions of Mascagni's work were more favourable, but his praise is tempered by criticism :—

"Very dramatic—a mixture of Church and World. But I fail to understand the violence, the paroxysms, the throwing about the woman you love. Still there is something in it that goes to your heart and impresses you in spite of yourself. The *intermezzo* is very touching, being so natural and quiet and coming [after] such a furious scene."

On April 21st he met Sullivan at the Gare du Nord and started for Biarritz the next day. From Biarritz he made the usual excursions to Bayonne, and St. Jean de Luz ; but the weather all the time of his stay was bad, and he was pulled down by a severe cold which he could not shake off. He greatly enjoyed, however, meeting his old friend Susan Phillips, the widow of the artist, who reminded him of the unpublished verses of Tennyson's, which Grove himself had given her some years before :

"'Life of the life within my blood,
Light of the light within mine eyes,
The May begins to bloom and bud,
And sweetly glow the vernal skies.

"'Come near me, stay not to be wooed,
It is not glorious to be wise;
Come, feed my lips with loving food,
Mine ear with low replies.'"

On the 7th he moved on to Pau, and on the following day paid a visit to Lourdes. Perhaps he was not in an appreciative mood. Anyhow, his impressions were the reverse of favourable. The vulgar organ playing caused him to explode:—

"What might not be made of the service, if conducted by a man of soul? Susan used the word 'tawdry,' which was very appropriate. The proportions of the church are very good. Glass good, but everything covered and bedaubed with memorials, and inscriptions in such taste and poorness of decoration that the whole was frightful. What must God be if He is pleased by things which simply displease His educated creatures!"

He was back in Paris on May 13th, and wrote from Meurice's that night to his brother Edmund in anything but his usual spirits: "I have not written to you because I have been uncomfortable all through, and not in the humour to write a nice letter." He goes on to say the weather was villainous most of the time. "I left all the Loire country behind me, Tours, Poitiers, etc., for I had no spirits or heart to stay there." He was quite disappointed with Biarritz, but found better weather at Pau:—

"The fact is I was three or four weeks too early, and (another thing) I will *never* try a purposeless journey again. I am afraid that I am too old to try an *archæological* journey again. Architecture does not interest me as it used to do, though of course it's not fair to try it without a companion. Perhaps I am wrong; but if I had gone to Vienna, it seems to me I should have had many more resources in the Libraries and Museums. However, it's no use saying *that*. Here am I after a month's absence with my cold just as bad as when I started, and feeling very little, if any, stronger. At any rate I am coming *home*, to my own doctor and my own house; and more than all, to my own *work*—for that is the real secret. It's just what old Dickens said: When you are in harness, you must keep up; but when you get away from the big wheels you just tumble down."

Grove was back at the College on May 16th, and for the next two months was completely absorbed in his work. The entries in his pocket-book relate to little else, and I note one characteristic memorandum : "N.B.—To have a map in my room with places of ex-pupils marked." Characteristic, again, is the quotation from Dr. Johnson : "A man should keep his friendships in constant repair," a principle on which Grove certainly did his best to act ; while on another page he writes : "Beethoven did for music what Johnson did for letters, he abolished patronage."

A group of letters (dated June 11th, 14th, 21st) to his brother Edmund deals with Grove's researches into the genesis of the yellowhammer's song in the Pastoral Symphony. He had applied to his brother for advice as to books of reference ; he had consulted Howard Saunders, Canon Tristram, and his old friend Flower at the Natural History Museum, who in turn sent him on to Günther and Sharpe. The result of his researches was ultimately embodied in an article on "The Birds in the Pastoral Symphony," which appeared in the special Beethoven number of the *Musical Times*, published on December 15th, 1892. In this paper Grove gives Schindler's story of the yellowhammer, and comes to the conclusion that Beethoven was simply "taking a rise out of" his Boswell, as the arpeggio passage does not correspond in any way to the song of the bird in question. The article, with its references to Yarrell's *British Birds*, Brehm's *Thierleben*, Naumann's *Vögel Deutschlands*, and the information gleaned from Dr. Steindachner of the Natural History Museum in Vienna, is thoroughly characteristic of Grove's patience and industry in following up a Beethoven trail.

CHAPTER XII

At Vienna in 1892—Interlaken and Ringgenburg—Address to Sir Walter Parratt—At Tennyson's Funeral—Letter from Thayer—Sullivan's generosity—Visit to the Riviera—Correspondence with Leighton—Ordered to Ragatz—The "Sublime" in Music—Trouble at the College—Opening of the New Buildings—Thoughts of retirement—Tour in Scotland—Grove resigns the Directorship—Generous appreciation of the Council—Tribute of his colleagues—Grove on his successor.

THE musical exhibition held in Vienna in the summer of 1892 naturally enough decided Grove's choice of a holiday resort, and on August 2nd he started for the Continent, breaking his journey at Bonn, where he paid a visit to the Beethoven House, and reaching Vienna on the 6th. This was his headquarters for a fortnight, and in spite of the intense heat Grove enjoyed himself greatly. First of all there was the exhibition, with a quantity of interesting treasures to examine; then there was the congenial companionship of Mandyczewski—who showed him a large number of hitherto unknown songs by Schubert, "many very early, but one of April, 1828, of the noblest class, called *Herbst*, equal to rank with *Wehmuth*"—and of other Viennese friends and acquaintances new and old. Then on August 12th he went to Baden and made the acquaintance of a Herr Rollett, who, though only a year older than himself, had seen Beethoven when a child, and remembered him distinctly—one can imagine Grove's envy! On the following day (his birthday) he made friends with another Beethoven enthusiast, Herr Frimmel, who was engaged on a work dealing with Beethoven's early years. On the same day he heard a performance of Beethoven's *Eroica* Symphony at a popular concert.

On the 16th he went (not for the first time) to look at the pictures by Van Dyck, Rubens, Frans Hals and Caravaggio in the Liechtenstein gallery, and on the 20th he had a long and interesting talk with Mandyczewski about Brahms and his methods of composition, duly noted down in his pocket-book:—

"Brahms is never satisfied with his music. When he looks at a piece a few weeks after he has written it, it always disappoints him. All he can say is that looking at his pieces he finds them more to his mind than those of any other contemporary composer.[1] He has the greatest hatred for exaggeration or want of truth, or for inaccurate reports spread about himself even to his own credit or advantage."

On the same afternoon he left Vienna for Interlaken, breaking his journey at Salzburg and Innsbruck. While he was in the train between Salzburg and Innsbruck he set down the following notes, eminently characteristic of the common sense that tempered his hero-worship, on the Schwarzspanierhaus:—

"I visited this twice (on this journey), once by myself and once with Barry. Its existence is doomed; most of the houses in the neighbourhood have come down, and are replaced by huge mansions of flats, and the sooner the S. itself goes the better, for it is in a squalid state; no attempt is made to commemorate it in any proper manner. . . . The longer it lies in such a condition, the greater does the contrast become between its poverty and wretchedness (not its age or its character) and the trimness of the new streets, and therefore I, for one, should be content to see it come down if some slab or other memorial were erected, fixing the spot."

Interlaken was reached on August 23rd, and on the 25th Grove was joined by Walter Parratt, with whom he drove over to Ringgenburg on the following day.

[1] Grove notes earlier in the year the reply which Brahms is said to have made to an English lady who showed him a new composition from her pen: "At my time of life I think everything beautiful."

They called at the parsonage and saw the *Pfarrer's* wife: the *Pfarrer* himself was teaching the school in the church—the little church "where Mendelssohn used to shut himself in and play to his heart's content after he lost his sister." Eventually the *Pfarrer* came out, and in twenty minutes' time "*we* shut *ourselves* in and had quite a solemn little service, Parratt playing three pieces by Bach and three by Mendelssohn . . . After a little talk and exchanging cards, I asked the *Pfarrer* if he would take charge of the inscription, and I found the place to put it in, and we then left, very much impressed and pleased." The inscription relates to Mendelssohn's connection with Ringgenburg. Grove further adds a memorandum—"Look up all the passages about Interlaken in M.'s letters, and have the good passages printed in large type, to be framed and hung up in the Interlaken Hotel."

On the following day Grove went to see the Staubbach waterfall, on the 28th he was at Beatenberg, and on the 29th he describes his pilgrimage to the wooden octagonal pavilion on the mountain side, north of the Aar, with an inscription commemorating the visits to Interlaken of Weber in 1811, of Mendelssohn in 1832, 1837, 1842, 1845, and 1847, and of Wagner in 1867. He also struck up an acquaintance with the director of the Kursaal band at Interlaken, whose father had been a hotel proprietor there on the occasion of Mendelssohn's first visit. On September 1st he was at Basle, on September 2nd at Paris, and he reached Sydenham at 10 p.m. on the following night.

A few days later he set off to Gloucester for the Festival, "where," as he writes to Miss Heath, "I liked Parry's *Job* very much indeed; and heard a very remarkable performance of the C minor Symphony in the Cathedral with an effect which I shall never forget." Then came a short visit to his brother at Brighton, and on the 19th he was back at the College. "I can't say," he writes to the same correspondent, "that I feel fit for the term; but I can't expect to do so any more. Life now must be a time of taking care, and doing *as much as one can*, and not minding being disappointed." He continues :—

"I found in a note-book of mine some things which Mandyczewski told me about Brahms, and will copy them out for you. They are not much, but I know them to be genuine. His sense of humour is very strong. A lady at Hanover wanted to make him play at an evening party, but he wouldn't. First he got her to stand in the curve of the grand piano while he stood at the keyboard, leaning across the lid so that it could not be opened, and talking hard to her all the time. And when at last she did get the lid opened, he at once struck the low C with his left hand and a high C sharp with his right, and said, 'How can I play on a piano that is so fearfully out of tune?'"

Shortly after the opening of the College, on Sept 29, 1892, it was Grove's pleasant task to present his colleague and dear friend, Walter Parratt, with an address of congratulation from the pupils on the honour of knighthood recently conferred on him. After his wont, Grove emphasized the significance of the occasion with an ancedote :—

"There is a beautiful story told about Mendelssohn, which I heard from the son of the man to whom it occurred, and which seems to me to bear on this occasion. Mendelssohn had been presented by the King of Prussia with the Order of Merit (a very great distinction). He was staying at Frankfurt with Mr. Speyer, the old city musician, when the star of the order arrived, and there was a good deal of joking. After breakfast, he and Mr. Speyer and a large party went out for a walk. They came to a bridge, the others went on, and Speyer stopped behind to pay the toll—about a halfpenny each. Then the toll-keeper said, 'That little gentleman—is that the Mr. Mendelssohn who writes the part-songs that we sing in our Choral Society?' 'The same,' said Speyer. 'Then, if you please, I should like to pay the toll for him myself.' Speyer ran on and told Mendelssohn what had happened. He was immensely pleased. 'Hm,' said he, 'I like that much better than the Order.' Now, my dear Parratt, you have the Order, and here is the toll-keeper's halfpenny."

Then follow the usual list of achievements by pupils past and present, and the usual caution against overwork—"if you would be warned by an old man who has done as much overwork as any of you"—frivolity, tale-bearing and idle gossip. "I know," he goes on, "these temptations as well as any one can, and I want to help you out of them; and I am going to give you some rules which I lately found in the life of St. Teresa, and which I think will be very serviceable." According to his wont, he tells them about his holiday abroad; "a little spoiled because I was disappointed of Sir Walter Parratt's companionship, and then of Bayreuth." But he had been to Vienna, and describes what he saw that specially interested him at the Exhibition there.

Grove attended Tennyson's funeral on October 12th, and has left an account of the impression it made upon him in the following letter to Mrs. Wodehouse:—

"LOWER SYDENHAM,
"*Sunday, Oct. 16th.*

"I know you'll like to hear my impressions of Wednesday's ceremonial. I thought it most impressive and interesting. The 'procession' I could not see, being one of it; but the general effect—the gloom, the extraordinary gathering of so many distinguished people, the exquisite beauty and propriety of the music (perhaps not the best in quality of composition, but beautifully prepared and unexceptional in taste and effect); the scene around the grave, where the sight of the Union Jack on the coffin was to me most touching—all combined to make it quite unforgettable. At the edge of the grave I found a man (F. Locker) who had been at school with me and the Dean when we were eight years old. . . . It was just what I wanted, and I should hardly have clung to your arm more sympathetically than I did to his.

"To return to the general effect—I could not help feeling strongly how far superior it was in taste and religious sentiment to anything in the same line that one would see in France or Germany. Less pomp, no doubt, and more absence of blaze and colour—but far more feeling. No doubt we owe the Abbey a great deal for the low tone; the endless arches and pillars reverberating every sound; but also I do think that our feeling about Eternal Life is very different and much higher than anything abroad, and therefore that we naturally have a more appropriate and impressive (in the true sense) way of commemorating the entrance of our dead into it."

By way of contrast to the serious tone of the above letter, one may note Grove's letters to the *Times* of October 14th and 22nd, giving his versions of the nonsense rhymes about Timbuctoo and Jehoshaphat. Grove quotes from the *Recollections* of John Adolphus, 1871, p. 224, the true version of the latter—

"The valiant King Sennacherib
Of any man could crack a rib,
But could not of Jehoshaphat,
I'll tell you why—he was so fat."

The author, according to John Adolphus, was "a man in my very young days"; and as Adolphus was born in 1768, it could not, Grove contends, have been Bishop Wilberforce, who was not born till 1805.

Grove's correspondence with A. W. Thayer, the American consul at Trieste, and author of the monumental biography of Beethoven, had begun as far back as in April 1864. What this long association had meant to Thayer can best be understood from the very touching letter, honourable alike to writer and recipient, which bears date November 17th, 1892:—

"THOU DEAR GOOD GROVE,—Drawing near the end of a rather long life of disappointments, I have one consolation in the thought that many a good man and some famous men have thought me worthy of something more than common, ordinary friendship. You have given me ample proof over and over again that such is your feeling for me. I am grateful, and return it in full strength. I little thought, August 17th, that three months would elapse before my writing the letter then promised. They have been miserable months, with head and eyes and other troubles, and there has also been some work to do that pressed; so that the few workable hours in the *week* (not *day*) had to be occupied with it, and correspondence must wait—except in cases of business letters, and the few that could not wait. About a fortnight since, my mind was freed from that work, and my body from the doctor, and I could turn to the mass of accumulated unanswered letters. But I am not yet able to work steadily for any length of time, and some days not at all, and the pile lowers slowly. I think, however, that I am gaining, and do not quite despair of yet being able to do some work, although in my 76th year. . . .

"... At my age there are not many years still ahead, and probably my savings will cover them; but suppose I utterly break down, and be obliged to incur heavy expenses—What then? Old age during the last year has taught me that he has come into my life, and what I have to do, if I am ever able to do it, must be done quickly—yes, the night cometh when no man can work.

"Some years ago, I forget how many, you proposed to give or obtain for me pecuniary aid. I refused then, and do now, to accept charity—I have (God knows how!) battled my way 75 years, and wish to still remain in harness. I can live, if no calamity occurs, upon what I have (using my capital) until the end comes. But I must abandon the hope of finishing the Beethoven book, for I cannot pay an assistant, nor can I go away now and then to recruit. ... Some years ago, I devised a plan, but have never taken any steps until recently to try it, and wrote not long since to a friend in the U. States upon it, but have no hope from that quarter. ...

"Head and eyes grow louder and louder in their warnings to stop. I obey.

"Remember me most kindly to Lady Grove. Believe me that any degree of affection on your part is amply returned by always,

"Your loving friend,

"A. W. Thayer."

Grove's own health was far from satisfactory, as will be seen from his letter to Miss Heath—a letter which contains the first explicit reference to the approaching realisation of his scheme of a Beethoven book, as well as a charming tribute to Sullivan:—

[*To* Miss L. Heath.]

"Lower Sydenham,

"*Nov.* 18, 1892.

"... I will write to Mrs. —— about you, because unless some one blows your trumpet for you, you don't proclaim yourself half enough—*à propos*, what a fine line that is of Milton's, 'Sonorous metal blowing martial sounds.' I dare say you seldom read Milton; he is not an English poet in the same sense as Shakespeare, or even Gray—or Tennyson, most so of all next to Shakespeare. ... I am very much pressed by Novello to publish my analyses of Beethoven's Symphonies, etc. I suppose I must: but I quake at the presumption of publishing such temporary and incomplete things in a permanent form. I have a tremendous respect for a *book*, and should not like to regret its publication after it was launched. You ask me how I am. Well, dear child, anything but well. I am getting so old, and so much under the dominion of my vile body, and so plagued with rheumatism, loss of memory, slowness, and all the other things that make age so insupportable that everything becomes a difficulty. Thank God you don't know anything about such matters. . . .

"PS.—I could not find your letter about the Leeds Festival when I was writing last night, but now I have got it, and I see I *did* tell you about Interlaken. Your account of your doings at Leeds is most interesting. Why didn't you say to Sullivan that you are a friend of mine? He would have been awfully nice to you. To me he is always what he was in 1863, when I first knew him—the same simple, good, gay creature that he was then. That was the second youth of my life. Everything budded and blossomed to me, and for the first time, though then forty-three, I understood poetry, music—all the world, and Sullivan is bound up with it. . . ."

No better commentary on this postscript can be conceived than the charming letter which Grove received from Sullivan a few weeks later:—

"CABBÉ-ROQUEBRUNE, ALPS MARITIMES,
"*Dec.* 13, 1892.

"DEAREST G.,—Your letter shows me there is one thing you must absolutely do without discussion, argument, or consideration. You must, the day after the College closes for its Christmas holidays, put yourself in the train and come straight down here. I have a lovely villa with a very large garden right down to the sea, and you can go to bed and get up when you like—you can be alone, or with me; we can walk or drive, or do or not do any mortal thing, and you shall be allowed *two hours* every morning or more to attend to your correspondence. I only stipulate that nothing shall be forwarded from the College except your own *personal* and *private* correspondence. I bar all official stuff, and about this I will stand no d——d nonsense. If you don't take a rest now, and take yourself away from your surroundings, you are acting little short of criminally. You have no family gathering to sacrifice at Christmas now. If you had, your life and health are of more importance, and no man, whether Christian, Mahometan, Jew, or Buddhist, has the right to treat his existence here on earth in a reckless, careless manner. Your visit will cost you not one farthing, as I will send you a first class return ticket

—London to Roquebrune—a more useful Christmas present than a piece of silver, which I might otherwise have sent you. Don't, dearest G., read this lightly and put it aside with a smile, and answer, 'Bless your dear heart, I can't come.' You *must* come. I am very much in earnest about this, and mean that you should have a rest—and a real rest, which shall cost you nothing.

"It is divine down here—such sea, sky, and sunshine. Ever your loving A."

Such an appeal—in which common sense, affection, and generosity were so happily combined—proved quite unanswerable,[1] and the satisfactory results of Grove's timely surrender are shown in a letter to one of his pupils a month later :—

"CABBÉ-ROQUEBRUNE, MONTE CARLO,
"*Jan.* 12, 1893.

" . . . I feel as if I had undergone a sort of collapse, had lost nerve, memory, interest in life—everything that can make one valuable. No doubt I have been shaken by this last laborious term; but I think I am making ground simply because I have been idle; and when I get back into harness again no doubt I shall find the benefit of that course. This place is quite or very nearly new to me. It is very beautiful, not so much from what one generally associates with beauty, because there is no wood but olives and other insignificant trees and the mountains are poor in outline, height, and surface. But the sea is a lovely colour, the sun is bright and the villages are entirely different from what they are in Northern Europe—quaint, very old-looking, and attached to the mountain sides in a peculiar way. I am half-way between Monte Carlo and Mentone at the very head of the bay which forms the inside of the curve leading from Marseilles to Genoa; in a nice convenient modern house which has the sea right in front and the railway behind. Sullivan and I get on like two brothers—we are resuming the close intercourse which we enjoyed twenty years ago: we agree perfectly, and I have absolute liberty. I have seen hardly any one I know and don't wish to see any one. To-morrow I am going by train to Alassio, three hours off towards Genoa. That is where we lost our darling Milly six

[1] It was vigorously backed by a letter from Grove's Registrar at the Royal College, Mr. George Watson, whose own health had suffered seriously from overwork. After begging Grove to be warned in time and take a rest before he was thoroughly knocked up, he adds: "I am never so happy as when I am doing something for you or working under your guidance.'

years ago, and I shall see her grave, the clergyman who buried her, and a lady who keeps her tomb in splendid order. . . . I meant to do a deal of reading, writing, and thinking and I have done neither—but still as I say I am no doubt imbibing a lot of strength. I shall go back next week some time. I have been to Monte Carlo and seen the gaming tables and cannot find any interest in them: indeed anything more dull and uninteresting I never saw. . . . I hope my life of F.M.B. has been of interest to you. Don't be surprised if you get two volumes of *Die Familie Mendelssohn* which I so often refer to. I ordered them to be sent to you before I left. . . ."

Lord Charles Bruce who had urged Grove to go away as soon as possible and stop away as long as possible, was only concerned lest he should undo the good of his holiday by returning too soon. Writing on January 15th, he says:—

"When I think of it, when since you have been connected with the College have you enjoyed a real holiday and rest? . . . Now what is to be said of what you call 'such a wicked act' on your part in running away? Why, first that in me you have an abettor of such unheard-of depravity. So you see as a *particeps criminis* I am in the same boat as yourself and we must make the best of it. . . . You owe it as a duty to the College to leave no stone unturned to get thoroughly strong and well. We are just arriving at a critical stage in its history, when we shall need your advice, assistance, and experience more than ever. We can never express what you have been as our Director during these last ten years, for there is no other man who could possibly have guided our fortunes at the College as you have done. So, dear friend, do not, I beg of you, think of hurrying back, and believe me that when I say this I feel I am truly speaking on behalf of my colleagues as well as of myself."

A few days later, January 19th, he writes:—

"I enclose you Knollys' reply which I think will make you happier. I was anxious that the Prince should know all about our dear Director, and I feel that an expression of H.R.H.'s wish as to his obtaining as much benefit from a prolonged stay abroad as possible would set his mind quite at ease and convince him that he cannot possibly be laying himself open to the imputation of shirking his duty."

On the 25th Lord Charles vigorously remonstrates with him for deciding to return at once, adding :—

"What was the Prince's message to you which you must regard as a command? 'The Prince hopes he will not think of moving just yet, and thinks he will be able to do his work much better on his return to England if he were to remain away as long as he finds that the South is doing him good.'"

Grove, however, was not to be dissuaded, and Lord Charles writing on January 31st admits that his [Grove's] letter was unanswerable. "I have felt all along that as soon as a desire for home, and a return to active life seized you, not even the geniality of a Sullivan and of a Mediterranean climate would do you any more good."

The visit to the Riviera undoubtedly did him some good, but by March his rheumatism was again very troublesome. "I have it in my back, shoulders, both knees, and can really hardly get about. I am afraid I must go to a regular topsawyer and be prescribed for." In the same letter he complains of the "ungentlemanlike treatment" which Miss Ethel Smyth, whose Mass had lately been produced at the Albert Hall, had received at the hands of many of the musical critics, and notes with satisfaction the election to an open scholarship at the Royal College of the son of an engine-driver. The speech delivered to the pupils on April 27, 1893, is remarkable for a little sermon on manners. Grove points out that the greatest artists, Joachim, Madame Schumann, Liszt, and Jenny Lind, were all people of education and refinement; and offers some sensible remarks on the trials and temptations of singers —the uncertainty of their instrument and the danger of indulging in *ad captandum* effects. He compliments one of the pupils who had greatly distinguished herself in the College opera, but tempers his praise with advice. She has made a splendid start, but a tremendous task is still to be accomplished before she can become a great singer. On May 8th he delivered an address at the College of Organists, of which he has left no fewer than three drafts, an instance of that laborious mode of preparation which he was beginning to find more and more of a tax upon his powers. Meantime he was steadily working away at his Beethoven book, and an appeal to the late Lord Leighton for information elicited the following answer, dated May 20th, 1893 :—

"What a wild, wild creature you are ! ! ! Who can show you amongst thousands of Arabesques the one that illustrates your passage in Beethoven ? The chief specimens of Ancient Arabesques known to us are those of Pompeii (*passim*) and of Rome (baths of Titus, house of Tiberius, etc.); of the Arabesques of the Renaissance the Vatican Loggie offer the most famous examples—if you look in at S. Kensington and (in the Art Library) look for the heading 'Arabesques' in the catalogue you will find all these things in reproductions. I hope you will come across your Pastoral Symphony and am meanwhile and always, yours sincerely, Fred Leighton."

Mr. William Watson had written a sonnet, referred to in the *Spectator* of May 20th, 1893, in which he spoke of Beethoven as pre-eminently a poet of grief. In the issue of May 27th Grove demurred to this view on very convincing grounds, going through several of Beethoven's greatest works, and showing how exhilarating they are :—

"No one was fuller of fun and humour, of the merest joking, unless it be Shakespeare ; and the two men stand together and pre-eminent for the way they mixed tragedy and comedy in the natural and promiscuous way in which they are mixed in life . . . To conclude, I repeat that Shakespeare was quite as much a poet of grief as Beethoven ; and it would be as incorrect to speak of the one as melancholy or sad, as it would be of the other."

When the end of the summer term came Grove was so overdone that, as he foresaw, he had to "go to a medical topsawyer to be prescribed for," with a result described in the following letter :—

[*To* MISS LOUIE HEATH.]

"LOWER SYDENHAM,

"*Aug.* 11, 7 A.M.

". . . . . College term ended a fortnight ago, but here I am, still kept back by Reports (now done) and other business, and unable to find out where I am to go in Germany for a *Kur* for the rheumatism and lumbago which have been worrying me so long. But I expect to be off next week. I am also kept by my book on the Beethoven Symphonies which I am doing for Novello, and for which I must give the printers some MS. before I go. It was intended to be a mere reprint of my Crystal Palace Programmes: but that won't do, and it is really a fresh work, based to a certain extent on them. I want to make a work which, while dealing not inadequately with the Symphonies from a musical point of view, shall be readable and attractive to *all* amateurs. I have done the first 4 and now am at work on the 5th.

"7. p.m. The most singular thing is their extraordinary diversity. Each one differs entirely from all those before or after it, just as Shakespeare's Plays do:—that is one of the points of resemblance between them. Of course there is plenty of biography and anecdotes, and I am told by one or two who have read what I have written that it is really interesting. I hope they are right. You shall tell me what you think some day.

"You ask about my rheumatism: well, I will tell you. I have hardly been free for a day from January, and often it has been as much as I can bear. I am resolved to go to a *Bad* and try to be cured of it. To-day I have seen Dr. Weber, the great authority, and he has given me the choice of three—Wildbad, Schlangenbad, and Ragatz. I think I shall choose Ragatz. It is near Chur and under the baths of Pfäffers in the Via Mala and the water runs down from them to it, in a lovely situation and near Switzerland. I may go if I like to a fourth—Baden near Vienna: *that* would be full of Beethoven whose favourite country place it was, and is lovely. But this time I fear I must go in for my cure, and keep away from such excitement as things connected with Beethoven, which would agitate me very much. I must this time really try to get well. . . . When you wrote you had been reading Miss Edgeworth and Poe. *Helen* I know very slightly, but it is not so good as her Irish stories, *Castle Rackrent*, *Patronage* and many others. She went into the heart of Irish humour, whereas of fashionable correct society she knows little or nothing. How well I remember reading Poe's Tales—'The Gold Bug' (as it was called at first), 'The Black Cat,' 'The Murder in the Rue Morgue.' I have not seen the book for 30 years, and yet the impression is just as fresh. So, too, *Hyperion*—lovely!! I read it in Bermuda in 1843 when I was just beginning to think and feel. Longfellow was not a great poet, but he was very near it, and was a thoroughly fine, honest, simple man. . . I have not been reading anything of late. Any book I read is about Beethoven . . . At College all goes well . . . ."

Grove started the following week, stayed a short while in Paris to arrange about singing lessons for one of his pupils, and then pushed on to Ragatz, where for the best part of a month he conscientiously carried out his treatment, and patiently submitted himself to the ministrations of a brawny Swedish *masseur*. At first he was decidedly stimulated by the change, and wrote in good spirits to his brother-in-law, Andrew Bradley, on the 23rd of August :—

". . . Why are you not here ? We should enjoy ourselves vastly and have such endless talks. This is a *vast* place—two large hotels joined together with 6 or 8 dependences in the midst of the most shady woods. Very few English or Americans (though I saw some enormous trunks coming in to-day—the elephants will no doubt appear at dinner). . . I was very tired when I got here Sunday night, but have begun my course of baths, put myself *en pension*, and squared everything. The bath was just like a first-rate London one ; a small octagon room, two feet deep in water flowing in and out, warm, but not quite hot. I rather looked forward to the bath as a large room with 60 or 80 people all in bathing dress floating about drinking coffee, reading, etc., from little floating tables ! Thus perish all our illusions. It is cooler to-day and the glass has gone down : up till now it has been fearful . . . . . I have made no friends yet, not even with my pillow, for I lay awake the whole of last night from 9 till 7. . . I am working away at my Beethoven. It haunts me and I wish I *dared* pitch into it for 10 hours a day, but I daren't. If it only turns out well ! But I fear its being too wordy. Do you think that compression is really a good thing if you're not writing for eternity ? I think not when one is writing for people who want it all explained. When Beethoven corrected, he always struck out ; when Schubert, he put in. I belong to the latter school, I think . . . .

"I cannot tell you what a pretty thing happened to me coming from Paris to Basle. I was all alone in the carriage and suddenly a large thistle-down floated in, and danced about in such a charming, coy, saucy way ! It was just like a person. She darted about, came up close to me, bobbed against my face and at last disappeared with quite a curtsey ! Do you remember the bird which Prosper Mérimée saw in the amphitheatre at Nîmes, which kept coming up close to him but would not be caught ? Mine was a far sweeter adventure and quite set me up."

In his note-book, under the date of August 31st, there are a number of rough notes on the subject of the Sublime, a subject which, as will be seen from the subjoined letter, exercised him a good ideal about this time :—

[*To* MRS. WODEHOUSE.]

"RAGATZ,
"*Sept.* 1, 1893.

"I so hoped to get your proof of no. 4 this morning, because I am so hungry for your criticisms! But I fear it can hardly come till to-morrow. I want to consult you on a most exciting and interesting thing which rushed into my mind in the dead of Tuesday night. Can Beethoven be called 'sublime' or, rather, what sublime passages can be found in his works—passages of the calibre of the 'Hallelujah'—'He rebuked the Red Sea'—'The people shall hear'—'Darkness,' etc? I really can think of none. It seems to me that sublimity involves the highest religious feeling—as it were the presence of God himself. Passages there are which 'touch the spirit's inmost deeps' such as the Horns in the Trio of the Eroica, the end of the Scherzo in no. 5, the wonderful place in the working out of the Adagio in no. 9, going into D flat, over which years ago I wrote *Vanitas Vanitatum*, but those go *deep*—now sublimity exalts one, brings one near the throne of God, and I am afraid one must admit that Beethoven has not any. Had Shakespeare either? They were both concerned with this earth and the *men and women* on it. Grand, magnificent, tender, touching, beautiful, mystical—all these are theirs, but all fall short of what I mean by sublimity. Milton was sublime—was Dante so? The picture of Satan who 'lay floating many a rood,' so vague and vast—the picture of death and Satan fronting one another in the 2nd. Book, do look at it. These are sublime; but I can't remember anything like that in Shakespeare. 'To be or not to be' never goes out of the mind of Hamlet. The dream in Richard the III.?

"Do tell me what you think. It quite frightens me to admit that there is anything which Beethoven had not, and yet, as I see at present, I must admit he had not *this*. . . . Beethoven and Shakespeare had too much humour. *Had Isaiah any humour?*"

[*To* ANDREW C. BRADLEY.]

"RAGATZ,
"*Sept.* 1, 11 P.M.

". . . Do tell me something about the *sublime*. How do you distinguish it from 'grand,' 'magnificent,' 'overwhelming,' etc.?

In the dead of the night it came into my mind: Had Beethoven written anything sublime? And then, from that, what sublimity was, and whether Shakespeare can be said to contain any such passage. I suppose Psalm xc, and Milton's description of Satan and Death fronting each other may stand for it in literature, and in music the Hallelujah Chorus, and the Darkness chorus in Israel, 'He rebuked the Red Sea,' etc. I suppose the Old Hundredth Psalm or even 'God save the King' if sung by a great body of people on some critical national occasion would be sublime, but does it not require the religious feeling, or religious words to bring sublimity into existence? Now I am afraid there are few if any examples of this in Beethoven. The overture to 'Leonora' at the place where the whole orchestra pull up and you hear a solitary trumpet behind the scenes (which I always fancy is a summons to the besieged city to surrender) is very near it (though I never could get any one to share my feeling), but the *whole piece* decidedly gives an impression of conflict and distress and *final triumph* which, grand and noble as it is, is not sublime. In other places there's a strong mystic feeling—over one of these I wrote long ago *Vanitas Vanitatum.* Everything goes so flat all of a sudden—But they are not sublime. Should not one feel as if one were suddenly in the other world before one's Maker? At any rate the religious feeling is indispensable, and that is rare in Beethoven. Is it not rare in Shakespeare too? Do they not both of them deal with *this world*—in all its aspects certainly, but still they don't go into the other world, don't deal with the supernatural as Milton or Isaiah do.

"John Wesley's hymn—

"'Lo! on a narrow neck of land,
'Twixt two unbounded seas I stand
And yet securely dwell.
A point of time, a moment's space,
May whelm me from this narrow place
And sink me down to Hell.'

is really sublime, isn't it?

"I do wish you would give me a few lines on this point: you must have thought it all out. One might say that in the Handel pieces I mentioned the words had something to do with it. But I don't remember in Beethoven's Masses (his greatest sacred works) any instances. In the Mass in D the *Dona nobis* has a very dramatic moment when you hear the drums and trumpets of the besiegers outside the wall, while the inhabitants are praying for peace, but it is too fiery and disturbing. . . ."

Writing to his brother Edmund a few days later, after describing the course of his cure he reverts to the same subject :—

"RAGATZ,
"*Sept.* 10*th.*

"The sublime, as I take it, must have a supernatural element in poetry or music. I don't find the C minor symphony has any of the sublime.

"*Personal* and *terrible* it is in the first movement, mystical in the Scherzo and connection with the Finale; and triumphantly magnificent in the Finale itself. But I find nothing which, like Handel's Darkness or 'People shall hear,' etc., makes me silent with awe. Nor in *Hamlet*, which I have just read, do I find anything of the same sort as I find in Milton where there are not a few passages that have the same effect. . . . The transitions in the early part of the Finale of Schumann's Symphony in B flat are really sublime : they make me think of the day of judgment."

Writing again on the 16th to his brother he notes the disappointing results of his "cure," and announces his resolve to go to Lucerne for a few days, returning on the 28th for the opening of the college. He has found out some lovely walks in the woods : he is hunting everywhere for his favourite Polytrichum moss, though so far with little success, and working at his Beethoven, though hindered by lack of books and music, but still making some progress. He continues :—

"It is delightful work studying and exploring these great creations—and as good as great! The 'sublime' question I must leave for more books. I have just read *Hamlet* again with delight. It and the *Merchant* are the only plays I care for. *Lear* annoys and tires me. *Macbeth* I never could read. *Othello* I love, but it's too dreadful a tragedy . . . . How extremely I do wish you were here. . . ."

In answering the above Mr. Edmund Grove apparently made reference to the Life of W. G. Ward, as a work likely to interest "G.," but the latter, writing on the 24th, confesses to an imperfect sympathy with Ward. He adds :—

"I was a member of the Metaphysical Society for a few months, but it did not suit me at all. No doubt the Church of Rome has wonderfully improved in vigour like the Church of England. I am always looking for the time when the modern scientific spirit shall invade it. It must come sooner or later. That, and the marriage of priests seem to me the two things that must happen. . . ."

As will have been seen from the foregoing letters Grove's spirits were certainly the better for his trip, though he was unable to write very enthusiastically about his "cure" or to derive much consolation from the assurance of his *masseur* that he had been suffering from sciatica and not lumbago. He had complained of coming out alone, but was so far reconciled to his companionless condition that he writes to his brother-in-law, Dean Bradley: "I get fonder of my own society than ever. I have always David or Milton or Gray or Tennyson at command, and like to walk up the torrent and shout their verses." He made some pleasant new acquaintances, but "I don't think that I shall be much afflicted at turning my back on them all. 'King James called for his old shoes' and I certainly love my old friends." Besides the books already mentioned he had with him Matthew Arnold's *Essays in Criticism* and Trollope's *Autobiography*, "very racy and good till you get tired of it." The news that the Lords had thrown out the Home Rule Bill gave him great satisfaction, but his anxiety on that score could not be wholly removed so long as Mr. Gladstone, "with his extraordinary personal influence on the middle and lower classes," remained in the political arena.

Towards the end of September he moved on to Lucerne for a short "after-cure," had a glimpse of the great peaks, and passing through Paris on October 1st was back at Sydenham next day. He speaks of himself as "considerably stronger but still full of pains," and to his bodily infirmities were added the grief which he felt at the death of two old friends. "Jowett's death," he writes to Dean Bradley on October 5th, "has filled me with sorrow. I did not hear even of his illness. Strange all these columns on him in the *Times* and no mention of

Stanley who fought his battle so fiercely." The Life of Stanley, which had been ultimately entrusted to Mr. R. E. Prothero, was now approaching completion, and Grove was in constant communication throughout October and November with Dean Bradley about the introductory chapter which the Dean had undertaken to write. The other friend was Sir William Smith. "I am going," he writes on October 12th, "to dear old Smith's funeral this morning. It is rather against the grain, as far as weather is concerned, but he was a very good friend of mine, and I should not like to be absent."

But his pains and aches and the deaths of his friends, distressing as they were, affected him but slightly in comparison with the shock caused by a painful disclosure at the College, which resulted in the sudden dismissal of one of the staff. Addressing the pupils he spoke of the incident as "the first disturbance to our harmony and enthusiasm—an incident so painful that it has given me a blow that I shall never get over." He then continued :—

"Believe me when I say this. I am an old man. I have lived a long life of action, of energy, of enthusiasm. I can't say that I have been able always to escape evil, but I do say that whenever I have departed from the strict line of right I have always found that the transgression has avenged itself, and has proved unmistakably by the results that I was wrong."

The difficulty of filling the vacancy thus created at the College proved a "dreadful crux," and he writes in great despondency to his brother Edmund on December 31st, 1893 :—

"Indeed distress is becoming terribly familiar to me, and if this recent business and the opening of the new College buildings were over, I should certainly make my bow. My life now is a perfect *chase*—always in pursuit of something which I can't overtake. My powers are deteriorating so fast that I ought not to occupy the post. I have enthusiasm still and a certain amount of superficial energy, but my memory, my grasp of things, and the power of keeping order and keeping up with my work are sadly gone, and the distress and annoyance of life are sad. I am literally unhappy from morning to night. . . . If I go on overworking I shall some day have a stroke which will wind me up altogether and prevent my doing the book on Beethoven, which I wished to do before I die. *That* would be a dreadful disappointment. On the other hand I can't go till the ship is in the new harbour."

Happily the "dreadful crux" was settled by a most admirable appointment, and there is a distinct rise of his mental barometer in the letter which he wrote to Miss Jones (now Mrs. S. P. Waddington) on February 10th :—

"LOWER SYDENHAM.

". . . . I was so sorry I could not come down to hear Mr. Waddington's *John Gilpin*, but it was quite impossible. That day I had an annoying and irritating committee in which I had to fight beasts (like St. Paul) for 4¼ hours, and then to go in, at once, to the evening College Concert without a moment in which to get my dinner. You may imagine I had rather have been with you! . . . I am very glad it went so well, but even his being a Leicestrian (or whatever is the right word) would not have secured the genuine applause you describe. *John Gilpin* was a happy thought, and it is evident it has been happily carried out. You are very mysterious about the 'new and more important work' which is to follow it. Do give me a hint: I am sure he won't mind, I know he is too fond of me for that. You are quite right; fond as he is of me, I am quite as much so of him, and daily do I regret that I can't see him oftener and profit more by his cleverness and sense and still more by his youth which is the greatest gift of all. . . ."

More cheerful, again, and more like his own vivacious self is the address delivered to his pupils on April 26th, 1894. The new buildings in Prince Consort Road were now finished, and after reading the usual list of successes, and mentioning the encouraging achievements of Messrs. Walford Davies, Walthew and Coleridge Taylor, Grove goes on to note that "before a week is over Charles Wood's setting of Mr. Swinburne's Ode on Music will have been performed at the opening of the new College buildings, he himself conducting."

In an interesting passage he urges on would-be composers the value of beauty: "Because you are in earnest in your compositions it is not necessary to be dry or ugly."

He points to the earlier works of Beethoven as illustrating his point: "However full they are of meaning, melody, beauty, and pleasantness reign throughout them, and this is very important. This characteristic in music is something like what I may call *manners* in life."

The portrait that follows is a piece of unconscious autobiography:—

"Everybody knows how delightful is a pleasant manner—what the Germans call on-coming or inviting. A person who meets you half-way; who not only says he is glad to see you, but who shows it, who grasps your hand—who says a kind word in a kind tone—whose face beams, whose eye lights up, when he addresses you! Now I see a strong analogy between that and melody and grace in music; without these *appealing* characteristics force and earnestness are seriously discounted, they can't get themselves expressed or appreciated. Now such *manners* in common life as I have been describing are not dishonest—they are quite consistent with the truest intentions, and in music *grace* may be employed without sacrificing any of the graver and sterner qualities. In fact both in life and music grace and beauty are the feather which wings the arrow."

Later on, *à propos* of manners, he reads the pupils a little sermon on the significance of the term "gentleman," a truly English word though other countries have attempted to borrow it in vain:—

"It is significant of the fusion of ranks and classes which distinguishes our country—is one of our peculiarities. A gentleman is not a rich man who has been expensively educated, wears expensive clothes and has lots of money to spend. One of the most perfect gentlemen I ever knew started in life as an under-gardener,[1] and retained his old simplicity of manners and speech after he was made a baronet and a member of Parliament. A gentleman is a *gentle man.* He is a man who thinks of others—other persons and things besides himself: tries to do all the good he can, to repress the evil which is so natural to us all, to be unselfish, refined, thoughtful; to make himself in sympathy with men and women, animals, trees, and flowers. Another man I knew who was of quite a humble origin. This man when walk-

[1] Sir Joseph Paxton.

ing along the road would never tread on a flower lying on the ground, never step on a beetle or worm, never tear off a branch from a tree as he went by. Now you may say that's nothing, *I don't think so.* I think these things are proofs of a thoughtful, *gentle* mind. Remember what is said in the New Testament as *the* characteristic of the greatest Man, and the sweetest Gentleman that ever lived—Jesus Christ. We are told of Him that 'a bruised reed He would not break, and smoking flax He would not quench.'"

Later on he makes an appeal to the pupils of Dr. (now Sir Hubert) Parry:—

"You all of you know that he was ill before Easter. But you are perhaps not aware how *very* serious it was. His doctors warned me then that unless his work were lightened the worst consequences would probably follow. Now Dr. Parry's lessons and lectures at College are only a part of his work. He is one of the greatest English musicians of the day, and as such is constantly being applied to for oratorios or overtures, or other such little compositions: *and he never refuses.* It is a characteristic of his beautiful nature. For instance he will never say *no* to any one of you who asks him for an extra ten minutes: never scold you or refuse to take you if you bring your work badly done. But I entreat you don't do it. Those ten minutes—those *little extra* worries are death to him: they are the things that send hard-worked men into their graves. You must carefully avoid them, or you may be responsible for something *very* serious indeed."

It has been noted that Grove invariably took great pains over these speeches, beginning with rough notes and often making two or three drafts before he was satisfied. And he was not insensible to the attitude of his listeners. Writing to his brother about a speech delivered in October 1893, he says:—

"I thought all the time that I was making a complete fiasco. These children are no critics. They hear one sentence or sentiment which carries them away, and then that colours the whole. As for myself I could not give you an idea of the trouble these things give me—for a fortnight I am simply in misery with an impending cloud. In fact it is so, now, about everything. All my old spring and facility is gone."

The question of his retirement, as is shown by repeated references in his correspondence, had for some time past seriously occupied his mind. It was therefore a considerable relief to him to be assured by Lord Charles Bruce on May 9th, a few days after the formal opening of the new buildings, that he need have no anxiety about the future: "There's not one of us from the Prince downwards, who does not feel how much we are indebted to you for what you have done. No one but you would have *created* the College as you have: that new Building would never have been there but for you." This assurance, moreover, Lord Charles informed him, was entirely independent of the desire of the Prince that his services should be recognised by the bestowal of some special distinction. Still the situation was not without its anxieties, as the following undated letter to Mrs. Frederick Lehmann clearly shows:—

"You *are* a brick—nothing short of it—to think of writing to me like that—a regular little soap-bubble of a note, all floating about with prismatic colours of the sweetest and brightest! And it was very *à propos*—a great deal of apropository about it (that's better!)—for I am sadly down on my luck—no not on my *luck*, but overdone and tired and full of pain, and Oh my dear, *so* old. You can't realise it. You, somewhere in the fifties, can't feel with an old hulk—an old seventy-four, the *Téméraire*—that's it exactly.

"But really and truly, my time's about come, and now that we've got into our new house [*i.e.* the new buildings] I must retire—only there are two questions: Who's to succeed me and, How am I to live? I can live on bread and cheese—well, but even that will be hard to pay for with nothing coming in—for I shall never make anything with my pen. . . . I have not taken the plunge yet, only talked to Arthur Sullivan and Lord Charles Bruce. The last two months has been a bad time, and my factotum Watson (a splendid fellow) has knocked up—all but paralysis—and left everything to me. H.R.H. has been very kind, praised me no end, and spoke quite affectionately. . . . Do you know that except Christmas Day I have not had one day's holiday since I came back from Ragatz on October 2. I had planned a little run into Scotland, Kenmore, St. Andrews, Portobello, &c., when Watson broke down and stopped it. . . ."

[*To* Miss L. Heath.]

"Lower Sydenham,
"*May* 22, 1894.

"... I am afraid there is no hope of my coming to see you myself. Watson[1] is away for at least a month—and that effectually prevents my escaping. I hope it's warm and fine with you. Here it is fine but sadly cold, with an East wind which shrivels all the lovely lime leaves. I was woke at 3.15 this morning by a cuckoo—long and loud—at my window, a rare thing now, though when we first came to Sydenham both cuckoos and nightingales were plenty.

"Did you ever hear or imagine that Beethoven was once commissioned by a *Boston* society (U.S.A.) to write an oratorio for them? It was so, though—in 1823. It's a curious fact, and more curious that in a life of him just published in Boston itself there is no mention of it. It was not known to a certain *Grove* when he wrote his Dictionary article, and as the Boston author has followed Grove strictly throughout, he has not noticed the important fact...."

Three days later he wrote to his elder brother, Mr. Thomas B. Grove :—

"Royal College,
"*May* 25, 1894.

"You are the first person to whom I write to tell you that Lord Rosebery has this morning offered me a C.B. ... It does not make it less pleasant that it is an honour which is very rarely given to any one not in the actual employment of the Government. It is given me by the desire of the Queen 'in recognition of the eminent services which you have rendered to the public in connection with the Royal College of Music.' ..."

Attendance at the Handel Festival prompted the following letter to his brother Edmund :—

"*June* 30, 1894.

"The question of the borrowings came often before me, and something was borne in on me which had not occurred to me before: that is, how extraordinarily Handel has turned the old phrases—Stradella's and Erba's—from their original purport! The voice is Jacob's voice but the hands are the hands of Esau. The solemnity of the new *words* invests the borrowed notes with a new purport and quite transforms them."

[1] The Registrar of the Royal College.

With the end of the term his spirits sank again in spite of the prospect of a holiday in the most congenial companionship :—

[*To* DEAN BRADLEY.]

"LOWER SYDENHAM,
"*Aug.* 6, 1894.

"How are you? Why are we parted in this unreasonable way? No two men on earth love one another more, and then why are we never to enjoy one another's society? I am very bad, dear old man : so prostrate, so uncomfortable—so torn with pains of body and needless vague pangs and fears of mind. And yet there are alleviations. I just now read myself to sleep with Matthew Arnold's poems. Surely he was a very great poet, or had a great deal of it in him. What passion in 'Laugh, my friends'! What deep mystic truth in 'Yes! in the sea of Life enisled' or 'We cannot kindle'! What ineffable delicate feeling in 'The Future'! and yet it all seems inchoate and embryonic, and never comes to real mature power of expression. Every year I think these poems that I mention have more power over me.

"I am sadly feeble, and feel really very anxious about myself. I have no will to decide anything, but I have written to Ned who is in north Scotland, and proposed to come to him. He is a good old fellow—loves me, and has much in common with me; and if he's going to stay there, I shall go and rest and heal me of my grievous wound—for somehow I have sustained a grievous wound. The past twelvemonth has brought me sadly down. I feel (though I have for long been aware that my powers were going) that somehow I have sustained a *bruise*. I am hurt somewhere and can't recover. . . ."

[*To* MISS L. HEATH.]

"LOWER SYDENHAM,
"*Aug.* 10, 1894.

" . . . I am afraid I have used you very badly, leaving all your dear words . . . unanswered, but really it was not to be helped. I feel about as prostrate as a poor wretch can feel, always with a pervading gloomy feeling that I have done wrong—that I am a criminal—that it is my fault that I can't be as vigorous as I used to be, and that it is through me that some misfortune is impending on the College I love so dearly. This is all or mostly imaginary; but it is not the less hard to bear. However, I am going to cut the knot somehow : on Sunday night I go northward to Perth and there meet my dear brother [Edmund] whose society I delight in, and who has given up his dearly beloved fishing at Loch Maree, to come to more genial climes with me. We shall go first to Kenmore and loaf about. Will there be any chance of my finding you at Broughty Ferry? . . ."

[*To the Same.*]

"HOTEL, KENMORE, PERTHSHIRE,
"*Aug.* 23.

" . . . I told you that I thought our plans would have to be altered and so they have, as far as my brother is concerned. He has to-day gone off to Edinburgh and thence to Brighton where his home is. But *I* stay till Monday and propose to come that day to Dundee and either sleep at Dundee or at your house, if your mother will be good enough to take me in. . . . Then the next morning I could go on with you to St. Andrews and get to Edinburgh that night. From there I have to go to see Parratt, who is in Wigtonshire somewhere, and then get home by Friday or Saturday. . . . It was very hard parting with old Ned [his brother] this afternoon, but it had to be done. He is *such* a good old fellow,—simply pure goodness (with very considerable wits too) . . ."

Shortly after his return home Grove received fresh proofs of Sullivan's affectionate solicitude on his behalf in the following letter:

"WALTON-ON-THAMES,
"*Sept.* 21, 1894.

"I have been trying to think of someone who could help you at the College. The difficulty is to find anyone of weight and authority, because altho' everything would be done in your name yet everyone would know that the initiative came from your aide-de-camp. And you want an organising and executive assistant, not a musical genius. I wish I could (perhaps I may) spend one whole day with you at the College. Then I could see whether I am not right in my opinion that you fritter away your time, strength, and spirits upon a thousand paltry details that you need not and might not attend to. In racing we don't put a valuable thoroughbred into a brougham to drive us to the station or to a plough or to a lawn-mower. But that is what you do with yourself and wonder you are not in condition to run classic races.

However, I have preached all in vain, over and over again. When are you coming to see my new little cottage? The grounds are the prettiest on the river almost."

At the address delivered on September 27th at the opening of the College Term Grove spoke with more than usual earnestness on the only aims worth pursuing:—

"It is pressing forward—your eye fixed on the goal—*that* is the proper attitude for good men and women. And what is the goal? Success? Money? Fame? Applause? All these are good in their way; but the goal, the point on which all our eyes are to be fixed as I hope, will not be any of these. To do well, to know that we have done our best; to feel that we have got the approbation not only of music-publishers and large audiences but of a few good men, of our own consciences, and of the Supreme Judge—call him God, or conscience, or Nature, or any other name as you like—*that*, my dear friends, is the only object, the only goal worth looking at! You'll forgive me for taking this grave view of our position thus early in the day, when perhaps some lighter remarks would have been more welcome. But you must take your Director as you find him. I have lived somewhat of a long life, I am going down the hill, I see the evening light—the light from the other world—on things more readily than you do, and take a more anxious view of the course which I have passed through, but which you are entering on."

As usual Grove insisted on the advantages of travel, and the importance of good handwriting: "Remember that the very greatest musicians all wrote beautiful hands." He eulogised the munificence of Mr. Samson Fox, who had provided the funds for the erection of the new buildings, and of Mr. George Donaldson, who had presented them with a valuable collection of works of art; he praised the ability and loyalty of the Professors; and finally he alluded to the extraordinary exertions of Mr. George Watson, the Registrar, who was unhappily disabled by severe illness.

In little more than a fortnight from the opening of the term Grove had drafted and despatched a letter to the Prince of Wales as President of the Council asking his permission to surrender his charge. One of the first persons to whom he communicated his resolve was the Bishop of Lichfield, as the following letter shows :—

"LOWER SYDENHAM,
"*Monday*, *Oct.* 15, 1894.

"I have acted on your advice which you gave me in your letter, and on Saturday sent in my resignation to the Prince. You may imagine how much it cost me to do so, and of course since the letter went all the objections to such a course have presented themselves in full force! But I have been thinking of it for a long time, and there really is no alternative. It is so easy to say, why don't you do less and let others work for you? But *to me* that is quite impossible. I can only say that I have done my best to carry out my duty, and that I have been beaten by age and overwork. . . . Yours always affectionately."

It need hardly be said that the taking of the final step caused him great distress, but in view of his loss of nerve, of spirits and above all of memory, he saw no other alternative. He was further strongly encouraged to adhere to his resolve by Lord Charles Bruce, whose affectionate letter of October 25th is worthy of reproduction :—

". . . . . I am strongly of opinion that you must not jeopardize your health and strength in the slightest degree. . . The Prince and others would agree that you must be relieved of your arduous duties and anxieties without delay. What I think quite conclusive is your own doctor's opinion and advice. Do not, my dear friend, I beg, hesitate in taking the final step, severe as the trial will be to you to do so. . . . You know how much it must cost me to say all this to you, but prompted as I am by my feelings of affection and friendship for you, I cannot forbear from speaking out as I have done in the interests of your welfare. Your intense loyalty and devotion to the College would, I know, well make you go on until you were ready to drop. But indeed, indeed, this must not be. With you there has ever been 'le courage,' but there comes a time to all of us, when 'la force' is no longer commensurate with it. Ever, dear friend, your attached, affectionate and sympathising friend, Charles Bruce."

Lord Charles's advice only related to the time at which the severance should take place, as Grove's resignation had been accepted by the Prince on the 17th of October.

A special meeting of the Council was summoned for Monday, November 5th, and a resolution was passed in which the Council placed on record, in language of a warmth rarely employed in official documents, their appreciation of Grove's unselfish and unceasing devotion to the College since its foundation; their affectionate esteem and regard for himself; and their deep regret that in view of the reasons assigned, it would not be fair to ask him to reconsider his decision. The resolution was moved by Prince Christian, and seconded by the late Duke of Westminster, both of whom spoke of the Director in terms of cordial eulogy, while Lord Thring, as the oldest man in the room, testified to Grove's singleness of purpose and generosity of temper. At a subsequent meeting of the Council, held on Wednesday, November 7th, on the motion of Sir Arthur Sullivan, it was decided "in recognition of the signal services rendered by him to the College as first Director to award Sir George Grove a special pension of £700 a year."

On the day of the first meeting Grove summed up his own view of the situation very clearly in a letter to Professor Andrew Bradley :—

"*Nov.* 5, 1894.

"DEAREST A. . . . To-day I am going to a Council Meeting at which I put my resignation into their hands. Easy to write of, old boy, but, by George, it's a pang and in this case a pang spread over three months, for I have been at it all that time. I *do* love the place so, and I felt up to the best part of the work, and could preach in a gay, half-serious fashion to my heart's content on my old theme of nothing being any good without religion, and religion being no good unless it showed itself in the practical shape of faith and unselfishness and good manners (i.e. grace), and then, if I saw them yawning, I read 'em a bit of Tennyson or Browning. But then that was not all, and the sad collapse of memory and presence of mind and courage showed me it was time to go. It will be hard work facing them (the Council, I mean) because they are all so dreadfully sorry for me to go—the things they write are quite absurd. What I should like now is to have a few weeks to myself to go abroad and get my body into better order. . . . I have been in bed since Thursday and once was rather frightened and thought rather plaintively of all my little Beethoven memorandums that would be wasted if I was not there to put them in their places.

"*Tuesday*, Nov. 6th. I went up yesterday and heard speeches from Prince Christian and Lord Thring which quite *surprised* me—first that so much could be said in praise of an individual, and secondly, that I was that individual. It really was most delightful. . . . ."

Keen as was the pang that Grove suffered, it was greatly eased by the generous, considerate and appreciative attitude of the Council from the Prince downwards, and by the unanimous and affectionate testimony of his colleagues and of the pupils, past as well as present, at the Royal College. For the next month he was literally deluged with these evidences of gratitude and attachment. The Council had resolved to offer him the first vacancy at their board, but his old friend Mr. E. H. Pember, K.C., at once wrote : "I don't like the idea of your having to wait for a place on the Council. Mine is at your disposal." As evidence of the feelings that prevailed between him and the teaching staff it may suffice to quote the testimony of Sir Charles Stanford :—

"I must just write you one line of the most heartfelt gratitude for all the love and kindness you've shown me all these years at the College, and for making the last ten the happiest I have ever spent. Any good I have done has all been from your loyal help and splendid initiative, and the effect of that will last longer than you or I. I've always felt somehow as if your influence was like Arnold's at Rugby, and certainly he was not loved and honoured more than you."

The private letters from Lord Thring, from Sir Edward Hamilton, from Mr. Charles Morley breathe the same spirit. Lord Charles Bruce wrote :

"You must not make yourself unhappy as to the future of the College. You have laid a sound foundation and built thereon a noble edifice with which your name will be ever identified. We, the Governing body, can never forget all you have done for us, for without you the College could not have become what it is, one of our most important National Institutions. We must all feel that we have no right to ask you to remain one moment longer than you think you ought to do, and now, alas! the time has come to which I have so often looked forward with the greatest sorrow, when we must think of your successor. I simply know of no one who can take your place, and yet I feel that the same good Providence, which, as it were, raised you for this special work, which has so prospered in your hands, will continue to watch over the destinies of the College. Hubert Parry is the only man who could succeed you. . . . ."

Sir Alexander Mackenzie, the head of the sister Institution, wrote: "It is good to look back on the seven years during which I have been in office and think that our intimacy has never been disturbed by a single jarring note." Letters poured in from his old friends—from Sir Charles Wilson, from Lady Paget, from Mr. G. L. Craik (of Macmillan's), from the Rev. W. Addis, from Mr. A. D. Coleridge, from old pupils and their parents—all inspired by the same regret and goodwill. The testimony of the secretarial staff was equally notable, and Mr. Watson, the Registrar, himself sadly shattered in health, wrote of Grove's decision as a terrible blow to him: "The College can never be the same to any of us, especially to those of us who have had the privilege of serving under you from the beginning."

To the consoling influence of all this appreciation and sympathy there remained to be added the encouragement and confidence inspired by the choice of his successor. For Lord Charles Bruce's expectation was realised; the post was offered to and accepted by Hubert Parry. Grove's satisfaction may be gathered from the following letters:—

[*To* MISS L. HEATH.]

"LOWER SYDENHAM,
"*Nov.* 24, 1894.

". . . . The last twelve months have pulled me about fearfully and in October I felt that I ought no longer to hesitate, so I made my bow. Both Prince and Council have been tremendously kind and generous. They gave me a good pension and then placed me on the Council, so that I shall always be about the place, and shall keep as many of the old ties unbroken as I can, till my own time comes. Parry is to succeed me and as I talked to him yesterday the sight of his dear young face and his cheery way comforted me in a way I cannot 'exclaim' to you. I have been sadly under a cloud for three months past, and now it seems to be lifting. It is far the best appointment that could be made. . . I am going to hear the *Eroica* today, only fancy. . ."

[*To* Dr. WALFORD DAVIES.]

"*Dec.* 1894.

"It has been a terrible wrench to me leaving my dear College. I did not know how much I should feel it till the moment actually came and even now I am not at all happy as to the result. One never knows what turn events will take—I often think that my health may go . . . . I think, perhaps, I may take a voyage. . . . certainly, I am perfectly satisfied with my successor. . . . I believe that he will look on the work a good deal from my point of view and think that the breeding up of *good* young men and women is as much the duty of the Director as making them good musicians.

"I think with great satisfaction on my efforts (they are no more) in that direction, and on the great goodness and teachableness of the pupils as a whole."

[*To* MISS FLORENCE COLERIDGE.]

"LOWER SYDENHAM,
"*Dec.* 23, 1894.

". . . . I left College on Friday, and it has been a horrid time, relieved, I must say, by the numbers of affectionate, appreciative letters like yours, which have broken my fall very much. I have got a huge bundle, and I literally can't tell you how much I value them. I am most encouraged by Parry's appointment. He has all my virtues and others which I never could aspire to. It depends upon the pupils to make him an excellent Director. If they put the same confidence in him that they have put in me, he will rise to the occasion; so please remember *that*, and act upon it to. . ."

As a pendant to the foregoing may be given the letter which Grove received from Sir Hubert Parry a few days later :—

"WILTON HOUSE, SALISBURY,
"*Dec.* 26, 1894.

"DEAREST OLD G. . . . . I can't express myself about the situation . . . I realize too vividly and painfully what it must be to you, with all your energies and sympathies fully alive, to be giving up a thing so engrossing and valuable as the College work. It's too painful to speak of. It may be a comfort to you to feel how intensely everyone from the topmost Professor to the smallest boy feels your going. I hope it is. I feel very strongly that my first efforts will be enveloped in gloom! It will be a long while before the place regains any of its cheerfulness. . . . ."

CHAPTER XIII

Grove's occupations—The Beethoven Book—Address to Mr. Manns—Sittings to Mr. Alfred Gilbert, R.A., and Mr. Charles Furse—Address from R.C.M. pupils—Death of Mr. Watson—Publication of the book on Beethoven's Symphonies, 1896—Grove's unabated interest in his old pupils—Their appreciation of his kindness—Trip to Scotland in 1896—St. Andrew's and Portobello—Grove's views on modern music—Death of Lord Charles Bruce—At Woodhall Spa in 1897—Revision of Thackeray's novels—Death of his brother Thomas—Last years and death—Personal traits and reminiscences by Mr. E. H. Pember, Mrs. Wodehouse, Rev. W. Addis, and Canon Ainger.

THOUGH the new year brought Grove relief from the immediate pressure of his College work, the burden of his correspondence still weighed heavily upon him, though the letters which had to be answered at this period were mostly of a pleasant nature.

[*To* MISS JEANNE BRETEY.]

"*Jan.* 10, 1895.

" . . . Your letter pleased me immensely . . . it is one of the very best that I have received; many feel grateful and affectionate towards me; but few know how to express their feelings as simply and clearly as you do. Many, many thanks to you for it. Yes, you are quite right: your coming to College was entirely my doing. I saw you and you pleased me very much. I said to myself, that girl has character and feeling, and, more than that, she is *good*. . . . And you have not disappointed me, but have gradually worked yourself up and now I hope you are on the high road to success. Isn't that a nice thing for *you* and for *me* to think about? Yes, I have given up the College! the last 14 months have been too much for me. Parry has succeeded me and has begun thoroughly well and I don't doubt that in course of time he will eclipse me. But still to all of you old pupils I shall always be the Director, and very happy I am that *le bon Dieu* has enabled me to do so much and has given me such numbers of loving, grateful, true-hearted friends. I left College on Thursday the 3rd, but I don't find my work decrease; there is an immense heap of letters and Christmas cards to be answered gradually; and then every day brings 12 or 15 fresh ones; and then I feel so tired and want a rest if I could get it! Your letter has acted quite like a cordial in reading it over again. Good-bye, my dear, kind friend. Write to me now and then and always tell me of your successes."

Grove soon settled down, however, to his Beethoven book, and with evidently good results, for writing to him on April 15th Mr. Dannreuther (with whom he was once more in frequent communication on technical matters connected with the Symphonies) speaks of the pleasure of meeting him and finding him "so bright and ardent." "I have often said," he continues, "that your enthusiasm is contagious, and I found it so again."

On April 6th he gave away the prizes at the Sydenham High School and delivered a short address on methods of study, impressing on his hearers the need of thoroughness and the "helpfulness of learning some first-rate things by heart. At odd times, in the morning when they were getting up, or in the evening when they were going to bed, they might learn a few lines of poetry, a passage out of the Bible, or some good prose book, which would be of great value to them. He had proved this by experience." He also emphasized the need of being accurate and never being showy, of having a high ideal and preferring to be beloved to being admired.

To this month also belongs a letter addressed to a Mr. Maxtone Graham, of Crieff, published in the *Strathearn Herald* of April 27, 1895. In this Grove makes complimentary allusions to Mr. Graham's lecture and offers a characteristic remark at the end of his letter:—

"Did you ever notice that at the first enumeration of the inhabitants of the world (Gen. iv. 20, 21, 22) they are divided into three great sections—herdsmen, *musicians*, and engineers? It struck me as very interesting when I first observed it."

On April 30th it was Grove's pleasant duty to take a leading part in the presentation of a Testimonial to Mr. August Manns, who had recently celebrated his seventieth birthday, and in view of their long and intimate association a peculiar interest attaches to Grove's generous tribute. He said:—

"The friends and admirers whom you see around you on this happy occasion have assembled for more than one purpose. First we desire to congratulate you on the attainment of a term of years which musicians are not very often permitted to reach. Secondly we wish to express our pleasure at your happy recovery from your recent severe illness. Thirdly we have to express our gratitude for your efforts at the head of the Crystal Palace orchestra by which the works of many of the great composers have been introduced to England by your means, in a manner well worthy of the fame of those great men. Fourthly, and this is a matter which rouses not only our artistic sentiments but the deep feelings of our hearts, we desire to express to you our warm thanks for the singularly happy position which you have taken and maintained since your advent among us with regard to English musicians. Foreigner as you are by birth, no Englishman could have given more encouragement to our native school than you have given by your cordial behaviour to a multitude of our composers and performers, by the extraordinary pains you have bestowed upon their works, and the careful and brilliant performances by which you have in many cases introduced them to the public. Such benefits as these can never fade from the memory, and we here try to tender you our heartfelt thanks for them, and our earnest hope that your beneficent and useful career may be still prolonged for many years.

"As your first friend in this country, I may be permitted to acknowledge before this distinguished assembly the honour and gratification which I have felt at working by your side for many years in the realization of your splendid design, and the pleasure which our uninterrupted friendship has given me."

Early in May Grove began to give sittings to Mr. Alfred Gilbert, R.A., for the bust by which his old pupils had determined to commemorate his connection with the College, and a little later on began to frequent Mr. Charles Furse's studio in Tite Street for a similar purpose,

Sir George Grove.

From a portrait taken by Charles W. Furse in 1895.

the professorial staff having subscribed to present him with his portrait. As a result of these sittings, which lasted intermittently till the end of August, a close sympathy sprang up between the painter and his subject. Grove speaks more than once of the pleasure he derived from the companionship of his new friend, and Mr. Charles Furse has tersely summarized his impressions in the following lines:—

"The two qualities I remember as being most lovable in him were, first, his gift of eternal youth, and secondly his charming deference to youth and the crude statement of its convictions and prejudices. I never painted a man who made the work of the painter so delightful. He would monologue on in the most racy way, while one was too preoccupied to do more than allow his talk to enter by the pores of one's skin, and in the intervals he would listen to anything one had to say with that genius for listening that sent one away with the conviction that one had been astonishingly 'on the spot.' It was only in perspective that one realized how his quick sympathy and kindly irony had given the needle to one's blunter wits."

When the presentation took place in December, 1895, Grove, in thanking his friends for their gift, added: "One unexpected pleasure you have given me is the friendship which has sprung up between the painter and myself during my sittings."

Early in June he paid his brother a visit at Preston, near Brighton, followed by a short circular tour to Winchester, Romsey, Christchurch and so back to Preston again. The change did him good and on his return he wrote in brighter spirits than for some time past to Miss Heath:—

"LOWER SYDENHAM,
"*June* 14.

"... The address is to be presented to me on Friday, July 12th, How I wish that you and all my other dear old friends would be present. Thank you for mentioning Rusty. He is here asleep on the sofa in my bedroom. I am very fond of him (or rather her, for the gender is always confused). He is now about 11 years old, which for a dog I suppose is equivalent to about 70 in a human being, and yet notwithstanding he can be very cheerful and lively when a cat is in question, and rushes about the lawn with a vigour which I think makes him repent afterwards. Do you know anything of the verses of any of the new 'poets'—Watson, Davidson and Le Gallienne, etc.? I have read some, but don't care for them. It all lacks workmanship, and accurate knowledge of nature. I stick to my old friends, Tennyson and Shakespeare and Browning. I had a private volume from a friend, Mr. Pember, the other day with a Greek story, and the story of Naaman, and four little poems on the four seasons, which seemed to me (Winter especially) really good.

"Do things take *hold of you* sometimes? They do so of me quite absurdly. All yesterday from 6 a.m. I was humming, howling, shouting the 1st variation in the Finale of Beethoven's Sonata in E, Op. 109. How lively it is! and also how bold! A variation? Wherein does the likeness to the theme consist? And yet there is no mistaking the resemblance. Look at the 6th and 7th bars. They are only a kind of *excursion* outside of the melody, and how beautiful they are—the A♮ and then the A♯, and then the G♮ further on. Oh dear, it is all magical, I think. . ."

Early in the year Grove had lost an old friend in Lady Paget, linked in his mind, as Sir James Paget wrote, with the happy time of 50 years ago, and on July 4th he was present at Huxley's funeral. "I was a very humble friend of his," he wrote to Sir Norman Lockyer, "but he was so good to me that I should like to see the last of him."

On July 12th he attended at the Royal College to receive the address signed by 488 pupils of the Royal College of Music, past and present, and presented in their name by his successor. In his reply, Grove began by acknowledging the splendid work done by his colleagues, the great ability of the Prince, and the devotion of the Registrar, Mr. Watson. For himself all he had done was to use every effort in his power to make successful use of his unrivalled opportunities: for "no man was ever so much helped by his colleagues and his pupils." He then continued:—

"One thing I have tried to show you—that ability and hard work are of no avail unless backed by character; that, great work as the study of music is, there is one thing still greater—to be good, to be unselfish, to be thoughtful of others; and hereafter when the bust which you intend to present me with shall be placed in this noble building, I trust that it may be recognised as the likeness of one to whom *that* was the great object of his life. For my successor I can only say that much as we owe him for the past, I predict that as Director he will be of still more service to the College."

When August came Grove was too busy with his symphony book to think of a regular holiday. His pocket-books are full of Beethoveniana, and I find in his almanac such entries as "At home: working hard at No. 9" or "At home: *Eroica.*" Busy though he was he did not forget his eldest grandchild's birthday, but sent her the following charming letter, dated August 21st, 1895:—

"MY DEAREST GLADYS—To-morrow is your birthday, and I have sent you my present, and this is to wish you many happy returns of the day. You will find the present a rather large one! It is an Atlas; that is, a book containing maps of all the countries in the world, so that when you read of a place you can at once find it out. Next time I come to your house I will write your name in it. Yesterday I went to call on Ernest von Glehn at his office. He was very nice and took me out and showed me the Tower Bridge, which I had never seen before, and liked it much. Then I called upon his brother Willy, and went to the *Times* office to get your Atlas. Then I called on Mr. Macmillan and had lunch, and then went to Bond Street, and then to the Club and at last home. I forgot to say your papa took me up to London in the morning and led me by a short cut to Ernest's office, through such a queer collection of narrow lanes and odd passages and places—one was a churchyard—as I never saw before. We went by the 'Monument,' which is an immense pillar, 200 feet high, set up after the Great Fire of London in 1666, to mark the place where it began. It is very curious, and some day I should like to show it you. You see I had quite an idle day, and got home two hours before dinner. Papa soon came in, and after dinner we sat under the trees in the dark and smoked, which I liked very much. The hedgehog has appeared again in the little place under the drawing-room window, and Russ was in great excitement about it yesterday, Granny says. I daresay it has made its escape out of there in the night. It is now six o'clock in the morning; and the first thing I do when I go down will be to look into that place and see if it is gone. . ."

Writing to a friend on September 1st, he says that he cannot get away till he has done the Beethoven book, and that he finds work "much harder and more tiresome than it used to be." He hoped, however, to get to Paris with his "dear friend Sir Walter Parratt" later on in the month, a project which was not realized. The postscript contains some trenchant remarks on Russian novelists and English translators :—

"I can't see the likeness between Tolstoi and Tourguénieff. Tolstoi is a missionary, and often a brutal one, but Tourguénieff is one of the greatest artists of our time. *Spring Floods* I know as *Eaux printanières* ; to me it is intensely mournful. The first reading was quite enough, but until that dreadful seducing woman appears on the scene it's equal to anything he ever wrote. There never was such a picture of a girl. But the English translations are simply *dreadful*."

Grove had recently spoken of his faithfulness to Shakespeare, Tennyson, and Browning, but his attachment to Clough, whom he learnt to admire and love in the early "sixties," also remained unimpaired :—

[*To* MRS. WODEHOUSE.]

"LOWER SYDENHAM,

"*Oct.* 1.

"How can I best thank you for your delightful note? By answering it at once. Every letter ought to be a conversation, and so here goes. The poem you mean is by Clough, and is one of the sweetest pieces in the world. The 3rd stanza is a little faulty, but when Beethoven played we should not have minded a phrase played clumsily here and there, and so here. But indeed Clough's part of the vol. is full of the highest poetry. 'The two ships' is particularly dear to me : I heard Arthur Stanley quote the two last stanzas at a Rugby dinner, when I was at the turning point of my life, and I have myself used them in a sermon at College. . . . Do you think it would tire you to hear some of my life of David, which I wrote for our children twenty-five years ago and have just found again? If not I should very much value your judgment on it, and I can't help fancying it would amuse you."

On October 28th occurs the entry in his almanac, "knocked down in Victoria Street by a hansom horse : not hurt." But though he escaped without injury from this, the last of his numerous cab accidents, his general health was once more giving him a good deal of uneasiness, and his doctor spoke of a tour to the West Indies. Yet he was still capable, as the following letter to his brother in November shows, of suddenly extricating himself from a mood of depression by the aid of a quotation or a humorous reminiscence :—

". . . I have had the most terrible spirits, and feel sadly weak, and unhinged to a great degree. You must not put down this extra ragged writing altogether to *that*, however, for I am bathing the finger of my left hand in a cup, and am so far *unimanous* —not *unanimous*, alas ! *À propos* : do you remember old Fuller's translation of an epigram on a certain Perkins, a left-handed theologian in Elizabeth's time ? of whom he says, that 'this Ehud, with a lefthanded pen, did so stab the Romish cause, &c.' The epigram was thus :—

Dextera quantumvis fuerit tibi manca, docendi
Pollebas mirâ dexteritate tamen.

and he Englishes it thus :—

"'Though Nature thee of thy right hand bereft,
Right well thou *writest* with the hand that's left.'"

In another undated letter to his brother, evidently written about the same time, he says :

". . . I do think at last that I have done No. 8. Quite four times over have I written it ! *Magna est perseverantia.* But it wanted care, because Beethoven seems to me more of a *buffoon* in it than in any other, and one can't say exactly that . . ."

So in a letter to Miss Heath, written on December 5th, he notes the approaching end of his labours :—

"I am glad that you heard the No. 7. Yes, it is a wonder : no other except the 9th gives such an impression of *size.* The same thing is done by Schubert in C, but in both cases I vainly ask why ? Doing the whole nine as I have been doing, it's curious how one feels the step up from No. 6 to No. 7. The three last seem to stand on a platform by themselves, even above the *Eroica*, C Minor and *Pastoral.* I think that it is that they are less music, and more the expression of the emotion of the composer. But it is very hard to express . . . . I am sadly 'down in the mouth,' why, I know not. I have now *done* 1—8, and No. 9 only waits the last touches, and I ought to be happy. BUT I AM NOT. In fact I am completely worked out, and till I have had a rest ought to do nothing. Perhaps (*le grand peut-être*) I am going to the *West Indies* for two months—February to March, But it is not definite enough to talk of. Lady Grove is very well and Rusty, though infirm and old, is charming, and as good as gold. . . . The Purcell commemorations were very interesting. especially the Abbey one. I never lost sense of its being a *service*, and found it very impressive. . . ."

One of the last entries in Grove's almanac for 1895 relates to the *début* of a former pupil, Miss Jessie Grimson, at the Crystal Palace ; just as one of his earliest efforts after his resignation was to interest himself in securing a hearing for a work by an old College boy—Mr. R. H. Walthew. Grove had compared himself on his retirement to the Peri at the gates of Paradise, whereon Mr. Walthew humorously replied, "I should think that Cincinnatus, after having saved Rome, returning to content and cabbages would be the better simile."

The idea of the West Indian trip was abandoned, and Grove remained at home all the winter, finishing up his book and seeing it through the press. In January 1896 he made a point of attending the funeral, at Bramshott, of his old friend Mr. Alexander Macmillan, and on February 15th he was grieved, though not surprised, to learn from his successor that "our dear good friend Watson has come to the end of his earthly labours," contributing the obituary notice which appeared in the *Times* of the 18th. Mr. George Watson had been successively organising secretary (1882), chief clerk (1883), Registrar (1884), and finally Secretary (1894) to the Royal College, as well as secretary and organiser of the Associated Board (1889), and in all these positions he had shown not merely incessant activity and excellent judgment, but the strongest personal attachment to Grove.

In March the long-awaited Symphony book was published, and met with a most gratifying reception. In the Preface, dated February 29th, he expresses his especial debt of gratitude to Mr. Edward F. Pember, Q.C., Dr. F. E. Gladstone, Mr. Victor Henkel, Mr. F. G. Shinn, Mr. F. G. Edwards, and Mr. S. P. Waddington ; but his private correspondence shows that he was also indebted for valuable assistance in regard to suggestions and revision to Mr. Dannreuther, Dr. Charles Wood, Mr. A. Jaeger (of Novello's), and many others. True to his often expressed intention, he placed in the forefront of his preface the statement that the book was a "humble endeavour to convey to others the method in which an amateur has obtained much pleasure and profit out of works which in their own lines are as great as Shakespeare's plays," adding that it would be presumptuous in him to attempt to interest professional musicians. None the less Grove's book, which Dr. Pole pronounced a "storehouse of knowledge perfectly amazing," emphatically killed two birds with one stone. It delighted the amateurs, while its wealth and wide range of illustration threw a flood of light on points which the professionals had been too apt to consider from the purely technical point of view.

His old friend Thayer, the biographer of Beethoven, was too ill to write in his own hand, but dictated a touching message of congratulation on the completion of Grove's "noble work," and amongst others who wrote to express their admiration were, Sir Theodore Martin, Professor Andrew Bradley, the Rev. A. G. Butler, and Felix Moscheles. The tribute of Mr. F. G. Edwards is specially worth quoting. He says :—

"The first time I spoke to you, I remember telling you of the very great stimulus in the study of the Symphonies which I received from your analyses at the Crystal Palace concerts years ago. Youthful impressions are very strong, and I remember thinking how delightful it would be to *know* 'G'! And since then I have more than once urged you to put the notices into permanent form, and lo! this has now been done! I am very glad, and so will be thousands of others who, by reason of its moderate price, will become the fortunate possessors of your most interesting and valuable book."

As has already been seen, Grove indulged in no idle form of words when he promised that his resignation would make no difference in the interest he took in those whom he used to call his children. The instances already recorded of his personal exertions on behalf of his *protégés* might be multiplied to any extent. It would be interesting to know how many persons from first to last in the musical profession and outside of it have owed their start in life to Grove's recommendation or advice. And his interventions were none the less welcome when they had no direct reference to appointments, engagements or salaries. As an example of the particularity of his interest in and care for individual students and their doings I am allowed by one of his most gifted pupils to quote the following letter:—

"LOWER SYDENHAM,
"*Friday Morning, April* 10, 1896.

"DEAR——,—Many thanks for your kind answer. I hope Brahms won't keep you waiting too long, but I fear it is not unlikely.

"While you are at Vienna be sure to go to Mödling. It is a small town of which Beethoven was very fond, because, amongst other reasons, of its being near a sort of wood, which he refers to as the Brühl or Briehl. You must on no account miss seeing this. It is a short distance out of Mödling on a small railroad which puts you down close to it. You will be there before the spring has gone, and will see it at its best. On the left, as you leave the line, is a rising wooded hill, and on the right the flat wood itself with roads through it and an inn, the Zwei Raben (or Drei, I am not sure which), which Beethoven used to frequent and where the village musicians played, whom he imitated in the Scherzo of the *Pastoral Symphony*. It is sure to interest and inspire you,—and there is a wonderful beauty about the whole place—not *grand*, but most *charming*. Pray don't forget to see it. Be sure you do not.

"Good-bye, a happy journey to you and a satisfactory visit to Brahms. He can't remember me, but please assure him of my earnest love and veneration.

"Always, dear——

"Yours affectionately,

"G. GROVE.

"P.S. If you can, go also to Baden, a little further away from Vienna. It's very interesting, and you should see the Helenen-Thal, a beautiful wooded spot, part of the town, where Beethoven used to delight to walk when *aufgeknöpft*."

Exertions of this sort are not always appreciated at the time by young people, but certainly Grove had seldom reason to complain of the ingratitude of his "children." The recipient of the last letter wrote shortly afterwards beginning, "Mein lieber, lieber Sir George, or as Brahms, when I saw him, spoke of you, *Sir Grove!*"—to sympathize with him over his low spirits and loss of memory, and continues:—

"But, my dear Sir George, we young ones catch sight of all the greatness of your life, the enthusiasm you've bestowed on us, which is so grandly infectious! Only yesterday Mrs. M—— and I happened to come across an account in print of your Schubert discoveries. These are actualities which we see. Take a look at them again through our outside eyes and you will surely find some comfort."

Here, too, is another letter from another old pupil, already occupying an important post as organist, who wrote in 1896 to report progress to his old Director:—

"I am never full of words where personal matters are concerned, but I cannot help telling you how frequently I look back with love and gratitude to the dear old days at the R.C.M. I went there so raw and ignorant and conceited and left so humble and un-self-satisfied: and I was so happy, and so well treated that the College has a *very* large pigeon-hole in my memory, with your picture on the door. Often I feel sorrow for the troubles which I added to your worries, but perhaps you feel as I do, and do not love those least who have sometimes been unkind to you. At all events it must please you to know there was a solid and true atmosphere about the R.C.M. which some of us will be doing our best to hand on far into the 20th Century."

Dr. Charles Wood, one of the first batch of scholars elected at the R.C.M., who subsequently received the unprecedented honour of being elected a Fellow of his College at Cambridge for his musical distinction, wrote in 1897 to say, "It has been perhaps the greatest pleasure and privilege of my life to have known you, and to be able to say that you are my friend." In this context we may also note that Mr. Coleridge Taylor dedicated his "Hiawatha's Wedding Feast" to Sir George Grove, and that Mr. S. P. Waddington, the Mendelssohn scholar, wrote *à propos* of this dedication to say how "exactly it expressed the sentiments I have always had since the days—which seem a long time ago now—when you first began to be good to me. It must be pleasant," he continues, "to feel that you have so many Benedictions from those you have befriended, now that your retirement has taken you out of immediate touch with them." In unison with these testimonies of the younger men may be joined that of a veteran colleague, Mr. Ernst Pauer, who after many years' residence in England, and half a century of teaching, returned in the spring of 1896, to spend the evening of his days in his native land. "I shall always remember with gratitude," wrote Mr. Pauer on April 12th, 1896, "the many proofs of goodwill shown by yourself to me, not only when I had already secured a firm footing in London, but also when I was a struggling beginner."

With the completion of his book on the Symphonies of Beethoven, Grove brought his literary labours to an end, so far as any important contributions to musical criticism were concerned. But his pen did not remain idle. For the performance of Handel's *Israel in Egypt* at Windsor on March 26th he contributed some interesting explanatory notes, in which he takes much the same line as Mr. Balfour in his well-known essay on Handel. That is to say, he justifies Handel's loans at any rate on the artistic, if not moral ground that when he borrowed a phrase or a subject he made it as much his own as if Erba, Stradella, Urio and Kerl had never existed. "Their phrases were contrapuntal passages, while his treatment put a life and an emotion into them which gave them an entirely new existence. . . . . Property in musical phrases in those days did not exist as it does now." Grove goes on to illustrate how lax Beethoven (and he might have added Haydn) was in his ideas on the subject of borrowing. He also notices the splendid after-thought in the chorus, "The People shall hear," viz. the thirty-three bars to the words, "All the inhabitants of Canaan shall melt away," which was written on a different kind of paper and wafered into the autograph score. "Coleridge has said that 'sublimity is Hebrew by birth'; and the wonderful effect of this chorus surely proves it." He also contributed to the *Scottish Musical Review* for June a sketch of his old friend Madame Schumann, who died on May 21st, 1896, specially emphasizing her single-hearted and serious devotion to her art, and the fact that she was "by suffering made strong."

Throughout the summer he attended the meetings of the Royal College Council and the Associated Board when his health permitted, and was occasionally seen at concerts—the recitals of Eugen d'Albert in particular attracted him. On July 4th he went to hear *Tristan* at Covent Garden, but, as the following letter to his brother Edmund shows, found himself more antagonistic than ever to the spirit of the opera :—

"On the whole *Tristan* did not appeal to me or please me. The story is one of wicked passion throughout—no variety; no relief; no subsidiary story. And the music has no relief or variety either. Think of *Fidelio*, and the difference between an opera founded on 'married love' and devotion, with all the by-play of Rocco and Marcelline, the incident of the prisoners, the soldiers, &c. It really left me very miserable, as if I were in the presence of a very strong man who was insisting on forcing bad, deleterious food and gloom and monotony on me. The theatre was crowded, the orchestra excellent, de Reszke *absolutely perfect* . . . Beethoven's sentence was more than ever deeply imprinted on my mind: 'I want an opera which shall interest me—something moral and elevating. Librettos like those which Mozart composed I have never been in such circumstances as to be able to set. I have never felt inclined to compose anything loose or immoral.' *This* gives the impression of being out of all law or order. No doubt it is so far a more faithful picture of the savage time in which the scene is laid; but why are we to have such times brought before us with such enormous ability? . . Several times in the course of the three acts there were touching and beautiful passages in the orchestra. But all of one character. Man cannot live by bread alone, but by *every word* that proceedeth out of the mouth of God.'

"This constantly occurred to me: this is not *music*. Fine *sounds*; but the form of *music*—the art (as one understands it) was not there!"

On the same date we find him writing to Mrs. Frederick Lehmann, who had asked him to pay her a visit at Portobello:—

"I went to hear *Tristan* on Saturday. My impression of it was that it was very long, very loud—but my soul revolted. Remember the lovely variety of *Fidelio*, and then think of that savage, diabolical story (it only wanted a fight of gladiators to make it quite brutal), 4½ hours long—as monotonous as *could* be . . . Oh dear! This is what we have come to *after Beethoven*! and all the house raving!"

On July 27th Grove started for Scotland, and reached St. Andrews the next day. There he found himself amongst friends, and wrote in something like the old spirit to Mrs. Lehmann a few days later:—

"RUSACK'S MARINE HOTEL, ST. ANDREWS,
"*Aug.* 31, 1896.

"DEAREST OLD FRIEND,—I must send you a line or two though they will be illegible, partly owing to the original sin of this writer, and partly owing to the vileness of his pen. Your Ernest has been awfully good to me: the way we have hunted one another backwards and forwards to our hotels is most amusing: but at last we met at E.'s hotel and had a very nice dinner—*à la mode ancienne*—splitting with jokes and stories all through (not without pathetic moments either). Ernest,[1] Guy,[2] Oswald[3] (a very nice fellow),

[1] Mr. Ernest Lehmann. [2] Sir Guy Campbell.
[3] Mr. John Oswald of Dunnikier.

and a certain G. of your acquaintance. It was really very nice. We go to-day to Mr. Oswald's house [Dunnikier] some 10 or 15 miles off till Monday morning (longer they cannot be absent from their irrepressible golf) and I think I shall enjoy it, though I confess I do feel dreadfully rusty now and then (but I don't *creak*, as old —— used to do) . . . . I have given up the Highlands; weather too unpromising. . . . Joppa ! ! how comic ! Do you remember Forbes's poem in *Punch* (100 years ago) describing his tour in the East—

"'Ease her, stop her,
Who's for Joppa?'

"But that was the real place. . ."

Grove enjoyed his short visit to Dunnikier: "My hosts were as pleasant and hospitable as one can conceive, and the place *most* beautiful, interesting and homelike," and on the following day, with Sir Guy Campbell as his travelling companion, he moved on to Portobello. There, as the guest of one of his dearest surviving friends, he stayed till the end of the month, making frequent excursions to Edinburgh, renewing old friendships—as with the Rev. William Addis, with whom he visited Melrose and Dryburgh on the 24th—and making new acquaintances. This was practically the last holiday visit that Grove ever paid at a distance from home, and it is pleasant to think that it was spent in such thoroughly congenial society. He went, however, both to the Hovingham Musical Festival in the last week of September in this year and to the Bristol Festival in the middle of October, and whenever there was a Beethoven symphony or concerto at the Crystal Palace or Richter concerts he was generally among the audience. As time went on his antagonism towards the new music grew more acute, and a month later he wrote with bitterness of the modern worship of ugliness:

[*To* MRS. F. LEHMANN.]

"LOWER SYDENHAM,
"*Nov.* 17, 1896.

"DEAREST OLD FRIEND,—A 1000 thanks. I answer you at once, lest you should be crowded out, though I fear I sha'n't interest or amuse you. I am anything but well; full of pain and of distress and fear. I lay awake from 4 this morning, fighting the devil—all about nothing, but just as bad as if I had disgrace and disaster before me. It's no use complaining, and as a rule I don't tell, but it is dreadful. I am just worn out with letters on mere routine, that I have to write myself. . . . I have seen A. S. [Arthur Sullivan] twice. He was thin, but I thought his face very much improved, and *very* nice to look at. We were quite on our old terms; but I had only two words with him. I am sorry about the small houses in Edinburgh; but on the other hand the *Mikado* is doing well here. The fact is that in music now (as there was in painting in Pre-Raphaelite times) composers and hearers worship ugliness,—that is directness in any art. There has come a turn or *kink* in the brains and heart-strings of composers; they have no affection—no love—for their music. That divine quality which made Mozart, Beethoven, Schubert, couch their thoughts in the most beautiful forms they could find, and return to their lovely phrases and subjects over and over again, giving the melodies to one instrument after another, with small appropriate changes, and loving it better every time they came back to it—that is now all dismissed in favour of sound and fury. . . And so the old school, with our dear Arthur as its latest product, must go, and wait in the background till the *fad* has passed, and reason comes back! The same thing happened in literature too, Carlyle setting the example. But there's a purer air and a bluer sky behind! these thoughts were forced on me by Schubert's 'unfinished' symphony last Saturday. . . ."

Grove's handwriting, owing to the rheumatic gout by which he was troubled, had begun to deteriorate sadly, and towards the end of 1896 he had recourse to the services of an amanuensis.

[*To* Miss Edith Fox.]

"Lower Sydenham,
"*Dec.* 7, 1896.

"I have got an amanuensis now for 4 hours every morning and it much relieves me, as she is very good and efficient. I am glad to hear you are working away so well, there is nothing like it: indeed what would Heaven be without work? Doesn't it strike you that the minds of men must have been in a very strange embryonic condition when the greatest possible good, the highest ideal, was placed in a sort of idle contemplation? One thing however is certain: how much one's power of work is lessened by growing old. By a chance yesterday I came across a book in which I used to paste all my letters to the *Spectator*, *Times*, *P.M.G.*, &c., and it fairly astonished me to find so many. I can't do the same now. . . .

P. S. Arthur's old dog, Vic., a companion of Russ's youth, is perhaps coming to spend the evening of his days with us!"

It was to this amanuensis that Grove dictated in the early spring of 1897 six copy-books full of discursive reminiscences from which I have already borrowed freely. Engagements that involved physical exertion, fatigue, or exposure he had now frequently to decline, though it was a keen disappointment to him not to attend the marriage of his old friend, Mr. Manns, on January 7th. But he was still ready as ever to place his pen at the service of his friends, and cheerfully acceded to the request of Mr. H. E. Krehbiel, the well-known New York musical critic, that he should write an introduction to the English edition of his book *How to Listen to Music*. I have said that Grove was extremely careful to abstain from *public* condemnation of the music he disliked, but in his private correspondence in later years there is certainly no uncertainty about his verdict on the moderns.

[*To* MRS. WODEHOUSE.]

"LOWER SYDENHAM,
"*March* 15, 1897.

". . . We had a fine concert on Saturday at the Crystal Palace. Joachim played the Beethoven Concerto as no one but he can play it; and among other things we had the *Genoveva* overture, which made a *wonderful effect*. It raised many thoughts in me. What can have happened to drag down music from the high level of beauty, interest, sense, force, grace, coherence and any other good quality, which it rises to in Beethoven and also (not so high) in Mendelssohn, down to the low level of ugliness and want of interest, that we had in Strauss's absurd farrago ("Also sprach Zarathustra") a week before and even—to a degree—in Wagner? *Noise* and *effect* seems to be so much the aim now. F.M.B., in 1836, or so, speaking of a new overture of Cherubini's, complains of it, as if the instruments were nothing and the effect everything,—and that explains a great deal. In Beethoven's Violin Concerto every instrument is treated with dignity and propriety, and each as finely drawn as if from the hand of Raffaelle or Titian. . . On

Monday I had a delightful time, when I went with Joachim to the rehearsal of the Monday Pop. at Piatti's house. They rehearsed Beethoven in C. op. 59, Haydn in G. and Brahms P.f and violin in G. (No I) in a small room, where the sound rushed through one's head, and one had not to listen for the effect as in those horrid big rooms. I think the Haydn struck me most of all. It was really wonderful for humour, grace, variety and the *beauty* of the phrases and harmonies, so different from the worship of ugliness we were talking about, which seems to possess writers of the present day. It was most impressive. I was not prepared for so much power in 'Papa Haydn.' It seemed to me like a solid basis or substratum to all the great music that has been made since on the same lines—a kind of foundation for Beethoven's wonderful edifice, through which his great genius shone plainly. I recalled a conversation which I had with Joachim after dinner one night about 1865 at Sterndale Bennett's house, *on the stairs*; when he held that Haydn was the greatest inventor of all—a judgment which I received with great difficulty then, but now agree with."

The death of Lord Charles Bruce on April 16th was deeply regretted by all the College authorities, by none more so than Grove. The two men were singularly dissimilar, yet an intimate affection had existed between them for many years, and their official relations had been of the utmost cordiality. A bleak easterly wind deterred Grove from journeying down to Wiltshire to attend the funeral, so that he was glad to learn from Sir Hubert Parry that the service had been just what it ought to be—quiet, respectful and dignified, and that their good friend had been laid to rest in a little churchyard remote from the bustle and strife of the world, and breathing the repose and calmness of the spacious downs. Another old and dear friend of nearly forty years' standing, Mrs. Phillips, the widow of the artist, passed away a month later. Grove was not one of those modern sentimentalists who care for animals *more* than human beings, but he was deeply attached to his dog-friends and sorely missed the faithful companion whose virtues are thus commended in his pocket-book. "In memory of Russ, a good, affectionate, faithful little dog. She died April 21, 1897, aged about 12 years. 'O Rus quando te aspiciam?'" In June his rheumatism once more began to make itself very troublesome, and he complains in a letter to his niece Miss Edith Fox that he is "killing himself writing letters to stupid people." In the same month Grove attended his last Handel Festival, and at the end of July went off to take the waters at Woodhall Spa in Lincolnshire. A few days before leaving London, however, he wrote to communicate a discovery to Mrs. Wodehouse :—

"LOWER SYDENHAM, S.E.,
"*July*, 15, 1897.

"I have made a discovery (?) in Shakespeare which I should like to know your opinion of. You know that the thrush's song consists of many repetitions of phrases like :—

Is there not a reference to this in verses 1, 2, 3 of Autolycus' Song in *The Winter's Tale*, in the 'with heigh' especially in verse 3, where it is repeated? Tennyson has made more of the same kind of thing in his 'Throstle,' but I can't help thinking that Shakespeare was on the same idea. No one seems to have noticed it before."

The discovery—his satisfaction with which was heightened by Mr. Aldis Wright's assurance that it had not been anticipated by anyone else—is duly recorded in a letter to the *Times* of August 2, 1897, in which Grove contends that stanza 3 of Autolycus's song in *The Winter's Tale* and Amiens's song in *As you Like It*, "Come hither, come hither, come hither," give the exact effect of the thrush's song, more elaborately indicated in Tennyson's "Throstle," "I know it, I know it, I know it."

Mrs. Richmond Ritchie (Miss Thackeray) was engaged at this time in passing the recent biographical edition of her father's works through the press, and Grove, who had always been not only an admirer but also a constant reader of Thackeray's novels, suggested to one of those connected with their publication that he would like to go carefully through *Vanity Fair*, correcting various errors and inaccuracies, due chiefly to careless proof-reading in the original edition, which had long, he said, been thorns in his flesh.

"The self-imposed task," writes Mrs. A. Murray Smith, "which he thoroughly enjoyed, occupied his enforced leisure during his stay at Woodhall Spa, and only sharpened his appetite for more. The *Newcomes*, *Pendennis*, and *Esmond* were all revised by the end of the year, after which he was unable to find time for any more. With reference to *Vanity Fair* he writes (July 29) to A. Murray Smith: 'Bless you for the copy. I read it diligently on the journey (to W. Spa) and did about 100 pages; every day I have worked well and hard, and this morning at 5.30 I finished it. . . . I am very glad to have read it carefully again; the first two-thirds are as good as can be, so full of wit, fun, solid goodness, and a freshness *unsurpassed*; the last one-third falls off. Perhaps he was tired; perhaps he had begun another book; perhaps that horrid slough of wickedness and absence of religion was enough to clip his wings. At any rate, mistakes or not, the book has risen beyond what I remembered it, though I have read it certainly twelve times. Now I have attended to every word.' On July 30th he returned the copy with about 100 minute points corrected, or with suggestions and queries, in the text, a precious volume indeed, as are also the three other novels which were revised by the same hand, to its present owners. He adds with reference to these notes: 'You must look it through page by page and there, few and scattered, you will find my suggestions; these you should look through, and finally I think they should go to Mrs. Ritchie.' As was afterwards done in the case of the other volumes, G.'s notes were copied out, carefully verified, and sent to Mrs. Ritchie, who, on October 10th, when the first three novels, *Vanity Fair* (July), the *Newcomes* and *Pendennis* (September), were completed, thanks G. in the following grateful words: 'I was ill when your dear, kind, sympathetic letter came, and I could not thank you for it nor for all your really valuable labour of love. . . . I went through all the notes, some seemed rather complicated but most of them *inevitably* to be carried out. I do thank you so very much and so sincerely. . . .' By November 10th, *Esmond* also was finished, and passed on to Mrs. Ritchie, who returned the copy (on December 10th) to A. Murray Smith, with the comment: 'What trouble kind Sir George has taken!' Some of G.'s notes on the margin of these volumes are most amusing. Thus he was much exercised by the vision of Master Omnium's Papa devouring the *Times* with his prawns for breakfast at Brighton: 'The shortest time for a coach to reach Brighton in 1818 must have been six hours, and I doubt if the papers in those days were published before 8, which would make them arrive at 2 . . . rather late even for a Crawley breakfast.' So minute again was his reading of every line that he notes that the title of a penny book given to Amelia should be the Washerwoman of *Finchley* not *Wandsworth* Common; probably it caught his eye in this case because he remembered the otherwise defunct little pamphlet. The misprint of 'cold bread and sausage' for Becky's supper in her lodgings is with similar minute slips carefully corrected. Dates he is very particular about, and there are constant queries, as, for instance, about the ages of Esmond, Frank, and Beatrix, which he finds differ in two passages—since set right as are all incorrect dates. In *Pendennis* is an elaborate note of the kind in which G. specially revelled, and which nobody else would even have noticed, with regard to Mr. Foker's evening paper—'Not in London. Surely it could not have penetrated so far as to Clavering, 25 hours' distance.' Then 'Professor *Sadiman's* researches in Zahara,' is corrected to *Sandiman*; and again the place of Miss Munifer's day school is noted as *Old*castle instead of *New*castle Street. In the *Newcomes* he delights in the opportunity for a musical note when Miss Cann is said to play old music of Handel's and Haydn's—*Don Juan* being referred to as one of her favourites; a few lines later on G. comments: 'Mozart? (for Haydn) He was much more known, and all the pieces quoted are by Mozart.'

Many more instances of G.'s minute and patient work might be given, but enough passages have been selected to show the type of his revision; it was truly, as Mrs. Ritchie herself remarks, 'a labour of love from first to last.'"

Grove relieved the tedium of his cure, after his wont, by visiting the churches and cathedrals of the neighbourhood—Boston on July 28th, Lincoln on August 7th, Heckington on August 14th—and making notes on their architecture and inscriptions. Early in August he received the news of A. W. Thayer's death, which severed a friendship which dated from their meeting in London in 1861, and had been continued in correspondence for upwards of thirty years. There are few more pathetic figures in modern literature than that of the patient American biographer of Beethoven, who devoted his life and his scanty means to a task which he did not live to finish, and which brought him practically no public recognition in his life-time. The value of his researches, however, was early recognised by Grove, and his sympathy and support went a long way to brighten Thayer's toilsome and secluded life. In return, Thayer's letters overflow with a gratitude that is all the more touching in that, poor though he was, he was prepared to make any sacrifices rather than forfeit his honourable independence. It is good to know that Grove, who had been one of his best friends in life, lived long enough to interest himself actively in the negotiations which led to the satisfactory completion of Thayer's monumental labours, and their ultimate publication in an English version.

On his return to Sydenham, Grove was occupied congenially enough in finally fulfilling the promise which he had made in the spring to his good friend Mr. F. G. Edwards to supply him with the materials for a biographical sketch in the *Musical Times*. There were few persons to whom Grove would have granted the request with greater pleasure, as Mr. Edwards had for many years rendered him valuable assistance in his Beethoven researches, and had repaid his master for the stimulus of his encouragement by a variety of helpful services discharged in the most loyal and affectionate spirit. Grove, as we have already seen, had employed an amanuensis to jot down some reminiscences, but Mr. Edwards was indefatigable by letters and interviews in eliciting all that he wished to know. The results of their correspondence and talks, supplemented by a good deal of independent inquiries conducted by Mr. Edwards, were embodied in the admirable illustrated sketch which appeared in the *Musical Times* of October, 1897, and was afterwards published separately in pamphlet form.

Always interested in "links with the past," Grove still from time to time contributed stray reminiscences to the

Press. One of these letters is to be found in the *Sydenham, Forest Hill and Penge Gazette* for September 25th, 1897, headed, "Some Sydenham Disappearances," in which he notes that when he first settled in Sydenham, in 1852, there were several fine specimens of the flowering ash (*Ornus Europæ*) in the village, the last of which had just been cut down. Grove also mentions the curious name of the house which for many years stood at the corner of West-hill and the Crystal Palace Park-road, "Roccles" (now altered to "Torrington") which he connects with "Rockhills" a few yards higher up the road and Beccles in Norfolk, as probable corruptions of some form of Ecclesia.

One of his very latest newspaper contributions was that in the *St. James's Gazette* of October 25th, in which Grove supports the version "Tom Hood" as against "Thomas": "'Thomas' is the name of a footman, and so it sounds. Tom Moore, Tom Hood, Tom Taylor, Tom Hughes, Tom Brown—make it Thomas, and how impossible the name becomes! Sir Thomas More, Thomas Arnold, are the exceptions which prove the rule."

The closing months of 1897 were marked by considerable fluctuations of his spirits. Going up to see the Nelson Column on Trafalgar day he speaks of being in as good spirits as Nelson himself on Trafalgar morning. A few days later he was distressed by learning of the severance of one of his cherished links with the past by the death of Mrs. Victor Benecke, Mendelssohn's daughter; and on November 9th his elder brother, Mr. Thomas Grove, of Penn, passed away at the ripe age of 85. Though much fonder of his younger brother Edmund, who was more akin to him in his interests and pursuits, while Thomas Grove was, in his own words, a man of the country, George Grove had a cordial respect for the head of the family, and that it was reciprocated was sufficiently proved by the terms of his brother's will.

This year (1897) was that in which Tschaikowsky's "Pathetic" Symphony was introduced to the English public, but Grove, who heard it at the Crystal Palace in October, did not altogether share the general *furore*. Writing to Mrs. Wodehouse, early in November, he says:—

"... How little logic there is in the music of the present day! Even Tschaikowsky goes in far too much for *emotion*. He's like the impressionist painters! A score of Beethoven is worth all the lot. ... I heard the H. Moll Symphonie of Schubert yesterday, and it struck me wonderfully. The beauty, the obvious intention to please and *benefit* those who heard it was irresistible. How can music have come down from that lofty, good level to what it now is? However, the pendulum is always swinging and it will rise again.

"... *Regret* is a strong word about the finale of No. 9. But there is no doubt that Beethoven was not easy about it. I am very glad he did not make the change. What *I* like about my book is that I have said from my heart how much love and gratitude Beethoven has created in me and what a strong *moral* ground there is in the creation of so much goodness. I feel towards him not as the clever *artist*, but as a great *poet* touching my deepest faculties as Shakespeare, Milton, Wordsworth, Tennyson, &c., have done. *That* is new, I think, or am I wrong?"

Grove's unabated interest in the Royal College was shown in December by his decision to present a number of his scores and books to the library. Writing to Mr. W. Barclay Squire on the subject, on December 6th, he says:

"It may be foolish to deprive myself of so many of my best loved books. However, every day I feel *certain* that I can't exist more than a week, and if I don't send them to-day, to-morrow morning I shall be thinking that I am too late. It's all along of Harcourt and the death duties."

On Christmas Eve Sir Arthur Sullivan wrote to congratulate him on having become "a landed proprietor": "Never mind the responsibility: it is a great thing to have something fixed and immovable, and you won't be expected to do the absurd generous things your poor brother did." By way of comment on this remark it may be enough to state that, though Grove benefited substantially by his brother's will, owing to the inevitable delay in winding up the estate he did not live long enough to derive any real satisfaction from the accession to his resources, while the business correspondence in which he was engaged caused him nothing but disquietude and worry.

At the beginning of 1898 Mr. Krehbiel of New York entered into communication with Grove with reference to the completion of Thayer's work, expressing his desire that Grove should undertake the English edition, or at any rate contribute a preface. This in turn led to an interesting correspondence with Mr. Edward Speyer, a firm friend and admirer of Thayer. Eventually Mr. Krehbiel himself undertook the English edition, which is being brought out in America. Continuous mental effort had become impossible, but he still attended committees, and went to an occasional concert. On January 27th the operatic performance of Mozart's masterpiece by the College pupils suggested to him the comment that *Don Juan*, like *Hamlet*, is full of quotations. Entries in his pocket-books, though greatly reduced in numbers, reveal his undiminished interest in his old pupils, and once and again a humorous saying is recorded, as *e.g.* that of the lady who, after a most impressive performance at the Crystal Palace observed, "You might have heard a mouse drop." But in the main his correspondence is saddened by the ever-present consciousness of his failing powers, and his loss of memory. When his friend Mr. C. A. Barry suggested that he should write something about Brahms, Grove replied on April 1st, 1898, that it was not the will but the power that was wanting :—

"The secret of writing has gone from me, never to come back. I have just been reading through my remarks in the programmes, on Beethoven No. 2, and *wondering where the words and the style came from*! I could no more do it now than I could fly. All is gone out of my head, and could only be brought back by an effort which would be impossible, and give me more anxiety than I could stand. Very grateful to you, but it can't be."

The entries in his almanac grew fewer and fewer, but it is curious to see how characteristic they remain—the date of Beethoven's death, the date on which a young friend was coming up for election at the Athenæum, the date of the Palestine Exploration Fund Meeting, the dates of the Crystal Palace concerts. Hitherto the most unfailing and regular of letter writers he found himself, even with the aid of an amanuensis, unable to cope with his correspondence, and for the first time in his life had often to leave letters unanswered. Old age had come upon him with a rush, and the suddenness of the onslaught left him saddened and dismayed, because he still retained the power of contrasting his past with his present self. Above all, the loss of his memory distressed him. "There was a time when I could remember anything," he writes, "but now everything has fled," on which Sullivan retorts (November 21st, 1898), "Dearest G., Your memory isn't worse than mine. Sometimes in making up my diary I have to think for half an hour what happened twenty-four hours before. *At all events your memory is strong enough when it comes to remembering your friends, dear old boy. Then it is always fresh and vigorous.*" The tone of Grove's letters in these last years is generally sad, often piteous, yet his self-pity was never querulous; in his saddest moods he was always able to sympathize with the troubles of others. There were moments, too, when his power of enjoying music and literature revived. On November 17th, 1898, he wrote to Mr. J. A. Fuller Maitland: "I heard Dohnanyi on Saturday, and took *great* courage. The moderation was so great! and his own little piece so beautiful." The loss of his friends affected him deeply. "I shall soon be alone," he writes to Mr. Spencer Lyttelton. "The old have all gone long since. Not a man who began at the Crystal Palace with me is now alive—save one—and now the generation below are going . . . Oh that it were all over and done. And yet I do cling to earth, and life and love very closely." And again to another friend he writes: "Oh, my dear, may you never live to be old." It is sad, as Mr. E. H. Pember writes, "to turn to his last year or two, and to think of him when his sensitiveness was smitten with the sadness of decay. The happy fact that he was at last freed from all anxieties as to the future of those about him, went for much, as it was bound to do with such a loving heart as his. But he did feel overmasteringly the loss of power, and the inevitable solitude of failing health. All his friends did their best to cheer him, but the well of cheerfulness in him had failed, and I know no human being to whom would have come with a heavier sadness the recognition of the fact, which must one day be brought home to us all, that a man must die alone. Poor old friend, unless all our dreams are vain, he has flung off the gloom now."

From early in January, 1899, his strength began to fail, while his memory grew progressively worse, and he was less and less able to stand the fatigue of journeys to London. But he corresponded regularly with Sir Hubert Parry, who kept him constantly informed as to the progress of affairs, and who, when Grove announced his intention of handing over to the College the bust by Mr. Gilbert, presented to him by his pupils, wrote at once to accept the gift and to assure the donor that they would give it a place of honour in the building. The last concerts that Grove attended, so far as I can make out, were those in the spring of 1899, when Dohnanyi and Joachim played at the Crystal Palace on successive Saturdays. Already the change in his appearance was painfully noticeable; he had lost his old vivacity, his features had become blunted, and his power of speech was affected. Amongst the last letters written in his own hand was that addressed to his brother-in-law, Dean Bradley, his life-long friend, on the occasion of the death of the Dean's stepmother:—

"LOWER SYDENHAM,
"*May* 4, 1899.

". . . What a relief, a blessed relief it must be to her—as far as one can comprehend it—to have the terrible weight and perplexity rolled away! . . . I have thought a good deal about the number of puzzles Heaven must have in it even to the cleverest or best man or woman. . . I am anything but well, and don't seem to get any better in any way. . .

"Have you by chance seen a book by a man whom one remembers at the Athenæum—Joshua Fitch by name, on 'The Two Arnolds'? I have known him for long very slightly but I am astonished at his book, and even find that it helps me over some weak places in Stanley's Arnold. Do get it and read it. . . I am afraid you are overdone. [In old times] I have only felt once or twice like that. Now I feel it constantly. Indeed nothing has changed more than [in regard to] my seeking for work. Now I always feel as if I had too much to do, instead of longing for more. . ."

On July 19th he addressed the following touching letter to the writer of this memoir:

"I was sorry—very sorry—to see your father's death in the paper last night. He was so very good to me, and I could ill spare him. Pray let me say how much I shall miss him. He valued me more than I deserved. . . He is one of the people I shall look for soonest. Think about me and pray for me. . ."

Grove lived nearly a year after writing this letter; but it would serve no helpful purpose to dwell in detail on the last flickerings of that bright spirit, which had brought sunshine and happiness into so many lives. He suffered from a progressive brain failure, which was really an old age change, though probably due in part to the excessive activity of his life. The machine, in a word, was worn out, and successive seizures of a paralytic nature left him each time weaker than before. During the winter of 1899 and the spring of 1900 he was chiefly confined to the garden, where he was wheeled about in a bath-chair. Throughout this long and painful period, all that medical aid could do was done by Dr. Green, for whom he had a strong affection; for the rest, whatever comfort and solace could be offered by loving care was rendered by his courageous and devoted wife. From time to time he saw some of his old friends, and as long as he retained consciousness was cheered by the constant visits of his sons and their wives. In the second week in May, 1900, he took to his bed, and sinking into a profound unconsciousness three days before the end, peacefully breathed his last on May 28th, 1900,

I have endeavoured as far as possible in the foregoing pages to confine myself to the autobiographical material placed at my disposal—to let "G." reveal himself with as little comment or criticism as possible. The picture must inevitably be inadequate, since regard is due to the living as well as to the dead, and the very passages which a biographer writing a hundred years hence would find most admirably characteristic and illuminating, merely serve to tantalise the compiler of a closely posthumous memoir. It must not be inferred from this that Grove's private correspondence was disfigured by personal acrimony, or spiced with scandal. There was neither malice nor venom in his nature; it was merely that in writing to his intimates he frequently adopted a strain which the self-repressed Briton would probably call gushing, and that he often discussed matters which it would be the profanation of friendship to commit to print, until the entire generation of the recipients had passed away. Much of what "G." wrote could only be appreciated by those who knew him: much, again, is unsuitable for the reasons which apply to all quasi-contemporary biographies. The very considerable portion that remains I have tried to weave together in the form of a continuous narrative, supplementing the absence of letters with the reminiscences of his contemporaries. The result is, I am only too well aware, somewhat in the nature of a patchwork; still it may serve to give some notion of the man, his work, and his character to those who never met him, as it can hardly fail, with all its shortcomings, to refresh and reanimate the affection of those who came within his sphere of influence. It only remains for me to supplement the narrative with a few words on the most salient traits of a singularly complex personality.

It has been said that our characters are to be read in our features, and there was certainly much in Grove's outer man that harmonized with his eager, mercurial, versatile temperament. In stature somewhat under middle height, at once squarely but loosely built, and of spare habit, he redeemed the comparative insignificance of his figure by the vivacity of his mien and the engaging charm of his physiognomy. He had no pretension to good looks, his features were too irregular for that, but the brow was open, the keen eyes and mobile mouth proclaimed him a humorist, and when his rugged countenance was lit up by the fire of affection or enthusiasm, it became quite beautiful to watch. Along with this varied play of facial expression he had, both in gait and gesture, a "quicksilverishness" unusual in an Englishman. Even into old age he retained the habit, when in good spirits, of executing a sort of little chassé step when he came into the room. And thus, though he had at command an intense and fervid earnestness of manner, he was perhaps too vivacious to shine on great ceremonial occasions, too mercurial to be imposing, too sensitive to be dignified. Until the close of his life he was in the habit of taking a good deal of exercise, but he was active rather than athletic. He never shared the modern enthusiasm for pastime, rather resented the worship of cricket and golf, and took little interest in sport, though he certainly went more than once to see the Derby. The diary he kept when he was in Jamaica shows that he constantly rode about the island, but he was no Centaur; indeed when he was a boy his indifferent horsemanship was rather a joke in the family. Yet he was capable of rising to the occasion. Thus one evening when he was driving out to dinner with some ladies, the coachman was discovered to be tipsy, whereupon "G." promptly mounted the box, took the reins and drove the carriage and pair safely to its destination. I am bound to add that when I told this story to one of his family, it provoked the unsympathetic comment, "I'm glad I wasn't sitting behind him." At one period of his residence in Sydenham, he was in the habit of riding before breakfast; the horse was tied up outside, and occasionally broke loose during family prayers. In the matter of dress he threw back to his Puritan forbears, he was neither slovenly nor smart, avoided colours, aimed at an efficient simplicity of attire, and cordially disliked bejewelled women. It was the same with his diet; in the whole course of his life I have never come across a single written complaint of what he ate or drank. His taste in wine and tobacco was of the simplest. He "hated champagne," drank Marsala, smoked cheap cigars, and, like Mr. Gladstone, drank tea at all hours with impunity. He talked too much at meals to pay close attention to the refinements of gastronomy, and a story is current of a city dinner at which, during the soup, Grove engaged his neighbour—a total stranger—in conversation with his usual vivacity until the other at last broke out, "Confound you, Sir! You made me swallow that last piece of green fat without thinking!"

His habits, as was natural in a man who filled so many different posts in a long life, varied in accordance with the work on which he was engaged, but until his health began to fail, he sat up late and rose early. He always had a book or books by his bedside, and constantly read himself to sleep. On Sundays he went regularly to church until his break-down, and for many years was in the habit of reading the lessons at St. Bartholomew's. There was nearly always a guest to lunch, and in the afternoon, when the weather was fine, he would sit in the garden, chatting with his family or friends, smoking a cigar, or playing with his dog. Of his devotion to his four-footed friends mention has already been made, but it may be added that at times he was wont to "refresh himself," as he put it, by putting the cat on the chimney-piece, letting it jump on to his shoulder, a distance of five feet or more, and then putting it back again. Another cat story belongs to the time when he was living in the Adelphi. The Groves had a cat which either died or had to be poisoned. "G." accordingly sallied forth to dispose of the corpse, intending to drop it over Waterloo Bridge, but his behaviour excited the suspicion of a policeman, who "shadowed" him so effectually that he never got a chance, and had to return home without fulfilling his purpose.

How so busy a man found time to be so voluminous and regular a correspondent is in a measure explained by his practice of devoting the early morning hours to his letters. The German historian, von Ranke, once remarked to a friend that the time the latter devoted to his private correspondence, if employed on literary work, would enable him to produce two good-sized volumes every year. This would probably be an under-estimate of the sacrifice that Grove made on the altar of friendship. He rose at six, or even earlier, made himself a cup of tea, and constantly wrote non-obligatory letters for a couple of hours before breakfast. The practice may have seriously diminished his printed output, large as that was, but it enabled him to keep his friendship in good repair, and to exert a stimulating influence on an immense number of minds whom he might otherwise have failed to reach. The majority of people are only really intimate with their contemporaries, but with his pen, as in his conversation, Grove was at his ease with all ages. He wrote too rapidly and too much to concern himself with literary felicities of expression; but he never wrote anything that did not contain something characteristic. It was said of his friend R. H. Hutton that "there was always a caress in his letters," and the same was true of Grove. "Dove sei amato bene?" he begins one note: "Where have you hidden your blessed self so long?" Or again, writing to Mrs. Lehmann: "Can't you recollect that you are a very weak fragile creetur and also awfully valuable to all your friends, and put yourself into a big jewel box and be looked at and aired only occasionally?" He wrote, in short, as he talked; he was always ready to communicate what he thought would interest or cheer or amuse the recipients, always anxious to know what they were doing or reading, or how they were getting on, always ready in his most depressed moods to exhibit pleasure in the successes of others. Hence it is not to be wondered at that a man who conducted his correspondence on these principles should find it difficult to employ the pen of another. Writing in 1880, he says, "I shall try to make her [his daughter] a kind of secretary to me, but I have no time for this. I never could show anyone how to do anything. I always must do it myself." At the Royal College he dictated a certain number of letters, but the vast majority were written by his own hand, and it was not until he was seventy-seven that he made any considerable use of the services of an amanuensis. Such a method, in a man constituted as he was, could not but interpose a barrier between him and his friends, and detract from the immediateness of the contract between mind and mind. This sensitive sympathy and two other striking traits—his essentially modern attitude and his realization of the maxim—

ἀεὶ γὰρ ἥβη τοῖς γέρουσιν εὖ μαθεῖν—

are admirably illustrated in the following tribute from his intimate friend Mr. E. H. Pember, K.C. :—

"The lovableness of the man, after all, was the dominant note in him. The love he was so ready to give drew attention no less than it provoked love. I have seldom known a man with sympathies at once so varied and so keen. Your sorrows and your joys he made his own. Whatever your art or calling might be, he always talked of it from the point of view of what it must be to you. If he told an anecdote he always gave you the notion, where it was possible, of laughing with the actors in it rather than at the situation. He essentially shared their fun. He had suffered much, as we all knew, and had his fits of depression and moments of discouragement, like any other; but his splendid cheerfulness overbore melancholy, and was in him, as I firmly believe, not merely the result of temperament, but the half-conscious outcome of an inward acknowledgment that life had, after all, brought him more than it had cost him, and it behoved him to wear gladness as a robe of gratitude. His thankfulness was thus to him almost a continual feast. Amongst other things, he was essentially modern. The past spoke to him, no doubt, but it did not say as much to him as to some of us. Perhaps this was owing not more to his natural bent than to the accidents of his career. I remember that he expressed this to me many years ago, by saying that Tennyson was far more to him than Shakespeare. Indeed, I used to hug the notion that I had had something to do with his having later on turned again with greater love to the older poet. He was a learner to the last, and was constantly turning up with some pleasant artistic or literary problem which had struck his fancy. I remember, for instance, his writing to me to ask how I should define the grand style in music and poetry, and express the conditions attaching to it; at another time he wanted to know whether I thought that poets ever consciously had tried to reproduce the sounds and rhythm of bird songs; and again, I recall his raising the point whether some of the finest aphorisms of men of genius might not be reminiscences improved upon, new treatments, as it were, of older themes, redrapings of simple proverbs, grand results of time. This habit of his helped to make him one of the most suggestive of talkers and correspondents, especially as, to use a phrase of his chief favourite, he did not always 'beat his music out,' but rather left you to do it for him—if you would."

With what Mr. Pember says about "G.'s" sense of humour may be linked a remark of Dean Bradley's: "George was always ready to fall down with laughter all his life long." He had a great store of good stories, and told them well, though he was never a self-possessed narrator, and would often explode with laughter at the thought of what was coming. Thus he would grow quite inarticulate in his efforts to relate the legend of the conscientious cat at St. James's Hall, which remained on the platform all the time Sarasate was playing Mendelssohn's violin concerto, so as to oblige him with a string in case he broke one.

Turning to his mental equipment and the use he made of it, one cannot but marvel at the amount of work he achieved in the domain of Biblical research, *belles lettres*, musical biography and criticism, considering that he was not a scholar or a linguist or a technical musician. He left school for the engineering "shops" at the age of sixteen, and was for the rest of his life his own teacher. But then he had been admirably grounded by Pritchard, he had great powers of assimilation, he was fortunate in his friendships, and, above all, there was never any one so ready to be impressed by the right thing. All the great enthusiasms were for worthy objects; he made no mistakes in his heroes; indeed it might be said of him that very few of his swans were geese. He was a delightful expositor; he shone as a narrator, interpreter, eulogist; he was a brilliant and persuasive advocate; but, to quote his own words, "I am no critic, bless you, and would rather love than condemn any day of the week." Nor did he shine in controversy. "I never attempted," he writes to his brother-in-law, "to answer a newspaper criticism but once, and the failure of that attempt cured me of ever repeating it." In a musical performance what chiefly impressed him was earnestness and simplicity. For the rest he was little concerned with the niceties of technique, and was infinitely more interested in the music than in the "reading." He was, however, fully conscious of these limitations, and never made the slightest pretence to any knowledge that he did not possess, and, when occasion demanded, invariably had recourse to experts to supplement his deficiencies—to Mr. Manns or Mr. Dannreuther, Mr. C. A. Barry or Dr. Charles Wood, to mention a few out of many whom he thus consulted. But it was not a case of employing a "ghost." "G." never made the slightest secret of his reliance on the technical knowledge of others to eke out the imperfections of his equipment. Wherever it was possible he acknowledged his indebtedness most scrupulously, though it is hardly necessary to say that he gave out far more in stimulation, suggestion, and enthusiasm than he received in the shape of technical information.

To define the precise extent of his musical accomplishments would be difficult. But in a letter to one of his relatives he puts it pretty plainly :—

> "*You* who execute music have an immense advantage over *us* who only listen to it. You don't realise how much you gain by having to go over and over a song till you can really sing it—till it becomes to you what many of the poems in *In Memoriam* are to me. I often think of that, and lament that with all my love, my knowledge of music is so much less intimate than it might be."

He was "no executant," though as a boy and a young man he had played the piano a little and sung in choral classes. Later on he had generally had the talent of the best professionals and amateurs at his disposal—if he wanted to hear anything in particular. When Dr. Charles Wood sent him his *Ode to the West Wind*, Grove wrote, "How I wish I could play it; but I am going to the Taylors to-morrow and I shall make him play it." To the same correspondent he wrote *à propos* of the opening "statements" of the C minor symphony, "I have very little ear for rhythm." When he was engaged on his article on Schubert for the *Dictionary of Music* he wrote to Sir Hubert Parry: "If with my patience and love of my subject I were only a musician! That's rather a confession, but I don't mind making it to you." With regard to his capacity for reading music, he could find his way well enough about the full score of a work that he had heard three or four times. By that time the written page became luminous, so to say, to his mind. The mere mental perusal of the score of a brand-new work conveyed as little to him as it does to most amateurs. No doubt these shortcomings account for the disinclination of a certain number of highly-equipped professional musicians to regard Grove in the light of a serious authority on their art. Against these few detractors I am content to pit the testimony of Dr. Richter, who declared to me his conviction that the services rendered by Grove in his picturesque and genial analysis of the symphonies of Beethoven, Schubert, Brahms, &c. were of incalculable value in educating the public. The secret of that power is very well expressed by Mrs. Wodehouse in the estimate of Grove she has most generously placed at my disposal:—

"In handling the great poets or musicians, his knowledge of their outer and inner lives, their friends, surroundings, and general circumstances, together with his minute loving study of every line and note of their works, gave Sir George a clue to the most abstruse and difficult passages which more practical and scientific musicians have rarely attained. In a letter Sir George wrote me early in the eighties, when he had nearly completed his biography of Schubert for the Dictionary, he says: 'Alas, I shall soon have to say good-bye to my beloved friend, Franz Schubert, and I do not know how to. We have been such inseparable companions for months and months, and close friends for years, and how lovable he is! I have got to know him so intimately—and yet—how *dare* I say so? In his great Symphony in C he towers so high, so far above but a very few of the "Chosen and Elect," that it is presumptuous in me to say I understand him. I can only gaze and worship him, and humbly thank God for having given us such a genius. Oh, my dear child, be grateful too for the privilege you have had given you of being able to hear, enjoy and appreciate his beautiful works. Fancy how poor you would have been, and how barren and poverty-stricken those natures are to whom music—such music!—is a sealed book.'

"The last letter he ever wrote me (September 1899, the writing of which is scarcely legible), was in answer to one of mine after I had heard Adela Verne practising the E♭ Beethoven Concerto, whilst she was staying with me at Minley, and in it he says: 'I agree with you about the "tenderness" and "everlasting freshness" of that concerto (*ewig jung und ewig neu*). There is no one like Beethoven for taking one off and out of misery, and making one forget all the ills of this life. And I do not believe one can ever exhaust the merits and virtues of his works until the very end. As I grow older and suffer the more, the meaning of Beethoven's music only deepens and becomes yet clearer to me. And so it will to you.'"

In regard to Grove's attitude towards composers generally, I again avail myself of some comments by Mrs. Wodehouse:—

"As regards Sir George's taste in music, he has often been accused of undue conservatism and even narrowness. But this surely is unjust, for if he could not pretend to admire, no one ever tried harder to be fair all round. Many and many a time he has written the same words to me about certain modern composers: 'Surely there must be something wrong in me that I cannot admire —— as others do, who are far better musicians and judges than I am.' And again: 'Do get ——'s songs and some of his pianoforte things. I feel sure there is beauty in them which I have failed to see, and which you must point out to me when we meet. His aims are always high and noble, but, dear me, something is lacking.' Or again, 'I do not mean to pass a judgment on —— yet: I mean to set hard to work and get to know it better. It shall not be my fault if I do not like it.'

"He would never tolerate one composer being held up at the expense of another, and always declared that each had his place in art, and were he really great he would live for ever. He never denied, for instance, the greatness of Wagner, and although he was never an ardent worshipper, and highly disapproved of some of Wagner's methods, yet I have many letters containing the most enthusiastic praise of certain of Wagner's works. 'Time is the best art-sifter,' he often said; and 'nothing will really die which is worthy to live,' was his answer to those who bewailed the ever increasing prevalence of fashion in music. He was faithful and loyal to his great gods in music, and perhaps unwilling to admit any blemishes in their works. In one of his letters he writes: 'Is it my fault that I love that ugly passage? [I do not remember what it was except that it was in Beethoven, for we had been corresponding about a certain phrase or chord of Beethoven which some editor wanted to alter.] I would not have a note of it altered. Would one wish to have a feature altered in a dear familiar face because it is not in accordance with the canons of beauty?—why, you would change its whole expression and character. No, no, there is a meaning and intention in every note Beethoven wrote.'"

The attachment of Grove to his special heroes was far removed from an ordinary admiration. I once asked him, when he was about seventy, had he ever met Mendelssohn. "No," he replied, "but if he were alive now, I'd go off to Germany and see him to-morrow." Here again, the testimony of Mrs. Wodehouse is valuable:—

"There was a certain paradox in Sir George's character which it is difficult to express. Of all men he was perhaps the most 'human' I have ever known, and at the same time the most reverent. In religion, poetry and music alike, there was with him a personal love and veneration of character, which inspired his treatment of the words or music of great men with close, intimate appreciation and insight. One day in September of 1897, when I was staying at Brighton with my mother, and he was staying at Preston with his brother, I remember so well getting a note from him saying he wanted to come and talk to me about something 'very near his heart.' He came and talked to my mother and to me about the Psalms and about David, for hours, and we felt that his love for David was so warm, and so vivid his understanding of David's whole character that it seemed as if David were a friend and contemporary. And yet this intimacy never degenerated into familiarity—it was ever reverent and spiritual."

To this illustration of the peculiar and intimate quality of Grove's hero-worship, I may add another, drawn from a letter written to his sister-in-law in 1879. *A propos* of the pleasures of literary creation, he says :—

"I can understand what you say about its being engrossing work. The only try I ever had at anything of the kind was my David, and I can recollect well that when I got him on to the slope leading down into the valley where Goliath stood roaring, my heart beat so that I could not write."

He always "preferred the attitude of the devotee to that of the critic," and herein, as Mrs. Wodehouse rightly says, the chief source of his influence was to be found :—

"I think the secret of his unique personality lay in the glorious enthusiasm which he not only possessed but also could impart to others. Hence his extraordinary influence on those with whom he came in contact. The driest and most mechanical work he could make interesting by his magical power (how often I felt this when working at the Index for the *Dictionary of Music*!), and hence also the zeal and devotion of those who worked with him, or for him, or under him. If we went to him in any difficulty, or feeling hopeless and disheartened, his warm, eager manner of throwing himself heart and soul into the subject showed us how to view it. He never minimised difficulties; and, on the other hand, his intuitive perception of any merit in a work supplied a never failing stimulant to fresh efforts. Sir George, again, never hesitated to speak of his own difficulties, doubts and failures, and would ask the advice and opinion of others in such an eager, humble manner that it gave one confidence and pleasure."

For a man who had achieved success in so many fields, and distinction in not a few, Grove was singularly free from anything approaching to complacency. He was incapable of blowing his own trumpet: indeed he seldom wrote a long letter without lamenting his own short-comings. When a friend congratulated him on the high standard of excellence attained by *Macmillan's Magazine*, he replied: "To me the magazine is nothing but a monthly failure," explaining that he never succeeded in achieving his aim, which was not to please the initiated, but to touch outsiders. He never compared himself with others except to his own disadvantage. If, for example, he was congratulated on his musical analyses, he never failed to impress upon his hearers the superior excellence and thoroughness of those of his old friend C. A. Barry or of Sir George Macfarren, by the side of whom he described himself as a mere door-keeper. He was perpetually conscious of the slow process of his mental development. "Here have I," he writes to his brother-in-law in 1877, "lately been going through states of feeling and appreciation of things which most people have at twenty-five and which I am only experiencing at fifty-seven." Sometimes his self-disparagement takes a truly comical form, as when he says [Oct. 10, 1862] of some lectures by Stanley: "They fill me alternately with malignant envy and with grovelling admiration." With this modesty may be noticed another cognate trait. Though he held himself responsible for any failures in his undertakings, he was always ready to give the full meed of praise to others, as any of his fellow-workers at the Royal College of Music or on the *Dictionary of Music* would readily admit.

Along with his vivid enthusiasm and keen pursuit of high ideals, there was in George Grove a considerable vein of shrewd common sense. He was certainly in many respects not a good manager—a defect happily supplied by a double portion in his wife: he was always ready to give £5 to a person in distress, whether he could afford it or not, he did an immense amount of admirable work for nothing, and was quite incapable of amassing a fortune or anything like it. But he had something like a genius for putting other people in the way of making a start in life. It was this gift that prompted so many young people, and especially his pupils at the Royal College of Music, to come to him for advice. It might be about their music, their public career, or their most private and trivial affairs; but Grove would listen to them all with the same unvarying interest and seldom failed to give them sound and practical counsel. And if the application was made by letter, the answer was sure to come, if not by return of post, at any rate in a day or two. As regards results it is good to think that very few of those whom he befriended failed to express their gratitude. On the only occasion on which he was treated by a pupil not merely with a want of respect and consideration, but with outrageous insolence, he showed a forbearance and magnanimity which few men in his position would have emulated. "Many old students," writes Mrs. Wodehouse, "have told me—perhaps years after—that they never forgot his words, and never repented having acted as he advised." Many instances have come within my own knowledge of Grove's benevolent and stimulating interest in his pupils and friends; and to those already recorded I may add the following typical example. The writer had been a pupil at the Royal College and on leaving had combined music-teaching with journalism. In December, 1894, she wrote to announce her appointment as assistant-editor to a popular and successful magazine, and to trace that appointment to Grove's encouragement:—

"It is exactly a year ago that you took the trouble to write me a most helpful letter, just when I was very despondent about my literary work. I wonder whether you remember the occasion? I had told you that it was no use my trying. I should never do anything at literary work, and I should give up ——'s *Journal*. You told me to persevere—and as I was in a *corner* I was to stick to it, and try to fill it as no one else could. You wrote four pages of encouragement, all to the same effect, and ended by saying, 'It's dogged does it.' I learnt the letter by heart, and then I set to work to *practise* it, and I have been grinding away *hard* in that *corner* ever since. Now the corner has grown to be a very large one! A few months ago, Messrs. —— told me that they were intending to start a new Magazine, and they offered me the post of Assistant-Editor—which rather astonished me! But I said I would like to try. And I did try, and now I have been Assistant-Editor for over two months, and I like the work immensely.

". . . Now I think you will have been worried quite long enough with this very egotistical letter; only I wished to tell you the result of that letter you wrote me last December; as, had it not been for that letter, I should have given up literary work long ago."

His versatility, the outcome largely of temperament, partly of opportunity, often inspired him with self-distrust. "My work lies too wide," he wrote in 1879, "I ought to concentrate it more." But if he suffered from the defect of this quality, so far as individual achievement went, it enabled him most effectually to combat the dangers of narrowness in his pupils. Here, again, I gladly avail myself of some excellent remarks by Mrs. Wodehouse :—

"His hatred of pedantry and affectation is well known, and he did his utmost to cure all young musicians by good-humoured banter of this failing. But he also never missed an opportunity of giving musicians interest in things outside their own profession and trying to develop their mental culture. In speaking to me of a very clever young composer, in whose works, however, one felt something was lacking, Sir George said : 'Wait a bit, I am going to give him lots of poetry to read and make him think about, and we shall talk about it this summer, and you will see his music will be quite different a year hence.' But it was not only over the young he had this power of arousing interest in a subject. All his friends and acquaintances felt the same when corresponding with him, for he would take up some subject with the utmost zeal and ask one's opinion about it or beg one to help him to work it out. Again, everything was worth telling him, as one might be sure of a letter back—usually by return of post, as he made it a habit never to let a letter lie unanswered more than a few hours ('until it got stale'), and if he could not write at length at the moment, he would send a line of warm acknowledgment first and then a few hours later a full long letter would follow."

Grove, as we have seen, was all his life a great and omnivorous reader, though at periods of stress he found no time to gratify his taste save in bed or in the train. He had certain pet aversions—theological novels and gratuitous tragedies amongst others—and distrusted writers who set too great store by style, but with few reserves all subjects interested him, from puns to the Pentateuch. Nonsense verses, "Limericks" and riddles are constantly entered in his pocket-books and he never tired of telling of the lover of nature who called attention to the beauty of the "autimnal tunts" or of the Frenchman who with unconscious wit replied to the salutation "Au reservoir" with "Tanks!"

Of his favourite poets—Tennyson, Matthew Arnold, Clough and Wordsworth—he knew a great portion by heart; and when one of his most intimate friends was lying seriously ill, in the summer of 1890, used to come almost every evening on his way from the College to Victoria to read or repeat without book his favourite poems to the invalid. Of modern novelists Thackeray was perhaps his chief favourite, but he had an immense admiration for Tourguénieff, and at one time would never go on a journey without taking *Pères et Enfants* or the *Nichée de Gentilshommes* in his pocket.[1] Many of his books bear the unmistakable impress of his eager mind, for not only are the margins crowded with notes containing cross references, comparisons of different editions, corrections or exclamations, but he also constantly made his own index, fixing in extra blank pages at the end of the volume for the purpose. The value of his method, if one is making a close study of any subject, is incontestable, but to any book which deserves careful reading it adds immensely in efficiency and interest. It is needless to remark that Grove was a reader, not a collector of books.

On his love of animals I have already dwelt. With regard to his love of nature a certain reservation must be made. That it was sincere I cannot doubt. Writing to one of his college "children" in April, 1893, after bewailing his loss of spirits and his ill health, he suddenly breaks out:—

> "How lovely the spring is! The mere look of the golden young lime-leaves against the pale blue sky in the morning is enough to make one thankful for all the beauty and joy that one sees around one. And then the sounds! And the delicious faint smells: as Tennyson says:—
>
> 'Sympathies how frail
> In sound and smell.'"

[1] Grove also possessed and greatly prized a portmanteau that had once belonged to Tourguénieff.

He was always enthusiastic in his admiration of grand mountain scenery, sunsets, cloud or storm effects. Mr. Arthur Grove tells me he delighted in watching thunderstorms; but I am inclined to agree with Mrs. Wodehouse that "the descriptions of nature by poets seemed to give him even more pleasure." So with the songs of birds: "I think his interest in the subject was derived from Beethoven's use of the yellowhammer's note and Tennyson's indication of the rhythm of the thrush's song in his *Throstle*."

Of Grove's higher thoughts on life here and hereafter, a good deal may be gleaned from the frequent references in the letters already quoted. Writing in the year 1884 to a friend who mentioned having prayed for him on his birthday he says, "I am naturally a very religious man," but adds that he was only beginning to find that "it is impossible to exist by one's self in one's own unaided thoughts. Even your dearest friends can't do that for you: no one can but God." His views as to a future life have already been illustrated; they are summed up in the words of the Nicene creed, "I look for the Resurrection of the dead, and the life of the world to come"; but there were moments when it was not enough for him to "look for" reunion after death; he longed for absolute proof. "I am so glad," he writes in 1888 to Dr. Charles Wood, "that you have set those beautiful verses of Vaughan—now that dear Louie Kellett has departed, it gives me an additional figure to think of as there. But, oh dear, if one could only believe—not only feel but believe—in the next world! Forgive me for this outburst! But if you had lost two daughters and half-a-dozen of the most intimate friends possible, you would feel the same." It is perhaps worth adding that he expressed the strongest disapproval of Walt Whitman's view of death. Death was terrible—it was nonsense to call it "lovely," "soothing," "delicate"; nor could he reconcile himself to the modern practice of lining graves with flowers. As for Grove's general position I am content to rely on the following interesting notes contributed by the Rev. William Addis, who conversed and corresponded with Grove more frequently on religion and theological questions than any other friend during the last twenty years of his life.

". . . To him religion was a Christian life, a humble and devout following of our Lord's example. He did not pretend to be a philosopher and hence with metaphysical subtleties and disputes about dogma he had scant sympathy. They simply repelled him. But more than once I have heard him repeat in solemn tones St. Paul's words, 'The foundation of the Lord standeth sure, having this seal, the Lord knoweth who are his. And let every one that nameth the name of Christ depart from iniquity.' He had a horror of all literature which tended to corrupt the mind: even of Gibbon he once spoke to me with severity for his needless detail on revolting subjects. He was also strongly averse to recklessness in disturbing the faith of good people. In this respect Lord Tennyson and he seem to have been of one mind. He had the highest value for family worship and for attendance at church. Through and through he was a loyal son of the Church and it was pleasant to hear the emphasis of his voice when he spoke of 'the manly religion of the Church of England.' His warmest admiration was given to men like Dr. Arnold, Frederick Maurice, and his dear friend Dean Stanley, and he certainly disliked excesses (or what he deemed such) in ritual or doctrine. Yet he was in no sense a party man. He loved the National Church for the incomparable beauty of its prayer-book, the glories of its past, the promise of its future. It is, he would say, an historical Church, and he appreciated it as a vast means of doing good to the nation. He was apt to be impatient with those who dissented from its communion, and still more with clergymen who felt scruples about their conformity. I need scarcely say that he abhorred the very notion of disestablishment, and was, though a sincere Liberal, the determined enemy of Radicalism in Church and State. I came to believe that his judgment on those matters was wholly wise and just, and I rejoice to think that I had the opportunity of expressing the entire agreement which I felt. I ought to add that there was no limit to his charity with regard to individuals. He honoured all men and especially all good men, whatever their theological or political opinions might be. He was tried—as who is not at times?—by doubt and misgiving. He had his sorrows: one great sorrow fell upon him during my stay at Sydenham, when a daughter, of whom any father might well be proud, was taken from him. For doubt and sorrow alike he found relief in strenuous and unremitting toil for the good of others. To us who knew him he has left a memorable example of unselfish devotion, of unfeigned humility and sweetness."

Few are likely to dissent from Mr. Addis's tribute to the consistent unselfishness of Grove's efforts. All through life it had been his rule, and in his old age he reached a level of energetic altruism in which he had few rivals. Probably no man of his age in our time had a larger number of young friends or is likely to have his memory kept green for a longer period in the grateful recollection of his survivors. In the highest sense he was at his best in his old age when, as Director of the Royal College, he sought at all times to impress on his young charges that character was more than efficiency. What he was like twenty years earlier, when his personal magnetism was at its strongest, and when even a few words with him gave the hearer a thrill, may best be gathered from the words of the Master of the Temple :—

"It was towards the close of the year 1868 that I first came to know George Grove. I was passionately fond of music, although then very ignorant of the orchestral and chamber works of the great composers. To such a state of musical destitution the Saturday concerts at the Crystal Palace were a revelation indeed, and my first introduction to Grove as one interested in his own dominant taste soon ripened into a very close and warm friendship. His wooden-faced cottage in Lower Sydenham, which we came to call the 'G. G. Block,' after one division of the seats at the Handel Festival, became to me for many years a second home. Often have I stayed with him and Mrs. Grove from the Friday till the Sunday morning, and written my Sunday sermon on the Saturday morning in his little (rather damp and underground) study, in a chaos of books, music, prints, and photographs. Grove was at that time nearly fifty years of age, and if past the prime of his various powers, certainly at the very height of his enthusiasms. What struck me about Grove was his seeming boundless capacity for work, in comparison with a like capacity for interest in all the tastes and pursuits of all his friends, notably of young men, musicians, or other artists, especially if they were poor, or perhaps unhappy in their family surroundings. Grove seemed to have time and strength for everything, He haunted concerts in London, as well as at Sydenham. He wrote articles and prefaces for journalists and editors. He apparently read everything new in the artistic or literary world, yet always kept himself in freshest touch with his old favourites, Coleridge, Lamb, Tennyson. His distance from town added materially to the fatigue of his life, with the necessary late hours and walkings in all weathers between home and railway station. We all loved him, but we all wondered how he could do it, and how long he would endure the strain. The present memoir will have proved how versatile he was—and that, not in the sense of having a smattering of many subjects. He was an expert in many, such as engineering, Biblical antiquities, music, and I never heard him discuss literary subjects, or those bearing on religion and criticism without his showing that he read and thought and formed opinions on these subjects at first hand, and never adopted the floating pronouncements of the hour. Added to all which, he was a humorist and a *raconteur* such as one seldom met. No wonder that he attracted men of all sorts, interested in any of his subjects, and exercised a kind of fascination over the young and aspiring. For with everything that he thought and said and wrote was blended that charm of enthusiasm which kindles love as well as admiration. It was a combination I have never met elsewhere. First-rate versatility, it has been said, is a gift of doubtful advantage to a man—moderate versatility a fatal disaster. Grove's particular order in this respect did not indeed bring him the success which consists of a large fortune. But the variety of his tastes and accomplishments in things on which he laid little stress and counted himself a mere amateur no doubt added largely to the effectiveness of his powers in matters where his main influence was exerted. It was the poetry in him, and the musical sense that enabled him to invest with such charm his articles in Smith's *Dictionary of the Bible*, not only when he treated such pathetic themes as the lives of Elijah and Elisha, but even when he dealt with the technical details of the geography or antiquities of Palestine. Notably did his width of culture and his passionate temperament colour all those analyses and descriptions of the great musical creations of Beethoven and Schubert, which have brought, to thousands of eager readers and hearers, music and literature into closer and more inspiring relation than has been achieved by any other critic. With the works of Schubert especially, that prolific genius who owes an incalculable debt to Grove for the spread of his music in England, Grove's name will be for ever associated, and this, not only because of the 'Unfinished' Symphony and the *Rosamunde* music. Up to the date of Grove's devoting himself to this master, it is no exaggeration to say that to nine out of ten of even accomplished amateurs in this country Schubert was known, as a writer of songs, by about a score of these, and therefore the most obvious and hackneyed. The figure in which Grove most often recurs to me is of one sitting close to the pianoforte with his elbow on his knee and his finger along his cheek, listening with rapt admiration to *Amyot Lyle* or the *Leiermann*, or '*Das sie hier gewesen*.' And it was largely the diffusive force of his own enthusiasm that encouraged great singers such as Stockhausen to introduce to English audiences such song-cycles as the *Winterreise* and the *Müller-lieder*, and perhaps even made it possible for Charles Hallé to gather audiences for two consecutive years to listen to the whole of Schubert's sonatas at his pianoforte recitals. Of the four hundred and odd songs that Schubert bequeathed to the world, even a Grove could not have made acquaintance with all. And it was one of my commonest experiences to receive notes from him by post, containing simply and solely, with a few words of ecstatic description, the name of some new song he had just heard or otherwise discovered. No musical amateur of the last half century probably did more than George Grove to infect a vast number of his fellow amateurs with enthusiasm for all that is best and noblest in music."

With Canon Ainger's tribute to the culture, the enthusiasm, and the fascination of George Grove, I bring this record to a close. The figure that I have sought to present to those who did not know him, and to recall to those who did is not that of a hero, but of a versatile, impulsive, generous, lovable man, who gave freely of his best to others without thought of reward or return, and who, for all his mercurial manysidedness, strove to leave the world better and happier than he found it. It is surely no unmeaning indication of the peculiar impression he created that no one who knew him well ever does or ever will speak of him except as "dear G."

INDEX

THE END

R. CLAY AND SONS, LTD., BREAD ST. HILL, E.C., AND BUNGAY, SUFFOLK.